DICTATORS AND DANGEROUS IDEAS

Uncensored Reflections in an Era of Turmoil

Paul Monk

ECHO BOOKS

This unabridged edition was first published in 2018 by Barrallier Books Pty Ltd, trading as Echo Books.

Registered Office: 35-37 Gordon Avenue, West Geelong, Victoria 3220, Australia.

www.echobooks.com.au

National Library of Australia cataloguing-in-publication information:

Creator: Monk, Paul M., author.

Title: Dictators and Dangerous Ideas: Uncensored reflections in an era of turmoil.

ISBN: 9780648355205 (Hardcover)

A catalogue record for this book is available from the National Library of Australia

Set in Garamond Premier Pro 12/17 and Trajan Pro

Book and cover images: Catherine Gordon

Cover image: *Book burning: The burning of books to suppress ideas is an ancient recourse of tyranny.*

Book and cover design by Peter Gamble, Canberra

for Claudia
with indelible memories of Venezuela
and of Spain, Switzerland, France, Italy and Israel
above all, perhaps, of Sils Maria
amor siempre

CONTENTS

Portrait of Paul Monk by cartoonist John Spooner.

Foreword

Timothy Garton Ash is the kind of political commentator I rather like. His coverage of the collapse of the Soviet bloc almost thirty years ago was luminous. Since then, he has risen to considerable eminence, as Isaiah Berlin Professorial Fellow at St Antony's College, Oxford; Senior Fellow at the Hoover Institution, at Stanford University; and winner of the Orwell Prize. In 2016, he gave us *Free Speech: Ten Principles for a Connected World;* an attempt to set out the principles of freedom of expression and inquiry for the 21st century. It is a very important topic and I want to evoke here the principles that he set out, by way of reflecting on the extent to which my own writing has been consistent with them.

Free Speech stands in the lineage of John Stuart Mill's famous defence of freedom of expression and inquiry, *On Liberty*, which was first published in 1859, the same year as Charles Darwin's *On the Origin of Species*. Both are classics which stand at the very threshold of modern liberal and scientific culture. They were both written in English by Englishmen at the high tide of British prestige and power. Culturally, linguistically and in terms of the political and civil liberties I enjoy and the worldview to which I subscribe, these are foundational texts. But, as Garton Ash declares at the very opening of his book, all this is now under sustained challenge from various quarters. If we wish to both preserve and extend such liberties in the present century, we have a great deal of work to do.

He states forthrightly:

> I contend that the way to live together well in this world-as city is to have more and better free speech. Since free speech has never meant unlimited speech—everyone spouting whatever comes into his or her head—that entails discussing where the limits to freedom of expression and information should lie in important areas such as privacy, religion, national security and the ways we talk about human difference. As important, it means identifying positive methods and styles that will enable us to use this defining gift of humankind to best advantage, in these conditions of unprecedented opportunity and risk.

He commented that he did not pretend to offer 'some kind of detached, universal view from nowhere—or everywhere.' He was, he declared, proud to call himself a liberal, in Mill's sense, not the contemporary American sense, and to argue for that position. My own outlook is very much the same. The best way to describe my own outlook would be that of a classical liberal.

I am passionately committed to and have spent a lifetime practising the individual liberties of inquiry, written expression and speech that are at issue here. I have refused, at every crucial point in my life, to subordinate those liberties to either authoritarian institutional constraints or collectivist ideologies of any kind. I have always been at ease with debate; always ill at ease with attempts to censor, denounce or 'de-platform' those with differing opinions, however much I may consider them ill-conceived or wrong-headed. The writings collected here, all written over the past three years or so, like those collected and published in my previous book *Opinions and Reflections* (Echo Books, 2015), surely exhibit this liberal spirit—unashamedly, unapologetically, even combatively. Do they, on the other hand, abide by the rules that Garton Ash suggests should govern free speech in our time?

On the assumption that only a few readers of this book will have read *Free Speech*, I will set out here the ten principles Garton Ash espouses in his book. In Part I of his book, Garton Ash surveys the present world, what he calls 'Cosmopolis', and then reflects on the ideals of freedom of speech and expression, comparing them with the realities of the contemporary world. I will not summarize here the arguments he advances in that part of his book, if only because all the pieces in this present book address those realities, from numerous different angles. I want, rather, simply to import here the ten principles Garton Ash enunciated in 2016 and offer them as a set of criteria by which to judge my own work.

In what he calls a 'User Guide' to his book, Garton Ash wrote of his ten principles:

> The ten principles that follow are distilled formulations of a modern liberal position on free speech...They have been extensively discussed with experts, and with anyone open to such a discussion, online and in person, from Oxford to Beijing and Cairo to Yangon, and then revised in the light of those debates...I believe these precepts are as close to right as I can make them. It seems to me that if everyone everywhere followed them, everyone everywhere would be better off. Now, if you, dear reader, think you have a better set of principles, please put them on the table. Then we can talk about it.

Of course, in order to do this—to table and talk about different sets of principles—we need to adhere to at least tacit shared principles, lest the discussion break down or be shut down by one or the other side. Garton Ash is suggesting that we will all be better off adhering to his ten principles just to the extent that we actually want to have a discussion or debate that goes somewhere. Wherever there are dictators or authoritarian bodies, of course, this is not quite what they have in mind; it's not how they operate; it's not what they permit those within their jurisdiction.

In order to get published in the newspapers and magazines where my pieces have appeared, I have at least tacitly had to observe various conventions of both style and form. I have not, however, had to conform to arbitrary rules regarding the opinions I actually express. I do not write in conformity with an editorial line and I do not avoid expressing opinions with which I know others, often many others and sometimes the majority of my readers, will disagree. But do I write in such a manner that, to borrow Garton Ash's locution, if everyone everywhere wrote in the same manner, then everyone everywhere would be better off? I think that is a good question not only to ask myself, but to ask my readers in a volume of this nature, which brings together a substantial collection of my opinions and reflections. I do not have a fixed opinion on the subject and would be genuinely interested in what others thought about it.

What, then, are Garton Ash's ten principles? They are as follows, in his words:

I. We—all human beings—must be free and able to express ourselves, and to seek, receive and impart information and ideas, regardless of frontiers.

II. We neither make threats of violence nor accept violent intimidation.

III. We allow no taboos against and seize every chance for the spread of knowledge.

IV. We require uncensored, diverse, trustworthy media so we can make well-informed decisions and participate fully in political life.

V. We express ourselves openly and with robust civility about all kinds of human difference.

VI. We respect the believer but not necessarily the content of the belief.

VII. We must be able to protect our privacy and to counter slurs on our reputation, but not prevent scrutiny that is in the public interest.

VIII. We must be empowered to challenge all limits to freedom of information justified on such grounds as national security.

IX. We defend the internet and other systems of communication against illegitimate encroachments by both public and private powers.

X. We decide for ourselves and face the consequences.

In the several hundred pages of this book that follow, you will see every one of these principles in action, I think. The three questions I ask myself are:

1. Have I violated any of these principles in my writing?
2. Have I fallen short of living up to them by holding back at any point?
3. Have I avoided subjects regarding which I should, perhaps, have articulate opinions?

Given that I have written (or spoken) about dictators in countries around the world, secret intelligence organizations, state secrets and counter-intelligence, coups, religious organizations and their adherents, terrorism, climate science, euthanasia, immigration, the American constitution, the teaching of history, the philosophy of science, Zionism, economics and the relationship between predictability and complex systems, I have left ample room for others to point to error or over confidence in the opinions I have expressed. But have I violated any of the ten principles of freedom of expression? I would like to think I have not and that this is one of the chief merits of the present book.

As for the second and third questions, however, I am less sure of my ground. Have I held back where I might have been more forthright on a given subject? Have I failed to dig deeply enough to ascertain what others, perhaps, regard as plain truths? Have I turned a blind eye to certain subjects for questionable reasons? Am I reflexively conservative and insufficiently open to the revision of basic tenets of my worldview? It's not difficult to think of answers to these questions that challenge me. Some of the pieces in this book have elicited challenges on these lines, whether by readers who are not acquainted with me personally or by friends and acquaintances. I have been called a 'neo-con' by one person, a 'highbrow neo-Nazi' by another, a 'white male patriarchal chauvinist' by a third. One pro-Erdogan Turkish diplomat, after my pieces on the events of 2016 in Turkey, asserted that I obviously 'hate Turks and Muslims'. My piece on Trump's electoral victory had me labelled on line a 'pseudo-intellectual cultural Marxist'.

Such denunciation goes with the territory, if one expresses robust opinions. I rejected all of the above characterizations directly. But it doesn't require very much reflection for me to realize, or more than elementary honesty and humility for me to acknowledge, that I do not write very much about Federal politics in Australia, about indigenous affairs, about the inequalities and indignities that exist in my own society, about matters of gender and sexuality, about pornography, about crime. There are many things I have not taken the time to inquire into very much at all, or to write about in the way that I write about international affairs. And I'll be the first to accept that there may well be assumptions embedded in some, perhaps even the greater part, of my writing which might be unimaginatively conservative, culturally weighted, gender weighted. It would be rather surprising, surely, if these things were not the case.

I am, after all, a white male over sixty years of age who has lived his life in a 'Western country', within a liberal democracy and has enjoyed what passes for a liberal education and a reasonably comfortable lifestyle. These things, in considerable measure, have shaped who I am and how I have perceived the world. How could they not have done so? Yet, whatever blinkers those traits may have left in place throughout my life, I have spent almost my entire life with a passionate desire to understand the world as it is in time and space, both scientifically and humanly. I have not consciously attempted to defend any unusual privilege or to gain any unwarranted advantage.

Rather, I have spent what modest resources I had or could muster in the pursuit of learning and the attempt to offer insight where I could. White I may be, but not racist. Male I may be, but not sexist. Three score years old I may be, but not, I hope, blind to the freshness or aspirations of the young. I have attempted to fill the role of scholar and public intellectual with integrity. I offer this book, as I have my others, not with a sense of vanity or self-importance, but by way of continuing to explore the vital domains of learning, liberty and public debate. I hope it will be seen in that light.

Quite recently, I received an email from an emeritus professor of human evolution in Canada, with whose work I have been familiar for almost a decade, and who has of late been reading my 2017 book, *The Secret Gospel According to Mark: The Extraordinary Life of a Catholic Existentialist*, with enormous appreciation. She is in her eighties and wrote the following on what she described as a 'grey day':

> You are in ascendancy and I am in decline
> And as that is the way of it, I must think that it's fine
> But truly I am feeling somewhat saddened by the thought
> That now I have forgotten all the things I ever taught
> The 'graceful' state of aging is yet another tale
> As steadily but all too fast my faculties will fail.

She has done wonderful work and is clearly a very fine person, but she feels her vitality waning and was, on that grey day, somewhat beset by this feeling. It was touching to receive the email.

Yet she expressed that melancholy thought poetically. We have never met; we live half a world away from each other; we are a generation apart in age; she is a woman and I a man; yet we have established a very personal, a very civilized rapport and mutual appreciation. The book of hers that first drew her to my attention was *Fire: The Spark That Ignited Human Evolution*. It inspired a long poem of mine called 'Fire and the Wheel'.[1] I would like to believe that, just to the extent that Timothy Garton Ash's ten principles are observed, such a dignified rapport is, in principle, possible between any two human beings. I hope that this anthology of my episodic writings (and speeches) will contribute in its own modest way to making the world a little more like that. And, dare I profess it, I do hope that my best writing is yet to come.

The pieces in this book have been published over the past three years in *The Age, The Australian, Quadrant, Australia Israel Review* and the *Australian Rationalist*. The original date and place of publication are not indicated piece by piece. Readers may occasionally be able to discern where a piece was published, but it is not germane, for the most part, to the views I advance in any given case. What I write is intended to derive its authority and appeal from what I have to say, not from where I say it. I trust that readers will see things in this light and not be tempted to second guess me and seek to find fault based on where my writing has appeared.

Paul Monk
Melbourne
24 April 2018

---

1   This poem can be found in *Credo and Twelve Poems: A Cosmological Manifesto* (Echo Books, 2016) pp. 79-81.

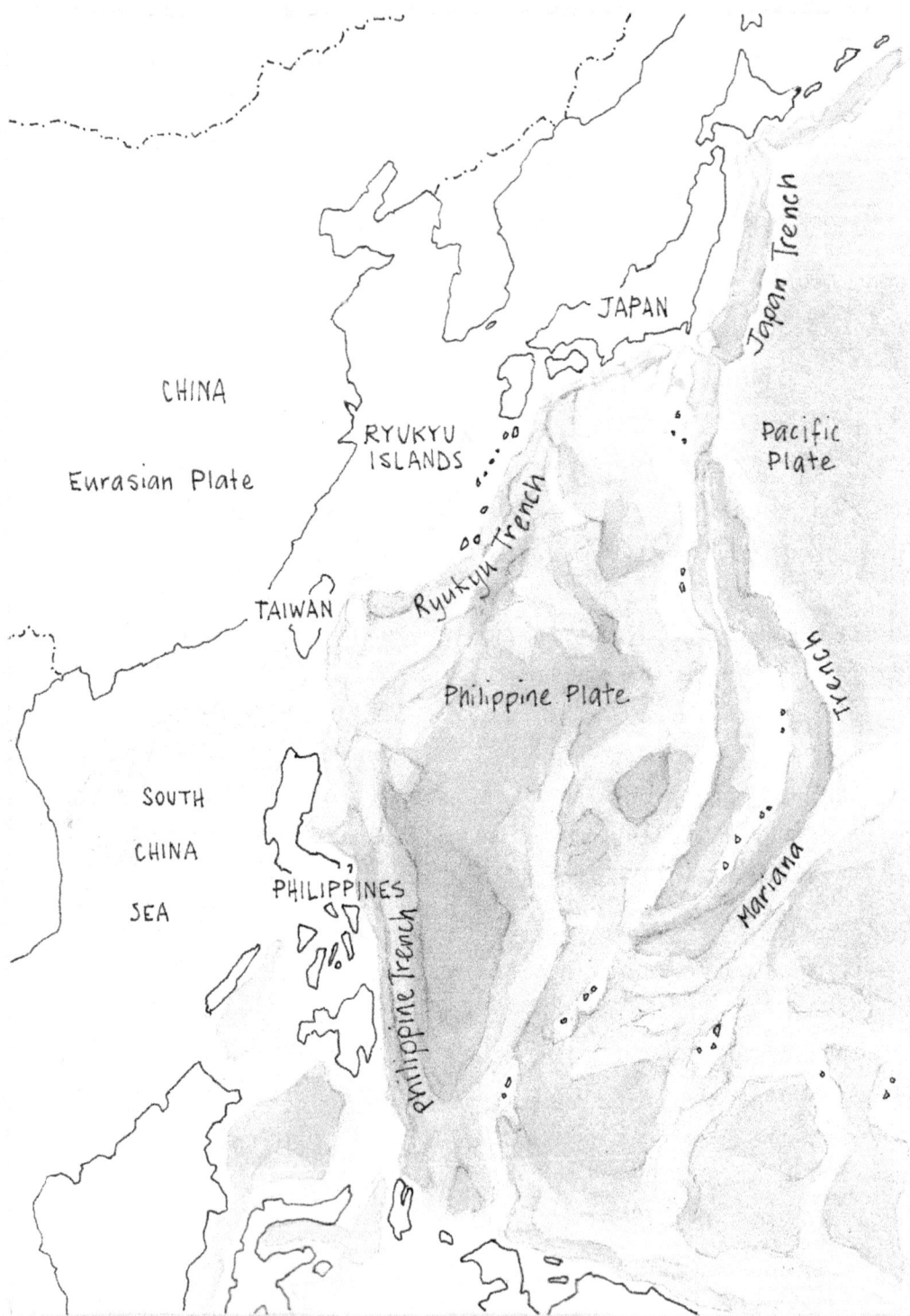

Geophysical and geopolitical fault-lines coincide in East Asia.

PART I: 2015

1: Fault line: China and the first island chain

China's military budget has just been increased by 10%, marking the 21st consecutive year in which its military spending has grown by a double digit increment. It is now the second biggest military spender in the world, after the United States. The difference is that the United States has worldwide commitments, providing security and reassurance to its many allies, including the EU and Japan. China, by contrast, protects no-one and nothing but itself. Why, therefore, is its military spending increasing even faster than its GDP (forecast to grow by roughly 7% this year)?

James Fanell, until recently the head of intelligence for the US Pacific Fleet, headquartered at Pearl Harbour, is in no doubt. He declared on 31 January, to a gathering of more than a hundred military professionals, among them several admirals, that China is preparing for war. 'Let's not deceive ourselves,' he remarked. 'The evidence I've been chewing on over the past fifteen years is overwhelming.' He argued that China's military rise, if left unchecked, 'will necessarily disrupt the peace and stability of our friends, partners and allies.' He urged that the US take deliberate and concerted steps to deter China from using its growing military capabilities to assert control of the South or East China Seas.

In a forthcoming study of these issues—*China's Coming War With Asia*—Jonathan Holslag, Professor of International Politics at the Free University of Brussels, argues that China's ambitions are, indeed, as Fanell describes them, but they are both understandable and justifiable—if seen from within China. He acknowledges that China's neighbours are not reconciled to its ambitions and that the United States has no intention of accommodating them. For that reason, he argues, we should expect some serious trouble in the not too distant future. He does not go so far as to predict a cataclysmic war between China and the United States, but he argues that the tensions between the two are likely to generate a prolonged period of rivalry and posturing along the rim of the Western Pacific and, by proxy, elsewhere in the world.

Holslag's message is of clear relevance to Australian strategic planners, who are currently working up the next Defence White Paper. Much of his book is taken up with going over fairly familiar ground regarding China's great shift after Mao Zedong's death and its impressive 'Meiji Restoration' since the late 1970s. The sharp end of his argument, however, is two pronged. First, he argues that China is a deeply dissatisfied rising power and that it will want to destroy the liberal world order we have become accustomed to since 1945 or since the end of the Cold War, just to the extent that its increasing power enables it to do so. Second, he argues that there is no evident way to satisfy China's ambitions while preserving the security of its neighbours and the liberal world order. He therefore, reluctantly and pessimistically, forecasts war in Asia.

Both the extent and proximity of the danger are, of course, the subject of much debate, here as well as in the United States and Japan. One Beijing-based Western commentator has recently stated that 'the sheer scale of the fiscal resources available to Beijing will soon give it the means to end the era of decisive US military superiority in the Asia-Pacific. Beijing might insist that it has modest military ambitions, and yet the underlying economic and strategic trends tell an altogether different story.' On certain projections, China's gross defence expenditure will grow rapidly and will increase from 2 to 4% of its GDP over the next ten to fifteen years.

'China claims that its rise is intended to be peaceful,' writes Andrew Krepinevich, in the March/April issue of *Foreign Affairs*, 'but its actions tell a different story: that of a revisionist power seeking to dominate the western Pacific.' He argues forthrightly that the response of the United States and other regional states should be 'Archipelagic Defence,' by which he means hi-tech defence of the first island chain—Japan, the Ryukyus, Taiwan and the Philippines—against Chinese revisionist claims and military intrusion. Quite certainly, this is the fault-line where the tectonic plates of American supremacy and Chinese ambition meet.

Holslag emphasizes just this point. 'The whole world,' he writes, 'has been echoing the complaints of Japan and the United States that China is seeking to deny access to its adjacent seas, whereas a formidable screen of sensors and steel is pulled up all along the first island chain around China.' It is precisely this 'screen' that Krepinevich is urging be strengthened in the immediate future. It is chiefly against that same screen that China has been developing a wide range of capabilities. It is important, therefore, to remind ourselves that the first island chain does not consist of abstract American defensive positions, but of a series of independent states, each of which has been actively seeking US assurances against the rising power of China. The situation would be very different if those states had been seeking Chinese support against an unwelcome US dominance.

The strategic debate in Australia must reckon with all this at two levels: our deep economic engagement with China and the possible consequences for our wider interests should the US retreat from the first island chain and an assertive China make good its claims to territorial control of the East and South China Seas. Hugh White, in particular, has been urging that we press the US to pull back and give China much of what it demands, but then resist if China starts to get out of hand. Malcolm Fraser and Paul Keating have been calling for us to abandon our alliance with the US altogether. The first island chain, however, is the only available defensive redoubt along which to guard against Chinese ambitions; and the US is the only power whose presence might deter China from going to war in Asia. Holslag quietly fears that trouble is unavoidable. He may be right.

2: Genocide by any other name

One of the strangest holdovers from the disasters of the 20th century is the refusal of the Turkish government to acknowledge the genocides of Armenians and Assyrians that were perpetrated under the Young Turks a century ago this year. Many governments, including our own, hesitate to call a spade a spade for fear of offending the Turkish government, but the Pope has recently called Turkey on the matter. At the very least, as Eugene Rogan observes in his newly published study *The Fall of the Ottomans: The Great War in the Middle East 1914-1920* (Allen Lane 2015), massive killing took place at the hands of the Turkish authorities of a nature and on a scale which made it genocide by any other name.

The Young Turks, who had come to power just before the First World War and in the wake of war in the Balkans that had displaced many Muslims, engaged in what has recently been termed 'ethnic cleansing', in an effort to stabilize their domain. Hundreds of thousands of Greek Christians were expelled from Ottoman territories before and during the First World War. This was to climax in the Greek war against Turkey the downfall of the Ottoman Empire and the expulsion of the Greeks from Smyrna in 1922.

The expulsion of the Greeks was ethnic cleansing, but it *wasn't* genocide. What happened to the Armenians and Assyrians in 1915-16 is another matter. They were deported wholesale from within their homelands and, in the process, either starved or slaughtered in very large numbers. The lowest estimates for Armenian dead are in the order of 800,000 and run as high as 1.5 million; while an estimated 250,000 Assyrians were also massacred. Pope Francis drew attention to this in the current ISIS context.

The Ottoman Empire, in 1915, was threatened on three fronts by enemy assault. The Russians were pressing an attack from the Caucasus, the British were thrusting northward from Basra in Mesopotamia and Anglo-French naval and land forces were striking at the Dardanelles and threatening Constantinople. Many Armenians openly hoped the Allies would bring down the Ottoman Empire, so that they could be released from bondage and have their own country.

Clearly, these circumstances exacerbated longstanding ethnic and religious tensions between Muslim Turks and their Armenian and other Christian subjects. The Young Turks viewed the Armenians as a bigger threat than the Greeks, largely because an Armenian nation state would have to be carved out of core Turkish territory, where Greece existed as an entirely separate nation (which had won its independence from the Ottomans a century before). The genocidal response, however, was shocking and cannot be glossed over any longer merely because the contemporary Turkish authorities object to it being pointed out.

Two key events precipitated the genocide: an uprising in the eastern Anatolian city of Van (in the heart of ancient Armenia) beginning on 20 April 1915 and the decision by the Turkish authorities on 24 April to 'decapitate' the ethnic Armenian leadership. More than two hundred Armenian political, intellectual and religious figures were arrested in Constantinople. Van was strategically located close to the borders with both Russia and Persia and its Armenian population, having suffered pogroms at Turkish and Kurdish hands for many years, actively sought Russian support. The Turkish government, for its part, feared that the large Armenian population in the capital would side with the Allies if things went badly on the Dardanelles.

The response to the Armenian uprising by the Turkish governor of Van, Cevdet Pasha, was to order the killing of all Armenian males over the age of twelve. That was the beginning of the murderous policy which, over the following twelve months was to generate wholesale deportations and killings. Mehmed Talat Pasha, one of the ruling triumvirate of Young Turks, submitted a bill to the Ottoman Council of Ministers on 26 May 1915 called the Deportation Law, calling for the wholesale deportation of the Armenian population from eastern Anatolia, with only three to five days' notice.

Alongside the public law, the Young Turks issued secret orders to the governors of the provinces of Anatolia that the Armenians were to be exterminated. Governors who demanded written instructions or who dissented were dismissed or even assassinated. Enver Pasha's secret intelligence service mobilized killing squads. Armenian villages were surrounded, the men separated from the women and children and then executed, while the women and children were sent on forced death marches. To all this there is abundant first hand testimony, Turkish, Armenian and foreign.

There is nothing peculiarly Turkish or Muslim about the horrors that were perpetrated. But the killing of well over one million Armenian and Assyrian Christians in 1915-16 *was* perpetrated by the Muslim Turkish government. Good relations with the current Muslim Turkish government cannot be based on pretending that none of this happened, but must be based on honesty about the horrors committed in the name of empire and religion, with a view to preventing or at least prosecuting such crimes in future.

Let's be clear that setting this record straight is not a matter of launching accusations against the state of Turkey in 2015, any more than setting the record straight about the atrocities of the Second World War is a case of making accusations against the current governments or citizens of Germany and Japan. Admission, at long last, that these terrible things happened would not make the present Turkish nation or government look bad.

What makes them look bad is their refusal to confess that the Young Turks presided over that genocidal ethnic cleansing. Dealing with the authoritarian government of Recip Tayyip

Erdogan on such a matter is unlikely to be rewarding. What we could do, in this country, however, which has numerous citizens of both Turkish and Armenian (as well as Greek) ethnic origin is to orchestrate a truth and reconciliation process in which realities can at last be acknowledged and a better future created—here, if not over there.

3: There is a lot to learn from earthquakes

We are in the first stages of reacting to the earthquake in Nepal: shock, rescue, emergency relief efforts and overall damage assessment. An estimated six thousand people have been killed and millions left homeless. The Nepalese government has responded ineptly and there could well be political consequences from the fallout. But beyond the immediate response to the natural catastrophe, there is a lot to reflect upon and internalize concerning the significance of earthquakes and our place in the natural world.

One of the most important things to register is that we have only, in the past half century or so, developed a serious science of seismology and a capacity to understand the nature, anticipate the probability and estimate the severity of earthquakes. None of that seems to have helped in the case of Nepal, because of the incompetence of the Nepalese authorities and the poverty and inaccessibility of much of the country. There were, apparently, some warnings, but no serious measures were put in place to prepare for what happened.

There are other places in the world where the same kind of thing could happen with even more devastating consequences. Tehran, for example, is a crowded, jerry-built city at serious risk from a catastrophic earthquake. It can be calculated with some confidence that there will be an earthquake at 7.0 or above on the Richter scale under Tehran every 300 years. It has not had one for as long as records have been kept, so we do not know where we sit in the 300 year time band. But should such a quake hit Tehran it would almost certainly kill huge numbers of people, because the city is vast and has not been designed to withstand a serious earthquake.

Seismology did not begin as a science until after the famous Lisbon earthquake of 1755 and even then it took two hundred years before it began to mature as a science. That quake was about 9.0 on the Richter scale, far bigger than the recent one in Nepal. It killed an unknown number of people (estimates range from 10,000 to 100,000) because it not only demolished the Portuguese capital of Lisbon and its surrounds, but generated tsunamis that hit lands on both sides of the Atlantic and are thought to have killed large numbers of people on the coasts of Morocco.

There was a great deal of speculation after the Lisbon earthquake regarding what it 'signified'. Theologians urged that it was a manifestation of the wrath of the Christian God. A number of more sceptical individuals pointed out that this seemed improbable, if only because the Alfama, the city's famous red-light district, had been one of the few parts of Lisbon to pretty much pass unscathed. The philosopher Immanuel Kant wrote the first theses on the possible natural causes of earthquakes, showing, as in so much of his work, both striking originality and considerable perceptiveness.

Voltaire was inspired to write his famous novel *Candide*; a picaresque reflection on the nature of the world and the human condition, lampooning the pious claim by the philosopher Leibniz that all was for the best in the best of all possible worlds. The great French *philosophe* swayed many readers with his ridicule of Leibniz's theodicy, but he was well short of being able to offer a science of the natural world or of the human condition within it. All that had to wait until the 20th century and even the last decades of the 20th century.

The key to earthquakes, it transpired, was continental drift and plate tectonics. The theory of continental drift was first conceived in 1911 by Alfred Wegener, but was rejected for the next fifty or sixty years by the scientific world. The story is beautifully told by James Lawrence Powell in *Four Revolutions in the Earth Sciences: From Heresy to Truth* (Columbia University Press, 2015).

Only in the past half century has continental drift been acknowledged as a reality. We now know that the Indian sub-continent was once an island land mass which has drifted northward over millions of years, colliding with the Eurasian landmass long before human beings emerged out of the primate past and pushing masses of rock upward to form the Himalayas and the Tibetan plateau. That inexorable geological force is the cause of the recent earthquake in Nepal.

This scientific breakthrough has gone along with revolutions in probability theory, the theory of complex systems and many other sciences to provide us with a better understanding of the natural world and our place within it than any earlier human culture or civilization. It was in 1944, for instance, that Charles Richter and Beno Gutenberg at Caltech established that there is a straightforward, power law relationship between the frequency and magnitude of earthquakes: the frequency decreases exponentially with the magnitude. The decrease in frequency forms almost a straight line.

This makes good forecasting, but not precise prediction, possible—rather as in meteorology. Fukushima was such a disaster because the nuclear plant was built to withstand an earthquake up to 8.0 on the Richter scale; nothing bigger being thought credible. What occurred was a massive 9.1 quake. The power law could have warned the designers, but they overlooked or ignored it. We suffer irregular economic and geo-political 'earthquakes' for much the same reason.

The most general lesson from all this is that earthquakes have nothing whatsoever to do with deities of any kind. They are wholly natural phenomena, caused by characteristics of the physical world which were not designed for our ease and comfort; or, indeed, 'designed' at all. We can, with good science and sound governance, take precautions against them. The same holds true for a wide range of natural and social phenomena in a complex world. Alas, far too many of us still fail to understand the world in a naturalistic and probabilistic way. As for governance—well, that calls for a lot of work, locally and globally.

4: It's not the Reformation Islam needs, but the Enlightenment

ISIS has just taken Ramadi and is close to the ancient ruin of Palmyra. While Western leaders persist in denying that ISIS is Islamic, everybody should be reading Ayaan Hirsi Ali's newly published manifesto, *Heretic: Why Islam Needs a Reformation Now* (Fourth Estate, 2015). It is a clarion call we all need to hear and heed. Her argument that Islam needs a Reformation—on the model of the 16th century Reformation in Europe—is problematic. She is actually calling for an Enlightenment to descend upon Islam. But she has what might be called a genuine moral compass. Her bold polemic should be read as widely as possible and discussed.

'For years, we have spent trillions on waging war against 'terror' and 'extremism'', she writes, but 'we have not bothered to develop an effective counter narrative, because from the outset we have denied that Islamic extremism is in any way related to Islam.' The counter narrative she suggests is that the ideas in question *are* rooted in Islam, not in socio-economic conditions, and that Islam needs a fundamental overhaul if it is to live in peace with the modern world and with itself. She is right, but the Reformation is the wrong model for her thinking.

She calls for at least five fundamental changes in Islamic belief and practice:

1. renunciation of Muhammed's semi-divine status and the claim that the Quran is a pure revelation from Allah (especially parts dating from Muhammed's time in Medina, when he became violent);
2. a shift from investment in the imagined after-life to concentration on life in the actual world;
3. the abandonment of sharia law in favour of civil law;
4. the abandonment of the practice of 'commanding right and forbidding wrong' which empowers vigilante gangs and obsessive individuals to harass others in the name of strict religious codes;
5. a radical revision of teachings about jihad, to remove the calls for Islam to be spread by force against infidels.

She is absolutely correct that these changes are needed, but they are not what an Islamic Luther or Calvin would have called for. They are the equivalent of saying to the Catholic Church in the 16th century that it should renounce the divinity of Jesus and the idea that the Bible was the revealed word of God; give up an emphasis on the afterlife; meld canon law in to civil law; renounce Papal authority and institute freedom of conscience and religious belief across the board.

The only one of these that Luther and Calvin brought to the table was the rejection of Papal authority. The changes *she* wants to see are what a Locke or Voltaire called for in the 17th and 18th centuries. She tacitly concedes this by quoting them, not Luther or Calvin, when it comes to freedom and civil law.

Sayyid Qutb, Egyptian theoretician of the Muslim Brotherhood in the 1960s, with his trenchant text *Milestones*, was a Muslim Calvin in his way. Tariq Ramadan, author of *The Messenger,* in 2006-07, has actually been hailed (in the *Washington Post*, no less) as the 'Muslim Martin Luther'. Yet they call for very different things than what Ayaan Hirsi Ali would like to see. They are critics of falling away from Islam and the secularization of Muslim societies. This has genuine parallels with the Reformation. What Hirsi Ali is calling for does not.

Reason, not blind adherence to the Quranic verses or the hadith (the sayings attributed to Muhammed), must guide Muslims to a better way, she insists. Reason is the Devil's whore, declared Martin Luther; and what is required is unquestioning faith in Biblical revelation. The consequence of the Reformation was one hundred and fifty years of religious war in Europe that tore Christendom apart, climaxing with the Thirty Years War (1618-48).

We are seeing something like that right now in the Middle East and Africa, not only in the atrocities of ISIS and Boko Haram, but in the regression of Turkey, the aggression of Iran and the growing commitment of Saudi Arabia and the Gulf States to war against both ISIS and Iran. None of this is progress. All of it bodes ill, both for the Middle East and for the rest of us.

Hirsi Ali is taking a necessary stand; but she is the same kind of heretic as Walter Kaufmann, author of *The Faith of a Heretic*, who renounced his parents' Lutheranism and then the Judaism of his grandparents, while remaining interested in and appreciative of the better elements of the Jewish and Christian religions. Hirsi Ali is not a believer. She is free and liberal minded. The dissidents within Islam or in the Muslim world that she champions should be championed, also, by us; but they are the equivalent of Giordano Bruno or Michael Servetus, not Luther or Calvin. Both were burned at the stake as heretics: Bruno by the Roman Inquisition; Servetus by Calvin in Geneva.

Hirsi Ali does not want to revive Islam as the 'true religion', but to see Islam reduced to a quiet cultural relic, like Christianity in Europe; with all the dogmatism and harshness stripped away. She claims that Muslim Reformation is coming, but it is already upon us. We should, all the more, as she urges, support dissidents in the Muslim world as we supported dissidents in the Communist bloc during the Cold War—but not in the name of a 'pure' Islam.

One of the finest current dissidents is the young Pakistani school girl, Malala Yousafzai, whom the Taliban tried to kill. She wrote: 'The extremists are afraid of books and pens. The power of education frightens them...They think that God is a tiny little conservative being who would send girls to Hell just because of going to school.' Quite so, but the adherents of this tiny, little conservative deity, are many and on the warpath. We misunderstand our dilemmas if we believe that they are not really Muslims.

5: *Going Clear* is all about civil liberties

If you are thinking about religion, social order and deradicalisation, you must see the new Alex Gibney documentary *Going Clear: Scientology and the Prison of Belief*. If you're not thinking about them, you're living in a cocoon. Based on Lawrence Wright's book *Going Clear: Scientology, Hollywood and the Prison of Belief* (2013), the film is a remarkably measured and candid exposé. But its importance goes way beyond Scientology. It addresses the general susceptibility of human beings to manipulation, the role of religion in society and the complexities associated with the civil liberties enshrined, in the case of the United States, in the First Amendment.

It's strength is a set of interviews with former Scientologists who have escaped the grip of the organization and spoken out. The common theme is that, in retrospect, they feel astonished at how they had succumbed to both the teachings and the manipulative control of the organization at all. Several of them, like Mike Rinder, Marty Rathbun and Paul Haggis, who were prominent figures in the organization for many years, express remorse, even shame, at the roles they played. It's rare to see such candid admissions of gullibility and culpability.

Superficially, it's possible to watch the film, feel astonished that these people—who come across as ordinary, decent folk—were taken in; and think that Scientology is a 'cult', which should be stripped of its tax exempt status and hounded out of existence. But the film is an invitation, at least implicitly, to think a lot further than that. How, exactly, would one go about defining 'cult' and hounding this particular one out of existence without threatening numerous other religious organizations and 'cults'—and without being seen as persecuting a 'religious' minority? There's the rub.

We are in the midst of a sustained debate about religion, minorities, law and the public good right now. We are discussing, among other things, 'deradicalisation' programs for Muslim youths caught up in jihadist propaganda and incitement to violence. Gibney's film is a very good pathway into thinking about this complex and delicate process, while having nothing to say about Islam at all. It confronts us with the question: How, in general, do we go about setting people free from noxious beliefs and the control of organizations which both teach such beliefs and manipulate those whom they convert?

Half a century ago, the psychologist Stanley Milgram conducted a famous set of experiments. He wanted to explore the susceptibility of human beings to following instructions of 'authority figures'. His findings were, famously, disturbing. He found that a surprisingly large number of the subjects were prepared to obey instructions from such figures well past the point of doing things that they felt uncomfortable doing, even in the absence of any form of coercion or pressure. If you add increments of such things, of course, the problem can get much worse.

As I watched the film, I kept thinking of the Maoist movement and the contemporary Chinese Communist Party, with their relentless thought control and coercive pressures on dissent or criticism. The Maoists were far worse than the Scientologists in terms of abuses; not just during the notorious Cultural Revolution, but before they ever seized power. The Party Rectification Movement at Yan'an, in the early 1940s, was a much larger and more brutal version of Scientology's practices in the past decade and more under David Miscavige. The Communist Party's ongoing thought control and repression in China are likewise worse than the abuses of Scientology.

It's because such thought control and repression can happen, in the name of religion or totalitarian ideology, that we have developed laws to protect civil rights. One comes out of a screening of *Going Clear* asking: How is it most appropriate and intelligent to respond when these things happen in the very midst of such freedoms? After all, Scientology took root in the United States and has protected itself from both taxation and the intrusion of the civil authorities under the codicils of the First Amendment. What is to be done in such cases?

It is sobering to reflect that banning the organization, or its books, or its practices might contravene civil liberties; whereas not doing so appears to permit rogues and scoundrels to get away with exploiting and abusing the vulnerability and gullibility of large numbers of people and piling up dynastic fortunes along the way. Yet Scientology is very far from being the only 'religion' to do this—in America or here.

We have a liberal, secular culture, but many religions. We cut people a lot of slack in terms of whatever they might choose to believe, however foolish, because we want to be left free to make up our own minds about things and so feel obliged to leave others to do the same. Every now and then, things happen which challenge this secular commitment. Scientology is one of them. It is only one, however, and by no means the most important or challenging one.

The refreshing thing is that Wright and Gibney have been able to research and expose it without infringing on anyone's civil liberties; indeed by exercising—and enabling others to exercise—such liberties. Gibney's film is a refresher course in what civil liberties are all about. Spend some time talking about it with your friends. Ask yourselves the difficult questions about how movements like Scientology are able to do what they do and why people are drawn to them. The exercise will be a conditioning for your, perhaps flabby, civil libertarian 'muscles'.

The Scientologists are denouncing Alex Gibney as a 'propagandist'. But, as *Esquire* magazine put it even five years ago, he is possibly 'the most important documentarian of our time'. His films include *We Steal Secrets: The Story of Wikileaks, Mea Maxima Culpa: Silence in the House of God* and *Enron: The Smartest Guys in the Room*. If you haven't seen those masterful 'propaganda' films, you should have. This one, too.

6: Ayaan Hirsi Ali's 'reformation' and the challenge of Islam

In the June issue of this magazine, Daryl McCann provided a thoughtful reflection on Ayaan Hirsi Ali's newly published manifesto, *Heretic: Why Islam Needs a Reformation Now* (Fourth Estate, 2015). He drew attention to the divergent reviews it has been getting, from ironical praise to angry condemnation. While generally supportive of her stance, he noted, in passing, that 'in her heart of hearts Ayaan Hirsi Ali remains an apostate and her true sympathies are for those who, like herself, are daring and fortunate enough to escape.' No-one reading her book, I believe, could avoid reaching the same conclusion. Hirsi Ali seeks to appeal to as many Muslims as possible to embrace modernity and tolerance, but what she seeks is not the Reformation. It is the Enlightenment. She evokes Locke and Voltaire, not Luther and Calvin, when she speaks most forthrightly about the principles and values that should prevail.

The crucial issue here, as Ayaan Hirsi Ali points out, is that we are engaged in a war of ideas and not merely the attempted suppression of a rogue 'death cult.' For years, we have spent trillions on waging war against 'terror' and 'extremism', she writes, but 'we have not bothered to develop an effective counter narrative, because from the outset we have denied that Islamic extremism is in any way related to Islam.' The counter narrative she suggests is that the problems we face *are* rooted in Islam, not in socio-economic conditions, and that Islam needs a fundamental overhaul if it is to live in peace with the modern world. As she points out, there are no Christian terrorists in the Middle East, although the Christians live under the same conditions as the Muslims. Indeed, they are suffering expulsion or suppression by Muslims in many places, even as Muslims demand greater acceptance within the West. There are also no Zoroastrian terrorists in Iran, although their religion has been suppressed by Muslims there for many centuries.

Hirsi Ali, for those who are not as yet acquainted with her life or work, is of Somali Muslim origin. She lived for periods of her childhood and early adolescence in Somalia, Saudi Arabia and Kenya, before fleeing the Islam of her family and an arranged marriage and seeking asylum in the Netherlands. To her enormous credit, once given such asylum, she worked her way into literacy and a university education, spoke out against the reactionary practices and intolerant beliefs of Islam and was elected to the Dutch Parliament. *Heretic* is her fourth book and has been written, like her previous book, *Infidel*, under the shadow of death threats from Muslim fanatics. She has not been cowed or silenced, but has married the celebrated historian of war and finance, Niall Ferguson, moved to America and continued her campaign for a far reaching overhaul of Islam globally. Her book merits sympathetic reading on all these counts.

She points out that she has been shunned not only by the Muslim establishment, but by many so-called 'liberals' in the West, whose mantra is that criticism of Islam or any suggestion that it is accountable for the violence perpetrated in its name, constitutes 'Islamophobia' and 'hate speech' that should not be given a platform. In her own words:

> Let me make my point in the simplest possible terms: Islam is not a religion of peace...
> For expressing the idea that Islamic violence is rooted not in social, economic or
> political conditions—or even in theological error—but rather in the foundational
> texts of Islam itself, I have been denounced as a bigot and an 'Islamophobe'. I have been
> silenced, shunned and shamed. In effect, I have been deemed to be a heretic, not just by
> Muslims—for whom I am already an apostate—but by some Western liberals as well,
> whose multicultural sensibilities are offended by such 'insensitive' pronouncements.

Her courage and lucidity are to be applauded. Note that she uses the word 'heretic' here less as a label put on her by Muslims than as one attached to her by 'liberals' who see her stance as 'Islamophobic'—and therefore inadmissible. If we have any sense at all, we will stand with Ayaan Hirsi Ali. We will do so, as Bernard-Henri Levy wrote in 2008, because this is the enlightened place to stand—against reactionary religious dogmatism, social oppression and terroristic violence.

A book with a similar outspoken message, Mona Eltahawy's *Headscarves and Hymens: Why the Middle East Needs a Sexual Revolution* (Weidenfeld & Nicolson, 2015) strikes a very similar note—and has suffered a very similar reception. She writes:

> There is no sugar-coating it. We Arab women live in a culture that is fundamentally
> hostile to us, enforced by men's contempt...Name me an Arab country and I'll recite
> a litany of abuses against women occurring in that country, abuses fuelled by a toxic
> mix of culture and religion that few seem willing to disentangle lest they blaspheme or
> offend.

'Enough, already!' is this brave woman's outcry. It doesn't matter what Muhammad thought or wrote or said; we do not live in the 7th century, but in the 21st century and it's time that this patriarchal, religiously-enforced culture was brought down and the situation of women in the Muslim world transformed. Who among us could disagree? Yet, of all people, 'liberal' feminists and post-colonial leftists seem ready to do so and to distance themselves from such radical stands as 'Islamophobic'. How do we move forward under these circumstances?

The story of Ayaan Hirsi Ali is instructive in that regard. Instead of being able to participate in a shared critical and free inquiry into the nature of Islam, she finds herself threatened, ostracised and rebuked for even raising certain issues. This has happened, of course, in many other circumstances—in religious controversies in the West, in ideological controversies during the Cold War and in debates over climate and the environment, among other things. This is precisely why she self-consciously calls herself a heretic. She knows that she has taken a stance that makes very many people uncomfortable. Her point is that this needs to be done and that any emancipated society committed to reason and liberty would accept at the very least her right to articulate such a point of view. She should be defended on this ground alone, quite apart from the merits of the specific arguments she has advanced. My purpose in writing this essay is chiefly to defend her—but also to question some of her arguments.

The Netherlands, where she first sought and gained refuge, was the seed-bed less of the Reformation (which it embraced in defiance of the Catholic Habsburg Empire), than of the processes of discussion and scholarship that slowly turned the Reformation into the Enlightenment in Europe. It was a drawn out process, but the critical response to Calvinism as well as to Catholicism slowly generated the stances which became the underpinnings of modern, restrained religion. These were Socinian (rejection of the divinity of Jesus of Nazareth) and Deist (distancing of belief in a Deity from belief in the specifically Judaeo-Christian one). Dogma was unpicked and rejected piece by piece. The work of Spinoza was a landmark in all this and he was execrated by Catholics, Protestants and orthodox Jews alike. Yet his critique of Biblical religion was fundamental to what, over the following century became the current of Enlightenment across much of Europe.

America, where Hirsi Ali now makes her home, was founded by refugees from religious persecution and grew as a republic, in the late 18th century as the Enlightenment was gaining ground and scepticism, Unitarianism (rejection of the Trinity) and Deism were becoming the common religious stance of educated Americans. So much was this so that Thomas Jefferson, in the early 19th century thought that Unitarianism might become the dominant religion in the United States. What Ayaan Hirsi Ali is seeking in the Islamic world of the 21st century is something like that makeover of dogmatic religion in Europe. But those of us who admire her courage and share her basic convictions would do well to remind ourselves that the process in Europe was very protracted, always incomplete and ended (insofar as it has ended) with a great many Europeans still adhering to various Christian beliefs. The matter is magisterially reviewed in J. G. A. Pocock's six volume reflection on Edward Gibbon and the Enlightenment, *Barbarism and Religion*.

Besieged by critics and denounced as an 'Islamophobe', Hirsi Ali declares passionately:

> My uncompromising statements on this topic have incited such vehement
> denunciations that one would think I had committed an act of violence myself. For
> today, it seems, speaking the truth about Islam is a crime. 'Hate speech' is the modern
> term for heresy. And in the present atmosphere, anything that makes Muslims feel
> uncomfortable is branded as 'hate'.

> In these pages it is my intention to make many people—not only Muslims but also Western apologists for Islam—uncomfortable. I am not going to do this by drawing cartoons. Rather, I intend to challenge centuries of religious orthodoxy with ideas and arguments that I am certain will be denounced as heretical...I intend to speak freely in the hope that others will debate equally freely with me on what needs to change in Islamic doctrine, rather than seeking to stifle discussion.

Here the divide yawns wide between those who identify themselves with the Western intellectual tradition and with the Enlightenment, on the one hand, and those who have wandered off into some kind of 'post-modern' relativism and spineless capitulationism, or anti-scientific nihilism, on the other. It is a scandal that we should need a Somali woman, taking refuge in the West, to stand up unapologetically for free discussion in the face of 'liberal' cant and reactionary religion.

There is, however, a gulf between what Hirsi Ali would like to see and the realities across the Muslim world that we confront. She expresses the belief that the tide is changing in favour of her 'Reformation', but the European Reformation was a long drawn out and violent process and did not in itself get Europe to religious toleration and secular peace. What she asks of Muslims is not only very radical, but at the end of the day *anti-religious*. She is calling for no less than the *abandonment* by mullahs around the world and their teeming followers of any serious commitment to the Quran or the Prophet on religious and dogmatic grounds. Even in the West, we have only ever gone part of the way down that road and there are still vast numbers of passionate and dogmatic Christians running around. Hirsi Ali is, in short, very much an infidel in the Muslim world as well as, apparently, a heretic on the Left. She is highly unlikely to see her hopes fulfilled any time soon.

Consider the five most fundamental changes in Islamic belief and practice that she calls for:

1. Renunciation of Muhammed's semi-divine and infallible status along with the literalist reading of the Quran, particularly those parts that were attributed to Muhammed's sojourn in Medina, where he started resorting to violence against unbelievers;

2. A shift from investment in an imagined life after death to concentration on life in the actual world, before death;

3. Abandonment of sharia law in favour of civil law;

4. Abandonment of the practice of 'commanding right and forbidding wrong' which empowers families, communities or vigilante gangs to harass others in the name of strict religious codes;

5. The radical revision of teachings about jihad, to remove the calls for Islam to be spread by force against infidels.

She is, I believe, absolutely correct that all these changes are needed, but they are not what an Islamic Luther or Calvin would have called for. They are the equivalent of saying to the Catholic Church in the 16th century that it should renounce the Trinity, the Incarnation, the Petrine magisterium of the Papacy, and the unique authority of the Bible as the revealed word of God; give up an emphasis on the afterlife; meld canon law into civil law; and institute freedom of conscience and religious belief across the board. Far more moderate demands by the likes of Luther and Calvin triggered religious wars and persecutions in Europe.

The only one of those changes that Luther and Calvin brought to the table was the rejection of the Petrine magisterium of the Papacy and the corrupt or fraudulent practices that it had engendered. The changes Hirsi Ali wants to see are what a Locke or Voltaire called for in the 17th and 18th centuries: toleration, scepticism and civil authority over religion. She tacitly concedes this by quoting them, not Luther or Calvin, when it comes to toleration, freedom of religious belief and civil law. In short, what she is calling for, in a single bound, is something that took Europe about 250 to 300 years to achieve. And Europe had the enormous advantages of having already gone through the Renaissance, having a pagan intellectual tradition of republican government and independent philosophical reflection to draw upon and being economically and geopolitically in the ascendant. None of these things apply to Islam in the 21st century. For all these reasons, the changes she calls for would be difficult to achieve even if there was widespread support for them among both Muslim intellectuals and the Muslim masses. Instead, she is meeting hostility and condescension left and right.

There is, however, an even more fundamental problem for the project she proposes. The very radicals whom she denounces (for very good reasons) are themselves the heroes of the Islamic Reformation. That 'Reformation' might be said to have begun with Muhammed ibn Abd al-Wahhab, in Saudi Arabia, in the late 18th century. The Ottoman caliphate attempted to suppress Wahhab, but his version of Islam predominates in Saudi Arabia now and has been exported by it around the world. The Muslim Brotherhood, from the 1920s, following the downfall of the Ottomans and the end of the caliphate, renewed the call for a Muslim 'Reformation'—a return to the 'purity' of scripture and the sayings of the Prophet. Sayyid Qutb, Egyptian theoretician of the Muslim Brotherhood in the 1960s, with his trenchant text *Milestones*, was a Muslim Calvin in his way. Tariq Ramadan, author of *The Messenger*, in 2006-07, has actually been hailed (in the *Washington Post*, no less) as the 'Muslim Martin Luther'. In a Western world based on religious dissent, these descriptions read like honorifics, but a revival of 'pure' Islam is the last thing anyone should want to see.

Hirsi Ali distinguishes between what she calls Mecca Muslims, Medina Muslims and Modifying Muslims. The first are those who accept the Quran and the hadith, but do not believe in trying to impose Islam (submission) on infidels by force. They nonetheless practice many things which are, to say the least, open to question; and many of them are susceptible to the call to jihad by radicals. The Medina Muslims are those who take as their exemplar the Muhammad who at Medina began to enforce Islam at the point of the sword. They insist on the imposition of Islam by jihad and denounce even the other religions of the Bible, Judaism and Christianity as false religions. Modifying Muslims are those who, like herself, seek to reconcile their broad Islamic cultural heritage with modernity and to leave behind the dogmatism and harshness of traditional Islam. She hopes they can draw the majority of Mecca Muslims to their side and isolate the Medina Muslims. Unfortunately, she undercuts her appeal to Mecca Muslims by basically repudiating Mecca. She leaves herself wide open to the retort that she is seeking to draw Muslims *away* from their religious traditions altogether, leaving only an empty shell behind as a cultural memory. She would perhaps have done better simply to espouse this goal outright.

Reason, not blind adherence to the Quranic verses or the hadith (the sayings attributed to Muhammed), must guide Muslims to a better way, she insists. Reason is the Devil's whore, declared Martin Luther; and what is required is unquestioning faith in Biblical revelation. Taking free initiatives to enhance well-being and prosperity is what Hirsi Ali would like to see Muslims doing; but Calvin preached predestination and insisted that only the grace of God, not works or freedom of the intellect could lead to salvation in a 'fallen' world. Neither preached or practised religious toleration or freedom of discussion. And the Catholic Church responded to them with the creation of the Roman Inquisition and the Counter-Reformation. The consequences of all this were one hundred and fifty years of religious war in Europe that tore Christendom apart, climaxing with the Thirty Years War (1618-48). All those trying to think their way through this morass would do well to read Mark Greengrass's *Christendom Destroyed: Europe 1517-1648*.

We are seeing something like the 16th century wars of religion right now in the Middle East and Africa, not only in the atrocities of ISIS and Boko Haram, but in the regression of Turkey, the theocratic regime in Iran and the growing commitment of Saudi Arabia and the Gulf States to war against both ISIS and Iran. None of this is progress. All of it bodes ill, both for the Middle East and for the rest of us. Moreover, within Saudi Arabia and such other states as Pakistan, contemporary Islamic practice is intolerant of other religions and repressive of women's rights just to the extent that it emphasizes a return to the Quran and the inerrancy of the Prophet. The cruel practices and repression of religious freedom that are endemic in such countries are certainly abhorrent to Ayaan Hirsi Ali—and rightly so—but they are deeply rooted in Islam. Rooting them out will mean rooting Islam up to a very large extent.

Pretending that things are otherwise and that Islam is basically a sound and peaceful religion is like pretending that the Chinese Communist Party is liberal and democratic at heart, when plainly it is nothing of the kind. If we are to move forward, we must begin by acknowledging and debating a few inescapable and rather dismal realities.

Hirsi Ali is taking a necessary stand; but she is the same kind of heretic as Walter Kaufmann, a German Jewish émigré, American philosopher and author of *The Faith of a Heretic*, among many other books. Kaufmann renounced his parents' Lutheranism at the age of eleven; because he decided he did not believe that Jesus was divine. He practised the Judaism of his grandparents for some years as an adolescent, but decided as a young adult that he did not believe in the existence of the old Deity or the claims of Judaism as a religion. He nonetheless remained interested in and appreciative of the better elements of the Jewish and Christian religions. He wrote fine books on Nietzsche, on the philosophy of religion and on existentialism—as a philosopher in America. Crucially, while he had to flee genocidal mania in Germany, he was free to think and change his opinions in the United States and to write without religious censorship.

Hirsi Ali, like Kaufmann, is not a believer. She is free and liberal minded, but is only able to think, write and speak as she does because she is *not* living in a Muslim society. Many of us in Australia are, similarly, able to inquire, write and speak as we see fit because we live in a secular, liberal society and not one dominated by any given religion. The finest and bravest dissidents within Islam or in the Muslim world that she champions should be championed, also, by us; but they are the equivalent of Giordano Bruno or Michael Servetus, rather than Martin Luther or John Calvin. Both were burned at the stake as heretics: Bruno by the Catholic Inquisition in Rome; Servetus by Calvin in Geneva. Bruno was a man of the Renaissance and a forerunner of the Scientific Revolution. Servetus was a pioneer of what came to be called Unitarianism, founded on a repudiation of the divinity of Jesus and an emphasis on Christian ethics in place of theological dogma. There have been comparable figures in the history of the Islamic world, but unlike the West, the world of Islam has remained mired in a theological and dogmatic religion, which has not only failed to come to terms with modernity, but in its 'Reformation' versions has actively turned against it.

Unlike the 16th century Christian Reformers, Hirsi Ali does not want to revive 'true religion' (Islam, rather than Christianity), but to see Islam reduced to a quiet cultural relic, as Christianity has been in much of Europe; with most of the dogmatism and harshness stripped away. She claims that Muslim Reformation is coming, but it has been upon us for some considerable time. The problem is that we have not been paying close attention. There is enormous ignorance and almost wilful blindness to all this in the West. It will not be going away any time soon, however; so it's high we time we sat up and paid it more serious—and critical—attention. We should, as she urges, support dissidents in the Muslim world as we supported dissidents in the Communist bloc during the Cold War. We should have the courage of our convictions and declare that the Prophet was a 7th century Arabian version of Joseph Smith, the Mormon founder, with the difference that he spread his religion by the sword across first tribal Arabia and then the declining Roman and Persian empires. Across all those lands it has long since become a cultural and political incubus on the backs of their peoples. Only quite fundamental change will set them free and it is opposed by ingrained traditions and prejudices.

In anything but a completely attenuated and nominal form, Islam is not deserving of our sympathy or support. That does not mean, of course, that human beings who happen to have been raised as Muslims should be treated as enemies. The whole project of modernization entails *separating* the human being from the believer and setting the human being free to change and grow. We need to reach out less to 'moderate Muslims' than to people of a moderate *temperament* and advance the argument that there are better ways and truer beliefs than old, fanatical religious dogmas. But to do that we need at least a broad consensus about what we stand for in such an exchange. Such a consensus seems to be lacking now in the West, if it ever existed. It would consist, however, of at least a few basic principles of civil government and civil society, as Natan Sharansky argued in *The Case for Democracy* and these would include the importance of critical reflection, freedom of expression and the subordination of religion to the secular authorities. If we cannot agree on at least those things, we cannot win the war of ideas with the Islam that is stalking the world in our time.

'The biggest obstacle to change within the Muslim world is precisely its suppression of the sort of critical thinking that I am attempting here,' writes Hirsi Ali. 'We who have known what it is to live without freedom watch with incredulity as you who call yourselves liberals—who claim to believe so fervently in individual liberty and minority rights—make common cause with the forces in the world that manifestly pose the greatest threats to that very freedom and those very minorities.' For this reason, she trumpets, 'We must no longer accept limitations on criticism of Islam.' In making this declaration, she is breaking with Islam, not simply with its more terroristic off-shoots. We should understand this very clearly, but be prepared for what it will entail. It will entail—it will require—a long and principled campaign not of 'intolerance' of Islam, but of the critical appraisal of it and the slow revision of it until it becomes itself tolerant in the way that much of Christianity has slowly become. That does not mean simply ISIS, but the cultures of Islam in Saudi Arabia, in Egypt, in Iran, in the Gulf States, in Pakistan. Right now, things are going in the opposite direction and the West is giving ground.

'*Our* civilization', Hirsi Ali declares, claiming a kind of cultural ownership that only citizenship in a Western liberal democracy could have brought her, 'learned, slowly and painfully, not to burn heretics, but to honour them.' True, but we would do well to remember that it was not until the second half of the 20th century that the Catholic Church, for example, announced that the Jews were not collectively culpable for the execution of Jesus of Nazareth under Pontius Pilate; publicly regretted its treatment of Galileo, accepted that Darwin had been on the right track as regards human evolution; and lifted its ban even on the works of the Jesuit visionary Teilhard de Chardin's works, *The Divine Milieu* and *The Phenomenon of Man.* Hirsi Ali hopes to see more rapid movement within Islam. It is a brave and bright hope, but the road is likely in fact to be long and painful. It is not a struggle that can be won by force, though the use of force may well be unavoidable in order to constrain at various points the mobilized Islamist forces. But it is a struggle that needs to be undertaken, if ever the mess in the Muslim world is to be sorted out and an attractive order put in place by the peoples of that world for their own sake.

It will be complicated by the divisions within Islam, not only between Mecca, Medina and Modifying Muslims, but between Sunni and Shi'ite Muslims and between rival states within the Islamic world. There are other, more obscure strands of Islam, also; and there will be those who will argue that Islam was once a great civilization—under the Umayyad and Abbasid caliphates—and that this alone is grounds enough for being restrained in our criticisms of Islam. There will also be those who will assert that all the trouble in the Middle East is the fault of the West—for its colonialism, its 'Orientalism', its greed for oil, its presumptuous and corrupt secularism, its interventions in Iraq and its inadequate assimilation of Muslims as citizens within Western polities. There is enough truth in this log of claims to make any debate on the subject fractious and acrimonious. But that simply means we need more judicious and fearless inquiry, not a moratorium on criticism of Islam or efforts to constrain violent Islamists. It's just that there will not be any quick, painless or simple solution for the foreseeable future.

Writing all this in the pages of *Quadrant*, I am conscious of its appointed role in the long and painful struggle against Communist totalitarianism. Throughout the Cold War, there were many who took the side of Communism within the West and who have never resiled from that stance. They campaigned long and hard to discredit anti-Communism and to insist, as Jean-Paul Sartre put it, even in the 1970s, that the Soviet Union was the trail blazer of progress and of a necessary 'revolution'. They derided and denounced the Congress for Cultural Freedom as a CIA front organization and *Quadrant* as a stalking horse for both the CIA and 'reaction'. All the while, of course, many activists on the Left—including, as it turned out, notorious terrorist groups—were taking funding from the KGB. Fortunately, that long struggle was won without triggering thermonuclear war. It was not won 'perfectly', since communist parties held onto power in China, North Korea, Vietnam and Cuba; while the remnants of the KGB took Russia back under Vladimir Putin to establish a dictatorial kleptocracy. But the war of ideas was won—at least until the turn of the century.

The struggle against Islam must also be won and won, ultimately, like the struggle against Communism, on the battlefield of ideas. It might be too much to hope that a new Congress for Cultural Freedom be convened with the express purpose of providing platforms and funding for organizations and magazines that are dedicated to freedom of expression in the struggle to transform and liberalize the Islamic world; but this would be a far more efficient and less costly investment than wars and attempts at nation-building by occupation. Hirsi Ali herself calls for some such thing. She hails the Congress for Cultural Freedom and its support for '*Encounter* (UK), *Preuves* (France) *Der Monat* (Germany) and *Quadrant* (Australia)'. Modelled on such efforts, she argues, 'there must be a concerted effort to turn people away from fundamentalist Islam'. Just as the West championed dissidents behind the Iron Curtain, it must now champion, support and protect dissidents in the Islamic world. It should provide platforms for the propagation of their names and ideas. It should promote scholarship that probes away at the history of Islam and the claims made in the name of Muhammed and his successors. And it must be prepared to stare down the Muslim equivalent of the Communist Party and its fellow travellers who will denounce all this as 'Islamophobia'.

Hirsi Ali names many such dissidents, across a spectrum of opinion from outright apostasy to moderate reform and spread across the Muslim world from Asia to West Africa. She laments that at present such people are dismissed as 'not representative', by mainstream Mecca (or Muslim Brotherhood) spokespeople and their 'liberal' allies in the West. But such individuals are heroic, as she puts it, precisely *because* they are not 'representative'. She has been dismissed on the same grounds; but it is an absurd argument. How 'representative' was Socrates? How 'representative ' was Giordano Bruno? How 'representative' was Charles Darwin? For that matter, one might retort to the Muslim Brotherhood and its liberal fellow travellers, how representative was Muhammed in pagan and tribal Arabia? The whole point of dissent and scientific inquiry is that one is *breaking ranks* with accepted opinion and established authority. The whole value of freedom of expression is that it exposes such opinion and authority to critical revision and challenges people to look at things with fresh eyes.

The individuals Hirsi Ali lauds are rare birds, trail blazers, heretics and free spirits. She names, in passing Tawfiq Hamid, Irshad Manji, Asra Nomani, Maajid Nawaz, Zuhdi Jasser, Saleem Ahmed, Yunis Qandil, Seyran Ates, Bassam Tibi. She names and gives the background to many others in an Appendix. Mona Eltahawy should be numbered among them.

Their names will be largely unfamiliar to most people in the West—rather like the names of similarly repressed and dismissed dissidents in China, under the boot of the Communist Party. Read her book and learn about them. She bravely asserts that they are beginning to turn the tide, but this is more hope than reality. The point is that the tide *must* be turned and it will only be turned if we lionize such people and support the stands they are taking against violent resistance and repression. They should be celebrated as we celebrate Locke and Voltaire, she writes (not Luther and Calvin, note well). There are many other figures, including religious believers, whom we might also celebrate, but the Enlightenment, which brought articulation of the case for toleration and civil government, has to constitute our common ground; not a 'liberalism' which recoils from criticism of Islam on confused and hypocritical grounds.

I was raised as a Catholic but, like Walter Kaufmann, I went my own way philosophically as a young man. I have always retained an appreciation of the Catholic Church and the Christian past, as Kaufmann did of the Christian and Judaic past. I regard much of that past as sublime: the writings of Augustine, Dante and Erasmus; Gregorian chant, Palestrina's madrigals, Bach and the great requiem masses of Mozart and Verdi. I am, also, aware of the complex history of the Islamic world and of some of the cosmopolitan achievements of scholars and traders in the world of the Arab caliphates between the 7th and 13th centuries. I would fully expect that in a modernized Islamic world such historical glories would continue to be cherished. But just as the 18th century Enlightenment brought a sweeping reassessment of the religious tradition of the West and articulated a new basis for civil government in a commercial age, so must a process of enlightenment in the Muslim world bring at last a sweeping reassessment of the claims to 'revelation' and 'authority' that give Islam its grip on the minds and moral cultures of one and a half billion human beings in the 21st century. We can, we should and I believe we must do all we can to encourage and assist that process, while staunchly resisting Islamist violence.

Let me conclude by returning to Ayaan Hirsi Ali's expression of appreciation for the Congress for Cultural Freedom and enlarging upon it. Only a generation after the end of the Cold War and the much heralded triumph of capitalism and liberal democratic ideas, the West is on the back foot and the liberal international order under siege by both Chinese and Russian authoritarianism and Islamic militancy. We should not want to see these forces gain more ground. Yet they cannot be halted merely by the use of force. Indeed, the capacity and willingness of the West to use force seems to have waned; sapped by the costs of seemingly fruitless wars in Afghanistan and Iraq; as well as by the self-inflicted economic disaster of 2007-08. There is a lot to feel gloomy about. But there is also a great deal to defend and extend. That is a cultural task and a matter of ideas and articulate debate. Neither complacency nor cynicism will serve us. We need, once more, to find the energy and imagination to champion the open society and the scientific enlightenment. We should do so unapologetically and vigorously. If we do not engage in the struggle of ideas of our time in this manner, we could lose—catastrophically. That's why we need a new Congress for Cultural Freedom, under any other name and however it is funded.

7: Let's have the truth about our spy catchers, Malcolm

One of the many reasons why it is a relief to see Malcolm Turnbull now Prime Minister is that it was he who, as a young lawyer, took on the secrecy and hypocrisy of the British government, in the *Spycatcher* trial, challenged the Official Secrets Act and successfully defended the publication of Peter Wright's controversial book, *Spycatcher*. That success marked him out a bright man with a big future. He is now in the pole position, at the pinnacle of his career, to crown his *Spycatcher* work with a major service to truth and justice in Australia—by releasing the Cook Report on Soviet penetration of ASIO throughout the Cold War.

The Cook Report is an historic document, written in 1993 or 1994 for then Prime Minister Paul Keating by former Ambassador to Washington and former head of ONA, Michael Cook. It was commissioned by Keating to follow up Operation Liver, a highly secret AFP investigation of ASIO. The conclusion Cook is said to have reached is that ASIO had been deeply penetrated over many years by at least four Soviet moles. His report has never been released and senior Labour figures are deeply reluctant to discuss it. Cook himself wrote to the author that neither Keating nor anybody else instructed him to 'give my report a high security classification. That I decided on my own for what I thought, and still think, were good reasons.'

He has declined to reveal what those reasons were or to defend them. It's time the new Prime Minister, twenty years after those events, overrode Cook's judgment and released this report so that the vexed question of the extent of Soviet penetration of ASIO and undermining of our security and intelligence operations during the Cold War can finally be told. If it was good enough for Peter Wright's speculative memoir to be published, over the objections of Whitehall and MI5, it is surely acceptable for an official document that cuts to the heart of our intelligence failures and difficulties in the Cold War to be released over whatever political or organizational objections have for so long made it one of the most closely held secrets in Canberra.

The second volume of the official history of ASIO has been published and we are none the wiser about the central challenge for which ASIO was created in the first place: hostile penetration of the Australian government and penetration of ASIO itself. Rumour has it that the third and final volume will contain revelations, but don't hold your breath. Given that penetration by the Soviets dates back to the 1940s in Canberra, why would we be made to wait for a volume covering the 1980s for a serious reckoning with his subject? And what confidence can we have that the matter will, in fact, be dealt with accurately and openly even there?

Demanding the release of the Cook Report is not an act hostile to ASIO. It is a patriotic demand that truth be known and justice be done. ASIO has an important role to fulfil in our time and its current head, Duncan Lewis, is an admirable figure to lead it in that role. There are, without doubt, serious threats to this country's security and intelligence operations from the rising power of China, the rogue power of Russia, Islamist terror networks and organized criminal cartels. Each of these is as formidable an enemy now as the Soviet Union ever was during the Cold War. And ASIO failed at its task during much of the Cold War, because it was outwitted and hobbled by Soviet penetration. It's high time that story was out in the open, both to point the blame where it belongs and to help ensure that such failures do not occur in the current phase of history, when new enemies with new technologies pose risks to the integrity of ASIO's work.

The anchor point for such an opening up of the secret records of the end of the Cold War is the knowledge, long since pieced together by historians, that Canberra was deeply penetrated in the 1940s, when Soviet spies operated openly in the offices of both H. V. Evatt, as Minister for External Affairs, and John Burton, as Secretary for External Affairs. Discovery of these spies was what led to the creation of ASIO. It seems clear that that was insufficient and that ASIO itself was penetrated at various points and perhaps throughout its Cold War history, seriously compromising both counter-espionage operations and our intelligence relationships with the United States and the United Kingdom.

It is, of course, possible that Cook's findings were tentative and that he recommended that his report not be released because he felt unable to prove beyond reasonable doubt who among the reported ten suspect figures pensioned off from ASIO at that time had in fact been the moles in question. It is possible that his report names foreign sources that he felt then and still feels now should not be disclosed. It is possible that his inquiry led him to the conclusion that the penetration of Canberra, well after the 1940s, went beyond ASIO and that revealing the full extent of what had had happened would truly set the proverbial cat among the pigeons.

Yet the film *The Gatekeepers* was made in Israel, a state under perennial siege and subject to endless controversy and it is stunningly candid about the challenges and failures, tactical, moral and political of Israeli counter-terrorism and counter-intelligence. Australia, a far more secure country, has no excuse for being less open or reflective about its security and intelligence past. The Cook Report identified a canker at the heart of our national security establishment. That canker will not be removed by pretending it doesn't exist. It is more important, Prime Minister, than *Spycatcher*. It is an official document written by a highly reputable civil servant. Remove this canker for us. Release the Cook Report now.

8: The future of religion in a complex world

Roberto Mangabeira Unger is a polymath of Brazilian extraction teaching at Harvard University. He has had an extraordinary career, both in the United States and in Brazil and has written many books. His 2014 book, *The Religion of the Future* (Harvard University Press), is a remarkable offering in several ways and ought to serve as the point of departure for a major global debate about the nature of religion and its place in the 21st century world. The book is global in sweep, deeply informed by the best scholarship on the history and philosophy of the world religions, intimately acquainted with movements in 20th century theology and philosophy and unflinchingly radical in its originality and socio-political vision.

Unger has a remarkable pedigree. His maternal grandfather, Octavio Mangabeira became professor of astronomy at the Polytechnic School in the Brazilian state of Bahia, gained mass popularity after delivering an inspired public lecture on Halley's Comet, in 1910, and ended up, in the 1920s, becoming Brazil's Minister for Foreign Affairs, before falling afoul of the dictator Getulio Vargas and suffering years of imprisonment and exile. He returned to Brazil in 1946, re-entered politics and became a senator in 1958. Octavio's brother Joao Mangabeira founded the Brazilian Socialist Party. Their sister Maria founded a religious order. Both of Unger's parents were intellectuals. His mother, Edyla Mangabeira, was a poet and journalist. His father, Artur Unger, was a German immigrant to the United States, where he became a successful lawyer.

Roberto Mangabeira Unger was born in Rio de Janeiro on 24 March 1947, when his parents, who were US citizens, were visiting Brazil. He grew up in New York, on Manhattan's Upper East Side, but would spend summers in Brazil with his grandfather, Octavio. These summers, he later testified, deeply shaped his understanding of politics. But his whole extended family was rich in influences that can be seen in his prolific, radical and wide-ranging writing. He was a leader of the Critical Legal Studies movement in the United States in the 1970s. He has written extensively on political theory, law and the nature of the self, always with an eye on what can activate human emancipation. His latest work, with cosmologist Lee Smolin, is *The Singular Universe and the Reality of Time: A Proposal in Natural Philosophy* (Cambridge University Press, 2015).

The Religion of the Future begins with a sweeping reflection on the religions that sprang from what Karl Jaspers, in the mid-20th century, called the Axial Age: the centuries in the middle of the last millennium before the birth of Jesus of Nazareth. In a tradition going back at least to Max Weber, Unger classifies the great belief systems of the world according to their existential orientation with regard to the human condition. Buddhism (and the Greek ethical philosophies of Platonism, Stoicism and Epicureanism) he sees as seeking to 'overcome the world', by attaining to a state of detachment, serenity and benevolence. Confucianism he sees as seeking to 'humanize the world' by ennobling and formalizing human relations in a world otherwise without meaning or purpose. The 'Semitic monotheisms' (Judaism, Christianity and Islam) he sees as 'struggling with the world'; seeking to console humanity for the flaws in its condition and redeem it in the name of a higher order of things.

Unger's perspective on all these religions is critical, but not polemical. He exhibits empathy for what each seems to be striving to do. He demonstrates a scholarly understanding of their sources as lucid and impressive as that of his great precursors like Weber, Jaspers and Toynbee. He argues that the existential orientations they offer will always remain human possibilities. In none of these crucial respects, therefore, can he be classified as anti-religious or any kind of secular vandal bent on the demolition of cultural traditions. Certainly there will be those who adhere to any one of the faiths he discusses who will want to put in a special case for their own set of beliefs. But the dispassionate reader is unlikely to find Unger crass or offensive in his general attitude towards religion as such or to any religion in particular.

That said, his vision is both radical and revolutionary when it comes to the work religion needs to do and the philosophical or metaphysical foundations on which it must from now on seek to place itself. In these respects, his argument is quite certain to occur as confronting to believers in any of the major religions and almost all of their more contemporary offshoots. He claims boldly that the modern sciences have now made clear beyond credible dispute that we must build for ourselves a religion 'beyond wishful thinking'. There is no deity running the universe with our good in mind, he claims. There is no possible way for us to grasp why we are here, only that we are. And there is no afterlife to compensate in any way for the shortness, incompleteness or painfulness of the brief lives we have. This reality is all the more confronting, he argues, because we are 'insatiable' in our appetites, imaginations and potential.

The perspective thus sketched out, in the opening pages of his book, has various elements in common with some of the most famous modern philosophers, from Schopenhauer and Nietzsche to Heidegger and Sartre. But one of the notable features of *The Religion of the Future* is that Unger delicately and lucidly distances himself from each and all of these thinkers in articulating his own position. He rejects Schopenhauer as too pessimistic and too prone to a kind of solipsism which offers no commitment to grappling with the world as it is. He rejects Nietzsche's 'Prometheanism' as a neo-paganism with no serious moral content. He also rejects as sterile Heidegger's neo-pagan worship of the radiance of times past and the mystery of existence itself. And he rejects Sartre's radicalism as anarchic and irresponsible, because it fails to acknowledge the human need for institutional structures and meaningful rituals. He calls such anarchism, in fact, 'the Sartrean heresy'.

Our mortality, our groundlessness and our insatiability, Unger claims, are ineradicable flaws in the human condition. No religion can do away with them, though each tries to come to terms with them or console us for them in different ways. Nor can the sciences overcome these flaws, because they are existential constants that knowledge of the world can illuminate but can never eliminate. Consequently, he argues, we need a religion that acknowledges these realities unflinchingly and builds itself unyieldingly on the granite foundation of existential realism that they provide. We might choose to turn away from these truths and try to shelter within the porches of the old religions, but we cannot in good faith do so much longer. We need, therefore, to rethink, refashion and reanimate our religious cultures in the light of the harsh realities that modern science and critical philosophy have brought home to us. We are a species of conscious animal on a small planet far out on a spiral arm of a galaxy in the middle of a cosmos that has given birth to us, but has no interest in our well-being.

Unger's belief that something along these lines *should* happen is well-founded. His apparent confidence that it *will* happen is less well-founded. His enunciation of how human social order should be pragmatically refashioned to take account of the three great existential constants and unleash human desire to fulfil its boundless potential is breathtaking in its boldness, wholly abstract in its reasoning and baffling in its complete failure to address practical obstacles, strategic wisdom or possible compromises with existing political and religious institutions. His program is spelled out in the fifth, sixth and seventh chapters of his book— Religious Revolution Now: Its Occasions and Instruments; Deep Freedom: The Politics of the Religion of the Future; and Becoming More Human By Becoming More Godlike: The Conduct of Life in the Religion of the Future. These chapters are worth reading and I read them very closely. But I read with a persistent sense of wonderment at Unger's unwillingness or inability to ground his poetic vision in any kind of immediate, plausible program.

Part of the problem is that he seems to have set out to simply provide a new vocabulary and worldview within which such a program might begin to take shape, rather than setting out to provide such a program itself. Another and more troubling problem, however, is that he pulls away from both scientific and social reality in the name of his 'religion of the future' as if the latter could be grounded purely in his critique of the old religions and the suggestiveness of his neologisms. He treats each of the old religions as if they had sprung from pure thought, the exemplary lives of their founders and the social need for what they offered. He fails to ground the phenomenon of religion itself in the long sweep of human evolution, as for example, Roy Rappaport did in *Ritual and Religion in the Making of Humanity* (1999), or Robert Bellah, in *Religion in Human Evolution: From the Palaeolithic to the Axial Age* (2011). Although Unger rejects all the metaphysics of the old religions, he at no point writes of human beings as *evolved* creatures. Instead, he consistently describes us as 'embodied spirits', a vague term wide open to abuse or misunderstanding.

A further consequence of Unger's rejection of a specifically naturalistic understanding of humanity is that he at no point so much as attempts to reconcile his enthusiasm for unleashing and fulfilling the 'insatiable' in humanity now with the ecological implications of even the current standards of living of seven billion human beings on the planet. The release this year of Pope Francis's encyclical on climate change and inequality, *On Care for Our Common Home*, has generated a wide spectrum of responses, some of them highly critical. Unger's 'religion of the future' seems to call for unbounded access to goods and services, unbounded liberties for individuals and strenuous demands for egalitarianism all at the same time. Yet he offers even *less* explanation than the Pontiff's encyclical as to how exactly all these desiderata are to be achieved. Nor does he dwell upon any but the haziest idea of the human future on Earth, because he insists that we should concentrate on being liberated 'now'. He often sounds like a new version of Herbert Marcuse preaching to the hermits of the Egyptian deserts.

He is writing at a time, of course, in which debate about the nature and future of religion is considerable. The old religions have not disappeared and secular society is, in a number of ways, floundering. Islam, in particular, is aggressively seeking to re-establish itself. The new little book *Islam and the Future of Tolerance*, a dialogue between atheist Sam Harris and Islamic reformer Maajid Nawaz (Harvard University Press, 2015) is, as Ayaan Hirsi Ali declares, an example of the kind of honest and civil dialogue that is badly needed. It would be interesting to see either or both of them in dialogue with Unger about 'the religion of the future'. His arguments would surely strike Harris as dangerously anti-rational and Nawaz as dangerously anti-Islamic. But an honest and civil dialogue should, at least be possible. The question is, what happens with regard to less civil interlocutors and where would Unger stand if and when the winds of violence and fanaticism blow? He never makes this clear in his book.

Mark Riebling's new book *Church of Spies: The Pope's Secret War Against Hitler* (Basic Books and Scribe, 2015) is a splendid and ground-breaking study in this problem. It is a highly illuminating new study of the vexed question of Pope Pius XII and the Third Reich, which shows the Pope struggling to reconcile his moral with his institutional and political commitments between 1939 and 1945. Riebling's history is rich in the human and institutional complexities that Unger entirely fails to address. Eugenio Pacelli (Pius XII), he points out, was a highly sophisticated, deeply religious man who was both an accomplished Papal diplomat before he became Pope and a man of profoundly humane moral principles who saw Hitler as a 'Satanic' figure and was appalled at both Nazi anti-Semitism and the Nazi persecution of the Catholic Church in the name of a crude neo-paganism.

Riebling recounts how Wilhelm Canaris and his fellow anti-Nazi conservatives within the Black Orchestra were sickened by Hitler's campaign to exterminate the Polish clergy and reached out to the Pope as an ally in the hope of bringing Hitler down in 1939. There is no such gripping, realistic scenario anywhere in Unger's book and this gravely weakens it as a vision of the 'religion of the future'.

Unger does not even articulate clear or tangible moral principles, only sweeping existential desiderata. There were reports, in mid-October this year, of 'civil war' at the pinnacle of the Catholic Church over moral teaching, with thirteen Cardinals, including Australia's George Pell, warning Pope Francis that the Church is in danger of collapsing, like liberal Protestant congregations, because of mooted compromises over both moral and dogmatic teaching. They may be correct. Whether such a 'collapse' would be a good or a bad thing, of course, is a matter on which opinions differ very widely. But Unger ought to have pondered in far more serious and practical terms how his proposed religion of the future would either infuse and renew institutions such as the Catholic Church, or replace them with newer, more soundly based and durable institutions. He does not do this. Indeed, he airily insists that all institutions need to be sufficiently plastic as to be ongoing experiments in emancipation. Whether in terms of moral principles, organizational coherence, ritual practices or soundness of belief, this looks deeply problematic. It would have been reassuring to see Unger at least acknowledge this.

Given both its sweep and its flaws, it isn't easy to enter a satisfactory net judgement on *The Religion of the Future*, but three conclusions seem to me inescapable: the book is too long and learned to be read by those most in need of rethinking their religious beliefs; it is too abstract and hopelessly utopian to be taken up in any but the loosest rhetorical manner by either religious reformers or the makers of public policy; and yet, in many ways, Unger is telling core truths and demonstrating poetic imagination in ways that are both refreshing and admirable. We need the kind of synoptic vision that he offers; a new 'synoptic gospel', if you like. We need the animated intelligence and generosity of feeling he exhibits. There are good reasons why we could do with an inspiring 'religion of the future' and why the old religions are inadequate to the realities with which we now live. Paradoxically, Unger tells us at the end that no religion was ever founded by a priest or a scribe; only by the charisma and exemplary lives of prophetic figures. Yet he has offered us a large book. Does he see himself as some kind of philosophical John the Baptist?

The most explicit account he provides of how he expects to be read is in a concluding 'Note on the Three Orientations and the Idea of the Axial Age' (pp. 445-456). In his own words:

> In the early parts of this book, I explored three major spiritual orientations exemplified by the world religions. I did so for the purpose of preparing the ground for the defence of a way of thinking that goes beyond what these orientations have in common.

> My argument can be read as an essay in the philosophy of religion, except that it is itself
> religious, and not simply an inquiry undertaken from the safe distance of uncommitted
> speculative thought. It might also be viewed as a theological text, except that it is a
> kind of anti-theology.

He draws upon the work of Weber and Jaspers on the sociology of religion but distances
himself from them. He claims that Weber's work on 'rationalization' and that of Jaspers on
the 'Axial Age' were merely a dubious attempt by 'the self-professed party of Enlightenment
in the North Atlantic world' to cast itself as the beleaguered heir to all that was reasonable
and restrained in history, against the storms of violent irrationalism that the 20th century had
brought forth and to give themselves a respectable genealogy. He repudiates, he tells us, the
idea that religion is 'the hazy penumbra and occasional ally of philosophy'. Rather, he claims,
'the task of religion begins where the instruments of the party of Enlightenment lose their
efficacy.'

This stand is likely, on the face of it, to appeal to many dogged adherents of the old religions,
who like to believe that their dogmas and spiritual raptures derive from a sphere beyond the
reach of reason and science. It is also likely to appeal to those countless adherents or founders
of contemporary cults or faddish notions who imagine that they are being transcendent when
they are simply losing their grip on reality. He claims to be challenging the old religions as well
as the Enlightenment, however, and appears oblivious to the risks entailed in his project:

> My argument about these past religious revolutions, about what they had in common
> as well as about the contrasting directions that they set, is motivated, directly and
> transparently, by a single purpose: the defence of another direction for the future. To
> take this direction, we must break with that common ground, undertaking religious
> revolution with new content and in new form. Nothing could be further from the
> intentions of the proponents of the Axial Age thesis.

He concludes that no priest or scribe ever founded a religion and that 'the commanding
purpose of the religious revolutions of the past was not to advance a disinterested view of the
world. It was to rescue mankind from its lack of imagination and of love.' It isn't altogether
clear whether, in ending his large book this way he wanted to imply that he had wasted his
time, being a mere scribe, prepared the way for commencing his public life as an exemplary
visionary, or opened up the ground on which the rest of us might hear and heed the call of
imagination and love issued by as yet unseen visionaries.

Does he believe that the old religions can be revolutionized from within by imagination
and love and come to form a cluster of renewed religions for the future, offering refreshed
versions of their old existential stances? He doesn't tell us. Does he believe that the literalist
and militant advocates of the old religions, most fearfully in our time the Islamists, are apostles

of imagination and love with access to truths that transcend those of the sciences? He takes no position on Islam specifically and makes no mention of religious fanaticism or dogmatism. Does he believe that his religion of the future is more likely to arise among unbelievers in the marketplace—where Nietzsche had his madman proclaim the death of God to the general scepticism and amusement of his listeners—or in the afflicted Muslim world, where armed fanatics are currently attempting to expel Christians, Jews and other 'infidels', to crush apostasy and to suppress moves towards female emancipation? He does not make any mention of these things. Does he believe his religion of the future can begin in our schools and take the next generation by storm? He demands a revolution in education, but makes no reference whatsoever to current or prospective curricula.

Although often puzzled, sceptical or frustrated by *The Religion of the Future*, I never gave up and read it word for word to the end. I do recommend that all those interested in the prospects for religious belief in the contemporary world read it and use it as a foil to their own thinking. Although there are many flaws in Unger's approach to things, his vast intellectual energy and passionate insistence on social and political openness are both consistently engaging and, at their best, quite compelling. The man is clearly immensely well-read and all the wonderful attainments of his family are evident in his manner and concerns. That said, I believe we need to ground an assessment of the future of religion in terms far more closely linked to the natural world, the 'crooked timber of humanity' and the cautious wisdom of modern secular culture than Unger allows. I have sketched out such a vision in my own new book, *Credo and Twelve Poems: A Cosmological Manifesto* (Echo Books, 2015). Yet I can imagine enjoying a very long and civilized exchange with Unger about the differences in our thinking and the vast scope for further thought. I hope that both our books will find readers among those whose religious beliefs are very different from either his or mine. Such readings and exchanges, I would like to think, will *give* us the religion of the future.

9: Niall Ferguson has produced a masterpiece

If your aspiration was to become an historian, you could hardly conceive of a better trajectory than that of Niall Ferguson: Glasgow Academy, Oxford, Cambridge, Harvard, the London School of Economics, the Hoover Institution at Stanford University, fifteen books, television documentaries, trenchant public commentary and now the biography of Henry Kissinger. It is an astounding record for a man still only 51 years old. And, into the bargain, he has married the beautiful and courageous Ayaan Hirsi Ali. The man is a prodigy.

This first volume of his Kissinger biography, *Kissinger 1923-1968: The Idealist*, is masterful. It exhibits a maturity of expression and judgement that are immensely impressive. It points irresistibly to the forthcoming second volume as perhaps Ferguson's crowning achievement. He was only 40 years of age, when Henry Kissinger approached him, in 2004, asking would he write an authorized biography. It was a remarkable tribute to the young historian that an elder statesman twice his age should make this request. Kissinger must have been impressed by Ferguson's body of work over the preceding decade, starting with *Paper and Iron: Hamburg Business and German Politics in the Era of Inflation, 1897–1927*, in 1995; and concluding in 2004 with *Colossus: The Rise and Fall of the American Empire*.

Ferguson already had many other projects on the drawing boards and was aware that writing a biography of Kissinger would not only be a massive undertaking, but 'would inevitably be savaged by Christopher Hitchens and others. And so, in early March 2004, after several meetings, telephone calls and letters, I said no'. This, he comments wryly, 'was to be my introduction to the diplomacy of Henry Kissinger', who wrote him exclaiming that it was a pity he had declined, both because 145 boxes containing his private papers going back 'at least to 1955 and probably to 1950', which he had believed lost, had turned up; and that 'our conversations had given me the confidence—after admittedly some hesitation—that you would have done a definitive—if not necessarily positive—evaluation.' Seduced by the allure of those papers, Ferguson consented.

The book is impressive in at least seven distinct ways: its mastery of a mass of detail; its architectonic balance; its felicity of expression; it's often striking and elegant *obiter dicta* about human experience, academic life and world affairs; its insightful and unflinching character sketches of successive American presidents and other prominent figures, as well of numerous other characters in the extraordinary story of Kissinger's first 45 years; its uniquely original and strikingly independent assessment of Henry Kissinger's character and development; and its magnificent stage setting for what is to come in the second volume, which will examine Kissinger as national security adviser and secretary of state.

Ferguson's sweeping works and outspoken stances as a public intellectual have drawn fire from both the political Left and academic or journalistic writers who find fault with his outlook or his work. Among those who have claimed to find fault with *Kissinger 1923-1968: The Idealist*, Greg Grandin, writing in *The Guardian*, in mid-October typifies just the kind of tendentious 'savaging' that Ferguson anticipated would come from the late Christopher Hitchens and others.

Grandin, whose own book, *Kissinger's Shadow*, is due out this December, asserts that Ferguson's book is an extended, but litigious, lazy and 'boring' defence of its subject. He insists that Ferguson has avoided the 'dark' side of Kissinger's character and motivation and that Ferguson is in error—deliberately and culpably—in rejecting the claim that Kissinger helped Richard Nixon sabotage the secret negotiations going on in Paris in 1968 with North Vietnam, in order to get the appointment as Nixon's national security adviser. He plainly has the same view of Kissinger as Hitchens set out in *The Trial of Henry Kissinger*: that he was a war criminal on a large scale and should be literally hanged for decisions that he actually or allegedly took while in office, regarding Indochina, Bangladesh, Chile and East Timor, among other things.

But Grandin is jumping the gun. Ferguson argues, very persuasively in my view, that Henry Kissinger was not motivated by 'dark' impulses, but by a highly intelligent, complex and perceptive commitment to statecraft and to finding ways to make American foreign and international security policy work better. He demonstrates meticulously that Kissinger did not sabotage the Johnson administration or connive in any malign way with Nixon and that he did not expect to become national security adviser at all, right up to the point when Nixon explicitly made him the offer in December 1968. He depends upon no convoluted or tendentious reasoning to make his demonstration, but on a detailed and judicious—not 'litigious'—assessment of the roles of many actors in the events leading up to the December 1968 appointment.

Determined to assert that Ferguson is out to exculpate Kissinger in volume two, Grandin appears not to have read most of volume one. In fact, Ferguson's long, deeply informed account of Kissinger's intellectual formation and his disillusionment with the Johnson administration's war in Vietnam as early as 1965, make compelling reading. One of the most eye opening revelations is that criticisms of Johnson's policies, of the workings of his national security decision-making apparatus and of the conduct of the war in Vietnam that have always been associated with Left-wing critics of the war and, in my own mind, with the thinking of Daniel Ellsberg before and after he leaked the *Pentagon Papers* to the *New York Times* (in 1971); can be found explicitly in papers and memoranda written by Henry Kissinger in 1965-66.

This is all the more striking because, at least in this volume, Ferguson hardly mentions Ellsberg and certainly shows no sign of having set out to argue that Kissinger anticipated Ellsberg's *Papers on the War* or more general public stance after 1971. Yet the precise wording used by Kissinger in a series of papers in the mid-1960s is so redolent of things Ellsberg wrote years later that I found myself wondering whether Ellsberg had, in fact, plagiarized Kissinger. The difference between the two, after 1968, was that Ellsberg defected from the inner councils of state and sought to change policy by leaking massive quantities of classified documents to the press. Kissinger sought to reshape the inner workings of those councils through his highly intelligent and quite transparent writings up to late 1968 and to take direct responsibility for their workings when offered the chance by Nixon, despite never having liked Nixon as either a person or a politician.

Central to the architecture of Ferguson's biography is his attempt to trace the development of Kissinger's thinking over decades. Grandin asserts that this makes Kissinger 'boring.' He could not be more mistaken. What is boring are the tired old clichés of the Left about Kissinger. In this new biography we can see Kissinger's gifted mind, his ideals, his use of history, his relationships with mentors, his analytical acumen, his political outlook and his attempts as an immigrant German Jew to grasp and then shape the machinery of foreign and security policy making in the United States. The book concludes with a very fine summation, in the fourteen page Epilogue, of what Ferguson calls the '*bildungsroman*' of Henry Kissinger—'the tale of his education through experience, some of it bitter.'

This Epilogue is in itself a beautiful piece of writing, opening with a reference to Goethe's famous *bildungsroman*, *Wilhelm Meister's Apprenticeship* and concluding with an invocation of the fifth century BCE anti-war comedy, *Peace*, by the brilliant Athenian playwright Aristophanes. It is a measure of the quality of Ferguson's mind that he has been able to avoid looking at the early life of Henry Kissinger through the jaundiced lenses that the Left would have had him wear; to examine the subject dispassionately; to have appreciated both the ironies in Kissinger's circuitous ascent to the West Wing of the White House; and the acute dilemmas that lay in wait for him as a scholar-statesman, when he got there.

As he remarks, Kissinger worked, throughout the 1960s, for Nelson Rockefeller, whose aristocratic liberal Republicanism he admired, despite the fact that Rockefeller was never going to become President; then was recommended to Nixon by both Rockefeller and Johnson. What he took on had already driven the Democrats, both liberal and conservative, to despair. He could have left it to others. He chose to take the poisoned chalice and attempt to deal intelligently with the vast challenges confronting the United States by the end of 1968.

What followed made him one of the towering figures of 20th century statecraft. Reading the second volume of Ferguson's biography will, therefore, be immensely absorbing. But make no mistake, in this first volume he, has produced a masterpiece and one that must be read in every graduate school of international relations, history and statecraft—attentively and thoughtfully, not in the superficial and supercilious manner that Grandin and his ilk have greeted it.

10: Australia needs a new grand strategy

The passage past Subi Reef recently by the *USS Lassen* is only the latest in a long string of maritime incidents from the Yellow Sea to the South China Sea which have highlighted the chronic stress being placed on regional security by China's territorial claims and great power ambitions. Australia's official response to it has been measured. As the Turnbull government settles in, however, and the new Defence white paper is completed, such incidents must be seen in the context of the review of the country's grand strategy.

Ross Babbage's recent monograph for the Menzies Research Center, *Game Plan: The Case for a New Australian Grand Strategy* is a concise attempt to sketch out the elements of such a new grand strategy. It is fewer than 100 pages in length, has been well received in senior military and security circles and deserves to be widely read and discussed. It is notable for its insistence that we strengthen our security alliance with the United States, not back away from it, as Paul Keating, the late Malcolm Fraser, former Deputy Secretary of Defence for Strategy Hugh White and others have been urging.

Babbage's argument is that Australia's peculiar geography has always made national defence a challenging task, but that we have now moved from the outer periphery of strategic affairs to centre stage in great power strategic rivalry. This is a premise broadly shared by both sides of the debate about the US alliance. A second shared premise is that a great power collision and war are to be avoided, if at all possible. Where the two sides part ways is in their assessments of the best means for avoiding what has been called 'the Thucydides trap': the collision between an existing (perhaps declining) hegemonic power and a rising power—of the kind that triggered catastrophic war in the 5th century BCE between the old power of Sparta and the rising power of Athens.

Far from believing, with Keating, Fraser and White, that we should jettison the US alliance and, in Keating's words, 'strike out on our own', Babbage urges that we must make ourselves 'the indispensable ally of the US in the Indo-Pacific.' Both the US and China, he points out, now view Australia as having significantly greater strategic importance than it had in any earlier era. The US sees us as a vital strategic anchor as China's rapidly growing military capabilities threaten the viability of long-established American military bases in East Asia and the Western Pacific, from Yokosuka to Guam.

Of course, this is precisely what the advocates of abandoning the alliance fear: that we will, as Malcolm Fraser put it, not long before he died, be dragged into America's wilful refusal to accommodate China's rise and its 'legitimate' great power ambitions. Everyone knows that we are rather torn between our trade with China (which has been very profitable and has vast future potential) and our strategic relationship (and cultural affinity) with the United States—and the Anglophone world more generally. What brings these two considerations together, however, is that our trade with China has occurred under the aegis of the liberal international order that the US has built and protected since 1945. That order is under challenge and China is the single biggest challenger.

America under President Obama has been showing many signs of becoming the same kind of 'weary titan' that Britain was by the eve of the First World War. It certainly does not seek war with China. But if it is to sustain the burden of deterring powers that seek to challenge the international liberal order, it needs allies and it needs defensive depth. Australia is crucial to it being able to reposition itself in a changing Asia to ensure these two things. Ironically, while White and others urge that China be accommodated as far as possible, the only solid fall-back position for the US on the Asian littoral if it gives some ground would be Australia. Babbage is urging that we think this through and take responsibility for its implications.

Much that is now unfolding was foreseen at the turn of the century by Paul Bracken, a strategic thinker at Yale University, in a pungent little book called *Fire in the East: The Rise of Asian Military Power and the Second Nuclear Age*. By and large, both distraction after 2001 and persistent optimism that China would come around to a more liberal and tractable stance as its economy grew, resulted in neglect of strategic realities in Asia, both here and in Washington. That neglect has to end. Given China's spiralling arms expenditure and insistence on making territorial claims that alarm most of its neighbours, elementary prudence dictates that we cannot responsibly allow things to drift any further.

One of Babbage's more striking recommendations is that we set out to become 'the center of intelligence excellence' for our neighbours and allies in the Eastern Indian and Western Pacific Oceans, as well as America's close confidante as the best informed nation in the South East Asian theatre. Such an ambition, of course, would require that intelligence collection, intelligence analysis, the political uses of intelligence and the counter-intelligence and counter-espionage functions be taken much more seriously, on a bipartisan basis, than they have been.

The absolutely crucial intelligence task, of course, is the willingness and capacity to cross-examine one's strategic policy assumptions. Neither here nor elsewhere has that generally been well done. The best thing that can be said for those who have challenged our commitment to the US alliance is that they are pushing us to re-examine assumptions about China, about the alliance with the United States, about our defence spending, about the probability of military conflict in this region and about our reliance on the international liberal order under which we have prospered for the past seventy years. We cannot, however, afford to drift while thinking. We need a serious and viable new game plan.

11: It's time to fully integrate our stranded boat people

The recent massacre of innocents in Paris and French President Francois Hollande's declaration of a 'merciless' war on ISIS, have heightened the danger of aggravated anti-Muslim sentiment in the West at large. The fact that huge numbers of refugees from the Middle East and North Africa are pouring into Europe and that a small number of them are likely to be ISIS infiltrators exacerbates this problem, even outside Europe.

Both problems are real and serious. But for this very reason it is time we, in Australia, took active and imaginative steps to integrate into our stable, multi-cultural society the tens of thousands of boat people stranded here and surviving in limbo on temporary bridging visas.

This issue has been divisive long enough. The core debate had to do with border security. That security has been established. But, as Scott Morrison, pointed out last May, before becoming Treasurer, we risk creating an impoverished and frustrated underclass 'vulnerable to the predations of criminals and extremists' unless we now embrace and integrate these people.

We need to remind ourselves that, with very few exceptions, they came here for either of two reasons: out of fear and desperation or, frankly, as economic migrants seeking a better life. We should demonstrate that here they can, indeed, live free from fear and that, if prepared to work hard like other waves of migrants, they do have a good chance at achieving the better life they dreamed of.

As Charles Bremner pointed out in *The Times* of London last Thursday, Muslim ghettos in Paris and in parts of Belgium have been the incubators in which the recent terrorist madness has bred. We should take deliberate steps to ensure, to the best of our ability, that such slums and ghettos do not develop in Australia's cities.

The first step would be to acknowledge the ordinary humanity of these stranded people, much as Bob Hawke embraced the tens of thousands of Chinese nationals stranded here after the atrocities committed by the Chinese Communist Party on 4 June 1989. These people are overwhelmingly from turbulent and unpleasant parts of the world. Our interest, as well as our principles, should dictate that we now say to them: 'You are strangers in our midst and we will make you welcome.'

The larger problem of stateless or displaced people in the outside world is huge and we can only make a modest contribution to addressing it. This would be both a good start and a prudent measure as regards our own social stability and cohesion, as Scott Morrison, who worked to secure our borders, has acknowledged. It would demonstrate that we are not ourselves merely fearful, much less paranoid; but humane and self-assured.

Among those sub-groups of asylum seekers who should receive particular understanding are two Muslim minority groups: the Hazaras and the Rohingyas. The former are the most persecuted ethnic minority in Central Asia, especially in Afghanistan and Iran. They are persecuted by fellow Muslims on ethnic as well as sectarian grounds. The Rohingyas are persecuted by hard-line Buddhists in Burma (Myanmar); not only by the fascistic junta that has so long tyrannized the country, but by the Burmese elite and the Buddhist monks.

It is six months since Mr Morrison's insightful remark. The horrors that have just occurred in Paris should serve as a wake-up call, not to appease brutal Islamists, but to embrace those who have sought our protection, to redouble our efforts to bolster our success as a humane melting pot society and to engage constructively in the immense international challenge of how to succour the tens of millions of stateless and uprooted people who have fallen foul of the world's more violent and heartless regimes.

Uthman Badar and others from Hizb ut Tahrir declared recently that it was 'oppressive' of Australian society to seek to assimilate Muslims and to require a commitment from them to democratic rules and values. It's time to show that, in fact, such assimilation and such rules are precisely what make Australia a place of authentic asylum and a place worth protecting. The risk we face right now is leaving just enough of our migrants out on the vulnerable fringes of our society that the firebrands of Hizb ut Tahrir and other Islamist bodies win more recruits to their benighted cause.

If we take this step—offering those now in our midst the path to citizenship thus far denied them—several things are likely to follow. Firstly, the best and most energetic among them, with the most to gain from being here, will seize that offer with both hands and become good citizens. Secondly, the few who have come with malign intentions will become more isolated and easier to detect. Thirdly, while our borders remain secure and our immigration policies sovereign, we will have refuted those who, often hypocritically, denounce our policies as inhumane and mean-spirited.

To secure these benefits, we should act not grudgingly or half-heartedly, but deliberately and decisively. The first step would be to engage with representatives from the different ethnic groups involved in order to determine to a first approximation the range of people we are dealing with and their current condition. The second step would be to convert temporary bridging visas into work visas and make clear that, while such visas will be revoked for those who gravitate towards militant Islamism, for the rest—the overwhelming majority—the way forward to permanent residency and ultimate citizenship is open.

This is a measure that should, at this juncture, win bipartisan support. It should bring together in the middle ground of considered policy, border security and humane initiative, all those from the Green Left to the Coalition benches. It would enable them to put aside for the moment their partisan political bickering and attempts at cheap point scoring and agree on a policy for both the national good and the moral good. Let's see it happen. Yes, Prime Minister?

12: Let's indeed have a conversation about Islam

Last Friday in these pages, Waleed Aly excoriated both Tony Abbott and that embarrassing buffoon running rogue in the US Republican primaries, Donald Trump. He deplored their ignorance about Islam and the muddle entailed in the conservative Catholic Tony Abbott calling for a Reformation and revolution within Islam. But then he added that 'this isn't really a conversation about Islam'; it's about a dubious brand of 'arch conservative' populist politics.

Very well, then. Let's actually *have* the conversation about Islam that we have to have. Let's begin with Waleed's striking observation that 'Islam's own version of the Reformation already occurred in the 18th century', giving birth to Wahhabism, the religious culture of the nation state of Saudi Arabia, al Qaeda and Islamic State. We have common ground here, since I have argued elsewhere at length that this is the case.

Where we differ is with regard to the claim Waleed then made: that the current 'affliction' of Islam stems from the 'utter destruction of the main institutions of religious learning' within the Islamic world 'in the colonial era', so that Muslims are now 'a people thoroughly disconnected from their own tradition.' The clear implication is that had there been no 'Reformation' within Islam and no colonial era, everything would have been just fine and dandy.

Now Waleed likes to cock a snook at 'arch conservatives', but here his posture is surely as romantically arch conservative as one could reasonably be. It reminds me of the claims of old fashioned Catholics who would assert in the 20th century that everything started going wrong in the West with the Reformation and had been going downhill ever since.

The much maligned B. A. Santamaria wrote thirty years or so ago that the West was in a sorry state 'compared with the bright promise of Christianity a thousand years ago'. Rather curiously, Waleed Aly seems to hold a similar position. Had he elaborated a little, we might have had him stating that a thousand years ago the civilization of the Umma, from Cordoba to Cairo and on to Baghdad, was admirable in many ways and more advanced than the tenth century Latin West, if not more than Song China.

But he felt it was more important to fire a broadside at the follies of Donald Trump than to spell out what he sees as the attractions of pre-colonial Islamic religious institutions. He might, had he spelled things out, have conceded that the divisions between Sunni and Shia Muslims long antedate the colonial era. He might have conceded that it was Berber fundamentalists from Morocco who sacked Cordoba a thousand years ago, not Christian reconquerors.

He might have conceded that Baghdad was sacked by the Mongols in 1258 and its schools and libraries destroyed, centuries before the colonial era. He might have added that the Umma ran a slave trade every bit as substantial in East Africa and the Indian Ocean for many centuries as the Atlantic slave trade. And he might have added that at many points prior to the colonial era heretics and infidels, Zoroastrian, Jewish, Christian or other, were persecuted by traditional Islam.

He might, not least, have admitted that Islam was spread, from Medina onward, by the sword across the Mediterranean world and Central Asia, not by missionaries with books and not by open minded philosophers. And he might, finally, have asked himself and his readers why, since the Wahhabists and other Islamic 'reformers' have been so reactionary and brutal, they have not been roundly rejected right across the Muslim world, starting with the most *religious* Muslims.

We should, certainly, have an intelligent conversation about Islam, but it cannot be a pious one in which it is pretended that there is some pristine form of the religion that is beyond reproach and which would have been and remained peaceful and compassionate, if only the colonial powers had not interfered with it. In implying something like this, without going so far as to explicitly claim it, Waleed is making things too easy for himself and actually stoking the fires of historical confusion and sectarian animosity that he professes to want to put out.

It is possible to admire elements of historic Islam and there were, in its heyday, certain thinkers and poets within the Umma whose work remains as impressive as that of the best thinkers from the pre-modern Western world. Not least among such figures is the celebrated 13th century Sufi poet Rumi, whose poem 'The Far Mosque' begins with the observation that: 'The place that Solomon made to worship in, called the Far Mosque, is not built of earth and water and stone, but of intention and wisdom and mystical conversation and compassionate action.'

Whether we are Muslims, Christians, Jews or atheists we could agree with the outlook of Rumi here and find in it a basis for civilized co-existence and a set of principles that elevate integrity and compassion above dogma and obscurantism. In the meantime, however, we have a serious problem with the Islamic 'Reformation', because it is tearing the Muslim world apart and assailing the West in a barbarous manner. It would be a relief to see Waleed agree that if this is the 'Reformation', then what is called for is neither its 'austere scripturalism' (his expression) nor an Islamic 'Counter-Reformation', but the *emancipation* of the Umma from the medieval traditions and tangled histories that weigh upon it like a nightmare.

This is the conversation about Islam that we need to have; just as we have been having it about Christianity and Judaism for centuries. If Waleed and his co-religionists are keen to have such a conversation, no obstacle stands in their way. But if, whatever their take on the Islamic past, they have a vision of Islam becoming the religion of the world at large and of some form of sharia law becoming ascendant over secular civil law; or if they remain ambivalent about the barbarities of their 'Reformers', then we all have a serious problem.

13: Duncan Lewis's dilemmas highlight the real problem

Perhaps the story of the past week has been controversy over the Director General of ASIO, Duncan Lewis, publicly rebuking a number of politicians and urging that they curb their outspokenness regarding Islam. Lewis made two crucial points: that intemperate criticism of Islam risked inflaming Muslim opinion, making ASIO's job harder; and that it was 'blasphemous, to the extent that I can comment on someone else's religion' to suggest that Islamist terrorism springs from Islam itself.

It is, surely, rather unusual for the head of the security service to rebuke senior politicians for their remarks; but that a man of Lewis's character and calibre felt the need to do so throws into high relief the delicate situation he believes we face within at least certain sections of the Muslim community. His task is to keep the lid on things. He fears that open criticism of Islam could blow that lid off. The problem is sufficiently delicate, it would appear, that he sees calls for a *reform* of Islam as inflammatory.

Yet the need for quite sweeping reforms and liberalization within the Islamic world is patent; whether in Shiite Iran, which groans under a theocratic tyranny; or reactionary monarchist Saudi Arabia, with its state-sponsored Wahhabist religion; or in any number of other Muslim countries, in which cruel penal codes, religious intolerance and misogyny are entrenched and oppressive. Islamists are trying to impose from Pakistan and Afghanistan, through much of the Middle East, in Libya, the Horn of Africa and parts of West Africa a brutal and misogynist rule. They declare this to be mandated by the Quran and not by any other authority.

It beggars belief that Duncan Lewis is oblivious to these realities. One must infer, therefore, that he simply thinks we should tip toe around them, lest we stir up a hornets nest. Doesn't this suggest that the Muslim community contains a large body of opinion that he fears could all too readily swing behind the jihadists if riled? There is clear empirical evidence from overseas that a substantial number of Muslims approve of what their violent co-religionists are doing. Without doubt, it is this body of opinion that the Islamists seek to mobilize in order to further their benighted cause. Is Lewis hoping against hope that, by exercising extraordinary restraint (and requiring it of our political representatives) we can avoid this happening here? I think we should assume so.

Not content, however, with calling for the use of temperate language on the part of political figures, he states that it is 'blasphemous' to suggest that terrorism springs from Islam, to the extent that he 'can comment on someone else's religion'. Here there are two problems, which throw into even higher relief the nature of our present difficulties. Firstly, the terrorism in question is uniformly practised in the name of Islam. This makes cleaning it up primarily a problem within Islam. Secondly, we are and must remain perfectly free to *comment* on the religious beliefs of others. We cannot maintain a free and secular society by pretending that anything done in the name of religion, or any religion itself, is immune from criticism.

The Islamists themselves, from Sayyid Qutb and Ayman al-Zawahiri of the Muslim Brotherhood and al Qaeda to the ruthless foot soldiers of the Taliban or of Boko Haram, to the merciless killers of ISIS declare outright that their jihad is sanctioned by the Quran. Even our own Waleed Aly describes their claims as an 'austere scripturalism'. Note that phrase. It simply will not do, therefore, to pretend that there is no basis for violent jihad in Islam and that it is offensive to call for major changes in how Islam is taught and held.

The question is not whether there is a problem with Islam, but what to do about it. Our answer, as a secular Western democracy must be to insist that Muslims can live alongside the rest of us on the understanding that they fully accept the rules of co-existence, which preclude religious fanaticism; require that their religion remain open to criticism and change; and encourage the adoption of cosmopolitan norms in the place of reactionary beliefs and practices. This may take a while, but it must be our common goal.

It is striking, therefore, that Duncan Lewis would imply that one cannot, past a certain point, even *comment* on someone else's religion. How, without freely doing so, could we ever have created a secular society or a scientific worldview? Two hundred and fifty years ago, Voltaire openly called for the abolition of Christianity and Judaism as infamous superstitions. Are we now to say that even calls for reforms within Islam are too inflammatory for public figures to utter?

There is no sound basis for treating religions as if they deserve inordinate respect—except the kind of prudence that Mr Lewis urges, out of a concern that religious rancour will get out of hand. But that means that it is the religious rancour that is the problem, not calls for its reform. Religious beliefs are all too often patently absurd. New-fangled cults and millenarian movements regularly remind us of this. Islam is by no means an exception and cannot be spared criticism merely because some of its adherents threaten violence on that account.

Duncan Lewis is a knight protector of the realm. We are fortunate to have him running ASIO. He is doing all he can to keep the peace and maintain social calm. Let's not, therefore, make too much of his recent remarks, or hound him on account of them. But let us not, on the other hand, lose our confidence or assurance so far as to self-censor when it comes to religion in general, including Islam, and the defence of civilized norms. What is called for is not silence or mealy-mouthed platitudes, but sustained honesty and well-informed debate about how to overcome rancorous religion and continue to build a prosperous, secure and cosmopolitan society.

14: Niall Ferguson's critics jump the gun

Harry Gelber's review (December 2015) of the first volume of Niall Ferguson's biography of Henry Kissinger—*Kissinger 1923-1968: The Idealist*—strikes the right note in describing it as 'the first half of what may yet turn out to be his masterpiece.' There is no question that Ferguson is poised to deliver something special in the second volume, which, he informs me, will take at least another three years. Even this first volume is a most impressive piece of work. Yet Ferguson's critics on the Left refuse to give him any credit for what he has accomplished. They insist that Kissinger was a malignant figure and that an honest account of his development would have revealed the taproot of the 'dark side' of his character.

Such critics, of whom Greg Grandin in *The Guardian* and Mario del Pero, in *The Washington Post*, are representative, insist that Ferguson has strained every fibre and every source to represent his subject as a 'tormented idealist', rather than as the 'cynical, amoral realist' that they see in him. Whatever one's assessment of Kissinger's work in public office, from December 1968, all talk of 'torment' and cynical realism is out of place in a dispassionate account of Kissinger's early life. His critics err egregiously by insisting on reading that early life through the lenses of their bitter denunciations of Kissinger's work as a statesman. Indeed, the claim that Kissinger was always a Kantian idealist at heart receives support from his own most recent work, *World Order: Reflections on the Character of Nations and the Course of History* (Allen Lane, Penguin, 2014); which they appear not to have bothered to read.

Gelber makes the odd statement that critical assessments of Kissinger's role in public life 'have centred on the two decades from 1960 to around 1980, when Kissinger was effectively in charge of the foreign policy of the world's greatest power.' In reality, he had very little influence on that foreign policy before 1969. What he did do, as Ferguson shows quite beautifully, is take a keen interest throughout the 1950s and 1960s in how US foreign policy was being conducted. He thought long and hard about the serious problems of strategy, containment, deterrence and counterinsurgency, wrote many papers, as well as several books and ran seminars at Harvard that brought together many of the finest academic minds to debate the issues of the epoch. If the critics know of evidence that, during these years, Kissinger was a dark and amoral character they have failed to bring it forward.

Mario del Pero asserts that, while Ferguson uncovered remarkable new sources for Kissinger's early life in Germany and his work as an American Counter-Intelligence Corps officer at the end of the Second World War, he failed to mine the rich literature on the Cold War and thus ended up with a superficial and distorted view of Kissinger's contribution to the war of ideas verging on hagiography. Del Pero, whose own modest accomplishments are unlikely to merit any kind of biography, concludes by disparaging the length of this first volume, given what he describes as the rather pedestrian character of its subject:

> His quasi-Delphic prose notwithstanding, Kissinger was in reality a fairly conventional thinker who followed the vogues of the times far more than shaping them. Despite what Ferguson wants us to believe, he rarely challenged power (or who was in power) as other international relations experts, like Hans Morgenthau and George Kennan, were prone to do. In advance of Volume 2, this often pleonastic and redundant first part thus leaves the reader wondering whether Kissinger as an intellectual — realist, idealist or however we choose to label him — truly deserves 1,000 pages.

The fastidious will differ in such matters, but I found the 1,000 pages consistently absorbing. Above all, I found them a deeply informative introduction to the life and mind of Henry Kissinger, precisely as del Pero put it, 'in advance of Volume 2'.

If your aspiration was to become a serious academic historian, you could hardly conceive of a better trajectory than that enjoyed by Niall Campbell Ferguson. He attended Glasgow Academy, then won a half scholarship to Oxford and did both his undergraduate degree (with first class honours) and his doctoral studies (on business and politics in Hamburg between 1914 and the hyper-inflation of 1923-24), at Magdalen College. He went on to teach at Cambridge University and New York University in the 1980s and 1990s and has produced fifteen major books since 1997. Now he is a professor at Harvard, and a fellow at Oxford, Stanford's prestigious Hoover Institution and the London School of Economics.

Born in Glasgow, in 1964, he was the son of a physician and a physics teacher, who brought him up as an atheist, which he remains. The grim, atheistic political philosopher Thomas Hobbes has been a major influence on his thinking. As a school-boy, he has related, he was inclined to the humanities, but was unable to decide whether to study English language and literature or history. Curiously, for a young atheist, it was reading of *War and Peace,* a work of literature by a devout (though highly heterodox) Christian, that persuaded him to become a historian. We all owe a debt of thanks to Leo Tolstoy for having so influenced him.

He was already well credentialed, but only 40 years of age, when the eighty year old Henry Kissinger approached him, in 2004, asking would he consider writing an authorized biography. It was a remarkable tribute to the young historian that an elder statesman—and no ordinary elder statesman—twice his age should approach him and ask him to write his biography. It can only have been that Kissinger had been impressed by Ferguson's body of work over the preceding decade, starting with *Paper and Iron: Hamburg Business and German Politics in the Era of Inflation, 1897–1927,* in 1995; and concluding in 2004 with *Colossus: The Rise and Fall of the American Empire.*

In between, he had written a two volume history of the house of Rothschild and world banking (1998-99), a history of the First World War, a study of alternatives and counterfactuals in history, a study of money in the modern world from 1700 to 2000 and, in 2003, *Empire: The Rise and Demise of the British World Order and the Lessons for Global Power*. He had covered much of the terrain that had always interested Kissinger, not only as a statesman, but as a person and a scholar. And, in 2004, Ferguson was appointed to the Laurence Tisch professorship in History at Harvard University, Kissinger's academic *alma mater*, where he had made his name as a scholar and strategic thinker long before he became Richard Nixon's national security adviser in late 1968.

In 2004, Ferguson already had many other projects on the drawing boards including his acclaimed book and television series *The Ascent of Money*. Writing a biography of Henry Kissinger would be a massive undertaking. Being a 'conservative', who supported Margaret Thatcher in the 1970s and 80s and endorsed the Anglo-American invasion of Iraq in 2003, he was aware that, as he writes in his Preface to this first volume of the biography, 'I would inevitably be savaged by Christopher Hitchens and others. And so, in early March 2004, after several meetings, telephone calls and letters, I said no'. This, he comments wryly, 'was to be my introduction to the diplomacy of Henry Kissinger.'

The octogenarian Kissinger wrote him exclaiming that it was a pity Ferguson had declined, both because he had only just rediscovered, in Kent, Connecticut, 145 boxes containing his private papers going back 'at least to 1955 and probably to 1950', which he had believed lost; and that 'our conversations had given me the confidence—after admittedly some hesitation— that you would have done a definitive—if not necessarily positive—evaluation. For that I am grateful, even as it magnifies my regret.' The diplomacy of the controversial old man prevailed. Ferguson comments laconically, 'A few weeks later I was in Kent, Connecticut, turning pages.'

The diplomat chose well and the scholar has delivered, in this first volume, a remarkable book. It is impressive in at least seven distinct ways: its mastery of a mass of detail; its architectonic balance; its felicity of expression; it's often striking and elegant *obiter dicta* about human experience, academic life and world affairs; its insightful and unflinching character sketches of successive American presidents and other prominent figures, as well of numerous other characters in the extraordinary story of Kissinger's first 45 years; its uniquely original and strikingly independent assessment of Henry Kissinger's character and development; and its magnificent stage setting for what is to come in the second volume, which will examine Kissinger as national security adviser and secretary of state.

Yet Greg Grandin, whose own book, *Kissinger's Shadow*, was released in the United States in December 2015, writing in *The Guardian*, in mid-October typifies just the kind of tendentious 'savaging' that Ferguson anticipated would come from the late Christopher Hitchens and others. He asserts that Ferguson's book is an extended, but litigious, lazy and 'boring' defence of its subject. He insists that Ferguson has avoided the 'dark' side of Kissinger's character and motivation and that Ferguson is in error—deliberately and culpably—in rejecting the claim that Kissinger helped Richard Nixon sabotage the secret negotiations going on in Paris in 1968 with North Vietnam, in order to get the appointment as Nixon's national security adviser.

But in taking this line of attack, Grandin is jumping the gun. Ferguson argues, very persuasively, that Kissinger was not motivated by 'dark' impulses, but by a highly intelligent, complex and perceptive commitment to statecraft and to finding ways to make American foreign and international security policy work better. Moreover, he demonstrates meticulously that Kissinger did *not* sabotage the Johnson administration or connive in any malign way with Nixon and that he did not expect to become national security adviser at all, right up to the point when Nixon explicitly made him the offer in December 1968. He engages in no convoluted or tendentious reasoning to make his demonstration, but offers a detailed and judicious—not 'litigious'—assessment of the roles of many actors in the events leading up to the December 1968 appointment.

Determined to assert that Ferguson is out to exculpate Kissinger in volume *two*, Grandin appears not to have even *read* most of volume one. In fact, Ferguson's long, deeply informed account of Kissinger's intellectual formation and his disillusionment with the Johnson administration's war in Vietnam as early as 1965, make compelling reading. One of the most eye opening revelations is that criticisms of Johnson's policies, of the workings of his national security decision-making apparatus and of the conduct of the war in Vietnam that have always been associated with Left-wing critics of the war and, in my own mind, with the thinking of Daniel Ellsberg before and after he leaked the *Pentagon Papers* to the *New York Times*, in 1971, can be found explicitly in papers and memoranda written by Henry Kissinger in 1965-66.

This is all the more striking because, at least in this volume, Ferguson hardly mentions Ellsberg and certainly shows no sign of having set out to argue that Kissinger anticipated Ellsberg's *Papers on the War* or more general public stance after 1971. The difference between the two was that Ellsberg defected from the inner councils of state and sought to change policy by leaking massive quantities of classified documents to the press. Kissinger sought to reshape the inner workings of those councils through his highly intelligent and quite transparent writings up to late 1968 and to take direct responsibility for their workings when offered the chance by Nixon, despite never having liked Nixon as either a person or a politician.

Being a Scotsman, Ferguson came to the study of the Vietnam War from a perspective independent from entrenched partisan disputation in the United States. His candour and detachment are epigrammatically summed up in his remark, at the beginning of Chapter 16, 'The Road to Vietnam':

> There are many ways of explaining why the United States came to grief so spectacularly in Vietnam. But the plain fact of it will always be astounding.

Anyone who thinks that the Vietnam War was an immoral war launched by 'evil' or imperialistic Americans has never understood the matter at all. Ferguson puts his finger on the fundamental problem at once in drawing attention to Robert McNamara's confession that the problem was 'above all, the failure of the American decision-making process itself.' And it is in this context that Ferguson's perceptive account of Kissinger's thinking about Vietnam is grounded. 'It has long been assumed', he writes, '- since Hans Morgenthau first asserted it in 1969—that Henry Kissinger 'supported' the Vietnam War throughout the 1960s and that this was indeed one of the key reasons Richard Nixon offered him the job of national security adviser. *This view is incorrect.*' The way in which Kissinger's thinking on Vietnam developed is set out beautifully by Ferguson. It confutes the Left-wing canard that a 'dark' Kissinger was at work on Vietnam in the lead-up to the White House years.

As early as 1962, Kissinger was critical of the handling of the Vietnam War by the Kennedy administration. He deplored what he saw as the cynical manipulation of the South Vietnamese government by the pragmatists of Camelot. In 1963-64, working for Nelson Rockefeller, he urged the liberal Republican to 'call on Johnson to tell the American people frankly just what this Nation's policies and objectives in Southeast Asia really are.' He was appalled by the Goldwater wing of the GOP and repelled by Nixon. The 1964 Republican convention struck Kissinger as akin to Nazi politics and worried him deeply. Johnson, of course, trounced Goldwater the hawk in the 1964 election, but then proceeded to escalate the Vietnam War in 1965. Kissinger had no hand in this. As Ferguson remarks, he 'could scarcely have been less responsible for the fateful decision to escalate the war in Vietnam'. But he did involve himself in attempting to understand it and offer critical analysis to the administration from outside the government.

'By the summer of 1965,' Ferguson relates, 'Vietnam had become not just the most important foreign policy challenge facing the United States but the only one and he thirsted to understand the problem better.' Those who are determined to depict Kissinger as a villain will assert that the Vietnam War was a war to prevent the self-determination of the people of Vietnam and that if Kissinger had been as Ferguson argues, an idealist, he would have denounced the war as simply wrong. Such critics have never conceded how violent and oppressive the Vietnamese Communist movement was. But they are, in any case, wrong about Kissinger. By August 1965, Ferguson shows us, Kissinger 'already knew one thing. This was a war that could not be won by military means. The only question worth discussing was how to negotiate an end to it. It was a question he was destined to spend the next eight years struggling to answer.'

Far from being or becoming a sinister rationalizer of escalation, Kissinger set about asking 'disquieting questions' about why the war was being fought at all, how it was being fought, how decision-making in Washington was being done and what the implications of the imbroglio were for the United States on the world stage. Just as LBJ was ratcheting up the war, Kissinger penned a memo in which he wrote:

> I am quite convinced that too much planning in the government and a great deal of military planning assumes that the opponent is stupid and that he will fight the kind of war for which one is best prepared. However...the essence of guerrilla warfare is never to fight the kind of war your opponent expects. Having moved very many large units into Vietnam...we must not become prisoners now of a large-unit mentality. Otherwise I think that we will face the problem of psychological exhaustion.

This, of course, is precisely what happened over the following three or four years. During that time, Kissinger reflected again and again on what was going wrong and its implications. Above all, and very early, he identified a syndrome of which Ellsberg was to write only years later: the lack of collective or institutional memory that bedevilled operations in Vietnam. When he visited Vietnam in August 1966, he found to his dismay, 'almost no-one who knew about conditions in October 1965...New people start with great enthusiasm but little sophistication. By the time they learn their job it is time for them to leave.' This is not the language of a dark and amoral 'realist'.

Writing in the early 1970s, Ellsberg was to make much of the idea that he had tried, in 1969, to get Kissinger to think about Vietnam in a critical way based on past mistakes. Yet Kissinger had been among the most lucid and candid critics of those mistakes for years before Ellsberg himself even became disillusioned with the Vietnam War. In Ellsberg's 2002 memoir *Secrets: A Memoir of Vietnam and the Pentagon Papers*, an enormous amount of space is given to discussion of Henry Kissinger. Ellsberg refers to his role in 1969 as an adviser to Kissinger, helping him to 'discover uncertainties and alternatives'. But Kissinger had been hard at work on this subject well before 1969. Reading Ferguson one gains a very different impression of Kissinger's pre-1969 thinking on Vietnam than that recorded in Ellsberg's memoir. It will, to say the least, be interesting, therefore, to see how Ferguson treats the relationship between the two men in the second volume of the biography.

Central to the architecture of Ferguson's biography is his attempt to trace the development of Kissinger's thinking over decades and not only about Vietnam in the 1960s. Grandin asserts that Ferguson's account makes Kissinger 'boring'. This seems to me a perverse judgement. Grandin, convinced that Kissinger was some kind of vaudeville villain, insists that the biographer should have shown the 'dark' side of Kissinger that he assumes must have been there. Instead of a Grandin melodrama, however, Ferguson sets the stage for a kind of tragic drama, which may be how the second volume will read. The really boring view of Kissinger is the tired old clichés of the Left. In this new biography we can see the slow development of Kissinger's personality, his immigrant patriotism, his ideals, his worldview, his relationships with mentors, his analytical acumen, his political outlook (which was anything but cynical) and his attempts to grasp and then shape the machinery of foreign and security policy making in the United States. The book concludes with a very fine summation, in the fourteen page Epilogue, of what Ferguson calls the *'bildungsroman'* of Henry Kissinger—'the tale of his education through experience, some of it bitter'.

One of the projects that Kissinger commenced in his youth, with his doctoral dissertation at Harvard, was an examination of the system of balance of power devised in Europe at the Congress of Vienna to prevent another cycle of disruptive wars on the Napoleonic scale. His dissertation was published under the title *A World Restored: Metternich, Castlereagh and the Problems of Peace 1812-1822*. Ferguson reveals that Kissinger planned to make this the first of a triptych of books taking the study up to the collapse of the system in 1914-15. The second volume, which he took to advanced draft form before abandoning, centred on Otto von Bismarck and the rise of Germany in the mid to late 19th century. Ferguson's discussion of this facet of Kissinger's life is fascinating and beautifully nuanced. Kissinger, he observes, was often accused after 1969 of aspiring to be an American Bismarck, but in fact Kissinger *never* so aspired. He appreciated the genius of Bismarck, but regarded his achievement as having been 'fatally flawed' and as opening the way, unintentionally, to the catastrophe of 1914. Ferguson's critics seem to have made no attempt to absorb this key finding by the biographer.

It would be interesting to know how the planned triptych would have played out, had Henry Kissinger abstained from public policy work and concentrated on historical scholarship. When George Weidenfeld, who had published *A World Restored* in 1957, approached Kissinger in early 1969 to inquire whether he had completed or planned to complete the Bismarck volume, Kissinger responded that he had not only abandoned it, but had burned the manuscript, having realized, as he put it to the publisher, after only a few weeks near the centre of power 'how much I still have to learn about how policy is really made.' As Ferguson found, Kissinger had not actually burned the manuscript. 'The incomplete manuscript survived, unread for more than half a century, in his private papers.' Having worked at a level even more exalted and challenging than Bismarck ever had, Kissinger of course was to write both his multi-volume memoirs and his two treatises on foreign and security policy, *Diplomacy* and *World Order*. The latter, published only in 2014, may be regarded as Henry Kissinger's mature reflection on the problems he had pondered over a very long lifetime. It is not a cynical or amoral piece of writing at all, but one fully consistent with Ferguson's account of how Kissinger's mind developed and worked.

The Epilogue to this first volume of the biography is in itself a beautiful piece of writing, opening with a reference to Goethe's famous bildungsroman, *Wilhelm Meister's Apprenticeship* and concluding with an invocation of the fifth century anti-war comedy, *Peace*, by the brilliant Athenian playwright Aristophanes. It is a measure of the quality of Ferguson's mind that he was able to avoid looking at the early life of Henry Kissinger through the jaundiced lenses that the Left would have had him wear; to examine the subject dispassionately; to have appreciated both the ironies in Kissinger's circuitous ascent to the West Wing of the White House and the acute dilemmas that lay in wait for him as a scholar-statesman. His accounts of Kissinger's relationships with his various mentors, not least among them the brilliant, conservative and very private German émigré Fritz Kraemer, whom Ferguson dubs a Mephistopheles to Kissinger's Faust, considerably enrich our understanding of how the young man developed.

Ferguson's argument that Kissinger was a Kantian idealist, not an amoral realist might stick in the craw of Kissinger's baying critics, but his argument is compelling. Kissinger worked for Nelson Rockefeller, whose aristocratic liberal Republicanism he admired, despite the fact that Rockefeller was never going to become President. Neither del Poro nor Grandin bothers to address why a cynical realist would have done this. What Kissinger took on from December 1968 had already driven the Democrats, both liberal and conservative, to despair. He chose to take the poisoned chalice and attempt to deal intelligently with the vast challenges confronting the United States. He did so not out of a lust for demonic power, but because he believed such challenges needed to be tackled with as much intelligence as possible. He then became one of the towering figures of 20th century statecraft. The second volume of Ferguson's biography is something to look forward to. But make no mistake, in this first volume he has produced a masterpiece and one that should be read attentively and thoughtfully, not in the superficial and supercilious manner that Greg Grandin and his ilk have greeted it.

Liu Xiaobo was awarded the Nobel Peace Prize while in a Chinese prison. The Nobel Committee put an empty chair on the stage to signify his absence. The Communist Party then blocked the term 'empty chair' on the internet in China.

PART II: 2016 (A)

1: Iranian ambitions in Arabia pre-date Muhammad

The growing tensions between Iran and Saudi Arabia—already at war by proxy in Syria and Yemen—need to be better understood by those making Western security policy. We are too easily distracted by the obvious and too little inclined to think deeper and longer about what is going on. The struggle between Persians and Arabs dates back a very long way and it has had outcomes in the past that may offer clues about what might unfold in the Middle East in the years ahead.

Certainly, this is a clash between a Sunni Arab power and a Shiite Iranian one. Certainly they are at odds over the fate of Syria's secular fascist dictator, Bashar al-Assad. Certainly, each of them has more at stake in that outcome than does any Western power. But precisely for this reason we need to look beneath these surface considerations to the deeper historical forces at work, in order to assess where our true interests in this conflict lie.

The most instructive antecedent to the present situation lies far further back than the famous Sykes Picot settlement at the end of the First World War, when the Ottoman Empire was dismantled and the nation states of the Middle East as we know it today were created out of its dismembered parts. It lies further back than the rise of the Ottoman Turks and their conquests in South-eastern Europe, the Middle East and Africa in the 16th century.

The antecedent in question in fact pre-dates the rise of Islam in the 7th century of the Common Era (CE). Only very recent scholarship has brought this long obscure history to light, but it repays careful study right now. It involved the clash of the Christian Ethiopians with a Jewish kingdom in what is now Yemen. It drew the Roman and Persian Empires into a war for influence in Arabia and the wider Middle East. It ended with the rise of Islam and its conquest of both those empires.

In the 4th century CE, the powerful kingdom of Ethiopia, which included the whole of the Horn of Africa (including Somalia), converted to Christianity, within a decade or so of the Emperor Constantine making Christianity the state religion of the Roman Empire. Not long afterwards, the Arabs of what is now Yemen, which had since Solomonic times been known as Saba or Sheba, but was known in Roman times as Himyar, converted to Judaism.

This was the crucible in which Islam germinated. It came from the clash of monotheisms and of arms in Arabia and not from the 'Archangel Gabriel'. The pagan Ethiopian kings had conquered Himyar in the 3rd century CE, but their rule there had lapsed decades before the conversions to monotheism on either side of the Red Sea. When, however, in the early 6th century, the Jewish king of Himyar began to persecute his Christian Arab subjects, the Ethiopian king, urged on by the Emperor Justin in Constantinople, crossed the Red Sea and overthrew Jewish rule.

That invasion set off a chain of events in which the Persians intervened on the side of the Jews, much as Iran has recently aided the Houthis in Yemen, while the Romans (from Constantinople) backed the Ethiopians. Both sides sought Arab allies and a series of wars lasting a century devastated the Middle East. The Emperor Justinian in Constantinople (the 'West', of the time) was committed to restoring the ancient extent of the Roman Empire, by reconquering Italy, North Africa and Spain, as well as checking Persian ambitions in the Middle East. The Persians, for their part, sought to restore the glories of the Persian Empire as it had been before the conquests of Alexander the Great, almost nine hundred years before.

Think, by way of analogy, of American hegemony and Iranian ambitions in this context. In the 6th and early 7th centuries, the fortunes of war ebbed and flowed. Late in the piece, in 614, the Persians took Palestine, including Jerusalem, and even overran Egypt. They were greeted as liberators by the Jews, who had long resented Roman domination. Arabia was not marginal to all this. It was a theatre of war and of the contention of ideas. Muhammed, forty four years old when Jerusalem fell to the Persians, witnessed the Romans retake everything that the Persians had overrun.

By 629 the Romans had retaken Jerusalem and their other Middle Eastern provinces, after the Emperor Heraclius inflicted a series of crushing defeats on the Persians. But the Arabs had, by then, begun to rally under the flag of Islam. In 636 they inflicted a devastating defeat on the Roman army in Palestine, then overran Syria and Egypt. In 644 they inflicted an equally crushing defeat on the Persians. The Roman Empire never recovered its Middle Eastern provinces and the Persian Empire ceased to exist by 651.

This massive transformation of the Middle Eastern world and the utter failure of the great powers of the time to foresee the rise of Arab monotheism and military power ought to be central to our strategic thinking right now about the implosion of the contemporary order in the Arab world. That is not only because Islam is central to the awful mess that is afflicting the area, but because our antecedent shows how basic assumptions about power and order can melt down in such conflicts.

Among the assumptions about power and order that are up for potential meltdown in our own time are the very foundations of Islam itself, both in the reactionary monarchy of Saudi Arabia with its brutal and aggressive state religion and in the oppressive, terror-sponsoring theocratic regime in Iran. We should want to see the two collide and implode, that a better and more modern order might arise on the ruins. But it is just as possible that even worse regimes could arise from the ashes of war. The 7th century lacked good options. We need quite urgently to ponder ours.

2: North Korea's a-bombs: a study in international relations

North Korea's four tests since 2006 suggest it has only nuclear firecrackers, not thermonuclear weapons. Yet the ugly nature of the Kim family tyranny and its bellicose rhetoric make its possession of even small nuclear weapons unsettling. The perennial worry is that Pyongyang will finally lose the plot altogether and trigger a catastrophic war in North East Asia.

All efforts to induce it to end its nuclear program, reform its grossly distorted economy and come out of the cold have failed. It regularly issues bizarre threats and continues to defy international sanctions and standards. Yet it remains confined to its bleak and impoverished bunker, incapable of much more than brutal bluster. All these things make it, from a detached point of view, a fascinating study in the nature of international security affairs and diplomacy.

A generation ago, before North Korea had in fact become a nuclear power, I was Japan and Koreas desk officer in the Defence Intelligence Organization. This gave me a ringside seat to watch the drama that developed after the end of the Cold War regarding North Korea's nuclear program. For a while, in 1991-92, it looked as though North Korea would play by the rules. It joined the UN and the NPT and agreed to IAEA inspections of its nuclear plant at Yongbyon.

Throughout 1993, however, the IAEA reported a long series of discrepancies and evasions in North Korea's compliance with the safeguards agreement. The resultant tension built up through to March 1994, then appeared to be resolved, with North Korea seemingly reaching an agreement to abide by inspections in exchange for assistance in developing peaceful nuclear technology and being supplied with quantities of fuel oil for its energy sector.

It's a matter of history now that the agreements reached in late 1994 and early 1995 unravelled. North Korea proceeded to repudiate all non-proliferation commitments and develop nuclear weapons. In the current context of uncertainties and misgivings about the nuclear agreement with Iran, it is worth revisiting the failure of the agreement with North Korea twenty years ago. The best account is by Joel Wit, Daniel Poneman and Robert Gallucci: *Going Critical: The First North Korean Nuclear Crisis* (Brookings Institution Press, 2004).

From within the intelligence world, in 1994, I followed the excruciating complexities of the case and concentrated on an effort to understand what was driving North Korean behaviour. As tensions reached a critical point, in early 1994, I was asked to brief the Secretary of Defence and the Chiefs of Staff Committee (COSC) on North Korea's nuclear program. A number of senior figures in Canberra feared there could be a war in Korea, with the aged North Korean dictator Kim Il-sung opting to go out with a bang. My task was to help them think it through.

I drew attention to three central drivers of North Korean behaviour. First, by the 1980s, when North Korea first began to build a nuclear reactor, South Korea was leaving the North behind economically. While the North was spending 25% of its GDP on the military and the South 'only' 6% (compare our current 1.8%), the South was spending twice as much in absolute terms, because its economy was so much bigger—and there was nothing the North could do to close that gap. It began, therefore, to seek a strategic equalizer.

Second, in 1989-91, the North watched with astonishment and dismay as the Soviet bloc in Eastern Europe collapsed, the US brushed aside Saddam Hussein in the Gulf War and then the Soviet Union itself fell apart. There were those who thought that North Korea would soon follow. In Pyongyang they had other ideas. The nuclear program was a key part of their strategy to survive by threat and bluff.

Third, I stated that we should not expect Kim Il-sung to go to war. In 1950, with everything in his favour, he did so and suffered a crushing defeat. Only Chinese intervention saved him from extinction. Had he been itching to have another crack at it, he might have done in 1975 or 1978, with the US on the back foot after Vietnam and Carter in the White House; but he baulked at the idea. As an old man with no allies and strong enemies he was extremely unlikely to do so in 1994.

Twenty years on, the US-led West looks less formidable and self-assured than immediately after the Cold War. North Korea's only ally, China, is displeased with it. North Korea remains deeply insecure. Old Kim's grandson is a brutal and immature despot, but is unlikely to start a war he cannot win. There is no easy or pleasant solution for dealing with him. Such is the nature of international affairs. Spare a thought for those whose job it is to deal with such matters.

3: It's time to embrace the Taiwan of Tsai Ingwen

The thumping victories by Tsai Ingwen and her political party the DPP (Democratic Progressive Party) in Taiwan's elections last Saturday are a breath of fresh air. They are similar, in this respect, to the revitalization of democratic politics in Latin America, with sweeping victories for the political opposition in Venezuela and for Mauricio Macri and the Let's Change Party in Argentina.

Nothing like this has happened in China since the election of the Constituent Assembly in 1912, which was aborted by the old imperial general Yuan Shikai, ushering in a century of warlordism, civil war and totalitarian government from which China is yet to emerge. Taiwan escaped Communist takeover in 1949 and has evolved a long way since then. It set an economic example to the Communist Party decades ago and is now setting it a brilliant political example.

While China under Xi Jinping is going backwards politically; Taiwan has just demonstrated that its democratic politics are very real; that genuine regime change is possible by completely peaceful means; and that merit can rise to the top. Tsai Ingwen is a very capable and impressive woman and, given that she commands a clear majority in the legislature, she should be able to govern in an effective manner. Her victory is the true coming of age of Taiwanese democracy.

The Communist Party's response has been negative and sour. Its mass media have censored reporting of the Taiwanese elections and even mention of Ms Tsai's name. Party-aligned academics have warned that if Tsai takes Taiwan down the path of independence it will prove a 'dead end'. The Foreign Ministry has declared, in classic Communist style, that China's commitment to its claim of territorial sovereignty over Taiwan is 'rock hard'. There has not been a hint of admiration or awe at the peaceful nature of the shift from Guomindang (Nationalist) rule to DPP rule, much less of respect for the rise of the accomplished Ms Tsai.

Yet they know very well who she is and how capable she is. She chaired Taiwan's Mainland Affairs Council and has always conducted relations with China intelligently and conservatively. If Beijing was being dispassionate about her win, this would have been acknowledged. But of course Beijing is anything but dispassionate about the matter of Taiwan and there is a considerable likelihood that it will, under Xi Jinping's fairly aggressive leadership, seek to put pressure on Taiwan to kowtow explicitly to the 'one China' line. This could lead to trouble and tensions in East Asia.

Given that China has been pushing the envelope on territorial claims in both the East and South China Seas under Xi Jinping, and is taken aback by Tsai's sweeping victory, it will be looking for ways to corral what it insists is a wayward province. We should not expect that it will embark on a ruinous war, but we must be prepared for tensions and diplomatic gamesmanship. Tsai Ingwen has already and rightly warned Beijing that any attempts on its part to pressure Taiwan will only have adverse effects on Cross Strait relations.

The strategic realities of East Asia are such that everyone has been playing a game of pretense about Taiwan for many years. The pretense is that Taiwan is really a part of China and not an independent country. In truth, however, Taiwan is very much a *de facto* independent country. It has its own currency, armed forces, government, foreign policy, education system and media. It is evolving politically and socially in a manner wholly independent of the repressive political culture of China. Its people clearly have no desire to be governed from Beijing; not even on the so-called 'one country, two systems' model applied to Hong Kong. That model is plainly degenerative and holds no attraction for the free people of Taiwan.

In my book *Thunder From the Silent Zone: Rethinking China* (2005), I argued that, contrary to the dogged insistence of the Communist Party that Taiwan is a renegade province of the People's Republic of China, Taiwan is an island state that Beijing would do well to recognize and befriend, not hector and seek to subdue. Taiwan was never an integral part of the Chinese Empire, only a peripheral and neglected outpost of the foreign Manchu dynasty from the late 17th century until Japan took it in 1895 after the Sino-Japanese War of 1894-95. The Chinese Nationalists took it from Japan in 1945, crushed Taiwanese resistance in a brutal crackdown in 1947-48 and ruled by martial law and dictatorship until the 1980s.

The DPP, heir to the resistance movements of the 1940s through to the early 1980s, has stood for democratization and independence for Taiwan since its founding, in 1986. It has now decisively and peacefully won the battle for public support in Taiwan. In this context, Beijing's claims to Taiwan are empty and oppressive. We can't expect, however, that Xi Jinping will accept this reality. Therefore, the presidency of Tsai Ingwen will be a challenging time. She is far too wise to provoke Beijing by declaring independence. She will simply keep calling for peaceful maintenance of the status quo—which is one of *de facto* Taiwanese independence— until the time when the Communist Party loses its stranglehold on China and something like Taiwan's democratic order comes to the core of the Chinese world. We should support her.

4: Reason in Western civilization: why I joined the Rationalist Society

For years now, I have heard people speak sceptically, even dismissively, about 'Western logic' or 'Cartesian rationalism', as if the ills of the modern world are largely to be blamed on an excess of reason in Western civilization. I feel pretty much at home in the Rationalist Society because I believe such notions are fundamentally erroneous. In writing this for readers of *The Australian Rationalist*, I am, in all probability, preaching to the converted, but even among members of the Rationalist Society of Australia there is, I suspect, quite a range of opinion as to what exactly rationalism is and what its benefits to Western civilization, or humanity at large, have actually been.

I'd like to think that the following brief reflections will find a fair degree of agreement in our circles, but more importantly that they will help stimulate a fruitful discussion *outside* the Society—in the wider society—about the role of reason in civilization. In other words, I am writing not to prove a point in a technical debate among rationalist philosophers, but to position myself, as a member of the Rationalist Society, in a wider conversation about the uses of reason in a civilized society.

Much as Daniel Kahneman, in *Thinking Fast and Slow*, offered a simplified concept of 'the mind' as consisting of what he calls System 1 and System 2, I suggest we begin not with a stance of Cartesian scepticism, but with a tripartite division of the world of reasoning into practical reasoning, formal reasoning and critical reasoning. Kahneman's System 1 is the intuitive brain; his System 2 the consciously reflective and methodical brain. The three types of reasoning I have listed have much in common with his two types of thinking.

Practical reasoning is largely a System 1 activity. It consists of what is often called common sense, with the added component of largely intuitive insights in practical affairs, whether as regards physical activities, manipulation of tools or tactical and strategic judgement 'on the fly'. *Formal* reasoning consists of logic and mathematics and is the science of inference. *Critical* reasoning has to do with the re-examination of assumptions, experiment, conjecture and the testing of hypotheses.

I differentiate between formal and critical reasoning because one of the central breakthroughs in the Western intellectual tradition was the shift from Aristotelian 'logic chopping' to (broadly) Baconian investigative science (whether one refers to Roger or to Francis Bacon). Again and again, more or less sound inference, proceeding on the basis of unexamined assumptions, has led people to all manner of erroneous conclusions. It is in surfacing and testing things taken for granted that the most dramatic progress tends to be made; though sound inference is still required to think clearly to new findings.

When I think of 'Western civilization', I am conscious of a heritage dating back at least 3,000 years—5,000 if we choose to include both Stone Henge and the Egyptians in our history of what is 'Western'. However, the role of reason in either the formal or critical senses has been much more episodic than continuous; and has largely been the work of small minorities of people living within 'Western' societies. It has not been the defining characteristic or virtue of the mass of Westerners at any point; nor is it now.

It cannot be stated too emphatically that merely being able to claim membership— as subject or citizen—of some Western society or other at any point between the Druidic Neolithic and the present time does not remotely guarantee that one is especially rational. Kahneman's System 2, as he insists, is a latent capability and a lazy one. Thinking rationally, whether in a formal or a critical sense, is hard work, requires specialist methods and is not something the majority of people do very much. Indeed, they tend to avoid it whenever they believe they can.

Practical reasoning is far older than either formal or critical reasoning. Those who built the pyramids or the Druidic henges plainly were capable of considerable practical reasoning. Indeed, their accomplishments point to fairly advanced geometric sophistication, as well as engineering and project management skills some five millennia ago. Practical reasoning, in its various forms, has underwritten the technological innovations and arts of our species from deep in the Palaeolithic.

Practical reasoning enabled our ancestors to out compete their hominin cousins, fight off predators in the wild, hunt down big game and devise agriculture after the end of the most recent ice age. Pat Shipman's new book *The Invaders: How Humans and Their Dogs Drove Neanderthals to Extinction* (Belknap, Harvard, 2015) is an illuminating study of this topic. Practical reasoning, grounded in hand/eye coordination, intuitive insight and improvisation, is what enables us to do almost everything that matters to us on a daily basis. It's not to be sneezed at.

Formal reasoning came much later. We associate it with the Greeks, but we need to be careful about several things here. *Practical* reason always was and is a human universal. *Formal* reasoning has appeared to varying degrees in a number of cultures. There are good reasons, however, for seeing the elaboration of the elements of geometry, the foundations of mathematics and the science of formal logic as having taken unprecedented and lasting steps forward in the Grecian world between the fifth and fourth centuries before the Common Era.

The works of Plato and Aristotle, of Euclid and the Hellenistic mathematicians were influential for good reasons; or more precisely because of the good reasoning that these thinkers generally did. They have all been superseded in the modern world; not because of some idle change of fashion, but because modern thinkers did a lot of hard work and developed better and better insights into both the nature of reasoning as such, the scope of mathematics and the nature of physical reality.

Critical reasoning overlaps with both practical and formal reasoning and can be seen at work in many times and places in an informal, improvised way. As a *systematic* approach to reality, however, it has been underdeveloped in most places at most times. Even now, it is seldom the default *modus operandi* even of physical or social scientists. They can as readily become the slaves of unexamined assumptions as anyone else and defend dogmas tenaciously. Consider how doggedly Einstein resisted the very idea of indeterminacy; or how long the scientific consensus of earth scientists was that there could not be any such thing as continental drift, based on the shifting of tectonic plates.

The refined methods for *practising* critical reasoning have taken a very long time to develop and require exquisite expertise to handle. They are the key to the stupendous scientific and, indeed, social advances of the recent past and they hold the keys to our future. Given the challenges we face as a species; given the quantity of data now coming on stream; the pace at which human industrial and information society is now moving; almost everything now depends on our capacities to exercise—and collectively act upon—*critical* reasoning.

Nate Silver's beautiful book *The Signal and the Noise: The Art and Science of Prediction* is a delightful field manual in this respect. It demonstrates again and again how indispensable the methods of critical reasoning are—as distinct from System 1 practical judgements or merely formal reasoning from assumed premises—if we are to understand and react intelligently to the complex physical and social world in which we now live. Richard Thaler and Cass Sunstein's *Nudge: Improving Decisions about Health, Wealth and Happiness* is an almost equally rewarding read in the application of critical reasoning to public policy and social choice.

When I think of rationalism and ponder it as largely the fruit of Western civilization (increasingly available globally), it is on these lines that I think. There is—and has long been— more than one school of thought that wants to insist on the limitations of reason or the 'soullessness' of rationalism. In my experience, this is chiefly a confused response, arising from a failure to comprehend the nature or uses of reason.

There is, however, a perfectly respectable philosophical tradition delineating the limits of reason. My own most recent favourite is Noson Yanofsky's *The Outer Limits of Reason: What Science, Mathematics and Logic Cannot Tell Us* (MIT Press, 2013). Discerning such limits, however, as Yanofsky rightly points out, does *not* give us a license to both freely invent and dogmatically declare adherence to imagined realities beyond the limits of reason, as religions and cults have always done. Rather, it requires of us a highly civilized discipline of mind:

to see that we do not know and cannot articulate 'realities' beyond these rigorously defined boundaries.

This leaves us, in the early 21st century, with an enormous amount of cleaning up, educating and social renovation to get on with—but with some excellent tools and methods to hand. I see the Australian Rationalist Society as a body committed philosophically to both this broad agenda and the use and continued refinement of these tools. And the task is now one not only of Western civilization, but of global civilization; since the whole species is now inescapably caught up in the same currents and dilemmas.

5: Karl Popper and the pre-Socratics

If I was asked to teach an undergraduate course on Rationality 101, I would begin by introducing the students to the work of Karl Popper; especially *Conjectures and Refutations, Objective Knowledge* and *The Open Society and Its Enemies*. Indeed, a good case could be made for having such a course consist entirely of acquainting undergraduates with the arguments in these three books and inducing them to think hard about them. Between them they cover principles vital to both natural and social science.

When I took first year philosophy, almost forty years ago, no such course was on offer. I remember an introductory course on Plato, which baffled me. The following year, I bought the superb Bollingen *Plato: The Collected Dialogues, including the Letters* and grappled with Plato privately. Interesting though that was, it did not convert me to Platonism. Popper, however, whose work I also read largely at my own initiative, did convert me to critical rationalism.

The decisive idea was the one he advanced in *Conjectures and Refutations*: interesting and productive beliefs are not to be had by either 'revelation' or deduction from 'first principles', but by generating and refuting conjectures. By such means three things have developed within cognitive culture over time: constructive imagination, analytical acumen and corrigible knowledge – i.e. beliefs that can be checked and updated or discarded, based on critical inquiry.

A year or so before he died in 1994, Popper published *The World of Parmenides: Essays on the Pre-Socratic Enlightenment*; an attempt to dig down to the roots of the scientific method among the 'natural philosophers' preceding Plato and Aristotle. Popper firmly believed that those two iconic figures had corrupted philosophy and brought scientific thinking to a halt. He believed it had originated, however, with Thales, Anaximander, Xenophanes, Heraclitus, Parmenides, Democritus and others; but had then been lost.

My own opinion in this regard differs from Popper's. I believe that scientific thinking of just the kind he applauded continued well beyond Plato and Aristotle, peaking among Hellenistic scientists between the end of the 4th and the middle of the 2nd century BCE, then ground to a halt; less because of the influence of Plato or Aristotle than because the cognitive culture that had produced Euclid, Eratosthenes, Herophilus, Aristarchus, Archimedes and many others was smothered by Roman pragmatism.[2]

Nevertheless, Popper's reflections on the Pre-Socratics make fascinating reading for those interested in the origins of scientific thinking. At the end of the Introduction to *The World of Parmenides*, Popper described the era of the Pre-Socratics as 'the greatest and most

---

2   For a compelling account of this question see Lucio Russo *The Forgotten Revolution: How Science Was Born in 300 BCE and Why It Had to be Reborn* (Springer Verlag, 2004).

inventive period in Greek philosophy; a period that came to an end with Aristotle's dogmatic epistemology, and from which even the most recent philosophy can be said hardly to have recovered.'

Leaving aside the fact that this ignores the remarkable findings of the Hellenistic scientists, Popper's book is interesting because of the fundamental cognitive breakthrough that he believes was made by the Pre-Socratics. As he wrote, 'The questions which the Pre-Socratics tried to answer were primarily cosmological questions, but there were also questions of the theory of knowledge. It is my belief that philosophy must return to cosmology and to a simple theory of knowledge.' The key to *The World of Parmenides* is Popper's analysis of the cosmology of Parmenides and how, by setting out to understand and refute it, Leucippus and Democritus derived the theory of atomism.

'There is a widespread belief,' Popper wrote, 'somewhat remotely due, I think, to the influence of Francis Bacon, that one should study the problems of the theory of knowledge in connection with our knowledge of an orange rather than our knowledge of the cosmos. I dissent from this belief...[because] Western science – and there seems to be no other – did not start with collecting observations of oranges, but with bold theories about the world.'

Note the term 'bold theories', not 'tall stories'. Popper is not concerned with competing myths here, but with conjectures that lend themselves to critical cross-examination, because grounded in evidence and reasoning. He cites the strikingly counter-intuitive and non-observational conjecture by Anaximander that the Earth was freely suspended in space and held stable by inertial forces, owing to its equidistance from all other heavenly bodies.

Popper comments: 'this idea of Anaximander's is one of the boldest, most revolutionary and most portentous ideas in the whole history of human thought. It made possible the theories of Aristarchus and Copernicus. But the step taken by Anaximander was even more difficult and audacious than [theirs]...To envisage the Earth as freely poised in mid-space and to say that it remains motionless because of its equidistance or equilibrium...is to anticipate to some extent even Newton's idea of immaterial and invisible gravitational forces.'

One of the central problems stumbled upon by the Pre-Socratics was that of change. What was the cosmos such that we could observe the mutability of things? How was such change possible at all? Parmenides postulated that there was, in fact, *no* change; that our perception of change was an illusion. This postulate was derived from his judgement that *what is is, while what is not is not*; from which it followed, he deduced, that there is no void and no room for movement or change. The cosmos is full: it is a single, dark, solid sphere, a 'block universe'.

This strange conclusion, Popper observed, 'may be described as the first hypothetico-deductive theory of the world. The atomists took it as such; and they asserted that it was refuted by experience, since motion does exist. Accepting the formal validity of Parmenides' argument, they inferred from the falsity of his conclusion the falsity of his premise. But this meant that the nothing – the void or empty space – *existed*.'

'Consequently there was now no need to assume that 'what is' – the full, that which fills some space – had no parts; for its parts could now be separated by the void. Thus there are many parts, each of which is 'full': there are full particles in the world, separated by empty space, each of them being 'full', undivided, indivisible, and unchanging. Thus, what exists is atoms and the void. In this way, the atomists arrived at a theory of change – a theory that dominated scientific thought until 1900.'

Atomism was elaborated by Epicurus (341-270 BCE) into a philosophy of life. It isn't clear how much of his thinking was derived from the hundred or so books written by Democritus, none of which has come down to us. But 'Epicureanism' became one of the enduring ethical and cosmological philosophies of the classical world. The great Latin poem *On the Nature of Things*, by Lucretius (99-55 BCE) distilled the thinking of Epicurus into verse and counselled a view of reality freed from the terrors and superstitions encouraged by religion.

The rediscovery of atomism, Stephen Greenblatt argues, in *The Swerve: How the Renaissance Began* (2011), began to undermine the grip of religion on public affairs and moral discourse from the 16th century and to provide a foundation for the emergence of modern science in the 17th century. Little by little, classical atomism developed into modern atomism, with the discovery of the elements and their compounds, the realization that atoms are not solid or unchangeable, but chiefly consist of space themselves; and the investigation of atomic physics. The irony is that conceptually all this springs from the conjecture of Parmenides that change was an illusion – and its critical refutation by Leucippus and Democritus.

Popper did not venture into the arena of biology, but a similar story holds in that regard, of course. The bold conjecture by Charles Darwin that natural selection had driven a process of evolution and that the observable changes in the biological world were due to such selection pressures, opened up the biosphere and the human past to inquiry in a way that no creation myth had ever done.

The 20th century saw developments and refinements of this theory, with the integration of genetics into the picture and then the realization, only thirty years or so ago, that evolution had proceeded not through a gradual, progressive process, but via many changes and catastrophes of a quite haphazard nature – punctuated equilibrium. Little by little, our understanding had to be adjusted in the light of the refutation of assumptions or poor inferences embedded in the original conjecture.

Popper's work helps to open up the thought processes by which such remarkable and fertile scientific conjectures have first emerged and then been refuted, reshaped and replaced to yield the scientific understanding of the cosmos and the biosphere that we now enjoy. That's why a course in Rationality 101 might well feature his key books; not because he is an 'authority', or because he got everything right; but because he drew attention to the role and nature of free thinking and critical rationalism in a most illuminating way.

6: A mole at the highest levels and an ASIO cover-up

Among the many rather disconcerting admissions made by Cardinal George Pell, in his recent testimony from Rome to the Royal Commission into Institutional Responses to Child Sexual Abuse, was that he had allowed a paedophile Catholic priest to retire on the grounds of ill health despite knowing of complaints made against him over several years and without asking to see evidence of his medical condition.

Pell commented, regarding the secrecy and complete lack of moral responsibility exhibited over decades in this matter, 'This was an extraordinary world—a world of crimes and cover-ups and people did not want to disturb the status quo.' Why, however, would senior figures in a body which purports to be the moral guide and guardian of society have any inclination to protect such a status quo? What possible excuse can they plead for having done so?

While bleakly fascinated by the ongoing proceedings of the Royal Commission, I have found myself drawing a comparison between the Catholic Church's negligent treatment of sexual offenders and our intelligence system's treatment of moles and traitors. I am referring to those who betrayed this country during the Cold War by working within our security and intelligence community as moles for the Communist world, chiefly the Soviet Union.

The sexual abuse scandal is all over the newspapers, but the quiet pensioning off of those who penetrated and undermined our security for decades has gone almost entirely unnoticed and no-one is being held to account for it. It has been done in the same manner as the retirement sanctioned by Cardinal Pell and the attitude to it appears to be similar: that the world of espionage and security is secretive and murky and it is best not to 'disturb the status quo'.

In the wake of the Cook Report, ASIO was culled extensively and many officers were quietly retired. The report itself is one of the most closely held documents in Canberra. It is said to have concluded that ASIO was penetrated during the Cold War not by one Soviet mole but by a clutch of them. What's worse is that there is compelling evidence that the problem went beyond ASIO. Yet no-one, on either side of politics, appears to want to open up this can of worms.

The official history of ASIO was an opportunity, in principle, for this matter to be brought out into the open. It has been used, instead, to continue a longstanding pattern of obfuscation and cover-up. Neither the first nor the second volumes comes close to addressing this crucial issue, but there is a telling passage on p. 411 of the second volume—John Blaxland's *The Protest Years*—which throws the matter into relief by its very ellipses and omissions.

The official historian relates that, in late 1974, ASIO discovered that the Soviet military intelligence (GRU) officer Vladimir Dobrogorskiy 'routinely drove to Haig Park in the Canberra suburb of Braddon'. On evening in December 1974 they put a surveillance team on him. That team spotted and watched a lone, agitated man in Haig Park at dusk apparently waiting to rendezvous with Dobrogorskiy. When he realized he was being watched, this agitated individual 'suddenly took fright and ran away'.

After a little further investigation, the conclusion drawn at ASIO was that the man was an Australian civil servant working for the Department of Defence, 'known to have very high security clearances' and known, also, to have 'travelled overseas to a communist country'. The official historian relates, however: 'But with little further to go on and no substantive accusations to make, ASIO was reluctant to ruin a man's career on the basis of only tenuous evidence. The case effectively stopped without a conclusion being drawn either way.'

Just so we're clear: a known GRU officer, operating under cover, makes a rendezvous with an Australian Defence official with very high security clearances at dusk in a public park, where the GRU officer is known to go regularly. This Australian official is found to have visited a communist country. He looks agitated and, when he realizes he is being watched, he takes fright and runs away. Yet ASIO concludes that it should not 'ruin a man's career on the basis of only tenuous evidence'. Really?

As a former intelligence analyst, I must say, this shocked me. But I am credibly informed that the communist country which that agitated individual had visited before 1974 was the Soviet Union; that he visited it again some years later, as a guest of the KGB; that he had numerous meetings with Soviet intelligence officers over many years; and yet rose to the highest levels in defence intelligence in the late 1970s and 1980s. I have been informed that the official historians know who he is, but that ASIO insisted they not cite his name and wanted to kill the story completely.

I submit that this is quite extraordinary and completely unacceptable. If there is an 'innocent' explanation for how all this can have happened, it needs rather urgently to be given. Perhaps the individual in question—whose name, for the moment, I withhold—was travelling to the Soviet Union and liaising with the GRU and the KGB as part of brilliant Australian black operation that fooled the Russians for years?[3] Somehow, I find that hard to believe.

---

3   Subsequent to this piece appearing in the press, I was informed by the official historian, John Blaxland, that this unnamed individual was not the person I seemed to be implying he was, i.e. Paul Dibb. Two other well informed specialists had told me they were confident it had been. I am prepared to believe the official historian. But that does not materially change the nature of the problem pointed out in my remarks. The basic details remain the same and the problem this points to is a serious one. The question of Dibb's innocence is addressed elsewhere in this book (see II:9 Bring the Cook report in from the cold wilderness of mirrors).

Yet the alternative is almost too awful to contemplate: that a Soviet mole was able to penetrate to the summit of our defence intelligence system, with access to virtually everything to do with our national security and our alliances with the United States, the UK and Canada, while meeting clandestinely with Soviet intelligence officers and visiting the Soviet Union itself. How was this even possible—unless?

But who wants to open up that 'unless?'? There's the rub. It would certainly and radically disturb the status quo. Who wants to know the truth? More precisely, who wants us, the citizen body, to know it?

7: Mao Zedong was the full catastrophe in China

With *The Cultural Revolution: A People's History* (2016), Frank Dikotter completes a trilogy on the catastrophic impact that Mao Zedong and his Communist Party inflicted on China between their seizure of power in 1949 and Mao's death in 1976. The first volume in the trilogy chronologically, though it was written second, was *The Tragedy of Liberation: A History of the Chinese Revolution 1945-57* (2013). It covers the civil war, the seizure of power, the mass terror campaigns that accompanied and followed that seizure of power, the vaunted Marxist-Leninist nationalization of the means of production, distribution and exchange and the crushing of intellectual and popular dissent in the 1957 Anti-Rightist Campaign—which was led by none other than Deng Xiaoping.

The second volume was *Mao's Great Famine: The History of China's Most Devastating Catastrophe 1958-62* (2010). It covers ground that others have covered before, but draws upon the latest research to drive home two astounding realities: that Mao Zedong wilfully inflicted on his own country in peacetime a famine that took the lives of tens of millions of Chinese peasants; and that the Communist Party, supposedly committed to liberation and progress, not only was unable or unwilling to prevent him from doing this, but provided the machinery for enforcing it in a way that no less totalitarian regime could have done. Even when evidence of the calamity became undeniable, Mao kept his job. Then he launched the next catastrophe: the Cultural Revolution, inflicting immense damage on an already reeling country.

As early as 1984 demographers concluded that the loss of life in the Great Famine had been at least 30 million. Archival research by the tenacious and very cautious Chinese journalist Yang Jisheng over many years established that, in fact, some 45 million people died from starvation and disease during the famine years. Yang's book *Tombstone: The Great Chinese Famine 1958-1962*, (2012) with an introduction by two eminent China scholars, Edward Friedman and Roderick MacFarquhar, brought this data out of secret Chinese archives and into worldwide circulation. Dikotter rendered the history of the famine more readable and put the data into its political context. The Communist Party continues to suppress scholarship and public discussion of the matter right up to the present.

The great British social democrat and China scholar Roderick MacFarquhar (born 1930) has been, as Dikotter acknowledges, the pre-eminent analyst of the terrifying nihilism Mao Zedong unleashed on China with the Cultural Revolution. His own three volume work, *The Origins of the Cultural Revolution* (1974, 1983, 1997) remains indispensable reading on this grim subject. In 2006, with Michael Schoenhals, he released a summary reflection on the matter under the title *Mao's Last Revolution* (2006). Dikotter has not only written a synthesis of earlier scholarship, including that of MacFarquhar; he has driven home once and for all the responsibility of Mao and those around him—including Mao's most senior colleagues Deng Xiaoping, Liu Shaoqi and Zhou Enlai—for the brutalization of China and the breathtaking abuse of political power over decades.

The Cultural Revolution: A People's History will, ideally, be read in conjunction with *The Tragedy of Liberation* and *Mao's Great Famine*, but it has been designed so that readers will gather from its opening chapters a summary understanding of the events and conditions that preceded the upheaval of the 1960s. It is, also, the most compact of the three books, covering a longer period than either of the other two in slightly fewer pages. In some ways, it is too compact. In chapter after chapter, the long succession of intrigues within the Communist Party and destructive mass campaigns in Chinese society are related in meticulous detail. But there are times when Dikotter might have paused more to discuss two things: the way in which the evidence has come to light and the enduring human impact of the suffering inflicted on China in the name of 'revolution'.

In a book published three years ago, the Sydney-based historian James Curran described the late Malcolm Fraser as having been, in the 1960s and 70s, 'a hard-line cold warrior prone to foaming at the mouth about the evils of Chinese communism'. He described the 1950s and 60s as a 'Menzian dark age' in Australian foreign policy; and made the remarkable assertion that the United States had, in the 1950s and 1960s, 'denied itself access to the great China market.' All three statements were astonishingly wrong-headed. Not least among the merits of Dikotter's book is that it shows just how stark the evils of Chinese Communism were.

There was *no* Menzian dark age in Australia. There was, however, very much a Maoist dark age in China. As for the 'great China market', Western capital was excluded from Mao's China not by choices made in Washington, but by those made in Beijing—until the 1980s. When China began to reform and open, after 1978, the West, led by the United States, bent over backwards to draw China out of its self-imposed shell of paranoia, autarky and propaganda and into the global economy. It was admitted to the WTO on remarkably generous terms. We are now beginning to see that those terms were too generous, in some ways. The Party remains obstinately totalitarian; its grip on the economy remains stultifying in important ways; and its mendacity and xenophobia in matters of history and political discourse remain unyielding.

These are among the reasons why we need work like that of Frank Dikotter. Consider the following three facts: after taking power in 1949, Mao and his Party perpetrated a political terror in which some millions of 'bad elements' were arrested and executed; millions more were sent to a system of forced labour and 're-education' camps; then forced collectivization and irrational economic policies killed 45 million in a few short years. Yet the Party's response was to double down on repression and 'socialist re-education', in which millions were abused, tortured and coerced, in mass campaigns led by Liu Shaoqi and Deng Xiaoping—the supposed pragmatists and 'moderates' within the Party. Then, suspecting that these very men were 'capitalist roaders', Mao unleashed his Cultural Revolution to hunt down and root out 'monsters and demons'.

It is impossible to do justice in a review of this nature to the detail in Dikotter's history. This book must be read so that people can grasp something of the enormity of the case. At a time when disillusionment with democratic politics, scepticism and even anger about Wall St bankers and frustration over the state of our schools and universities is widespread, it is sobering to contemplate the stark contrast between the modest shortcomings of liberal democratic capitalism in the West and the nightmare that was 'progressive' revolutionary Communism. The historian of the Soviet GULAG and the Stalinist monstering of Eastern Europe, Anne Applebaum, acclaimed *The Tragedy of Revolution* as essential reading for anyone who wants to understand the current regime in China. This is equally true of *The Cultural Revolution*.

The prominent left-wing poet and essayist Hu Feng (1902-85) was arrested in 1955, along with seventy seven other intellectuals, for defending freedom of speech. He remained in prison for the next 25 years. Did things improve under Deng Xiaoping and his heirs? Ask Wei Jingsheng, who was sentenced to fourteen years in prison in 1979 by Deng for the very same charge—using 'so-called freedom of speech' to 'stir up trouble'. Liu Xiaobo, born in 1955, the year Hu Feng was imprisoned, was arrested in 2009 for helping draft the Charter 08 manifesto, calling for liberal democratic reforms in China. He was tried for 'inciting subversion of state power' and sentenced to eleven years in prison and two years' deprivation of political rights. Dikotter shows that the Communist Party in China has only ever varied between the systematically repressive and the truly monstrous. During the Cultural Revolution it was truly monstrous. Mao Zedong was inescapably responsible for the catastrophe, but no-one in the Party can escape blame for it; including leading Party figures who fell afoul of it. They had created this monster and had participated in its brutal and totalitarian practices.

Dare to rebel! Bombard the headquarters! Root out reactionaries and spies! Go down to the countryside to learn from the peasants! Denounce and purge hidden counter-revolutionaries among the Party's old guard! Root out the May Sixteenth conspiracy at all levels of state and society! These were the slogans of the Cultural Revolution. Under those banners tens of millions of people had their lives turned upside down and several million were killed or driven to suicide. The statistics are numbing. The message ought be clear: never again let such regimes come to power and do not allow the memory of their travesties of 'liberation' to be suppressed by the Party's ongoing lies about its own past. Above all, understand in the light of this history why liberal democratic norms are so precious and must never be surrendered to fanatical mass movements or political cults.

8: Mamamia, let's focus on the economy

Late last week, a tabloid style story popped up on my computer declaring that Malcolm Turnbull had been 'caught' at an exclusive gentlemen's club. This was eye-catching. My instant reaction was the astonished thought that the PM had done what Kevin Rudd did in New York a few years ago and gone to an upmarket strip club. 'Really?', I thought, 'That's hard to believe, in all the circumstances.'

Hooked by the meretricious headline, I checked the piece out. It was one Alys Gagnon, on the blog site Mamamia, asserting that 'Malcolm Turnbull's lunch at an exclusive gentlemen's club shows the truth about the campaign'; where the club in question was the old and eminently respectable Athenaeum Club on Collins St, Melbourne. I then wondered what it could possibly be about attending the Athenaeum Club that would show 'the truth about the campaign'?

The nature of my astonishment had taken a u-turn. It wasn't what Malcolm Turnbull had done that was astonishing. It was what Ms Gagnon was claiming. Her beef was that the club is 'one of the last strongholds of institutionalised misogyny, because it is still the kind of place where women aren't welcome.' 'It's entirely unacceptable', she asserted, 'for the Prime Minister to dine in a venue that by its nature discriminates against half the population.'

Entirely inappropriate? I've dined—and given speeches—at the Athenaeum Club, as well as the Melbourne Club, the Australian Club and the Savage Club and I'm no-one's idea of a misogynist. Nor, quite obviously, is Malcolm Turnbull. There have been women present at all the talks I've given and I'd be very surprised if they were not present when Malcolm spoke. Whatever one's view of these old businessmen's clubs, reprimanding a public figure for talking at one is over the top. As for 'the truth about the campaign', let's get a little more serious.

Assume, just for the sake of argument, that the Athenaeum Club really is a reactionary and misogynist institution; would it follow from such a premise that it is 'entirely inappropriate' for the Prime Minister to have lunch or give a talk there? One can think of many places in our society in which dubious or tendentious views are held. Would Ms Gagnon deem it entirely inappropriate for the Prime Minister to appear at *any* of them? Mamamia! What a fatuous proposition.

But she did not confine herself to wanting to impose sanctions on both the Athenaeum Club and the Prime Minister from the redoubt of her little blogging pulpit. She went on to claim that this lunch was a blunder on the Prime Minister's part—or that of his election campaign team—from which he might find it difficult to recover. She quoted Senator Claire Moore, the Opposition spokesperson on women's issues as stating that 'This just shows how out of touch Mr Turnbull really is.'

Truly? This nutty bit of agitprop really doesn't wash. Malcolm Turnbull has been in the public eye for many years and his progressive views are well known. To accuse him of misogyny is just absurd. Did Mamamia consider asking Lucy Turnbull whether she believes she is shackled to a male chauvinist in their darkly hetero-normal marriage? It seems not. Comment, we are told, was sought from the PM's office and from Senator Cash, but had not been received when the blog was posted. Doubtless, Mamamia hoped for an embarrassed apology. She was, instead, treated with the bemused disdain its silly column deserved.

What *is* the truth of this election campaign? It is that the outcome is of considerable importance to the nation. One might hope that, given the substantive issues at stake, commentary would focus relentlessly on them and the electoral strategies of the major parties. Mamamia's little tirade about the Athenaeum Club is representative of a blizzard of feckless chatter that serves only to distract voters from the core issues and clutter up the blogosphere.

The problem with much social media commentary is that it exacerbates the worst vices of old fashioned tabloid media and fails abysmally to deepen public understanding of truly important issues. Achieving such a deepened public understanding is, of course, a notoriously difficult business. It takes first rate journalists and editors or public figures to accomplish it on any given issue. But paparazzi-style pouncing on political leaders in efforts to generate sensations or scandals are a direct abuse of the public mind, not a service to it.

The truth about this campaign is that the Turnbull government has been soft and cautious in its policy formulation and is internally divided on ideological grounds. These are its weaknesses in the present campaign. It should never have come to this, given Malcolm Turnbull's public standing six months ago. The Bill Shorten-led Opposition, on the other hand, has taken the astonishing and disturbing stance that there are no economic lessons for it to learn from the Rudd-Gillard debacle and that increased spending and borrowing are 'fairer' to the country at large than fiscal responsibility and debt reduction.

Everything other than these fundamentals is relatively peripheral. We need to return a government, in both houses, that can restore and strengthen the kind of fiscal order and vibrant economic growth that we experienced under the Howard government, on the back of the bipartisan reforms of the 1980s and 1990s. All single issue demands—including possible future moves to a republican constitution, gay marriage and indigenous affairs—are logically subordinate to this bigger picture and should be commonly understood as such.

Mamamia's assertion that the PM's lunch at the Athenaeum Club revealed the truth about the election campaign is utter nonsense. It might, on the other hand, be ventured that the kind of distracting, irresponsible, blatantly partisan blogging that proliferates in the 'new media' reveals the truth not about this election campaign as such, but about the growing governance problems of liberal democracies. We need a sound, not a fractured and distracted public policy debate.

9: Bring the Cook report in from the cold wilderness of mirrors

Last Saturday's *Inquirer* story about Paul Dibb's annoyance at the innuendo that has swirled around him for decades and that security investigations into his *bona fides* were held at all was both fascinating and important. He was cleared by all investigations, he reveals, including the 1994 Cook Report. This is news. I have called for years for the release of the Cook Report precisely so that we can finally be clear where suspicions were confirmed and where they were dispelled and, in each case, on what grounds. Dibb's important story is another illustration of why we need the Cook Report in the public domain at long last.

Dibb feels aggrieved, but while so much of the story remains classified, the kinds of conspiracy theory he detests are all but impossible to put to rest. He allows that there appears to have been a Soviet mole in ASIO during his time. The Cook Report, which seems to have exonerated him, is said to have concluded that there had been *multiple* moles in ASIO and perhaps elsewhere. Yet the government insists that the Cook Report will not be released even in redacted form—as *60 Minutes* was recently informed. Questions about it remain unanswered and, therefore, suspicions and perhaps unwarranted ones remain in circulation.

My own interest in the suspicions long levelled at Paul Dibb date back to when I applied to work in Defence in 1989. I was asked a lot of questions about my contacts with him, when I had been a PhD student at the ANU. It was plain that those questioning me regarded Dibb with suspicion. Even prior to that, while still a student, I had been warned to be careful about him by someone who declared he was 'morally certain' that the suspicions were justified. This has never meant that I accepted the charges against him. He was a very interesting figure and plainly held in high regard by many. He also did me a favour by inviting me for a beer in 1985 to talk about my future plans.

I always felt, therefore, that there was a puzzle to be resolved about where these allegations were coming from. Dibb's own account of his story goes some way toward showing where the confusion has arisen. His own determination to clear his name is understandable, but as he himself says, he was in fact, for many years, operating in a wilderness of mirrors by working in Joint Intelligence, working under cover for ASIO and making extensive contacts with KGB and GRU officers based in the Soviet Embassy. He will privately know, whatever his wounded feelings, that this complex set of intelligence activities was always going to mean that counter-intelligence and counter-espionage staff would worry about him being doubled or played.

Nor should it surprise him that, once started by rumour or fear, conspiracy theories can be devilishly difficult to extinguish. My own company has for many years run a professional workshop on conspiracy theory and critical thinking, designed to get participants to see how easily and even intractably they can become tangled up in conspiracy theory and how exacting the steps are to finding one's way out again. The case study we chiefly use is the long-running cluster of conspiracy theories about the assassination of President Kennedy, in 1963. Bankers, lawyers, military officers, intelligence analysts and others all struggle in the quicksand of the case.

For three reasons, therefore, I read last Saturday's story and the following reports with great interest: I have known Dibb somewhat for more than thirty years and worked in intelligence myself; I was suspected of being some kind of protégé of his; and I run a consulting company that unpicks conspiracy theories and coaches people in critical thinking. We even ran training workshops for ASIO itself for some years and for the CIA. Against that background, I must say that the story Dibb has shared with this newspaper throws into relief why he found himself the subject of so much innuendo for so long. It would, surely, have been a good idea to get all this and a good deal more out into the open long ago.

He could do us all a great service by expanding considerably on his story. He tells us, for example, that he approached the Soviet Embassy in 1965, was photographed by ASIO, called in to talk to Don Marshall and, a week later, introduced to the Deputy Director Ron Richards and asked to work for ASIO against the KGB and GRU. He was given a doctored copy of a Cabinet-in-Confidence document to proffer to his Soviet intelligence contacts as 'chicken feed' and encouraged to try to induce one or more of them to defect. He agreed, provided that his career was protected. A moment's reflection on this scenario inevitably prompts a host of questions, with no presumption as to the answers.

To begin with, what was the cover story for offering the Soviets a classified Cabinet document? Was Dibb supposed to be posing as someone willing to keep supplying classified material to the other side? On what terms? This was several years before he travelled, by his own account, to the Soviet Union, in 1968. What had transpired in between as regards their sense of his *bona fides* and utility? Koshlyakov, his contact and a KGB spy handler, is quoted as saying they always thought he worked for ASIO. Does that mean his ASIO cover was blown by a Soviet mole in ASIO? The KGB must have seized the opportunity in Russia, in 1968, to put the hard word on him. Where, when and how? Did ASIO believe the young geographer could outwit highly trained KGB and GRU officers? Was he himself outwitted and played? How did things change when, in 1970, he joined JIO? Such questions are neither naïve nor malign. They simply arise automatically from the story as told and beg for answers.

10: Andalusia was not all it is cracked up to be

There is a widely held belief that in Spain, during the European Middle Ages, Islam, Christianity and Judaism co-existed peacefully and fruitfully under a tolerant and enlightened Islamic hegemony. It is comforting and even inspiring story that has been drawn upon to underpin the so-called 'Toledo Principles' regarding religious toleration in our time—an important point of reference. Dario Fernandez-Morera, associate professor of Spanish and Portuguese at Northwestern University, with a PhD from Harvard, has written a stunning book which upends this myth.

The myth has been used to suggest that Islam was a higher civilization than that of medieval Europe, whose destruction should be lamented. The great Spanish poet Federico Garcia Lorca, a century ago, saw it that way. Barack Obama and *The Economist* have both cited Muslim Andalusia as evidence that Islam has been a religion of peace and tolerance. This makes the myth of Andalusia a beacon of hope for working with Islam in today's world on non-sectarian lines and with a common commitment to civilized norms.

Perhaps the most notable articulation of this vision is Maria Rosa Menocal's *The Ornament of the World: How Muslims, Jews and Christians Created a Culture of Tolerance in Medieval Spain* (2002). It receives reinforcement in David Levering Lewis's *God's Crucible: Islam and the Making of Europe, 570-1215* (2008). But it has deep roots. Edward Gibbon, in his famous 18th century history of the decline and fall of the Roman Empire, wrote in glowing terms of the 10th century Umayyad caliphate in Spain as a beacon of enlightenment, learning and urban living, at a time when Europe was plunged in bigotry, ignorance and poverty.

As someone who has long taken this vision for granted, it came as a considerable shock to me to discover that this conventional wisdom is unfounded. Fernandez-Morera's forensic cross-examination of the matter systematically refutes this beguiling fable. The picture that he draws, both in outline and in detail, is starkly different from the conventional one, troubling in what it reveals and compelling in its arguments. From this point forward, if you do not acquaint yourself with its arguments and evidence, you will be wandering in a fog of illusion.

If we are to satisfactorily resolve current disputes about 'Islamophobia' and the future of Islam as a world religion, this book is required reading. Serious reviewers abroad have greeted it as a desperately needed corrective to delusion and propaganda. That will invite pushback from those who either remain committed to the myth or believe that it is too important a beacon to allow it to be extinguished in this manner.

However, Fernandez-Morera argues trenchantly that we must shake off the sense of the superiority of Islam to medieval European culture. He makes the point, for example, that, given Islam's antipathy to graphic art and music, had Europe been Islamised in the 8th century, we would never have had Gregorian chant, orchestral music or opera. No Bach, Mozart, Beethoven or Verdi. No Caravaggio, Michelangelo or Titian. Think about that, at least as a thought experiment.

He shows that the Muslim invaders of Spain, in the 8th century, did not arrive as a higher civilization conquering Visigothic barbarians. They arrived as barbarians intruding on a strongly Romanized, Catholic and materially sophisticated culture. As other scholarship has shown, the Arabs, in the 7th and 8th centuries, were barbarian invaders every bit as much as the Germans or Bulgars in Europe. They plundered, enslaved and sacked from the Middle East across North Africa and eastwards to Central Asia and India. As the great Muslim historian Ibn Khaldun would put it in the 14th century, war in the name of religion was integral to Islam.

Secondly, it argues that Islam, in general, was not the vehicle through which classical Greek learning was preserved, as is so often claimed. It was chiefly Constantinople that archived and protected the patrimony of Greek antiquity, philosophical, medical and mathematical. The Arabs acquired all this through Greek Christian scholars translating the classics for them. Greeks from the East and Christians in the West later revived such learning for themselves. Meanwhile, the rise of Islam had disrupted the flow of both trade and ideas between the Greek east and the Latin west, thus harming not fertilizing European civilization.

Even these background theses will strike many readers as controversial, but they are only the beginning. Fernandez-Morera argues that Islam in Spain, far from setting a high bar of tolerance, was characterized by plunder, domination, the harsh application of sharia law, the persecution of Christians or Jews who openly avowed their non-Muslim beliefs and the violent suppression of 'heresies' and apostasy within the Muslim community itself.

He makes, moreover, the point that the Christian and Jewish communities themselves tended towards dogmatism, enclosure against the other religions and the fierce persecution of both heretics and apostates. The regime in Andalusia, he remarks, has been extolled as a *convivencia*, but in reality it was an unstable and oppressive Muslim protection racket and what he dubs a *precaria co-existencia* between the three monotheistic religions, which finally disintegrated.

Chapter 4 'The Myth of Umayyad Tolerance: Inquisitions, Beheadings, Impalings and Crucifixions' and Chapter 5 'Women in Islamic Spain: Female Circumcision, Stoning, Veils and Sexual Slavery' show us the realities that the myth has airbrushed from history. The Moroccan Muslim feminist Fatema Mernissi and others have laboured to argue that the sexual slaves in Andalusian harems were somehow 'free' women. Fernandez-Morera draws attention to the considerably greater *actual* freedom of women in Christian Spain, by contrast, both in terms of everyday outdoor work and their access to political power.

The indulgent view of Andalusia has been based on neglect of primary sources and selective adulation of worldly Muslim rulers, as if they were representative of the clerical *ulama* and Muslim masses. In fact, as he shows, both mullahs and masses tended to bigotry and anti-Semitism. There were anti-Semitic pogroms every bit as violent and irrational as those in Christian Europe. And large numbers of Christians were expelled at times to North Africa.

Among the many shocks to my relatively settled beliefs in reading this book was learning of the atrocities committed, both publicly and privately, by Muslim rulers I had long seen as models of enlightened despotism; notably Abd al-Rahman I (731-788) and his descendant two centuries later Abd al-Rahman III. Both committed deeply abhorrent deeds of torture and murder.

Far more shocking, however, is Fernandez-Morera's relentless documentation of the grip that harsh sharia law had on Spain under the Maliki school of Islamic jurisprudence; something endorsed even by the celebrated 12th century philosopher from Cordoba, Averroes. It was neither pluralist nor 'secular'. It offers no model at all for what we might want or do now in civil society.

I learned things reading this book that I wish were not true. I accepted none of them merely on the author's say so, but read closely his argument and his voluminous documentation. Here and there, in detail, I found fault with him. The overall impact, however, was profound. His book will surely run into hostility and dismissal of the kind that has been hurled at Ayaan Hirsi Ali. But Fernandez-Morera is a formidable scholar. Those who dismiss his book will only expose their own prejudices in the process.

The classic works of Patricia Crone or Jon Wansbrough on the origins of Islam are the best comparison with what Fernandez-Morera has achieved. They demonstrated that the Qur'an as a canonical text dates from long after the traditional death of Muhammed (632 CE) and the hadiths (sayings attributed to Muhammed) were overwhelmingly just made up by story-tellers long after he was gone.

Crone's *Meccan Trade and the Rise of Islam* (1987) argued that the traditional story of Mecca as a trading centre where Muhammed started his religion simply does not stand up to scrutiny. Islam cannot have begun at Mecca (or Medina) even though everyone takes those things as historical fact. Yet this extraordinary finding has never sunk in. It will come as a stunning surprise to most readers of this review.

Religious myths, of which the 'historical' founding of Islam and the Andalusian paradise are two, are remarkably tenacious. Those whose goal is enlightenment without illusions and tolerance that does not consist of walking on eggshells, have a lot of work to do. Crone and Fernandez-Morera provide a strong foundation. It needs building on.

The Myth of the Andalusian Paradise is vital work. Rather than accepting conventional or politically correct views about Islamic Spain, read Dario Fernandez-Morera. We *do* need the 'cultural secularism' that Maria Rosa Menocal and others think they can point to in Muslim Andalusia. We do need to find a way for those who still adhere to the old religions to live in reasonable harmony. We should want a cosmopolitan order here and abroad. What we cannot do is take Muslim rule in Spain as our model for accomplishing that laudable goal. We need to invent something new. There is no Andalusian Golden Age to emulate.

11: The dragon, alas, remains China's symbol

Today, 4 June, is the 27ᵗʰ anniversary of the crushing by tanks and gunfire of the student democracy movement in Beijing and the imposition of martial law across China in violation of the country's constitution. Many hundreds of innocent people were killed in cold blood. The Communist Party did what communist parties have always done: it asserted its dictatorship 'of the workers and peasants' against the people with the ruthless use of force.

You won't find this recalled in the official Chinese media this weekend. You won't even find it mentioned in most of the Chinese community media in Australia, because Chinese community newspapers and radio stations have been taken over by proxies for the Chinese Communist Party and follow its editorial dictates: a flagrant interference with press freedom in this country, the like of which would never be permitted to any foreign country or media group in China. Just ask Google. And the ABC's news site in Shanghai omits any mention of 'bad news' about China.

We can recall the bloody crackdown of 1989 year after year, but there are a few larger points that need to be made about both its significance and the failure of political reform in China to measure up to the hopes not only of the democratic world outside China, but of the finest writers, scientists and journalists *inside* China. For 4 June 1989 was a watershed in China's modern history every bit as significant as the famous nationalist demonstrations of 4 May 1919. It demonstrated that the dictatorship would not submit to the rule of law or honour the civil and human rights set down in its own hollow constitution.

Deng Xiaoping, the pint-sized dictator, had declared that China would replace the 'rule of man' with the 'rule of law'. He abandoned that idea in the face of calls for actual liberalization. He had always been a hardliner in this regard. As far back as the 1950s, he played a leading role in repression and abuses far worse than those of 1989. His chosen successors have continued to set their faces against freedom. Xi Jinping, the new uber-boss of the party machine, directly discourages even the discussion of freedom of speech, human rights and civil society.

This is the sombre reality of the huge country which is our single largest trading partner and one with which we have generally run a healthy surplus. Yet, while so many of us deplore the things we dislike about the United States and worry about the current presidential election contest, with its three strikingly divergent contestants, relatively few of us focus on the lack of any such open contest of ideas or scope for criticism and complaint in China.

Why is that? Baffled ignorance on the part of many is one cause. Relentless Communist Party propaganda is another. Craven preference for trade interests over political principles or human rights is another. Yet the xenophobia, 'exceptionalism' and political brutality of China under the Communist Party are every bit as ugly as anything we are seeing in the United States. We need to think about this more seriously than we do—especially if, as various pundits keep insisting, we are at the beginning of 'the Chinese century'.

When people complain to me about the state of Australian democracy (to say nothing of American democracy), I generally respond that in China or Russia or Iran or any number of other anti-democratic countries, people like me get censored, beaten up, put under house arrest, gaoled or killed. I therefore regard all such regimes as my enemies. People like me were crushed under tanks in Tiananmen Square on 4 June 1989. People like me and people I personally know are, to this day, victimized, imprisoned or driven into exile by the regime in China.

There was a time when many of us hoped—inside and outside China—that the economic reforms of the 1980s would be followed, sooner rather than later, by judicial, political and press reforms. We hoped that China would follow the liberalization path blazed by little Taiwan in the 1980s and 1990s, from dictatorship and martial law to democratic pluralism, the flowering of civil society and the ending of repression. It did not happen and it is not happening.

In 1988, a man after my own heart, Yan Jiaqi, then a close political adviser to Chinese Premier Zhao Ziyang and Director of the Institute of Political Science in the Chinese Academy of Social Sciences, gave a keynote speech entitled 'China is no longer a dragon'. He argued that the old imperial symbol of the dragon gave China the image of authoritarianism and threatening power, but that this was 'inappropriate for a nation seeking to be a democracy.'

The dragon should be replaced, he urged, by a symbol more consistent with the idea of the rule of law, enshrined in a constitution that genuinely protected civil and political rights and enabled the citizenry to form their own associations and political movements. But the Communist Party is not moving towards democracy in any meaningful sense of that term. Yan came to understand this on 4 June 1989. He fled his motherland and has lived in exile since.

If there is one figure we should lionize, as a symbol of our flickering hopes for 'the Chinese century', it has to be the neglected political prisoner Liu Xiaobo, one of the key architects of Charter 08, which called, once again, upon the Communist Party to relent in its repression, to ease its dictatorship, to take responsibility for the authentic liberation of the Chinese people. He languishes in prison for no other reason than that he helped author this charter.

Liu Xiaobo was awarded the Nobel Peace Prize for his advocacy of fundamental human rights. The Communist Party refused to allow him to go to Stockholm to receive the award and denounced it as 'an obscenity'. That is the feral mood of the regime in Beijing and its is deeply unpleasant and undemocratic.

12: Is there a final solution to Tehran's vicious anti-Semitism?

Since Barack Obama came to office, in 2008, he has bent over backwards to mend the fences with the theocratic regime in Iran. He has pleaded *mea culpa* over the famous CIA intervention in Iran (with MI6) in 1953. He has sought cooperation to bring stability to the Middle East (with no success whatsoever). He has struck a problematic nuclear deal with Iran. It is problematic because the regime in Tehran is constitutionally truculent and brutal.

Our own government, since Julie Bishop became Foreign Minister, has also taken a conciliatory approach to Iran. Given the many other distractions of both international affairs and domestic politics, this policy has largely gone unnoticed. It's time it was put under greater scrutiny. That was driven home last month by a particularly nasty government sponsored cartoon competition in Tehran to lampoon the Holocaust.

If you didn't hear about this, you should sit up and pay a little attention. As veteran Middle East analysts Reuel Marc Gerecht and Ray Takeyh observed in the *Washington Post* on 27 May, vicious anti-Semitism, Holocaust denial and virulent anti-Zionism are part of the Islamic regime's DNA. The Ayatollah Khomeini, godfather of the whole malevolent enterprise, detested the Jews racially and wanted to see Israel wiped off the map.

The regime in Tehran remains committed to these views and goals. It engages in anti-Semitic and anti-Zionist propaganda in order to burnish its pretensions as a leading power in the Muslim Middle East, at a time when the Arab powers, Saudi Arabia and Egypt, see Iran as a dangerously ambitious state; and Turkey, under Erdogan, is seeking to stage a kind of neo-Ottoman revival. The easing of economic sanctions seems unlikely to moderate Iran's behaviour in this regard.

So, what was this cartoon competition and what makes it so disturbing? It was first held in Tehran in 2006, under Mahmoud Ahmadinejad. Cartoonists were invited to mock the Holocaust or the very idea of the Holocaust, since leading figures in the regime have again and again expressed scepticism as to whether it even occurred. When called to account, regime spokespeople (well, spokesmen, since they are invariably male) tend to equivocate. But the cartoons don't.

The first prize this year was awarded to a cartoon which showed what very much looks like the entrance to Auschwitz sitting on top of a cash register that has $6 million in it. It was drawn by a French cartoonist notorious for his anti-Semitic views. It is worth juxtaposing this exercise and award with the global expressions of outrage by radical Muslims and their secular allies over cartoons lampooning Muhammed. It seems that one 7th century man's reactionary views must not be held up to ridicule, but the murder of six million people is a subject for mockery.

That fact alone tells us a good deal about the regime in Tehran. It's smooth-tongued, US-educated Foreign Minister, Javad Zarif, dances around the question of whether the Holocaust occurred or on what scale. He denied, in a late August interview with the *New Yorker*, that the Iranian government sponsored the cartoon competition. That, not to put too fine a point on it, is a bare-faced lie. The competition is orchestrated by bodies—the Islamic Propaganda Organization and the Owj Media and Arts Organization—which report directly to Supreme clerical leader Ali Khamenei and the Iranian Revolutionary Guards Corps (IRGC).

Speaking to a US university audience recently, Zarif was asked did he or did he not acknowledge the historical reality of the Holocaust. He said that during the Second World War atrocities were committed and a lot of Jews were among those killed; but he then insisted on adding that the real question is why the Palestinians have been made to suffer for this. 'What did they have to do with the atrocities committed in Europe?' he asked.

There is an answer to that question with which nobody in his audience confronted him. The Palestinian Grand Mufti of Jerusalem and many of the Arab League leaders in the 1930s and 1940s were openly pro-Nazi and the Grand Mufti called for the extermination of the Jews, not only in Europe but in Palestine. Two state solutions proposed by the Peel Commission, in 1937, and by the UN, in 1947, were flatly rejected by these Arab leaders, even though accepted by the Zionist movement. The consequence was the war of 1948, which the Arabs resoundingly lost.

The unpleasant truth is that Iran officially and unrepentantly continues to peddle pernicious and genocidal propaganda. That is the moral character of the regime. If we are to deal with it realistically, we cannot afford to blink at this fact. Our goal must be not to avert our eyes and tell ourselves that they don't do things like this cartoon competition, or they don't really mean it, but to seek by all means within our power (limited though they are) to hold them to account and push for change.

Early this year, David Cesarani's *Final Solution: The Fate of the Jews 1933-49* was published, offering a superb synthesis of the breakthrough new scholarship on the Holocaust which has been accomplished since the end of the Cold War. It was published posthumously, as he died while it was in press. No-one who wishes to speak responsibly on human rights and the Holocaust has any excuse for not reading it. Ali Khamenei and Javad Zarif ought to be required to do so.

On 1 November 2005, the UN General Assembly declared 27 January International Holocaust Remembrance Day, because it agreed, as Cesarani remarked, that the Holocaust is the global benchmark for moral evil. That is, therefore, the benchmark against which to judge the cartoons presented in Tehran last month. That is the benchmark by which to judge the anti-Semitic rhetoric of Tehran. And, when we seek to open channels of dialogue with Tehran, this is a matter we must bear in mind. Julie Bishop, take note.

13: Erdogan's crackdown is deeply disturbing

There is something deeply disturbing about the direction in which Recip Tayyip Erdogan and his Justice and Development Party are taking Turkey. Writing in this newspaper last week, John Lyons compared the sweeping purges to McCarthyism in the United States, in the 1950s. That was altogether the wrong analogy. The scale and arbitrariness of what is happening are, rather, akin to Hitler's state of emergency after the Reichstag fire in 1933, or Stalin's reaction to the assassination of Sergei Kirov in 1934, than to the United States in the 1950s. There is also an analogy with the Islamist revolution in Iran in 1979-81.

In the wake of a coup attempt whose source remains mysterious and which fizzled within hours, Erdogan's regime began arresting or dismissing from their posts tens and tens of thousands of people: military officers, soldiers, police, school teachers, academics, judges and civil servants. The scale and speed of the reaction have been breathtaking and *cannot possibly* be based on evidence of complicity in the failed coup. They can only be based on lists long prepared of those deemed to be politically and ideologically opposed to the Erdogan regime. Such opposition is not a crime and by no means indicates treason or conspiracy.

The rhetoric of the Erdogan regime has, also, been startling. The call to reintroduce the death penalty is chilling. The insistence, without the provision of any credible evidence, that the coup was a conspiracy orchestrated by exiled Sufi cleric Fethullah Gulen in the United States, the arrogation by the regime under the 30 day state of emergency to take extra-legal steps to 'cleanse' the state apparatus and armed forces of perceived enemies are all worrying indications that the Erdogan's agenda is not the restoration of democracy, but the installation of an Islamist dictatorship. This is where the analogy with Iran under Ayatollah Khomeini arises.

The Reichstag fire of 27 February 1933 was exploited by Hitler to declare a state of emergency in Germany and basically abolish the rule of law. The clearest account is by Ian Kershaw in the first volume of his magisterial biography of Hitler (1998). As he points out, the fire was not itself a Nazi conspiracy, but came as a surprise. Goebbels, when informed of it, thought the report was a bad joke. Hitler thought it was the signal for a Communist uprising. Wild allegations to this effect were quickly made, but no credible evidence was ever produced. Bear that in mind when reading of allegations against the Gulenists.

Hitler, driven by vengeful phobias rather than evidence, declared to his closest colleagues: 'This is a God-given signal...If this fire is, as I believe, the work of the Communists, then we must crush out this murderous pest with an iron fist!' Erdogan himself, whether or not he was consciously mimicking Hitler, declared almost at once that the coup attempt was a 'God-given' chance to crush the opposition. He is proceeding to attempt exactly that. If he does, as he has threatened, reintroduce the death penalty, we should note very closely who is put to death. Given that Erdogan has been on the record as declaring that democracy is just a train you use to get to your destination, then you get off it, what we are seeing looks distinctly like disembarkation.

Stalin did something similar in 1934-35, in a prelude to the Great Terror of 1936-38, in which, according to the KGB's own records, some 750,000 people were executed and the GULAG crammed with others. In Stalin's case, it was not the Communists who were the target, of course, but a wide range of political oppositionists in Leningrad and around the country, who were labelled 'White Guard elements' and 'counter-revolutionaries'. He then used the same pretext to arrest many of his opponents from within even the Bolshevik opposition. Again, the analogy is striking.

Perhaps the best account of the Kirov murder and its consequences is by Oleg Khlevniuk, in his 2015 biography of Stalin, based on unprecedented access to Soviet archives. What he makes clear is that, contrary to various conspiracy theories that have been around for decades, Stalin did not *arrange* the murder of Kirov, but he did exploit it to accuse his political rivals (and former allies) Grigory Zinoviev and Lev Kamenev of having planned it. They were convicted, but based on 'blatantly fabricated' evidence. As things stand, there are disturbing signs that this is the game Erdogan is playing.

He has become a serious problem and it could soon get much worse. Spurned by the EU, he has in effect declared 'there is a world elsewhere' and has taken his stand under the banner of radical Islam. He has become a Putin-like figure and his Turkey is now a highly unreliable member of NATO, a looming danger to its small European and Mediterranean neighbours (think Cyprus to begin with) and a further case of the implosion of order in the Middle East. Whatever our perceptions or sympathies with regard to Turkey's domestic affairs, these geopolitical concerns must be thought through both quickly and very realistically, lest things unravel in a very serious way indeed.

In May last year, Erdogan gave a public speech to a huge crowd in Istanbul, on the 562nd anniversary of the Ottoman conquest of Constantinople in 1453. He lionized not just that conquest—which no-one in the West should celebrate—but the Muslim conquests as a whole, beginning with the first raids and small wars by Muhammed. The crowd roared its approval and a chant went up, 'Here is the army! Here is the commander!' Make no mistake, Erdogan has a strong base of support in Turkey—as Hitler did in Germany. Neither his reasonableness nor his intentions can be trusted. His Turkey has become a problem for Europe for the first time since the murderous wholesale expulsion of Turkey's Greeks, in the 1920s. A great deal now depends on how that problem is handled, diplomatically and strategically.

14: Voltaire would have been hounded for his *Mahomet*

On 23 July, Waleed Aly will be presented with the Voltaire Award for free speech from Liberty Victoria. It would be rather charming were he to give a speech on that occasion reflecting on Voltaire's play *Mahomet,* which depicted Islam as based on false miracles, personal ambition and ruthless fanaticism. Aly has for some time been the go to person for commentary on Islam and avoiding what is widely dubbed 'Islamophobia'. It is safe to say he does not share Voltaire's assessment of Islam.

Yet Voltaire remains a figure for our time, just because free speech on the subject of Islam has become extraordinarily problematic. Imagine *Mahomet* being produced in Paris today! The truth is, if we tactually want to buttress a tolerant, multi-cultural society, we have to confront more honestly the underlying realities that generate 'Islamophobia', however awkward this may be, especially for those like Aly who are stranded between Islamic culture and secular society. The occasion of the Voltaire Award for free speech is an opportunity for Aly to make this clear.

In April this year, Aly was interviewed for ninety minutes by Robert Manne under the rubric 'Islam: What Are We Afraid of? Waleed Aly and Robert Manne in conversation?' Their conversation was lucid, temperate and fascinating. In some ways, it was a model of intellectual discourse in civil society. The problem is, they did not answer their own question; to say nothing of answering it as Voltaire would have done.

Aly observed correctly that Islamist terrorism has only gotten worse since the invasion of Afghanistan in 2001 and especially since the invasion of Iraq in 2003. He distinguished thoughtfully between European, American and Australian reactions to Muslim immigration and made intelligent points about ISIS, Iraq, Syria and the debacle of the briefly promising Arab Spring. He described the short rule in Egypt by 'the Brotherhood', meaning the Muslim Brotherhood, as 'a disaster'.

However, neither he nor Manne raised serious questions about Islam itself; simply gliding over it as 'one of the world's great religions'; the fear of which is, implicitly, irrational, phobic, ignorant and, in Aly's words, hardly worth engaging with. They described ISIS as a rogue operation whose atrocities (which both deplored as barbarities) have nothing to do with Islam as such, but are aberrant even by the standards of al-Qaeda.

Aly compared beheadings by ISIS to the Jacobin terror in 1793 France, but didn't mention beheadings in the history of Islam. Nor did Manne ask him about them. Neither mentioned movements towards Islamization—from North Africa via Turkey to Indonesia—or the disturbing phenomenon of Muslim 'militants' murdering journalists and others for insulting Muhammad or mocking Islam.

Consequently, they failed to explain why there would be any reason to feel uneasy about or even hostile to the growing presence of Islam in the West. One might have expected at least passing reference to the many centuries of confrontation between Europe and an expansionist Islam, Arabic and Ottoman, right up to the late 17th century. But the only confrontations discussed were the Western invasions of Afghanistan and Iraq after 9/11.

Clearly, this is an immensely sensitive subject and it is easy to lapse into polemic about it, inflaming rather than tempering debate. If, however, we are to answer the question 'Islam: What are we afraid of?' we cannot avoid raising certain characteristics of Islam which do in fact give cause for concern to many people in the West—and many of those trapped in Muslim dominated states. We know far more than Voltaire did and what we know is not reassuring.

Karen Armstrong has portrayed Muhammad as 'a prophet for our time'. But the classic Muslim sources (Ibn Ishaq, Ibn Kathir, Waqidi, al-Tabari, going back to the 8th and 9th centuries) make clear that he was a very dubious figure even in his own time. He founded a religion at the point of a sword, plundered infidels, arranged for the murder of his critics (even poets), massacred or expelled communities of Jews in Arabia, condemned apostates to death, was an unscrupulous polygamist and taught that women were inferior to men.

The Muslim sources themselves are completely explicit on all these points. It is simply dishonest to pretend that none of this is true; or to pass it off on the basis that Christianity and even Judaism also have their dark or dubious characteristics. The modern world (Voltaire being a leader) fought its way free of Judaeo-Christian dogmatism and error through trenchant criticism of religious claims and practices. There are no good grounds for sparing Islam similar critical treatment; all the more so because we are seeking to integrate into Western societies millions of human beings who happen to be Muslims.

Outside the West, the problem is much worse. In wide swathes of the Muslim world, other religions are persecuted and apostates are hunted to death with judicial sanction. Blasphemy is violently attacked and Muslim 'heretics' hounded. Homosexuals are condemned to death. Women and girls are denied freedom and education. The Jews are viciously denounced on racist and religious grounds, quite apart from the political issue of Zionism.

What are we afraid of, then? A world in which, from Bangladesh to West Africa, a savage version of Islam is being championed by armed groups; in which the Indonesian Ulama Council has issued fatwas denouncing secularism, pluralism and liberalism as 'sipilis' (syphilis); in which the President of Turkey last year publicly lionized historic Muslim conquests and called for the reconquest of Europe by Muslim immigration.

All these things cause unease and fear. Should they not? We need to address them honestly and intelligently, not dismiss fear of Islam as phobic or bigoted. It would have been good had Manne asked Aly questions about these difficult matters and had Aly addressed them. In accepting his Voltaire Award, Aly needs to step up and champion freedom of speech in the Muslim world and freedom to criticise Islam itself, including 'the Prophet'—as Voltaire himself did.

George Mallory and his colleagues attempted three times to climb Mount Everest in 1921. 1922 and 1924. On the third attempt, Mallory fell to his death 800 feet from the summit.

INTERMEZZO:
FIVE SPEECHES

1: Chinese espionage and Australia's national interest (2012)[4]

Good afternoon. It's delightful to see the extent of interest, within the CBD, in Chinese spying. There's no doubt that the subject of spies and conspiracies and all manner of dark arts holds a perennial fascination for a great many people. Personally, I'm a Le Carré fan, because his novels are more sombre and realistic than the popular spy genre. And, as I put it to a veteran of ASIO about a decade ago, when he approached me about the unfinished business of Soviet penetration of Australia's intelligence and policy circles during the Cold War, 'When it comes to such matters, I am unequivocally one of Smiley's people.' For those of you unacquainted with the work of George Smiley, I recommend Le Carré's marvellous end of Cold War novel *The Secret Pilgrim*. It was published in 1991 and dedicated to Alec Guinness who had starred as Smiley in BBC TV productions of Le Carré's classic 1970s Smiley novels *Tinker, Tailor, Soldier, Spy* and *Smiley's People*. The dedication was warranted. Guinness was a superb Smiley and I don't think Gary Oldman, in the recent feature film of *Tinker, Tailor, Soldier, Spy*, laid a glove on him.

I identify with Smiley, because I have never subscribed to the cynical view that the West is the enemy of historical progress or the revolution and deserves betrayal, as the Cambridge Five and their very numerous colleagues in treachery apparently believed in the 1930s and afterwards. Also because I believe that Australia was deeply compromised by traitors during the Cold War; by some of its own citizens, who became moles for the Soviet intelligence services. I despise the Left's unyielding insistence that such allegations are paranoia and that, in any case, those who spied for Stalin and his successors were somehow 'romantic' or 'idealistic' figures. I grew up thinking of Stalin as the Dark Lord and the Kremlin as the Dark Tower and the more I have learned about both the more I see those childhood archetypes as largely justified. Finally, it seems clear to me, from what information I have been able to gather over the years, that virtually none of those who worked for the dark side in Australia during the Cold War have ever been identified or exposed to public obloquy. In particular, those who did so right through to the end of the Cold War have got away scot free.

I cannot emphasize sufficiently in this context that Australia was rather poorly served during the Cold War by its counter-intelligence services, in large measure because they were deeply penetrated by the Soviet Union. This remains a subject that the Australian government is extraordinarily reticent about. That makes it possible for the Left to get away with the old Cold War canard that ASIO was a right-wing organization obsessed with allegedly mythical reds under the bed. It turns out that the reds were not merely under the bed; they were in it. Yet it remains one of the most troubling aspects of post-Cold War revelations about Soviet espionage

4   A speech delivered at the Athenaeum Club, Melbourne, 21 March 2012.

that so much has come out about previously unconfirmed or altogether unknown Soviet spies in the United States, Britain, France, Germany and elsewhere and nothing of any substance at all about such spies in Australia. There is, however, a good deal of evidence to suggest that Australia was perhaps more deeply penetrated than any other Western country during the Cold War and that this has been deliberately covered up over the past twenty years.

In late 2009, in an opinion column in *The Australian*, I drew attention to the anomalous fact that the KGB files on Australia have somehow never seen the light of day, despite the publication of two fat volumes on the Mitrokhin revelations from the KGB archive. I noted that there were, indeed, revelations to be had about Soviet spies in Australia, but these had been suppressed. I claimed that this had been done at the request of the Keating government. I added that, as Prime Minister, Paul Keating had, nonetheless, quietly set up two inquiries into Soviet penetration of Canberra and specifically of ASIO. Those inquiries were Operation Liver, by the Australian Federal Police; and a separate inquiry by senior diplomat and former head of ONA, Michael Cook. The AFP inquiry, I stated, was terminated by Attorney General Michael Lavarch with the exclamation, 'This has got to stop. There's no knowing where it will end!' One mole, I am given to understand, worked inside ASIO from 1952 until 1985 and ended up as head of security vetting. According to my understanding, Cook deduced that there were still four Soviet moles inside ASIO at the end of the Cold War and more than a dozen suspects.

As several serious, well-informed and responsible individuals have exclaimed to me since that piece came out, the silence in response to it was deafening. There was not a word of retort from Michael Cook, Paul Keating, Michael Lavarch, the AFP, ASIO or anyone else in a position to state that I was in error in any particular. Disconcertingly, there was no response, either, from the conservative side of politics. In the weeks following, I met with both the Inspector General for Intelligence and Security, Ian Carnell, and the Director General of ASIO, David Irvine, and neither gave me any ground for believing that I was in error in what I had claimed. Well before I had written it, I met with Michael Cook and asked him whether the claim put to me that he had identified four Soviet moles in ASIO was correct. In a conversation that had been perfectly serious, his only response to this question was to say that he would not be divulging any information on that subject. You may draw your own conclusions from all this. But there are grounds for believing that ASIO was not the only Australian agency penetrated by Soviet moles and that none of the other moles have been exposed either.

We are here this afternoon, of course, to talk primarily about Chinese espionage, but I ask you: if what I stated about Soviet Russian penetration of ASIO is in substance correct, and given that there has never been any public accounting for that debacle; what basis do we have right now for confidence in the effectiveness of our counter-intelligence services against the Chinese?

My own view is that we have very little basis for confidence. The Russians counted on ideology and venality to place moles in the West. They continued to have successes right through to the end of the Cold War. The Chinese have advantages that the Soviet Union never enjoyed: a booming economy, a huge trade relationship with their target countries, not least Australia; interested lobby groups working on their behalf; very large pools of Chinese migrants in this and other Western countries; huge numbers of students and tourists coming here and to the other leading Western countries every year; and a widespread view that they are now a capitalist country set to overtake the United States, which encourages both apologias on their behalf and band wagoning.

Let me tell you a little story that is both amusing in a dark kind of way and instructive for our present purposes. How many of you have heard of Katrina Leung? In the 1970s, she became a leading figure in the Chinese community in Los Angeles. In 1982, she was quietly recruited by the FBI, America's ASIO. With their support, she was given American citizenship in 1984. She was codenamed Bureau Source 410; otherwise known as PARLOUR MAID. For twenty years, while remaining a high profile figure in Los Angeles and the person it was said that you had to go to if you wanted to get something done in China; she travelled back and forth to Beijing, meeting an incredible range of people and reporting back to the FBI's top Chinese-speaking counter-intelligence specialists in California, James Smith and William Cleveland. She quickly became the FBI's top secret source on China, the Chinese political leadership and the Chinese Ministry of State Security. The FBI paid her $1.7 million during those years for her seemingly stunning intelligence on what top Chinese leaders were thinking. Briefings based on her reports went all the way to the White House.

There was just one problem. Even before she was recruited by the FBI, Katrina Leung was working for the Chinese intelligence service. She continued to do so for all those twenty years. Moreover, from shortly after the time he recruited her, James Smith became and remained her lover. From 1987, so did William Cleveland. Both would visit her and confide in her. Smith took briefcases full of classified documents to her home and she would filch them, copy them and transmit them to Beijing. In December 1990, the National Security Agency (NSA) intercepted a telephone conversation in Chinese between a woman in Los Angeles and her MSS handler in Beijing whose name was Mao Guoha, in which she revealed to him, among other things, that William Cleveland was about to make a trip to China. The NSA sent the intercept to the FBI. It was passed on to Cleveland. When he listened to it, he recognized the woman's voice at once: it was that of Katrina Leung.

Cleveland and Smith realized they had a serious problem. They covered it up for the next twelve years and kept up their sexual liaisons with PARLOUR MAID. They kept her on the pay roll and Smith kept taking briefcases full of classified documents to Leung's house when going there for trysts. She kept reporting to her MSS handler. Right up until 2002, neither Smith nor Cleveland apparently guessed what the other was up to with PARLOUR MAID. That, you might say, was need to know, compartmented information. She, meanwhile, kept sixteen foreign bank accounts, travelled to China at will, betrayed a string of sensitive FBI operations to the MSS and was paid handsomely by the FBI while doing all this. They thought they had a brilliant penetration operation running; but while their top agents were certainly penetrating Katrina Leung, she was penetrating the FBI in a manner that put the legendary Mata Hari in the shade. And when, eventually, she was exposed and brought to book, the FBI's lawyers bungled the prosecution and she was given so nominal a penalty that she exclaimed in court, 'I love America!' As well she might! But her loyalties had clearly been to China.

There almost seems to be an element of Keystone Cops to this story. One can only groan at the extraordinary incompetence of the FBI and the stunning susceptibility of the Bureau's most highly rated, Chinese speaking counter-intelligence officers to the oldest lure in the book of spies. But the case raises a set of questions which, I suggest, are what we are actually here today to ponder. First, how much Chinese espionage of all kinds happens? Second, how much of it happens here in Australia? Third, what does China gain from its espionage? Fourth, are we any better placed to thwart it than the FBI? And finally, does it really matter, at the end of the day? I shall approach these questions step by step and, by the time I am through, I hope you will have formed a sufficiently clear view of the terrain for us to have an interesting conversation about it. But the short answers to the foregoing five questions are:

i. A very great deal;

ii. Plenty;

iii. The biggest haul of data and intelligence you can imagine;

iv. Our lot are even less effective than the FBI; and

v. It all depends on how the economics works out, because that will determine whether the West, including Australia, continues to thrive or ends up floundering in some kind of Asian century; apart from which China itself faces grave challenges in the years ahead.

I cannot prove these things here and now. I offer my judgments not as one with privileged information on the subject, but as a former senior intelligence analyst who has always taken an interest in the subject and keeps an eye on developments. You may take my observations for what they are worth.

China's spy agencies are headed by the huge Ministry of State Security (MSS), whose headquarters are out near the old Summer Palace in Beijing. The Chinese name for the MSS is Guojia Anquan Bu or GAB. You might say that Chinese espionage, with its fabled history dating back into the mists of time and enshrined in the vaunted treatises of Sun Tzu, is the 'gift of the GAB.' It relies on tens of thousands of Chinese speakers with the gift of the gab travelling abroad, asking questions and reporting back to Beijing Centre—as well as the new dark arts of cyber espionage. It is targeting anyone and anything that can yield the Chinese Communist Party an advantage in its quest to make China the world's greatest power by mid-century. Whether this is the best way to go about that ambitious goal is, of course, another matter; but that it is the goal and that the GAB is deeply involved in pursuing it there can be no doubt. It is now far better resourced and more sophisticated than ever it was in the days of Mao Zedong or the fabulous Fu Manchu.

The GAB has twelve bureaux:

1. Recruitment for both domestic and overseas service
2. Spy handling under diplomatic or commercial cover
3. Taiwan, Hong Kong and Macao operations
4. Technology: wiretapping, communications, photography
5. Internal security: domestic surveillance
6. Counter-intelligence
7. Intelligence analysis and reporting
8. Research
9. Counter-surveillance and counter-defection
10. Scientific and technical intelligence
11. Computers and computer security
12. Foreign liaison and cooperation

Academically speaking, MSS spies are trained in the agency's own university, the Institute of International Relations, in Beijing. Spying tradecraft is taught at the Institute of Cadre Management in Suzhou, which as some of you may know is located not far from Shanghai. It also happens to be the city from which, according to long standing tradition, the most beautiful women in China come. I remarked on this, many years ago, to a Chinese businessman sitting next to me on a flight from Beijing to Shanghai. He quipped, 'You are well informed! But I wouldn't go looking for them in Suzhou these days. They're all in Guangzhou, because that's where the new money is.' My guess is that, these days, Suzhou hangs onto a few.

Long after Stalin's time, many a recruit to the KGB felt the lure of what was seen as an elite, front line service in the global battle against the evil empire of imperialism. Kim Philby, in his memoir, spoke of his own secret recruitment by the KGB in such terms, but did not apparently see his recruitment by MI-6 in the same glamorous light. Imagine the sense of patriotism, pride and prestige for young Chinese men and women entering into such training now, at a time when so many Chinese believe that their country is set to become, in their own life times, the greatest economic power and perhaps even the greatest military power in the world and maybe in history. Lee Kuan Yew, in 1996, remarked of China, 'This is not just another big player. This is the biggest player in the history of man.' In the same year, then Chinese Premier Zou Jiahua, at a conference of Chinese intelligence agencies, praised 'the tens of thousands of nameless heroes who cherish and loyally serve their motherland...quietly fighting in their specialized posts abroad.' This is what we are up against.

Note Zou Jiahua's mention of tens of thousands. Who was he talking about? Plainly not Chinese spies as the word 'spies' is commonly understood in the West; not secret agents reporting to case officers in the Chinese Embassy or planted inside foreign governments. As Madame Fu Ying remarked some years ago, in response to the defector Chen Yonglin's claim that there were about a thousand Chinese agents in Australia, 'If I had a thousand spies working for me, I wouldn't have time to play golf.' She was right. If she had been running a thousand spies she wouldn't have time to play golf. But ambassadors don't handle spies. And China doesn't handle most of its spies through its embassies. To assume that it does would be to fall into the trap of believing that China's espionage service works in just the same way as the old Soviet intelligence services or the American or Australian intelligence services. It doesn't. And this will be important to understand in any serious effort, should we mount one, to counter the Chinese intelligence program in Australia.

Paul Moore, a specialist in classical Chinese language and literature and some time head of the FBI's whole China division, told US historian David Wise:

> if a beach was an espionage target, the Russians would send in a sub, frogmen would steal ashore in the dark of night and with great secrecy collect several buckets of sand and take them back to Moscow. The US would target the beach with satellites and produce reams of data. The Chinese would send in a thousand tourists, each assigned to collect a single grain of sand. When they returned, they would be asked to shake out their towels. And they would end up knowing more about the sand than anyone else. China does not normally pay money for intelligence, unlike the KGB and the CIA. Typically, you help them and they help you develop an export business. They don't develop intelligence relationships with people, but general relationships, which may end up having an intelligence dimension. They don't so much steal information as put sources in a position where they will be indiscreet or generous with information under false pretences.

This might be dubbed 'Moore's Law'.

Let me underscore a few crucial aspects of Moore's Law. The MSS doesn't target the vulnerable so much as the eager. It doesn't offer money so much as it offers contacts in China and assistance in setting up or furthering a business or a research project there. It will make appeals not to ideology but to helpfulness and friendship and a desire to see China modernize. It also places numerous agents among first generation Chinese immigrants, whether in the US or here. In the US there are currently some 2,600 Chinese diplomatic and consular officers, 25,000 visiting Chinese delegates each year; 127,000 Chinese students in schools and universities; and millions of Chinese citizens—1.2 million in California alone—with its large defense and aerospace industries and Silicon Valley. The counter-intelligence task here is incomparably more difficult than anything faced during the Cold War struggle with the KGB and the GRU. It's like trying to find bombs hidden in shipping containers at America's ports.

The absolute numbers of Chinese in Australia are smaller, but the proportional numbers are certainly very substantial. Remember the Joel Fitzgibbon affair of three years ago in this context. Here's the key press report from May 2009, as written up by well-known investigative journalist Philip Dorling:

> Associates of the businesswoman Helen Liu claim Chinese intelligence services asked them to cultivate a relationship with Joel Fitzgibbon and his father, Eric Fitzgibbon, after they were flown first-class to China in 1993. Sources with close ties to the company that paid for the trip also allege that Chinese agents had electronically monitored the pair during their visit.
>
> It was on this trip that Mr Fitzgibbon, then a NSW ALP official, and Eric Fitzgibbon, then a federal MP, first met Ms Liu, who has since become what the Defence Minister has described as 'a very close' family friend. Sources familiar with the details of the trip allege Chinese spies eavesdropped on the private conversations of Eric Fitzgibbon, who as a serving MP had attracted their interest.
>
> The sources, who are close to Ms Liu's then business partner, Humphrey Xu, confirmed the trip was organised and paid for by Mr Xu through his company Diamond Hill International. According to the sources, Chinese intelligence officials expressed interest in the Fitzgibbons' preparedness to accept benefits from Mr Xu and Ms Liu, and encouraged them to continue to develop their relationship with the Fitzgibbon family.
>
> When asked about the 1993 trip, Joel Fitzgibbon said in March this year that he went in a private capacity and that his father 'was invited to turn the first sod at a tourist development in China'. Both Joel and Eric Fitzgibbon deny receiving $US20,000 for their services on the all-expenses-paid 1993 trip. Eric Fitzgibbon declared the trip in the House of Representatives register of members' interests.
>
> In late 1995, Diamond Hill International contributed $20,000 to Joel Fitzgibbon's campaign for the 1996 federal election. At the time, the donation was declared by the NSW Labor Party as a donation to a 'party unit' with no direct reference to Mr Fitzgibbon. In 1996 the personal and business relationship between Mr Xu and Ms Liu broke apart and she took control of several joint companies including Diamond Hill International and Wincopy. Wincopy subsequently donated $20,000 to Joel Fitzgibbon's 1998 re-election campaign. Her companies gave a further $50,000 to the NSW ALP between 2001 and 2007. Ms Liu has denied ever being involved in spying.

'She's just a Chinese business woman with whom I am friends and who happens to have good Party connections,' was the Fitzgibbon defence. Exactly so; although the nature of the gifts and contributions looks highly suspicious. But such gifts and contributions, such friendships, are the way it works and the target may never know what the game is until deeply into it. The donations to Joel Fitzgibbon's election campaigns are straight out of the Katrina Leung playbook. That Mr Fitzgibbon may not have done anything so much as questionable doesn't alter the troubling reality of the situation. It simply highlights the great difficulty in countering the ancient Chinese art of espionage. And let's be clear: the Fitzgibbon case was high profile only because he was Minister of Defence. It would be naïve to believe that it is anything but the tip of an iceberg of considerable proportions.

Chinese espionage right now is occurring on a scale that dwarfs what the Soviet Union accomplished during the height of the Cold War. This is not something widely appreciated. It has three sources or enablers. Firstly, China, unlike the Soviet Union, is now a commercially thriving state, doing vast volumes of trade all over the world. This gives it both the incentive and the means to conduct espionage of every kind to an extent that the Soviet Union could only have envied. Secondly, there is a huge Chinese diaspora and China's intelligence services, unlike their Soviet counterparts, have always depended primarily upon first generation Chinese immigrants to foreign countries and students or tourists travelling abroad, to gather much of their intelligence for them, a grain at a time.

Thirdly, China is now conducting cyber espionage—something that was never possible for the Soviet Union. It was not technically possible in the Cold War years and, in any case, information science was one of the many areas in which the Soviet Union was left behind by the West in the 1970s and 1980s. Consider the 17,526 documents purloined by the Cambridge Five over twenty years and more, then think of WikiLeaks. Bradley Manning downloaded 250,000 documents onto a flash drive in about as much time as it would have taken Kim Philby to hold a single meeting with his KGB controller.

For years now, business people travelling to China have been warned either not to bring laptops and cell phones with them, or to never leave them unguarded; because the MSS targets them and copies their content. Michael Hayden, former CIA and NSA chief, issued this warning not so long ago; but the well-informed have known it for quite a bit longer. Moreover, few foreigners have ever realized the extent to which the MSS collects intelligence on them into vast data bases for future reference. If you have heard tales of the files collected by the FBI under J. Edgar Hoover or by ASIO during the Cold War, you have a faint inkling of what the MSS has done domestically and abroad for decades.

And such collection often takes place, as you might expect on a little reflection, in the most apparently innocuous ways. This is intensive in the United States, targeting think tanks and policy centres, for example; and has been even more so since China's reform and opening era began than in the Mao years. Australia may be provincial, by comparison, but the same is true here. Think Chinese restaurants and ask how many Soviet restaurants ever operated in the West at any point between 1917 and 1991. Even now, Russian restaurants are as rare as hen's teeth. Chinese restaurants are everywhere. Think the Mafia and pizza parlours.

In recent years, Western security and counter-intelligence organizations, including our own, have warned repeatedly that financial firms, banks and law practices are targets of cyber invasion by the Chinese. It need hardly be said that the same holds true for government departments, ministerial offices and the headquarters and personnel of leading firms doing business in China. In 2009, MI-5 disseminated a fourteen-page white paper to a number of financial institutions warning of hacking by the Chinese. Such cyber espionage, MI-5 added, is backed up by 'honey traps' set to ensnare British businessmen. It's a case, of course, of the two oldest professions in the world, as the saying has it, becoming interwoven, as they so often have been. All of you, I'm sure, remember the brouhaha that ensued when Google announced that it had detected highly sophisticated Chinese hacking of its own cyber networks. The sophistication of these attacks was described as 'staggering' and, while Beijing routinely denies that it bears any responsibility for them, no-one of any seriousness or standing believes these disclaimers.

It's important to register two things here: the scale on which Chinese cyber espionage is now being conducted and the fact that it's happening here as well as elsewhere. 'They are stealing everything that isn't bolted down, and it's getting exponentially worse,' according to Mike Rogers, a Republican Congressman from Michigan and chairman of America's Permanent Select Committee on Intelligence. Economic and technological cyber espionage is intended to enable China to leapfrog over its American and other foreign competitors to further its goal of becoming the world's largest economy, according to a U.S. intelligence report of November last year. As national security and counter-terrorism specialist Richard Clarke has expressed it, 'What has been happening over the course of the last five years is that China...has been hacking its way into every corporation it can find listed in Dun & Bradstreet.'

Clarke is a former special adviser on cyber security to President George W. Bush. Speaking at a conference on the subject last October, he stated that the Chinese have targeted every corporation in the U.S., in Asia, in Germany. They are 'using a vacuum cleaner to suck data out in terabytes and petabytes. I don't think you can overstate the damage to this country that has already been done.' According to a Bloomberg editorial of mid-December last year, 'The electronic theft of proprietary information from U.S. companies has reached the level of grand larceny on a national scale. One declassified government estimate put the value of information stolen in the last year—everything from blueprints to merger plans—at almost

$500 billion.' One specialist has described all this as the greatest illegal transfer of wealth in the form of intellectual property in history.

This grand larceny is the fruit of an operation originally launched in 1986, under the title Program 863 to close the gap with the West in areas such as nanotechnology, biotechnology and computers. Program 863 operates in such a way that the MSS and the Foreign Ministry can routinely disclaim any responsibility for it. Indeed, it would appear that much of it is conducted under the auspices of Chinese military intelligence and by special task forces created to make plausible deniability feasible. Given the extent of Australia's trade with China, there is no good reason to believe that our own companies and ministries have not been targeted in the same way. I have no privileged information on what Chinese human and cyber spies have accomplished, you'll be disappointed to learn; but our large mining companies are certain to be a target rich environment for Chinese espionage. One must assume they look to their own cyber defences and personnel security. I need hardly add that Chinese espionage will be strongly centred, also, on our defence alliance with the United States, our force structure plans and our intelligence agencies.

At a time when there are prominent figures in this country openly calling for us to distance ourselves from the United States and draw closer to China, the counter-intelligence challenge is becoming acute. It becomes ever easier for Chinese operatives to develop relationships and ask questions in the name of 'balance' and 'friendship'. But let me share a few anecdotes about successful, old-fashioned Chinese espionage in the United States. Over the past thirty or forty years, Chinese spies have penetrated the CIA and US nuclear weapons laboratories and have passed to China crucial technological intelligence on some of the most sophisticated weapons in the US arsenal, including the neutron bomb, the W-70 warhead, the W-88 thermonuclear warhead for the Trident submarines and stealth technology. Spies such as Gwo-bao Min, Wen Ho Lee and Larry Wu-tai Chin are not exactly household names, but if the story of Chinese espionage in America was better known, these would be names as famous as the top Soviet spies of an earlier era, such as Julius and Ethel Rosenberg and Klaus Fuchs.

Gwo-bao Min, for example, worked at the Lawrence Livermore Laboratories on missile defence and had access to the designs of every US nuclear missile. He had come to the US in 1963, got a doctorate in aerospace engineering from the University of Michigan in 1970 and joined Livermore in 1975. In 1979 he travelled to China and Chinese friends who helped him with his visa steered him to China's nuclear scientists for close questioning. That visit to China in 1979 by Gwo-bao Min became a focal point in the investigation that the FBI launched many years later in an effort to determine who had leaked the secrets of so many American nuclear weapons technologies to the Chinese.

Another key suspect in that case was Wen Ho Lee. Lee worked in X Division at Los Alamos, the most highly sensitive part of the laboratory where America's nuclear bombs have been designed ever since the Manhattan Project in the 1940s. He downloaded vast quantities of highly classified data without accounting for why; made trips to China about which he lied; made contact with Gwo-bao Min and lied about that; and yet when prosecuted for espionage was acquitted and apologized to by the trial judge, because the case could not be proven beyond reasonable doubt. He walked free, sued for damages and accepted $1,645,000 in an out of court settlement in 2006. Like Katrina Leung, he must have decided that he loved America.

Larry Wu-tai Chin was born in Beijing in 1922 and began working as a translator for the Americans in 1944 in Fuzhou. By 1948 he was working in the US consulate in Shanghai. When the US pulled out of mainland China, he found himself in Korea; where he worked as an interpreter, interviewing Chinese POWs, in 1951. In 1952, he joined the CIA's fledgling Foreign Broadcast Information Service and was based in Okinawa. For years within FBIS, he had access to CIA reports, including those from covert agents in the Chinese world. He used to make regular visits to Hong Kong. In 1961 he was transferred by FBIS to California and in 1965 was granted US citizenship. He was given a TOP SECRET security clearance and, in 1970, transferred to the CIA's FBIS headquarters in Rosslyn, Virginia. He now had very high level access to classified information and this remained the case right up to the point in July 1981, when at the age of fifty nine, he retired.

At a special ceremony on his retirement, Chin was presented with a Career Intelligence Medal as the CIA's best translator by CIA deputy director Bobby Inman. A week later, he flew to Hong Kong, where an MSS officer paid him a retirement bonus of $US40,000—the equivalent in today's terms of at least several times that amount. He had been spying for the Chinese Communists since 1944. He betrayed Chinese POWs that he had interviewed in Korea. In all probability a good many of them were incarcerated or executed on their return to China. He used to meet his case officer, Ou Qiming, on those visits to Hong Kong from Okinawa, all the way back in the 1950s. He had had an emergency contact in New York in the 1970s; one Father Mark Cheung, a Catholic priest at the Church of the Transfiguration in Chinatown. Cheung really was a priest. The MSS had sent him to a Catholic seminary to become a mole inside the Catholic Church. All the while, he had a wife inside China. When he visited her, he threw off his priestly attire and resumed his personal identity.

Chin, having been handsomely paid over the years and having invested his gains in properties, thirty one of which he owned in the Washington DC area alone; lived comfortably in retirement. But over three years from 1982, two Chinese sources informed the CIA of Chin's career as a spy and his cover was blown when their testimony led the FBI to hard evidence of his espionage. For once, the FBI got its man. He was arrested in late 1985, and put on trial. Convicted on charges that could carry two life terms, he committed suicide in prison by self-asphyxiation, on 21 February 1986, before he could even be sentenced. Isn't it remarkable to think that this man had worked for the Chinese intelligence service for 37 years as a mole inside US intelligence and the CIA without ever being detected and that only Chinese defectors blew his cover? It's almost enough to make one a little paranoid. But paranoia is not what I advise.

Now, you might ask, 'What is the evidence that any such spies have operated in Australia?' After all, we don't have nuclear weapons or stealth aircraft or other high profile targets for Chinese espionage. Well, the question of evidence regarding espionage in Australia in general is a strange and elusive subject; and the targets of foreign espionage here are often indirect. Throughout the Cold War, we were seen by the Soviet Union as a prime target because of our close relationship with the United States, Britain and Canada. It is clear that high level intelligence was going to the KGB out of H. V. Evatt's office when he was Chifley's Minister for External Affairs. Several of his staff, including Alan Dalziel, have always been suspected of being Soviet spies. Des Ball recently gave it as his opinion that John Burton, Secretary for External Affairs, and even Evatt himself, may have been spies and were certainly fellow travellers indulgent of actual spies in their midst.

In 1981, CIA veteran Ted Shackley told Brian Toohey that Australia had been more deeply penetrated by the Soviets than any other Western country. Think about that. He was convinced that there was a high level Soviet mole in either Defence, Foreign Affairs or the office of the Prime Minister at that time. A decade later, Oleg Kalugin, a former senior KGB official, wrote of having had a mole in ASIO. And these moles were interested chiefly in Australia as a key regional ally of the United States. There can be no serious doubt that Chinese espionage in Australia in our time, like Soviet espionage during the Cold War, is directed at US secrets confided to the Australian government; at the nature of the Australian alliance with the United States; and, of course, also at inside information regarding commodities trade and the Australian economy. There is also relentless pressure on Chinese dissidents in exile, whether they are democracy and human rights activists, Tibetans, Uyghurs or Taiwanese.

Fear of espionage has, for a hundred years, been prone to stir up popular fantasy and paranoia. I do not seek to stoke any such fire. I do believe, however, that Chinese espionage is a serious issue. I am not inclined to believe that our intelligence services are on top of the problem and I have no confidence in the willingness or capacity of our diplomatic cadre or immigration officials to stand up against any but the most blatant Chinese offences. It has been refreshing to see that, based on warnings from ASIO, the Government has banned the

Chinese telecom giant Huawei from bidding for involvement in the National Broadband Network project, over the hypocritical objections of Beijing.

But for the most part, of course, the MSS does not commit 'blatant' offences. It knows its business rather well, as I trust my handful of anecdotes showed. Rather, however, than use all these points as a platform from which to declare that we need to double and redouble our counter-intelligence budget, I prefer to ask a provocative question: How much does this espionage really matter, when all is said and done? I ask that question because, as a moment's reflection will remind you, despite the scale and success of Soviet espionage, the West won the Cold War. And it was not counter-intelligence and espionage that won it for us; though what role it played is fascinating to ponder.

We need to be realistic about the challenge we face, without becoming paranoid. Many years studying the history of Western intelligence and working inside it have left me with the belief that, all things considered, the secret world is considerably overrated. Too much is kept secret and the whole game of secrecy feeds on itself. The books of William Burrows—*Deep Black* (1986) and *By Any Means Necessary* (2001)—are excellent inquiries into the work of America's U-2, SR-71 and KH-11 aerial and satellite surveillance programs of the Cold War.

The Soviet Union was seen, by many of the most senior officers who ran these programs, as so malevolent and so secretive that enormous expense was justified in spying on it, just as almost unlimited expense was said to be justified in building up a nuclear arsenal to intimidate it. Even so, there was much that was never learned and much that was misinterpreted. The system that was supposed to guard us fed paranoia on the Soviet side and more than once came perilously close to triggering thermonuclear war. Meanwhile, the CIA, shaped by Dulles to be as ruthless and secretive as the KGB, engaged in activities that often reflected very badly on the United States. I have studied those activities.

The Soviet Union fell, in the end because of its own economic and social deficiencies. Our task in the years ahead is not to stop the Chinese from spying on us, but to manage our economic and political affairs better than they do. The West has done far more damage to itself through economic mismanagement than the Soviet Union or China has ever done to it through espionage. The debts that are now all but bankrupting the United States, the EU and Japan were not caused by Chinese spies. China's surge in economic growth was not accomplished by China's spies. Nor will China's massive thefts avail it very much, unless it is able to become far more technologically creative and unless we continue to fumble the economic football. Sure, China is pouring resources into a huge peacetime military build-up, but the most acute imbalances and shifting balances in the world are those of productivity and solvency. If we are to get our counter-intelligence and defence strategies right, we must keep a sense of proportion here and ensure that we fight only those battles that really matter and only when we can win them.

The chief battle, then and now, is economic and right now the West is losing the battle. In 2010, Nobel laureate in economics Robert Fogel estimated that, by 2040, China's GDP will have soared to $US123 trillion, or about eight times the current US GDP; and that China's gross domestic product will be 40% of world output, or twice the combined output of the US and the EU. That, he concluded, is what economic hegemony will look like. At the same time, the US Congressional Budget Office was estimating that US national debt would climb to as much as 700% of GDP by 2080.

We live in a time of such extravagant and alarming projections, including the more alarming climate change scenarios. They should be used to concentrate the mind. They should not be permitted to take it over. I am sceptical of such long range linear extrapolations. China, as it own premier pointed out quite publicly just last week, faces enormous hurdles in the years immediately ahead and 2080 is a very long way off.

As Yogi Berra famously said, 'It ain't over til it's over'. Do you know what a jumping land mine is? When you step on a pressure land mine it blows off your feet and leaves you crippled and bleeding on the ground. A jumping land mine doesn't explode when you step on it. It waits until you step off it. Then it pops up to about groin height before detonating. Very unpleasant. Having accumulated three trillion dollars and Euros in foreign exchange reserves and created an economy enormously dependent on exports to the US and the EU, China is standing right now on a gigantic jumping land mine.

It's biggest intelligence challenge is figuring out what to do to rebalance its economy and hedge against the weakening of both the dollar and the euro. It faces immense demographic and institutional challenges in the coming decade or two and, as Wen Jiabao expressed it only a week ago; China could face an historical tragedy and an upheaval on the scale of the Cultural Revolution if it fails to negotiate these challenges. That, I suggest, is the perspective in which to set both Robert Fogel's extravagant curve and our own concerns about Chinese spies.

Naturally, there will be some among you who will have been thinking just now that we, too, may have stepped onto a big jumping land mine: over dependence on commodity exports to China at the expense of the more balanced and forward looking development and management of our own economy. You would be correct. Our own greatest intelligence challenge in the years immediately ahead, therefore, is to think this one through. Sure, we would be prudent to keep a watchful eye on economic and strategic espionage by Chinese spies; but we should remember the main game, keep our eye on the prize and understand that the expensive and secretive world of espionage is, as often as not, inefficient, counter-productive and even irrelevant.

Writing after the end of the Cold War, former KGB head of counter-intelligence, Oleg Kalugin, remarked wryly that there may have been some in the CIA who truly believed the KGB was efficient, adroit and masterful, but that those inside it knew it to be corrupt, inefficient, plagued by ideological obsessions and often groping in the dark. Don't fall for myths and nightmares and, whatever you do, don't imagine that what really counts in the world is secret intelligence. What counts is clear strategic thinking and economic efficiency. We are short of both these days—and it's not China's fault.

2: Israel and Zionism (2014)

Good evening, leaders of UIA, honoured guests, ladies and gentlemen. It is an honour and a pleasure to have been invited to address you this evening. I will keep my remarks brief, in the hope that we can have a little more time for questions, because I would very much like to hear what is on your own minds.

Earlier this year, I was bemused when, in his *Diary of a Foreign Minister*, Bob Carr declared—and let me quote his precise wording here:

> Paul Monk, I think, is one of Australia's best intellectuals—no, the best; this is another case of him leaping over the various divides and factional camps, the culture wars.

He was referring to a piece I had written about China.

My first thought was that Robert Manne would get his nose out of joint at the idea that anyone other than him might be considered the country's best intellectual. But I sent Bob a copy of my 2009 book, *The West in a Nutshell*, with an inscription inside the cover to the effect that I have always admired his sense of humour.

I mention this, of course, because of Bob's recent declaration that he had moved across to the Palestinian side as regards the intractable situation between Israel and the Palestinian Arabs. That step left me even more bemused, I have to say, than his unexpected and perhaps ill-considered remark about my intellectual standing.

I am, as I have remarked in more than one context, a visceral secular political Zionist and I do not see merit in the stance taken by our erstwhile foreign minister. Perhaps the best clue to his rhetoric is the opening line to his diary entry for the day immediately following his remarks about me:

> I dance, I sing, I fly through the air. I am the master entertainer.

We might see his flourish about Israel and the Palestinians as a political song and dance routine for the benefit of audiences in Western Sydney and the famous latte sipping left-wing elites who certainly do not share his estimation of my intellectual standing.

Mind you, on the next page of his book, he records that he told Kerry O'Brien in a *Four Corners* interview that the emerging upheaval in Syria was:

> a crisis for the 'dictator for life' model that Arab nationalism had imposed on the Middle East.

There, perhaps, he was actually close to the mark.

It is that subject that I chiefly wish to address this evening. But, since this is an address to the United Israel Appeal, I want to begin with a few brief remarks about my own visits to Israel.

I have been there twice: in 2007 and in 2013. I attended the Herzliya conference in 2007 and visited Masada, the Old City of Jerusalem and the Jezreel Valley. Last year I roamed more widely. Jay Sekulow remarks, towards the end of his book *Rise of ISIS*, newly published by Simon and Schuster:

> Every time I fly into Israel, I'm moved by what I see. Israel is a beautiful land, where the desert has literally bloomed.

He has had far more visits that I have, but I concur with his experience and judgement. After landing in Tel Aviv last year, I took a cab down to Jerusalem. Along the way I had a wonderful conversation with the cab driver, Noah Greenberg.

He told me that his grandparents and parents had come to Palestine in the 1920s; that he had been born in 1948 and had literally grown up with Israel. 'When my family came here', he said to me, 'there were just a few Jews, a few Arabs and some desert. Now, it is a good country.' Israel is a good country. It is a free country, a strong country, a prospering country, an innovative country and compared with any of its Arab neighbours without exception a just and equitable country.

In Jerusalem I had a rolling series of excellent one on one meetings. Among them was a dinner with Amotz Asa-El, who will be known to many of you by name if not in person. We spoke at length about Israeli journalism and public affairs and the impasse with the Palestinians. But we discussed, also, the situation in Egypt, the troubles in Syria, the challenge of Iran, the divisions within the Arab Muslim world and the retreat of the US from hegemony in the Middle East.

We also discovered a common interest in the history of Judaism and the Jewish Diasporas, in the debates among religious and political Zionists, in Jewish intellectual life over the centuries and in contemporary literature and film. Amotz spoke of George Steiner being a religious Zionist, or more precisely anti-Zionist; something I had not known, despite reading all of Steiner's books over the past thirty or forty years.

We spoke of Gershom Scholem and the deep roots of the return. We talked about the books each of us is writing. I asked Amotz what he thought of two remarkable films starring Maximilian Schell: *The Man in the Glass Booth* and *The Chosen*. He didn't know of the first and had not seen the second, though he was acquainted with Chaim Potok's novel, on which it is based.

This is what is known as liberal intellectual discourse. There was nothing in it of jargon ridden ideology or partisan point scoring. It is one of the things that has characterized Jewish intellectual culture around the world throughout the 20th century and explains why, if I have my facts right, no less than 32% of Nobel Prizes have gone to Jews. I would be surprised if even one has gone to a radical Islamist.

I visited Beersheba last year and at my own request had a meeting with Professor Addy Pross. I had read and been deeply impressed by his 2012 book *What Is Life? From Chemistry to Biology.* He and his wife Nella, both chemists, have been at the university in Beersheba for forty years and have seen it grow from a rudimentary and small establishment into a flourishing world class campus with 20,000 students. It is a microcosm of the flourishing of Israel, despite a constant state of siege.

I had a wonderful afternoon with them talking, quite literally about life, the universe and everything. They are a most charming couple and their simple home is lovely, the garden with its flower beds; the walls with Nella's excellent art works. This is the Israel I relate to and admire: flourishing, humane, open, brimming with intelligent people and with 21st century thinking.

But that brings us to the question of the prospect in the 21st century, which by some indices is troubling and not least in the Middle East. Consider just seven current realities:

- The so-called Arab Spring has become a bleak Arab Winter, not least in Syria.
- Turkey has gone from being a secular democracy and strategic ally of Israel to being an increasingly Islamist state under Erdogan and an ally of Hamas.
- Iran has foxed with the EU and the US for a decade and looks set to achieve nuclear capability possibly before Barack Obama completes his presidency.
- The United States has, under President Obama, shown itself very reluctant to engage in more than marginal conflict in the Middle East and has distanced itself from Israel perhaps more than any US administration since 1948
- Fatah and Hamas have formed a notional unity government, which demonstrates that Fatah can no more be a partner for peace than Hamas
- The emergence of ISIS (and also Boko Haram) shows that the attempts since 2001 to dismantle Islamist terrorism have fallen a long way short of their objectives.
- The international left-wing and anti-Semitic lawfare against Israel continues unabated and was intensified during and after Israel's exasperated effort to bring Hamas to heel or to its senses in Operation Protective Edge.

To any one of these topics, to say nothing of the perennial question of the West Bank and the fruitless eighty year search for a two state solution, we could devote a whole evening, I'm sure you will all agree. Here and now, I have time only to stake out an indicative position in the most general terms.

It is this: in Jeremy Kagan's beautiful 1981 film of Chaim Potok's 1967 novel *The Chosen*, the great Austrian actor Maximilian Schell, who incidentally died in February this year at the age of 83, plays the part of David Malter, a Modern Orthodox Talmud scholar in Brooklyn from the school of the great nineteenth century Rabbis Hildesheimer and Hirsch. He tells a meeting of New York Jews:

We here have a responsibility to protect the lives of the men, women and children in Palestine who are now threatened with Arab aggression. Millions of us have already died...Only a Jewish state can give meaning to these savage acts. Only a Jewish state can guarantee that it will never happen again. We don't need sympathy. We need money, we need supplies, we need action, now...Let us prove to all the world that we mean what we say, when we say: Never again! Never again! Never again!

The state he longed for survived the attack he was describing in 1948. It pre-empted another attack in 1967, the very year *The Chosen* was published. It fought off a third attack in 1973, launched on Yom Kippur itself. During the intervening years and well beyond 1973, it took in hundreds of thousands of Jewish refugees expelled from across the Arab world and hundreds of thousands who left Europe, especially the Soviet Union, to find a Jewish home.

The Zionist project has, from almost every point of view been a resounding success. But as you all know, Zionism itself has been both contentious within the Jewish religious community from the outset and internally divided between the original Zionism of Chaim Weizmann and the Revisionist Zionism of Ze'ev Jabotinsky, since at least the 1920s. I think it would be correct to state that what has won Israel its current level of security and prosperity has been Revisionist Zionism. The Iron Wall that Jabotinksy called for has been built, not because this was the ideal approach to building Israel, but because all overtures to the Arab world about finding agreement on a different path have been rejected.

By common consent, this leaves contemporary Israel with a challenge: How is the Arab (and Iranian) world to be won over to accepting Israel and seeing it as an opportunity instead of a mortal enemy? In current circumstances, that question cannot find a clear, simple or short term answer. Yet it must underpin Israel's evolving sense of itself, if the moral idealism and social vision of the original Zionists is to be brought into better balance with the hard-headed *realpolitik* of Likud, the children of Jabotinksy.

Israel remains eminently worth defending and championing. Your cause is a sound one, a moral one and still an existential one, but this question I would think has become, more than ever, the central one. I hope that a creative and fruitful answer to it can be found, but let us understand one another: such an answer will not be found by appeasing radical Islam or the incitement of genocidal anti-Semitism among Israel's many enemies both in the Middle East and around the world. To them we should in unison repeat the vow of David Malter in 1948: Never again! Never again! Never again!

3: On what is important: Mount Everest as a metaphor (2014)[5]

Writing to his friend, the Cambridge political scientist Goldie Lowes Dickinson, in 1913, Bertrand Russell confessed to a feeling that a great many of what we now call knowledge workers must often feel:

> We here in Cambridge all keep each other going by the unquestioned assumption that what we do is important, but I often wonder if it really is. What is important, I wonder? Scott and his companions dying in the blizzard seem to me impervious to doubt—and his record of it has a really great simplicity. But intellect, except at white heat, is very apt to be trivial.

That one of the leading intellectuals of his time should long to be 'impervious to doubt', at least as regards the importance of what he was doing, is food for thought. That he should have admired the heroic exploits of explorers, on the other hand, seems completely understandable.

This evening I would like to argue that the greatest intellectual work is precisely that which is pervious to doubt, which challenges itself again and again. The worst kind of intellectual work is that which is impervious to doubt. But I will explore this idea and its implications for leadership and innovation against the background of mountaineering and, in particular, the heroic and unsuccessful efforts by Russell's contemporaries, in the early 1920s, to scale Mount Everest for the first time.

Let me explain at once what I mean when I say that the greatest intellectual work is precisely that which is 'pervious to doubt'. We speak rather often of the need for people to have the courage of their convictions, but serious thinking actually requires the opposite. It demands that we be capable of critically cross-examining our convictions and those of others to probe for flaws, illusions, biases and errors. The greater the stakes and the more entrenched a conventional belief or common assumption is, the more courage this requires.

We should not be reduced to hopeless confusion by chronic doubt. That is not at all what I am saying. Rather, we are first rate thinkers just to the extent that we can see in a complex and important field the grounds for our existing beliefs; or those of some major strategic commitment on behalf of our company, our client, our government, or public opinion and then see our way through to pinpointing errors and pointing the way to a new framing of the problem and a better grounded assessment of the reality.

It is curious, in a way, that Bertrand Russell, of all people, should have envied Scott or other explorers exposed to mortal hazards. After all, in the course of a long life, he sought to

5   Reflections on Wade Davis's *Into the Silence*, an address to the KWS Legal team, 30 November 2014.

challenge many orthodoxies and to use his acute reasoning powers to point to what he regarded as better approaches to government, education, religion, arms control and so forth. Did he not regard these forays as being important? Did he not believe that sound approaches to reasoning in public policy were actually more important than hazardous expeditions to remote places?

He once remarked that many people would rather die than change their minds and in fact they do. Yet he declared himself in awe of those impervious to doubt about their commitments even in the face of death in a blizzard. I think we would do well to reframe his way of looking at this matter. I want to suggest that the reason we may well admire explorers of the natural world, right up to astronauts walking on the Moon, is not that they are (if they are) impervious to doubt, but precisely because they embody the tenacious will to overcome challenges in the face of doubt and to deepen our collective understanding of both what is so and what is possible.

What is required in terms of thinking, instrumentation and the revision of opinion or perception here is, I think, beautifully captured in an anecdote some of you may have heard before. It concerns the Austrian philosopher Ludwig Wittgenstein and the old pre-Copernican notion that the Sun circled around the Earth. The story goes that one day a student remarked to Wittgenstein, 'You know, it isn't really surprising, is it, that people used to think that the Sun circles around the Earth; because it looks like that's what happens.' To which the philosopher responded, 'Really? So, what would it look like if, actually, the Earth revolved around the Sun while rotating on its axis?'

The answer, of course, is that it would—and does—look exactly the same. It's just that unless you inquire closely and calculate carefully and have the intellectual training to conduct the necessary calculations, you will never see behind what looks like the truth to what is actually the truth. To do such things, in any field, whether in geophysical exploration or intellectual inquiry, requires being pervious to doubt and having the courage of one's doubts, one's questions, one's willingness to entertain radical new possibilities, to experiment, to think hard and to be prepared to both fail and admit to failure.

This is where the matter of mountaineering becomes interesting as a metaphor and where we can learn a little by, as it were, unpacking the instinctive respect we tend to have for those who actually do climb serious mountains. I have never climbed a mountain of any consequence, much less put life or limb at risk in doing so. Two years ago, however, I read an extraordinary book by the explorer and prolific author Wade Davis. It was called *Into the Silence: The Great War, Mallory and the Conquest of Everest*. If you have neither heard of it nor read it, or have heard of it but not read it, I urge you to get yourself a copy and read it slowly, digesting its endless richness.

This evening, of course, I will only be touching on a little of what is in the book and from a particular angle. My own point of entry for reading the book had nothing to do with mountaineering, everything to do with the scaling of Everest as a metaphor for striving to reach the summit of one's aspirations. I have had melanoma in me for a decade and in 2012 had two substantial operations—the fifteenth and sixteenth in eight years—to remove clusters of tumours from my right leg. I was on crutches for weeks and unable to exercise properly for months. But I had a highly ambitious book I wanted to finish—or die trying.

Your own context, at least as the KWS Law team, is different, whatever your personal situations. You are a new and still small law firm. The world of legal practice is evolving rapidly on the global stage and you are, collectively taking on challenges and seeking to mould yourselves into a highly effective, international team that can scale new heights. That, I take it, is the place from which you might listen to talk about mountaineering and, in particular, about one of the most famous as well as, let it be said, ill-fated, mountaineering teams of all: the British teams around George Mallory who attempted in 1921, 1922 and again in 1924 to climb Mount Everest for the first time. They failed each time, while getting a little closer to the summit on each occasion. On the final attempt, Mallory lost his life, leaving behind a beloved wife and three young children.

In elite sport these days, athletes often undertake training or adventure routines designed to test their endurance. Those who attempted to climb Everest with Mallory had already been through endurance tests of the most extraordinary nature. In particular, they had endured the First World War. Of the twenty-six climbers who participated in one or more of the three expeditions, twenty had seen the worst of the fighting. Six had been severely wounded, two others nearly killed by disease at the front, one hospitalized twice with shell shock. Three, as army surgeons, dealt for the duration with the agonies of the dying. Two lost brothers killed in action. All had endured the unprecedented mass killing, the extraordinary artillery barrages, the mounds of shattered bodies in the mud, the bones and the decaying faces of the dead.

But there was more to them than this. One after another, in the early pages of his book, which is to say the first couple of hundred pages, Davis introduces them as individuals. They were, the war quite apart, a group of men who had extended themselves in many ways and exhibited a remarkable range of skills, a rare depth of character. The names Arthur Wakefield, Howard Somervell, Francis Younghusband, Charles Bruce, Alexander Kellas, John Noel, Charles Kenneth Howard-Bury, George Ingle Finch, F. M. Bailey, Henry Morshead, Charles Bell, and Alexander Wollaston are in all probability unknown to you. But in the pages of Wade Davis they come alive like heroes from the Homeric epics, not because he overdraws their exploits, but precisely because their exploits and characters, soberly described, were so impressive.

Let me give you a little sense of this by sketching a few of their profiles for you. Take Arthur Wakefield, for example. A devout Anglican and churchgoer—before the Great War—he was, as described by Davis, 'ferociously strong, a champion boxer and rower at university, with brilliant blue eyes and a penchant for adventure that led him, in 1900, to suspend his medical studies and sign up as a cavalry trooper and sharpshooter' in the Boer War. After the war he completed his medical training in Edinburgh and Heidelberg, then went to work as a missionary doctor in Newfoundland and Labrador from 1908. For the following six years, he 'lived a life of considerable hardship: intense cold in winter, clouds of mosquitoes in summer, a diet of little but flour and grease, molasses, tea, caribou meat and salted fish.'

'Dedicated to God and King, impervious to physical suffering, possessed of medical skills that seemed wizardly to the scores of people he saved', Wakefield, when the balloon went up, in August 1914, raised the first five hundred of the Newfoundland Regiment. He knew them all as if they had been his foster sons and swelled with pride as they clutched their rifles, fixed with bayonets, marched to their ship with cheering crowds and broke into a rousing rendition of Auld Lang Syne. Two years later, by happenstance, he was manning the casualty clearing station at the very sector of the front on the Somme where the regiment was stationed on the eve of Haig's gigantic offensive. Yet it was weeks after the notorious opening day of the Somme before he learned their fate. They had been slaughtered by German machine guns on the parapet of their own trenches. Of 810 who went over the top, only sixty eight survived the day unscathed.

Then there was Charles Kenneth Howard-Bury: a brilliant writer, a fine photographer (when it was still a challenging art), a keen and accomplished naturalist, fluent in 27 Asian and European languages, a man who travelled widely in Siberia, Central Asia, China, India and Tibet at his own initiative, heir to a vast estate in Ireland whose main house had originally been built as a hunting lodge in 1740. When the war broke out, in August 1914, he immediately took a commission in the army. He became one of the most decorated officers in the war, winning every citation for valour except the Victoria Cross. He fought throughout the war and that he survived was statistically a miracle, given the massive attrition rate of the unit he led fearlessly and constantly. He was to become the team leader of the first assault on Everest, in 1921.

A third was Henry Morsehead, of whom Davies writes: 'he was a man of action and deed, a true explorer, decisive and contained in temperament, ferociously strong and fit, at five foot nine a pocket Hercules, as one friend described him, hard as nails, utterly indifferent to personal comfort, blessed with an impregnable digestive tract, fully capable of eating anything or nothing, of going without food or even water for days. Trained as a military engineer, with a specialty in topography, mapping and the design and construction of fortifications, he'd joined the Survey of India in 1906. Thereafter, he'd embarked on a series of extraordinary expeditions, none more dramatic than a number of thrusts up the Brahmaputra from the southern side of the Himalayas to the jungles of northeast Assam and, ultimately, into the heart of the Tsangpo Gorge.'

One of my favourites is Fredrick Marshman Bailey. Bailey was a British intelligence officer and one of the last protagonists of the Great Game—the legendary struggle for supremacy between the Russians and the British Empire in Central Asia and along the Himalayas. Bailey is described by Davis as having been a master of disguises, travelling at different times as a Buddhist priest, an Austrian soldier and an Armenian prisoner of war. He became such a headache in places like Tashkent and Samarkand to the nascent Bolshevik regime in 1918-19 that he lived with a Soviet bounty on his head for the rest of his days—and he lived until 1967.

Bailey was also a gifted naturalist and his clandestine work as a spy gave him many opportunities to pursue his hobbies of photography, butterfly collecting, ornithology and trophy hunting in lands most of us even now would regard as both harsh and exotic. His personal bird collection is now held in the American Museum of Natural History, New York. His papers and extensive photograph collections are held in the British Library, London. He also wrote books about his experiences and married into a wealthy family. Now there is a remarkable life. As Tom Lehrer once quipped about Gustav Mahler, Walter Gropius and Franz Werfel, 'It's people like this who make you realize how little you've accomplished!' He famously added, of course, 'It is a sobering thought, for example, that Mozart, when he was my age, had been dead for two years!'

Now, let's take stock of these remarkable individuals. You see, the salient thing here is that all the impressive accomplishments I have listed had been completed before any of these men attempted to climb Mount Everest. From almost any reasonable point of view, none of them had anything to prove. They certainly did not need to risk their lives more than they had already done or demonstrate that they had exceptional powers of endurance or commitment. Yet this, in 1921, again in 1922 and yet again in 1924, is what they did. They did it, as Davis makes clear, for many of the same reasons that test pilots in the 1960s became astronauts in the race to put a man in space and then on the Moon. They did it because the British Empire, or visionary people at the pinnacle of it, like John F. Kennedy in 1961, had issued a challenge.

Davis describes, as he puts it, the literal measurement of India, in the Survey of India, begun in 1806 and still proceeding in the first decade of the 20th century, as 'the greatest scientific undertaking of the nineteenth century.' It was the work of the surveyors of India that discovered Mount Everest to be the highest mountain in the world. The Himalayas as a mountain range fired the imaginations of the British surveyors: more than a thousand mountains each soaring above 20,000 feet, rising out of the heat and dust of the north

Indian plain and the jungles of Burma. It was only in 1846, however, that the exploration of them pinpointed 'a rugged knot of mountains some 140 miles west of Kangchenjunga, then considered the highest point on Earth.'

Here I pick up Davis's account. As you listen to it, bear in mind everything I began by saying about being pervious to doubt and about thinking, instrumentation and revision of opinion:

> Compared with the stunningly beautiful massif of Kangchenjunga, which dominates the sky beyond Darjeeling, these distant summits were unassuming, mere fragments of white on a dark horizon. [The leader of the 1846 party, John] Armstrong designated the highest simply Peak B. During subsequent seasons it remained hidden in cloud and it was not until November 1849 that another officer of the survey, James Nicolson, was able to make a series of observations from six different stations, the closest being some 108 miles from the mountain, by then known as Peak XV. Only in 1854, at the headquarters of the Survey of India in Dehra Dun and in Calcutta, did work begin on Nicolson's computations.
>
> Andrew Waugh, Surveyor General of India, assigned the task to a brilliant Indian, Radanath Sikhdar. Given the distance of the sightings and the problem of atmospheric refraction, the challenge was enormous. It took two years for Sikhdar to determine that this unknown summit was, at 29,002 feet, fully a thousand feet higher than any other known mountain on Earth. It was a most impressive feat of computation. The actual elevation of the mountain, measured today by satellite technology, is 29,035 feet. But the mountain itself has been rising at the rate of a centimetre a year for the last several centuries. In the nineteenth century, when Sikhdar did his calculations, the summit of the mountain, in all likelihood, would have been some five feet lower. Thus, with pencil, paper and mathematical wizardry, Sikhdar was off by only twenty eight feet.

Once this was established, that sharp spire of a white peak, fully a thousand feet higher than any other mountain in the world, became an object of aspiration and, for years before the Great War wrought catastrophic havoc on the world of European empires, the geographers, explorers and imperial propagandists of the British Empire found themselves yearning to mount an expedition to scale it.

If my objective this evening was to acquaint you with how that was done, I would be well into it by now. But of course my intention is rather different. It is to tantalize you with the very idea of that expedition or what became several expeditions; with the idea of the diverse and accomplished people who came together to form the team that made those attempts on the summit. I cannot, as I remarked early on, too highly recommend the book, but especially as a wonderful source of metaphors that you might individually and collectively draw upon in the next few years as you mount your own expeditions and build your own team.

Lest that seem a little grandiose, it may be worth recalling that, in 2005, when he first took over as senior coach at Hawthorn, Alastair Clarkson specifically evoked John F. Kennedy's famous speech about putting a man on the Moon and declared that Hawthorn should set itself the target, metaphorically speaking, of putting a man on the Moon within five years, by which he meant winning a premiership. He won his first within three years and has now won three, with the last two coming back to back last year and this year. He and they have fulfilled and over fulfilled their goals.

Late last year, after Hawthorn had won the second of these three premierships, I was approached by the club and asked to help them raise the bar in terms of decision-making processes within the coaching panel. My company worked with them this season and we were impressed by their honesty and openness to innovation. We are now represented on their newly created Innovation Committee and I must say, although I grew up and have been throughout my adult life a Collingwood supporter, I found it very sweet to be associated with Hawthorn's exceptional performance this season, capped off by a stunning performance and record breaking victory in the Grand Final.

But I mention all that chiefly to emphasize the matter of metaphors of aspiration. The one I have advanced this evening has been climbing Mount Everest. Doing so, is still a serious challenge to this day and people still die or lose body parts in the effort. But doing it the first time, back in the early 1920s, that was crazy brave. You are, I suggest, at that point in your endeavours. So the question is:

What is your Peak B, or Peak XV?

In other words, what is the shimmering peak off in the distance, far from your tea plantations in Darjeeling, that might lure you onto greater heights, quite literally? What observations have you made of it? From how many points? How have you set about computing its height relative to where you are? Who is your Radanath Sikhdar, who with pencil and paper will get the measurements right for you? What will it take to first measure, then reconnoitre and then scale that peak?

Perhaps, more important than all these questions, is the spiritual one: what spirit, what approach to life itself will you bring, as individuals and as a team, to this endeavour? At the end of his marvellous book, having taken us in fascinating detail through the terrain and human drama of the three expeditions, climaxing in the deaths of George Mallory and his sole climbing companion at 28,000 feet, Sandy Irvine, Wade Davis concludes with the following reflection:

Mallory and Irvine may not have reached the summit of Mount Everest, but they did, on that fateful day, climb higher than any human being before them, reaching heights that would not be attained again for nearly thirty years.

Mallory held nothing back, he writes:

> Because for him, as for all of his generation, death was but a frail barrier that men crossed smiling and gallant, every day. They had seen so much of death that life mattered less than the moments of being alive.

I do not, of course, suggest that you work yourselves to death in building your company. I simply pose the existential question: for you as individuals and as a team what ultimately matters? The answers you find to that question will shape how you work together, what goals you set for yourselves and how you go about achieving them. And as I understand it, you have gathered here this evening largely to begin reflecting on those things.

I mentioned earlier that the context in which I myself read *Into the Silence* was the sense, in 2012, that the relentless assault on my right leg of a melanoma that kept recurring no matter how many tumours were cut out of my leg, portended a metastasis and a mortal battle in the near future. Last year, the metastasis began. My doctors at once urged that I begin a course of oncogene inhibitor tablets, though they were likely to have significant side effects, might not work and, even if they worked, would only be effective for a median period of nine months.

I demurred, while I thought through what ultimately mattered to me existentially. It quickly became clear that mere survival, if increasingly depleted and without final hope of remission, meant very little to me. What did matter was the completion, if at all possible, of at least one and preferably several of the creative writing projects I already had on my drawing board. The moments of working on them, it was crystal clear to me; the prospect of finishing them and seeing them into print and of being able to leave them with family and friends, meant far more to me than merely hanging around.

The chief such project is a wildly ambitious work of literary art called *Darkness over Love: A Complete Fiction.* As I read Wade Davis's book, I came to think of my own endeavour on the model of Mallory's famous attempt on Everest. Does that mean I expect to fail and to die without attaining my goal? Given the scope of the project, as well as my health problems over the past decade, those possibilities can hardly be denied. Indeed, they are surely, on the balance of probabilities, more likely than the chance that I will succeed. Yet, as Davis concluded, we admire Mallory for what he attempted and for how close he got to his goal.

Eighteen months since I learned of the metastases and with my body still proving resilient, I feel more inclined than at any point since my project began to try to press on to the summit. Three months ago, knowing that the summit was still some considerable distance away and that time might be against me, I arranged for the publication of a 421 page book titled *Darkness over Love: A Writer's Workbook.* It was conceived as soon as the metastases were discovered last year. It will be in print within a fortnight. I think of it as my high altitude base camp for the next stage in the climb, to be undertaken in 2015, health permitting.

This is my existential project and I am increasingly arranging my life around it. The questions I would leave you with are simply these five:

I.   What is your project?
II.   Where is your base camp right now?
III. Who are the people in your team?
IV. Why are you in the team?
V.   How will your team reach the summit?

Let me suggest that in answering each and every one of these questions, you need to remain in all humility pervious to doubt. That is where exploration occurs. That is where you find your true answers and the sources of your inspiration.

4: How to teach history to school students (2015)[6]

I have been asked to address you and talk with you about how to bring history and world affairs alive in the minds of young people in our time. It is an honour to have been asked to do so and I look forward very much to discussing with you the nature of your work, hearing your own thoughts and pondering with you the ways in which your work can be made more fruitful. I left Aquinas College just over forty years ago. I was already keenly interested in history when I started secondary school and pursued that interest on an extra-curricular basis throughout my six years here.

Oddly enough, history was the only subject in my Year 12 exams for which I did not get a Distinction. Since I got 99 for two subjects and 66 for Australian History, my mother has always sworn that the history result had been printed upside down, due to a printer's error and should also have read 99. The result stands, however. Yet I went on to major in History— ancient, medieval and modern—at the University of Melbourne, none the worse for that embarrassing printer's error; which goes to show that historic setbacks need not put an end to hope or progress.

This afternoon, I would like to share with you three passages from very different books as a basis for reflection and a way to kick-start a conversation with you about the teaching of history in our time. I'll read them, since I do not have them memorized, but the whole presentation should take not much more than twenty five minutes or so, leaving us a good deal of time for what I trust will be a very lively discussion.

A: Igniting young imaginations–J. R. R. Tolkien *The Lord of the Rings*:

The first and longest passage is not from a book of history, but a work of literature that you may have read when you were younger. This book was read to me in 1967, by a young woman called Kathleen Gill, in fifth grade at St John the Evangelist's primary school, in Mitcham. It made an indelible impression. That impression began with the passage I am about to read to you. Along with many other passages in the novel, it set me on the road that goes ever on and on, in a quest to understand the world outside the little, comfortable world in which I was born and raised. Thirty seven years afterwards, I read it to a beautiful woman from Venezuela who had not even been born when the book was read to me. She promptly dubbed me Frodo Baggins and still calls me Frodo to this day. We were married a few months after I shared the passage with her.

Let me read it to you and then reflect on why it has always seemed to me to be a great provocation to taking an interest in the outside world and in history:

---

6   'The White Spaces Beyond the Borders of the Shire', an address to teachers at Aquinas College, Ringwood, 29 October 2015

As time went on, people began to notice that Frodo also showed signs of good 'preservation': outwardly he retained the appearance of a robust and energetic hobbit just out of his tweens. 'Some folk have all the luck', they said; but it was not until Frodo approached the usually more sober age of fifty that they began to think it queer.

Frodo himself, after the first shock, found that being his own master and the Mr Baggins of Bag End was rather pleasant. For some years he was quite happy and did not worry much about the future. But half unknown to himself the regret that he had not gone with Bilbo was steadily growing. He found himself wondering at times, especially in the autumn, about the wild lands, and strange visions of mountains that he had never seen came into his dreams. He began to say to himself, 'Perhaps I shall cross the River myself one day.' To which the other half of his mind always replied, 'Not yet.'

So it went on, until his forties were running out and his fiftieth birthday was drawing near: fifty was a number that he felt was somehow significant (or ominous); it was at any rate at that age that adventure had suddenly befallen Bilbo. Frodo began to feel restless and the old paths seemed too well-trodden. He looked at maps and wondered what lay beyond their edges: maps made in the Shire showed mostly white spaces beyond its borders. He took to wandering farther afield and more often by himself: and Merry and his other friends watched him anxiously. Often he was seen walking and talking with the strange wayfarers that began at this time to appear in the Shire.

There were rumours of strange things happening in the world outside; and as Gandalf had not at that time appeared or sent any message for several years, Frodo gathered all the news he could. Elves, who seldom walked in the Shire, could now be seen passing westward through the woods in the evening, passing and not returning; but they were leaving Middle-earth and were no longer concerned with its troubles. There were, however, dwarves on the road in unusual numbers. The ancient East-West Road ran through the Shire to its end at the Grey Havens, and dwarves had always used it on the way to their mines in the Blue Mountains. They were the hobbits' chief source of news from distant parts—if they wanted any: as a rule dwarves said little and hobbits asked no more. But now Frodo often met strange dwarves of far countries, seeking refuge in the West. They were troubled and some spoke in whispers of the Enemy and of the Land of Mordor.

That name the hobbits only knew in legends of the dark past, like a shadow in the background of their memories; but it was ominous and disquieting. It seemed that the evil power in Mirkwood had been driven out by the White Council only to reappear in greater strength in the old strongholds of Mordor. The Dark Tower had been rebuilt it was said. From there the power was spreading far and wide, and away far east and south there were wars and growing fear. Orcs were multiplying again in the mountains. Trolls were abroad; no longer dull-witted, but cunning and armed with dreadful weapons. And there were murmured hints of creatures more terrible than all these, but they had no name.

Little of all this, of course, reached the ears of ordinary hobbits. But even the deafest and most stay-at-home began to hear queer tales; and those whose business took them to the borders saw strange things...

Very early in my life, I took to calling the eastern suburbs of Melbourne, from which your students and many of you come, the Shire. Even before *The Lord of the Rings* was read to me at ten years of age, I had an interest in the white spaces beyond the borders of the Shire. When I was nine years old I found my father's old Year 11 history textbook, *Medieval and Modern Times* and made it my own, poring over its many coloured maps of the world which filled in the white spaces. But the passage I have just read to you lit up my imagination in a very personal and profound way. Listening to such a story, it was far easier to begin to think of oneself as a hobbit on the borderlands of history, rather than simply as a reader about things long ago and far away.

Don't you think that that passage, even now, has striking resonances? Don't we ourselves, right now, live at a time of ominous and disquieting developments in the outside world? Don't we have 'strange wayfarers' coming to this quiet, comfortable country of ours, seeking refuge in the West? Aren't events at our borders a subject of controversy and concern? Don't we, don't you, as teachers, readily think of real world parallels to the White Council, 'the evil in Mirkwood' and wars away east and south—even if they are chiefly north and west from here? Don't you find it easy, living and teaching in Ringwood and its surrounds, to imagine yourselves as living in the Shire, surrounded by hobbits who, as a rule, exhibit little interest in what is going on outside the borders of the Shire? Isn't the whole of the chapter from which this passage is taken, 'The Shadow of the Past', an evocation of history itself? As teachers, you should always remember that your primary task is to make your students vividly aware of the shadow of the past.

You might anchor that endeavour to the remark by American novelist William Faulkner, 'The past isn't dead. It isn't even past.' That, of course, is what Frodo Baggins discovered, when Gandalf informed him that the ring left to him by his Uncle Bilbo was the One Ring, on which the doom of Middle-earth itself hung. Having demonstrated to Frodo that his ring is the One Ring, Gandalf warns the startled hobbit that Sauron greatly desires the ring, but must not get it. 'Frodo sat silent and motionless', Tolkien tells us. 'Fear seemed to stretch out a vast hand, like a dark cloud rising in the East and looming up to engulf him. 'This ring', he stammered. 'How, how on earth did it come to me?' 'Ah!' Gandalf exclaims, 'That is a very long story. The beginnings lie back in the Black Years, which only the lore-masters now remember. If I were to tell you all that tale, we would still be sitting here when Spring had passed into Winter.' You, sitting here, are such lore masters; at least here at this College. Your task is not, of course, to tell your young charges that they possess the One Ring, but it is, I suggest, to bring alive in them, if you can, the sense of being very much part of stunning histories, explaining how the world came to be as it now is, that go back into the deep past.

B: The very idea of serious history–Thucydides *The Peloponnesian War*

This brings us to my second reading—from the first really serious and systematic work of narrative and analytical history written anywhere on Earth: the history of the Peloponnesian war. It was written 2,400 years ago and remains a masterpiece of historical and geopolitical writing even now. It is the excellent Landmark edition of this book that I can be seen reading, as if it was a Bible, in the photo of me that the College put up this year on the Honour Board. I chose it because *The Peloponnesian War*, by the exiled Athenian general Thucydides, is a primer of enduring value in the nature of war and human affairs; and these have been my central preoccupation since boyhood. Here are its opening lines:

> Thucydides, an Athenian, wrote the history of the war between the Peloponnesians and the Athenians, beginning at the moment that it broke out, and believing that it would be a great war, and more worthy of relation than any that had preceded it...

What set Thucydides apart from the beginning was his high seriousness in trying to get things right, based on evidence and critical reason and not merely the partial, forgetful or confused accounts accepted by those around him.

'On the whole', he claimed in his prologue to the history, reflecting on the legends of the Trojan War and the general problem of gleaning reliable evidence from the past, or even from events that had occurred in the war itself:

> the conclusions I have drawn from the proofs quoted may, I believe, safely be relied upon. Assuredly, they will not be disturbed either by the verses of a poet displaying the exaggeration of his craft, or by the compositions of the chroniclers that are attractive at truth's expense; the subjects they treat of being out of reach of evidence and time having robbed most of them of historical value by enthroning them in the realm of legend. Turning from these, we can rest satisfied with having proceeded upon the clearest data and having arrived at conclusions as exact as can be expected in matters of such antiquity...

> With reference to the narrative of events, far from permitting myself to derive it from the first source that came to hand, I did not even trust my own impressions, but it rests partly on what I saw myself, partly on what others saw for me, the accuracy of the report always being tried by the most severe and detailed tests possible. My conclusions have cost me some labour from the want of coincidence between accounts of the same occurrences by different eye-witnesses, arising sometimes from imperfect memory, sometimes from undue partiality for one side or the other. The absence of romance in my history will, I fear, detract somewhat from its interest; but if it be judged useful by those enquirers who desire an exact knowledge of the past as an aid to the understanding of the future, which in the course of human affairs must resemble if it does not reflect the past, I shall be content. In fine, I have written my work not as an essay which is to win the applause of the moment, but as a possession for all time.

The language—being a 19th century translation—is a little archaic, but the position is a powerful one. Here, as the historian himself declares, we are coming to grips not with romance or fable, but with mature analysis of deadly serious matters. Yet, from the point of view of your young charges, there may be little difference, because of the remoteness from their experience of the world of ancient times and also of the kind of grim affairs that Thucydides was determined to both record accurately and analyse correctly.

I began reading about ancient Greece when I was at primary school, but my first copy of *The Peloponnesian War* was given to me whimsically by my English teacher, Michael Mithen, here at Aquinas College, back in 1971, when I was in Year 9. That hardback copy was Rex Warner's translation of the classic book for Penguin. It was not a personal gift or something urged upon me as a classic. Michael was then the College librarian and one day, as he was cleaning out the library, getting rid of books he seems to have thought did not serve any very useful purpose at the school, he found *The Peloponnesian War* on the shelves. Turning to me, he said, quite matter of factly, 'Here, Monk. You might find this interesting'—and tossed it to me without any special reverence or recommendation He never subsequently inquired whether I had read it or what I had made of it. But he had chosen the right person to give it to; and he had given me one of the great treasures of classical literature.

We need, I suggest, to be active in this manner, seizing the moment to give or recommend classics to our students; looking for opportunities to put before their eyes and place in their hands the kind of books or ideas that are of enduring power and value, even if the gift does not come to fruition, or even if we never learn about the ways in which it does. Michael died decades ago and never lived to see me graduate in history from the University of Melbourne, or take my doctorate in international relations from the Australian National University. That casual gift of his, however, is something I have never forgotten. I now own several different translations of *The Peloponnesian War*, as well as other books about it and about Thucydides. One of the most insightful is Clifford Orwin's *The Humanity of Thucydides*, which I purchased at the Blackwells bookshop at Oxford University in 1996, when I had just resigned from the intelligence service and felt as much an exile as Thucydides must have after the citizens of Athens exiled him, early in the Peloponnesian war.

History is not, Thucydides teaches us, merely about dry facts as such or even dramatic stories. It is about evidence, inference and incisive explanation, because only these things enable us to grasp the meaning and significance of what has happened and what has shaped the world we live in. It is about opening up a window into the past in such a way that those who have a need to understand it will be able to see, with as clear a view as possible, what governed it and with what consequences. We should, while seeking by all means to engage the imaginations of our students, seek constantly to draw their attention to and focus their attention on the difference between truth and fiction, partiality and objectivity, romantic tales and political seriousness. This can be done in many ways and perhaps it is best to do it, whatever specific aspect or period of history you are teaching, by choosing episodes from history in which something was at stake and where passionate arguments have been had about both the truth and the meaning of what happened. The point of the lesson is less to insist that they believe a particular account than that they come to appreciate and wonder at how scrupulous we need to be about evidence and reasoning if we are to get anywhere close to a reliable account of those things. That was the primary observation of Thucydides and it is still, I believe, the most important thing to impress upon your students.

C: Dramatic history in the recent past–Mark Riebling *Church of Spies: The Pope's War Against Hitler*

And so we come to my third reading; the briefest of the three, but the one that brings all this together. Aquinas College is a Catholic institution; one of the finest in the archdiocese. It has a clear and sound Catholic social justice ethos. That ethos is rooted in theology; but simply to understand what Catholicism is, where its doctrines and institutions and values have come from, is an exercise less in theology than in history. This is especially so if we wish to grasp how others see the Catholic Church—from outside. I was in early primary school when the Second Vatican Council was held in Rome, in the early 1960s. My last year at primary school was the year that Pope Paul VI issued the famous and controversial encyclical *Humanae Vitae*. He was Pope throughout my years here at Aquinas.

However, by the time I left school, I was thoroughly confused about Catholicism and the history of religion more generally. I found that I could not simply accept doctrines or traditions that I did not understand, nor could I proceed with a normal or professional life without getting clarification of these matters. That is why I undertook an Arts degree at the University of Melbourne, studying the classical world, philosophy, Reformation history, modern revolutions and other matters. History was my access to comprehension of what it meant to be a Catholic, as well as what it meant to be some other kind of Christian, what it meant to be a liberal, an atheist, a materialist, a Marxist revolutionary; not because I was committed to being any of these things, but because I was determined to understand the world I lived in.

My third reading relates to a particularly dramatic and important episode in modern history; an episode which took place when my parents were still very young and more than a decade before I was born. It is from a stunning work of historical scholarship just published in the past few months, here in Melbourne by Scribe, the publisher that produced my book on

China a decade ago. It is Mark Riebling's *Church of Spies: The Pope's War Against Hitler*. Many of you may be aware that Pope Pius XII has been very widely attacked both as a pre-Vatican II conservative and as having failed to speak out against the Holocaust during the Second World War. There is a considerable literature on these subjects. I have long been acquainted with that literature. I remain deeply interested in it.

Riebling's compelling, meticulously researched history has transformed my understanding of Pius XII, his role during the Second World War and the role of Catholics in the resistance to Hitler. Let me emphasize that: this book has transformed my understanding of and I would add my esteem for Pope Pius XII. For Catholics, this book should be required reading. It is profoundly important and deeply stirring history of the best kind. It delves into the secret archives of the Vatican, those of the intelligence agencies and diplomatic services of the United States and several European countries, the private diaries and memoirs of numerous figures involved, a lifetime ago, in one of the greatest dramas of all time—the struggle for Western civilization against Nazism.

The passage I want to quote is a brief few lines from the Epilogue to Riebling's book. I urge you to read the whole book and to put it into the hands of your students, male and female. But I want to link it to the current encyclical of Pope Francis, *On Care for Our Common Home*, addressing the challenges of climate change and inequality, which has been released this year and has caused quite a stir. Here is the passage from Riebling's book:

> 'The task of this hour is to rebuild the world', the Pope said in a 9 May [1945] radio speech, as the guns fell silent in Europe. 'On our knees in spirit before the tombs, before the ravines blackened by blood, before the countless corpses of inhuman massacres, it seems to us that they, the fallen, are warning us, the survivors: Let there arise from the earth, wherein we have been planted as grains of wheat, the moulders and masters of a better universe.'

He knew, as he spoke these words, of how bravely Catholic resistance figures, in Germany and elsewhere, had striven since at least 1939 to foil the designs of Hitler and to document and frustrate his diabolical policies of conquest and genocide. He knew that many of them had paid with their lives. He had been appalled by Hitler's genocide of the Jews and his rape of the continent of Europe. He knew that profound social and political renewal on a moral basis was necessary in Europe. Over the following years, until his death in 1958, he was to play a significant role in seeking to bring such renewal about, even as the Cold War and the nuclear arms race threatened to bring calamities even worse—worse by an order of magnitude—than what had just happened in the Second World War.

The Second World War was a far more terrible war than the Peloponnesian War and was the real world counterpart to Tolkien's War of the Ring. As you may be aware,

Tolkien was in fact writing *The Lord of the Rings* during and after the Second World War. His son Christopher was in the Royal Air Force and Tolkien would send him draft chapters of *The Fellowship of the Ring* and *The Two Towers* as he wrote them, during the war years. Pope Pius XII was deeply and inextricably involved in the war at the highest levels and was seen by Hitler, correctly, as one of his most profound and dangerous enemies—on both moral and institutional grounds. You see, Pius XII, contrary to the claims of his many detractors, played the role of Gandalf in that great historical drama.

Mark Riebling's history, drawing on an astounding range of primary sources, which again and again took my breath away, has brought all this to light—seventy years after the end of the Second World War. It is a spy story, but an utterly real one and more truly dramatic than any fiction. Riebling tells that story not in overblown melodramatic terms, but in terms that Thucydides, the master of sombre and level-headed prose, would have approved. His book is one that, theology and the authority of the clergy entirely aside, ought to inspire you, both as Catholics and as history teachers. And when we reflect on the words of Pope Pius XII that I quoted; words spoken over radio to millions, amid the ruins of Europe, but in the moment of hard won victory over absolute evil, we should all feel a sense of vocation, of calling: to understand serious history, to pass on that understanding to our young; to motivate them, even if they are ordinary hobbits, to want to be among those planted grains who will rise from the earth to help mould a better universe.

That is the true subject of the conversation I want to have with you. What are your questions and concerns?

5: Australia and the Asian Century: The Reflections of a Dilettante (2015)[7]

In this morning's press there was a report that China has awarded the 2015 Confucius Peace Prize to none other than Robert Mugabe, the corrupt, brutal, incompetent dictator of Zimbabwe for 'overcoming a number of difficulties and contributing to building the government, economy and order in Zimbabwe, while continuing to work actively at the age of 91 for peace in Africa.'

The Confucius Prizes were introduced after the Chinese Communist Party became riled at the awarding of the 2010 Nobel Peace Prize to Liu Xiaobo, one of the chief architects of Charter 2008, which called for political liberalization and respect for human rights in China. The Chinese Communist Party denounced that award as 'an obscenity'. Its own award to Mugabe is simply, almost comically grotesque.

There are two sides to this coin, however. On the one hand, there is the ugly face of the Chinese Communist state with its unrepentant support for vicious dictatorships around the world, such as Mugabe's, or that of Kim Jong-Un in North Korea. The flip side of this is that China, so long as it is ruled by this mentality, will be largely unable to win the trust and confidence of the advanced, democratic and liberal states around the world, which now include many of its neighbours.

What the award to Mugabe demonstrates is that China remains a nasty dictatorship, whatever soothing rhetoric it might put out from time to time, such as when Xi Jinping travels abroad. This is the China which is viewed with growing apprehension by almost all its neighbours as it military power rapidly grows. But the award also shows that China lacks an authentic capacity to build what is often called 'soft power' and, as long as this remains the case, the probability is that coalitions of more liberal states will align against it to keep its pretensions and ambitions in check.

It's a pleasure to be here this afternoon. Some months ago I chaired a public debate on religious belief and civil society at the State Library. I remarked that I saw such a debate as belonging to a great tradition dating back to the classical world. It reminded me, I quipped, of the debates St Paul had with the Stoics and Epicureans on the Areopagus in Athens two thousand years ago, as recounted in Acts of the Apostles, chapter 17.

This afternoon, similarly, stands in a great Western tradition—and I emphasize Western tradition—of public and open-ended discourse about matters of common concern. This kind of gathering is what you might call an Athenian one of a different kind in its open and free canvasing of matters of public moment. Kurt Raaflaub's *The Discovery of Freedom in Ancient*

---

7   An address to the University of the Third Age, 23 October 2015

Greece and Josiah Ober's *The Athenian Revolution* are leading explorations of the idea of freedom of speech and public discourse.

I am Paul, but not St Paul and I have come here to talk not of God and resurrection, but of worldly affairs in a frank and open manner and to discuss them with you. I have been introduced as an expert of kinds, but that's not how I see myself. I have given my remarks the sub-title 'The Reflections of a Dilettante', because I see myself as a thoughtful generalist, not an expert specialist. I am not here to deliver a lecture, but to open a conversation with you about matters of common concern.

You are here because of your interests and concerns as citizens of a Western democracy on the fringes of the Asian world. I am here because I undertook, decades ago initially, to study Western history, then international relations during the Cold War, but have developed a keen interest in Asia because of what has been happening in my lifetime and because of its importance for Australia's future. . The subject of my doctoral dissertation was US counter-insurgency strategy throughout the Cold War, in Southeast Asia and Central America.

I then went to work for the Defence Intelligence Organization and was assigned to concentrate on Asia as an intelligence analyst for the Australian government at the very time when Japan began to stagnate, China began to rise, North Korea developed its nuclear weapons, Hong Kong was being prepared to be handed back to China after a century as a British crown colony and Taiwan was democratizing. It was 1990 and Ross Garnaut had just published his report *Australia and the Northeast Asian Ascendancy*.

For the past twenty years, having left government service in 1995, I have been a public intellectual and a businessman; a somewhat unusual combination. My business has been applied cognitive science, or in layman's language critical thinking skills. Over the past decade, starting with a book called *Thunder from the Silent Zone: Rethinking China*, I have had six books published. I have a seventh due out within a couple of months and several more in the works.

The fourth of my books was called *The West in a Nutshell*. The sixth is called *Opinions and Reflections: A Free Mind at Work 1990-2015*. I am, in other words, not short of opinions; but I am not an ideologue or a lobbyist—unless freedom and civilized values are considered an ideology and insistence on freedom of expression lobbying. I am, like you, simply a thinking citizen in an open society.

'Australia and the Asian Century' presupposes something that may not turn out to be the case—that the 21st century will be dominated by Asia. It is not self-evident that that is what will happen. But there are countless topics subsumed within this large one. We cannot cover them all and I certainly do not claim to be an expert on them all. I do, however, have an unusually independent way of looking at things. My writing might be considered sufficient proof of that. My work as a trainer and consultant in critical thinking skills has honed that independence over the past fifteen years.

This should be our point of departure for a conversation: not that I am the expert, telling you what is going to happen, or what to believe is true; but that I am an educated Australian whose background and experience have fitted him to at least have considered opinions on the broad outlines of this subject—opinions I am very comfortable sharing with you, out of an interest in the great conversation we as Australians all need to have about these important matters.

That conversation has to do not simply with how we might better 'fit in' with Asia or become part of it, but with how we buttress and further develop our identity as a cosmopolitan society whose civilizational roots and institutional origins are both Western and British. Bret Stephens, in a thoughtful and sombre column in *The Wall Street Journal* and *The Australian* this morning, has lamented the nihilism and passivity that appear to have gripped Europe and which now threaten it, he fears with disintegration.

He expressed alarm at Angela Merkel's strange and feeble offer to Turkey to facilitate its entry into the EU in exchange for a deal over Syrian refugees. As Stephens observes:

> This is *machtpolitik* in reverse, in which the Chancellor is begging small favours from weaker powers on temporary matters in exchange for broad concessions with far-reaching ramifications. There are 75 million Turks whose per capita income doesn't match that of Panamanians. The country is led by an elected Islamist with an autocratic streak, prone to anti-Semitic outbursts, who openly supports Hamas, denies the Armenian genocide, jails journalists in record numbers and orchestrates Soviet-style show-trials against his political opponents. Turkey also has borders with Syria, Iraq and Iran. These would become Europe's borders in the event of Turkish membership.

Australia does not have land borders with any part of Asia, but if we did we could face similar dilemmas. As it is, we have had heated and protracted debates about border security and real or alleged international obligations. We are a humane and multi-cultural society—arguably the most impressive on Earth—but we should not become confused or nihilistic about the things that are necessary if we are to remain this way. There can be no ignoring the fact that as we take in large numbers of Muslim immigrants, we must assimilate them into liberal norms and the culture of tolerance or create for ourselves an intractable social problem.

I have never become an academic boffin or business specialist whose job it is to scrutinize the minutiae of developments in Asia and make expert prognostications about where everything is heading. I am a generalist who has since boyhood been interested primarily in the big picture. I am a sceptic when it comes to prophecies and prognoses. I am a practitioner of the art of careful reasoning. I'd like to have you all understand those things as a basis for our conversation.

Let me begin, therefore, by quoting three short paragraphs from a book called *The Long Boom: A Future History of the World 1980-2020*, by Peter Schwartz, Peter Leyden and Joel Hyatt. It was published in 2000. Its message is summed up in the following words:

> We are watching the beginnings of a global economic boom on a scale never experienced before. We have entered a period of sustained growth that could eventually double the world's economy every dozen years and bring increasing prosperity for—quite literally—billions of people on the planet. We are riding the early waves of a 25-year run of a greatly expanding economy that will do much to solve seemingly intractable problems like poverty and to ease tensions throughout the world. And we'll do it without blowing the lid off the environment.
>
> If this holds true, historians will look back on our era as an extraordinary moment. They will chronicle the 40-year period from 1980 to 2020 as the key years of a remarkable transformation. In the developed countries of the West, new technology will lead to big productivity increases that will cause high economic growth—actually, waves of technology will continue to roll out through the early part of the 21st century.
>
> And then the relentless process of globalization, the opening up of national economies and the integration of markets, will drive the growth through much of the rest of the world. An unprecedented alignment of an ascendant Asia, a revitalized America, and a reintegrated greater Europe—including a recovered Russia—together will create an economic juggernaut that pulls along most other regions of the planet. These two megatrends—fundamental technological change and a new ethos of openness—will transform our world into the beginnings of a global civilization, a new civilization of civilizations, that will blossom through the coming century.

Well, here we are in late 2015 and this is not what is happening. All sorts of things have gone wrong from this rosy Schwartzian point of view, starting with the e-tech stock bubble bursting, then 9/11, followed by the wars in Afghanistan and Iraq, then the GFC, the economic crisis in Europe, the implosion of the Arab Muslim world that was initially greeted as the so-called 'Arab Spring' and now the slowing of the Chinese growth surge, which only a short while ago was widely believed to be unstoppable. None of that surprises me, but it does interest me a great deal.

This is not to say that the 21st century will be all doom and gloom, though that is a view that has its advocates. My own business partner calls himself an 'apocalyptarian'. He believes that we have so trashed the planet and are so committed to economic growth and consumption that we are headed over a cliff like lemmings. He is an acute climate alarmist who would see Matt Ridley as a dangerous, deluded or disingenuous ratbag. I don't try so much to cheer him up as to temper his gloomy certainty with scepticism, emphasizing how uncertain things actually are and how very many dynamic forces are at work that could lead to various possible futures.

Before the turn of the century, I wrote a long essay about the rise of China, in which I cautioned that too many economists and geopolitical analysts were committed to what I called the Linear Ascent Model: the idea that China would rise inexorably and grow endlessly at the rapid rates of the 1990s. We needed, I argued, to temper our enthusiasm—or alarm, as the case may be—and consider various different possible futures.

In 2005, my book *Thunder From the Silent Zone: Rethinking China* spelled this out at greater length. I sketched out four scenarios for China's future. I called them Mutation, Maturation, Militarization and Metastasis. Ten years on, the verdict is still very much out as to what the future of China will be even within the relatively near future. A refreshingly independent China analyst in Sydney wrote to me a few months ago, remarking that my book had been ten years ahead of its time and should be read now by as many people as possible.

Let me briefly explain what I mean by each of these four scenarios. Mutation is what we all hoped to see in the 1980s, as did many Chinese students and reformers, such as the late Zhao Ziyang and his predecessor Hu Yaobang. It would entail not only economic liberalization, but political liberalization, an independent judiciary, a free press and a tenable regime of human rights, none of which currently exist in China. This path was open to some extent until 1989. The Party then slammed it shut and it has remained firmly shut under Jiang Zemin, Hu Jintao and now Xi Jinping.

Maturation roughly equates to China's economic growth levelling off at the middle-income level that it has reached in this decade and thus growing old before it grows rich, while inheriting from the decades of rapid growth massive environmental problems, huge public debts, a ramshackle health and welfare system, yawning inequalities and high expectations among hundreds of millions of people of a better life. Simply holding China together under these conditions could prove an immense task. We need to remember that even after thirty years of super-charged economic growth, China's GDP per capita is still a fraction of our own, some $6,000 per head compared with our $50,000.

Militarization is a scenario in which, as I pointed out a decade ago, China pours resources into a military build-up and then, whether out of an excess of hubris or as a means for diverting popular dissatisfactions onto foreign enemies, uses its newfound power in military adventures abroad. Over the decade since my book appeared in print, China's military budget has continued to grow faster than its GDP, in double digit increments annually. Ten years ago, it spent less than Japan, Britain or France. It now spends more than the three of them combined. Only the United States spends more, but it has global commitments to protect numerous allies; China's forces are for its protection alone. And its unambiguous aspiration is to displace the United States as the dominant power in Asia and the Western Pacific by the middle of this century.

Metastasis is a scenario in which the dictatorial habits of the Communist Party, the environmental costs of rapid growth, the huge pressures of an immense and ageing population with a sever gender imbalance and the inflow of ideas and commodities from the outside world lead to an implosion of the Communist polity with no competent or legitimate body in any position to replace it. This, like each of the other scenarios, has some evidence to support it. The key thing is to look at the many shifting variables in the overall equation and not to succumb to facile and unreflective assumptions or predictions about what 'will' happen.

The same, as my citation from *The Long Boom* will have suggested, applies to the world at large. Whether we are talking about the capacity of the United States to demonstrate resilience and renew itself, the scope for India to really get on its feet and deal with its huge challenges, the capacity of Indonesia to sustain its still very new experiment in nation building and economic development, the capacity of Japan to deal with the world's most heavily indebted developed economy and most rapidly ageing and shrinking population, the question of territorial and power political rivalries between these major states, or the long-standing problem of a truculent and totalitarian little state in North Korea forever threatening to cause mayhem, the future is full of divergent possibilities.

Australia's place in all this is privileged and full of promise, provided that we conduct our affairs with intelligence and imagination. The recent spate of instability at the top, from Howard to Rudd to Gillard, back to Rudd, then quickly to Abbott and within two years to Turnbull seems almost like Italian politics and has not been especially inspiring or edifying. But we have come out of it all with Malcolm Turnbull as prime minister, which is by most counts and according to a majority of Australians, pretty much the best possible outcome of all. Our luck has held. Now what we need are several terms of good management.

We should remind ourselves that, in the 1970s, during the Whitlam and Fraser years, Australia began to look as though it was becoming if not politically Italian then economically Argentinian. Reforms were called for in order to open up our economy, make it more competitive and flexible, as globalization and technological innovation threatened to leave us stranded behind protectionist walls. It was, paradoxically, the ALP that led those free market reforms. Bob Hawke and Paul Keating still squabble over who should really get the credit, but the truth is that each simply provided the political leadership which made it possible for ideas developed by others to rise to the fore and become public policy.

Among those economic reforms was the floating of the dollar. By most accounts the reforms collectively, but the floating of the dollar specifically, enabled Australia to ride out the Asian economic crisis in the late 1990s and enjoy a long period of sustained economic growth during the prime ministership of John Howard. That is an antecedent well worth bearing in mind as we look ahead to what has been dubbed the Asian century; because there will be shocks ahead and we need to be able to ride them out with that kind of flexibility, if at all possible.

A key aspect of that flexibility will be our strategic and diplomatic adroitness in Asia. Ross Babbage recently authored a short monograph called *Game Plan: The Case for a New Australian Grand Strategy*, in which he argued that Australia strengthen its alliance with the United States and its links with a number of key Asian neighbours to hedge against the rising power of China and the danger that China will become more and more assertive in the years ahead.

This will, I am sure, be one of the main topics you will want to discuss, so I won't dwell on it here. But you will be aware that many subordinate strategic debates are taking place in this context, such as that about the new submarines, about the basing of US marines at Darwin, about the leasing of Darwin harbour to a Chinese corporation by the Northern Territory government for 99 years, about telecommunications, about foreign investment rules, about China's claims and moves in the South and East China Seas, about the decision of the Abe government to begin rearming Japan in an alliance context.

Ross Babbage argues that Australia is seen in Washington as a crucial ally and an anchor to the south of Asia for its own grand strategy. Ours, he writes, should be to embrace that and deepen our inter-operability with American forces. We can and should become, he argues, host to a much wider range of US combat and combat support units and a leading provider of strategic intelligence analysis in and on Asia.

'The challenge of providing effective security for Australia has been demanding in the past, but it is now truly daunting,' Babbage declares—not because the Asian powers are necessarily going to become predatory, but because Australia has moved from being a strategic backwater to being a frontline state, positioned at a crucial point on the greatest strategic tectonic plate on the planet.

At the same time, we have negotiated a free trade agreement with China. We do not seek conflict with China. We have profited enormously from its economic rise after the abandonment of Maoism and the opening up of its economy to foreign direct investment and trade. We have been taken aback by the recent slowdown in its growth and the signs that its apparently unflappable planners have begun to run out of viable macro-economic policy tools for many of the same reasons that those in Washington and the EU appear to have done.

Should we feel as daunted as the more pessimistic pundits suggest? Only, I suggest, if that leads to clear thinking and deeply intelligent strategic and macro-economic decisions. Pessimism is not dictated by circumstances. It is a mood. Australia is well-placed to adapt with that kind of intelligence and practicality, but it won't happen by luck alone; it requires good management. An important part of good management is prudence. It was imprudent of Wall St banks to leverage themselves to the extent that they did in the decade leading up to the GFC. It was imprudent of the Federal Reserve and Treasury to allow them to do so; just as it was imprudent of them to dismiss Brooksley Born's call for a real debate about how best to regulate the new derivatives that were proliferating at the turn of the century.

It would be similarly imprudent of us to bet on China being restrained and tractable over the decades ahead and to jettison the US alliance, as Malcolm Fraser urged before he died and Paul Keating has been urging; but equally imprudent for us to assume that it will be aggressive and expansionist and therefore to take steps that might help trigger in China the very forces we would prefer to see contained. It would be desirable for us to diversify our economic options beyond commodity exports, to deepen our capacity to employ our rising generation in productive and wealth creating ways; but it would be foolish to believe we can readily do this by demanding that the government pick winners and protect particular industries—although this is, in important respects, what the East Asian states have done, using a mercantilist economic strategy, from Japan to South Korea and Taiwan and now China..

The mantra has been repeated tirelessly for a generation now that Australians must become 'Asia literate', but it isn't clear that we have made striking progress in this direction. Clearly, larger numbers of Australians than ever before have worked in Asia, travelled in Asia, taught Asian students and followed the outpouring of news from Asia. I had dinner last Monday with three men of my own age. We all grew up in the same Catholic parish, all our parents were DLP activists and we went to the same Catholic primary school. We have all worked in or on China over the past twenty five years and have all moved on from both the politics and religion of our parents. Those are signs of the times.

But Asian languages have not 'taken' in our schools. Almost no white Australians make the effort now to master Chinese, Japanese, Indonesian or other Asian tongues. Native speakers of immigrant stock do most of this—and they are hard to compete with in HSC exams. Moreover, unless I am misreading the data, fewer and fewer Australian students are studying basic science or history. It's difficult, in fact, to design and foster a curriculum that would adequately address the challenges and opportunities before us. But we are hardly alone in that respect. Rather than panicking, we need to keep thinking and mooting our options—just as we are doing this afternoon.

I made a commitment that I would talk for no more than 20 minutes and then open the floor to discussion. I'm sure you will agree that I have done no more in my 20 minutes than touch on broad themes, but I hope I have said enough to draw you into an animated and open-ended conversation on this afternoon's vast and exciting topic. I addressed 500 Year 12 students on much the same topic several years ago and offered two prizes to encourage good questions. The prizes were my books on China and on Western civilization. I was delighted by the forest of hands that went up and by the questions. I don't imagine that I need to offer prizes to the members of this audience; but I do have the same books to offer this afternoon, as well as another more recent one—*Opinions and Reflections: A Free Mind at Work 1990-2015*. You can purchase a copy of any one of them, but what I chiefly look forward to is the discussion with you. Let's go.

Edward Snowden: are even the liberal democracies becoming 'Orwellian' surveillance states? Not nearly as rapidly as China and Russia.

PART III: 2016 (B)

1: Sonia Kruger's cry from the heart

In the wake of the atrocity in Nice, Sonia Kruger, like many of us, felt emotionally convulsed. She called for a halt to Muslim immigration. For this she was almost instantly denounced as a 'racist'. That, in saying what she did, she made reference to a newspaper piece by Andrew Bolt was damning in the eyes of many of her critics. Yet, as she expressed it on Tuesday, this is a complex matter and we must be able to talk about it openly, if we are to come up with solutions that keep this country peaceful and safe.

There are several matters that got tangled up in her *cri de cœur*, prompted, as she said, by her feelings as a mother and the outcry that followed: first, the definition of racism; second, the distinction between those who happen to be Muslims by culture or belief and those who seek to impose Islam by terror and intimidation; third, the practical matter of immigration criteria; and fourth, the elementary principles governing an open society. Let's address these one at a time.

It is vital to separate charges of racism from criticism of religion. Islam is not an ethnicity, not a 'race', even if it did begin as a tribal Arabic cult. Any sound progressive should by now be across the fact, moreover, that the very notion of 'race' is incoherent. But it becomes even more incoherent when those who express concern about Islam are charged with racism.

Wanting to keep Muslims out would, for one thing, extend across very many ethnic groups, from numerous African cultures, to Arabs, Turks, Persians, Malays, Indonesians and others. And in all these ethnic groups there are people who are not Muslim at all. So, the charge of racism is absurd and confused. Seeking to keep Muslims out would be akin to seeking to exclude, say, Mormons, Scientologists or Buddhists, though no-one is suggesting we do those things. Religion, not ethnicity, is the central issue.

Now, within countries or regions in which Islam is dominant, there are many people who would like to flee to more open and tolerant countries (such as ours), because they find the brand of Islam around them oppressive or reactionary. This does not mean that they repudiate their Muslim culture or traditions, any more than, say, Christian dissenters fleeing persecution in Christian Europe for the New World intended to give up Christianity, as they understood it. We should, surely, feel pretty comfortable welcoming such people, as a general rule.

What many people in the West are increasingly alarmed by, however, is the aggressive attempt by Islamic militants of various stripes to reinforce Muslim rule of a conservative kind, wherever they can; and also spread it into the West. This is a matter of growing and justified concern. There are strong currents flowing right now in this respect that we should be seeking to divert from our shores, if we value our peace and safety. The question is not whether we have the right and even the duty to stem that tide. It is how we can most intelligently do so, consistent with our values and principles.

This is where immigration criteria become paramount. The Prime Minister has responded to the media brouhaha over Sonia Kruger's emotional outburst by declaring that Australia has and has long had a non-discriminatory immigration policy. Long is an elastic word, of course. Many of us now alive can still remember the White Australia Policy and it is worth remembering, all *soi disant* (forgive my French in the present circumstances) progressives should be reminded, that it was the ALP, not the Liberal Party that most staunchly defended this discriminatory policy.

Yet such non-discrimination depends crucially on the willingness and ability of immigrants to blend into the secular and open society that has grown from 19th century liberal and utilitarian foundations in Australia. Most have done so, from the Jews to the Vietnamese. Muslims of different backgrounds need to do the same; lest they become a problem for themselves and the rest of us.

Trevor Phillips, the non-white British Labour politician and anti-racism leader, who originally coined the term 'Islamophobia' declared recently: '

> We are now in a different world from the 60s and 70s. What we should be talking about is how we reach an integrated society, one in which people are equal under the law, where there are some common values...They want to come here not just because of jobs but because they like this country—its tolerance, its eccentricity, its parliamentary democracy, its energy in the big cities.

However, speaking in April, Phillips, the former head of Britain's Equalities and Human Rights Commission, said he had 'got almost everything wrong' on Muslim immigration and is now concerned at how large numbers of Muslims in the West are creating 'nations within nations.'

We in Australia need to be clear about our goals as a nation in this regard, every bit as much as Britain does. If we seek to include Muslims within a cohesive, secular society, we need them to give up the ideas of dominance and religious militancy, exclusion and apartness from 'infidels' that characterise conservative Islam. If, for whatever reason, this does not happen, then we run the risk of alien and potentially hostile enclaves developing in our society and of mullahs and their followers seeking Islamization within our borders.

Here, therefore, is how we should surely shape up the debate. We see Islam as a religious, not a racial issue. We do not want, or *should* not want to import religious fanatics to these shores, or encourage them to believe that they are welcome to pursue their agendas here. The question is, how do we hold that line without becoming discriminatory on sweeping racial or religious grounds? That, surely, is a debate we can have in measured and rational terms. It is, in any case, the debate we *must* have.

2: We must champion apostasy from Islam

About six weeks ago, in a televised address during Ramadan, the leading Muslim cleric in Egypt, Ahmed al-Tayeb, Grand Imam of al-Azhar University in Cairo, who is hailed as one of the leading 'moderate' teachers in the Islamic world, denounced apostasy from Islam as 'grand treason'. He stated categorically:

> Those learned in Islam and the imams of the four schools of jurisprudence consider apostasy a crime and agree that the apostate must either renounce his apostasy or else be killed.

This prominent cleric has been a critic of ISIS, of Salafist radicals and of the Muslim Brotherhood. He was appointed by former dictator, President Hosni Mubarak as Grand Mufti of Egypt and has been welcomed by Pope Francis to the Vatican. Yet here he is backing condign penalties for apostasy from his religion.

Pew Centre surveys across the Muslim world show that many Muslims do *not* support such penalties; though a majority of Muslims in Egypt, Palestine, Jordan, Pakistan, Afghanistan and Malaysia do so. In (Sunni) Saudi Arabia, Sudan and Somalia, as well as (Shia) Iran death for apostasy is official state policy and has been defiantly defended against UN principles of the universal human right to freedom of religion.

Whether or not you are Christian (of any denomination), or some other religion, or no religion at all—and the census this week asks you that question—you have a stake in this matter, as a citizen of Australia and a resident of the Western world. Remember that, in the long struggle for religious liberty and freedom of expression in the West, the right to apostasy—the right to reject religious orthodoxy or religion itself—was one of the hardest rights to secure. Now we take it for granted. That battle has most definitely *not* been won in the Islamic world. Ahmed al-Tayeb's televised address is just one more sobering indication of this fact.

This issue should concern us, because the West in general is taking in more and more Muslim immigrants. Either we are clear that we intend to assimilate them into a culture of secular norms and freedoms, or we encourage Islamic mullahs—especially if they are Wahhabis from Saudi Arabia or Shias from Iran—to believe that they can perpetuate the culture of fear and intimidation within Islam that prevails in so much of the Muslim world. This is the cutting edge of the current fraught debate about Muslim immigration and religious tolerance. The imam's address in Cairo, as well as numerous other developments show that we cannot afford complacency or indifference. We should be on the front foot.

The debate over whether or not apostasy calls for the death penalty has a long history in Islam, but it now needs to end with an unequivocal denunciation of the very idea of intimidation for apostasy, to say nothing of the death penalty. In that regard, there is serious work to do. The Muslim Brotherhood advocate Tariq Ramadan has gone so far as to say, 'free and conscious choice and willing submission are foundational to the very definition of Islam. Therefore, someone leaving Islam or converting to another religion must be free to do so and her/his choice must be respected.'

That, however, is far from being the prevailing norm within the Muslim world and the eminent Egyptian cleric has just made things worse and more confused. Apostates again and again find themselves in danger. Even if they are not arrested and condemned for a private renunciation of Islam, they face severe threats if they seek to speak out against it. Both cases are documented in Ibn Warraq's illuminating book of 2003, *Leaving Islam: Apostates Speak Out*. If you are interested in freedom of religion and the debate about Islam in Australia, this book is required reading.

As a case in point, Syed Ahsan Gilani, a young Pakistani activist who, in 2012, co-founded the Atheist & Agnostic Alliance Pakistan, deserves our attention. Having grown up a practicing Sunni Muslim, he rejected Islam in his late teens, concluding that the Qur'an was full of obscurantist mumbo-jumbo. He has worked over the past four years for the acceptance of religious dissent in his own country and to provide counsel and support for those leaving Islam. Now *there* is a young man who deserves the Voltaire Award for freedom of speech! He is not a celebrated TV personality and media star, with a comfortable lectureship at a good university.

My own favourite figure from the early centuries of Islam is the great philosophical sceptic and apostate al-Rawandi, who lived in the early 9th century. He held that prophecy in general and that of Muhammad in particular was nonsense and that reason not faith should guide our thinking. He wrote that the Qur'an, far from being a work of inerrant revelation, was neither clear nor comprehensible, nor of any practical value. If this individual could have the insight and courage to so argue at the time of Islam's first ascendancy, we have no excuse at all for doing otherwise.

A century after al-Rawandi, the great al-Razi rejected dogmatism, taught that no authority was beyond criticism and was scathing of those 'billy goats with long beards', the mullahs, who spouted lies and imposed on the feckless masses blind obedience to the 'words of the master'. An admirer of the Greek philosophers, Plato, Aristotle, Epicurus and others, he taught that critical reason is superior to claims of 'revelation' and that 'salvation' is possible only through philosophy.

Do not, therefore, corrupt young minds with the Qur'an, is the lesson of al-Razi. Rather, give them Aristotle's *Eudaemian Ethics* and encourage them to develop critical minds, public spirited virtues and scientific knowledge. This must, surely, be the message of the West in our time. This should be our answer to Ahmed al-Tayeb's Ramadan address: we wish, like al-Rawandi and al-Razi, to see the world enlightened and liberated, not subject to dogmatic religion, which everyone should feel free to leave behind.

3: Turkey's purges: Reichstag fire pretext or defence of democratic institutions?

On the night of 15-16 July, there was what appeared to be an unexpected and badly bungled attempted *coup d'état* in Turkey. Over 200 people lost their lives in the violence. The Erdogan government swiftly exerted complete control and began arresting or standing down an astounding number of military officers, policemen, judges, civil servants and, most mysteriously of all, school teachers and academics. Some 2,000 of those arrested were accused only of having 'insulted' Erdogan.

Almost none of this makes sense. There was no build-up of tensions suggesting a possible coup. Allegations by the Erdogan government that it had been orchestrated from the United States by the Sufi cleric in exile Fethullah Gulen were not only categorically denied by Gulen, but were without any evident foundation. There has, subsequently, been speculation that the coup was either a provocation organized by Erdogan's own security forces as a pretext to crack down on his real or perceived enemies; or that it was a rushed and abortive attempt by secularists in the military to head off a purge that they had learned was coming anyway. Yet Erdogan accused Gulen.

There was very soon an excellent summation of the matter on Wikipedia, but well before it appeared the scale of the crackdown and the obvious purging of people who cannot possibly have had anything to do with a coup attempt led me to write a column for *The Australian* in which I attempted to put the unfolding drama into a serious historical context. The scale and arbitrariness of what was happening were, I suggested, akin to Hitler's state of emergency after the Reichstag fire in 1933, or Stalin's reaction to the assassination of Sergei Kirov in 1934, than to the United States in the 1950s. Others had seen the analogy with the Reichstag fire. None, to my knowledge, had drawn the analogy with Stalin and the Kirov murder.

The strangest aspect of the whole matter is the accusation that the mastermind behind the coup was Gulen. The regime seeks to move away from Turkey's secular political culture in the direction of an Islamized state. Erdogan has made that clear for some time. That has aroused concern among secular Turkish citizens and within the EU, which Turkey aspired to join. The armed forces had been the bulwark of the secular order for decades. But Gulen is not a secularist. He is the leader of a deeply resourced Islamist movement which seeks, by its own account, to modernize Islam and create a cadre of Muslims educated and trained to run a modern country. For all the accusations Erdogan and his ministers have made, they have nowhere spelled out why Gulen would have wanted to overthrow the Justice and Development Party.

The rhetoric of the Erdogan regime has been startling. It has threatened to go to war with any country that protects Gulen, which is astonishing, not least because the United States currently does so. The call to reintroduce the death penalty is chilling. The insistence, without the provision of any credible evidence, that the coup was a conspiracy orchestrated by Gulen from the United States; the arrogation by the regime of powers under the three month state of emergency to take extra-legal steps to 'cleanse' the state apparatus and armed forces of perceived enemies are all worrying indications that the Erdogan's agenda is not the restoration of democracy, but the installation of an Islamist dictatorship. What, exactly, therefore does he hold against the Gulen movement? There has been no clarification.

One thing has become clear in the wake of the coup: the Gulen movement is very large and well organized. Given the long history of violent conflicts within Islam, it must be assumed that there were deep tensions between Erdogan and Gulen and that the Turkish President has decided to both discredit and crush a rival whom he sees as a danger to his own ambitions. The Reichstag fire of 27 February 1933 was exploited by Hitler to declare a state of emergency in Germany and basically abolish the rule of law. He thought it was the signal for a Communist uprising. Wild allegations to this effect were quickly made, but no credible evidence was ever produced. Bear that in mind when reading of allegations against the Gulenists.

Hitler, driven by vengeful phobias rather than evidence, declared to his closest colleagues: 'This is a God-given signal...If this fire is, as I believe, the work of the Communists, then we must crush out this murderous pest with an iron fist!' Erdogan himself, whether or not he was consciously mimicking Hitler, declared almost at once that the coup attempt was a 'God-given' chance to crush the opposition. He is proceeding to attempt exactly that. If he does, as he has threatened, reintroduce the death penalty, we should note very closely who is put to death. Given that Erdogan has been on the record as declaring that democracy is just a train you use to get to your destination, then you get off it, what we are seeing looks distinctly like disembarkation.

Stalin did something similar in 1934-35, in a prelude to the Great Terror of 1936-38, in which, according to the KGB's own records, some 750,000 people were executed and the GULAG crammed with others. In Stalin's case, it was not the Communists who were the target, of course, but a wide range of political oppositionists in Leningrad and around the country, who were labelled 'White Guard elements' and 'counter-revolutionaries'. He then used the same pretext to arrest many of his opponents from within even the Bolshevik opposition. Again, the analogy is striking.

Perhaps the best account of the Kirov murder and its consequences is by Oleg Khlevniuk, in his 2015 biography of Stalin, based on unprecedented access to Soviet archives. What he makes clear is that, contrary to various conspiracy theories that have been around for decades, Stalin did not *arrange* the murder of Kirov. He did, however, exploit it to accuse his political rivals (and former allies) Grigori Zinoviev and Lev Kamenev of having planned it. They were convicted, but based on 'blatantly fabricated' evidence. As things stand, there are disturbing signs that this is the game Erdogan is playing. But thus far there does not seem to be even fabricated evidence against Gulen, only sweeping accusations.

Erdogan has now become a serious problem and it could soon get much worse—just as Putin has become a greater and greater danger over the past decade and a half. Spurned by the EU, Erdogan has in effect declared 'there is a world elsewhere' and has taken his stand under the banner of radical Islam. He has become a Putin-like figure and his Turkey is now a highly unreliable member of NATO, a looming danger to its small European and Mediterranean neighbours (think Cyprus to begin with) and a further case of the implosion of order in the Middle East. Whatever our perceptions or sympathies with regard to Turkey's domestic affairs, these geopolitical concerns must be thought through both quickly and very realistically, lest things unravel in a very serious way indeed.

In May last year, Erdogan gave a public speech to a huge crowd in Istanbul, on the 562nd anniversary of the Ottoman conquest of Constantinople in 1453. He lionized not just that conquest—which no-one in the West should celebrate—but the Muslim conquests as a whole, beginning with the first raids and small wars by Muhammed. The crowd roared its approval and a chant went up, 'Here is the army! Here is the commander!' Make no mistake, Erdogan has a strong base of support in Turkey—as Hitler did in Germany. Neither his reasonableness nor his intentions can be trusted. His Turkey has become a problem for Europe for the first time since the murderous wholesale expulsion of Turkey's Greeks, in the 1920s. A great deal now depends on how that problem is handled, diplomatically and strategically.

After much of this appeared in my column in *The Australian* in the last week of July, the Turkish Ambassador, Vakur Gokdenizler, took the somewhat unusual step of responding in a letter to the editor of the paper:

> I am appalled by Paul Monk's article ('Make no mistake: this is Erdogan's Reichstag fire', 27/7) and think his criticisms of the measures the Turkish government was forced to take were extreme. Given the seriousness of the challenges that Turkey is facing, his analogy of the events of July 15 with that of the Reichstag fire is incredible.
>
> The bloody coup attempt staged by a faction of the Turkish armed forces targeting our democratic and legitimate government and our constitutional order was defeated by the command chain of the Turkish armed forces together with the Turkish people who stood up against it.
>
> In the same manner, all political parties and members of the Turkish national assembly stood by democracy and democratic institutions. The joint declaration issued during the extraordinary meeting of the assembly on July 16 is a testimony to this unity.

When I shared this with a good friend who is a specialist on Putin's Russia and human rights and democracy more generally, he replied simply, 'High praise indeed!'

His Excellency would, no doubt, be just as appalled by a limerick I wrote in the wake of the abortive (or staged) coup:

> There once was a despot in Turkey
>
> Whose motives were really quite murky.
>
> He claimed to love justice,
>
> But his actions non-plussed us;
>
> And his rhetoric? Well, that was just quirky.

Will maestro Erdogan and his cronies prove me wrong and enlarge the rule of law and civil liberty in Turkey, rather than compress it? I would be relieved to see it. I don't believe I shall.

4: Edward Snowden and the open society

Think Inc, is a new venture that is doing wonderful work bringing cutting edge thinking to Australia across the spectrum of science and civil society. They recently hosted a public forum in which Edward Snowden was beamed in from Moscow. The evening was a great success and there seems to have been no attempt by the authorities, domestic or foreign, to sabotage or censor it in any way. Snowden's theme was the open society and its enemies; a classic Popperian topic. But he was talking about technologies that did not exist in Karl Popper's day. It is the implications of those new technologies that sit at the heart of Snowden's actions and his exile.

The Rationalist Society of Australia has been given a complete transcript of Snowden's interview that evening by Julian Morrow of *The Chaser*. We are publishing an edited version of the transcript in this issue of the magazine. Here, as a set of prefatory remarks, I'd like to draw attention to a number of the most salient points Snowden made in the course of over an hour. Having previously expressed some scepticism about his actions and his exile in Moscow and not having been particularly impressed by the documentary about him, *Citizen Four*, I must say that I was most impressed by him in person and am delighted that Think Inc was able to set up the forum for him to speak live.

I should add that it is not, of course, only Popper's work that comes to mind in the context of Snowden's actions, experience and articulate opinions. Wolfgang Sofsky's *Privacy: A Manifesto* (2009) and Tzvetan Todorov's *The Inner Enemies of Democracy* (2014) are recent books that take up at length the key questions of freedom of speech and the dangers to our liberties from government secrecy and surveillance. There is a broad tradition going back to Athens and to the figure of Socrates that hails freedom of critical inquiry and speech against government—or popular—censorship and harassment. And we should remember that Socrates was condemned to death not by a tyrant but by the Athenian democracy itself, for challenging its prejudices.

Yet among the most outspoken critics of Snowden and his disclosures, the great Russian exile and champion of democracy, civil liberty and human rights, Garry Kasparov, is especially notable. Writing in his 2015 book *Winter Is Coming: Why Vladimir Putin and the Enemies of the Free World Must Be Stopped*, Kasparov dismissed Snowden as a 'negligible figure' and wrote, scathingly:

> Snowden's first statement from Russia...included Putin's Russia—a police state and patron of despotism worldwide—on his list of nations that 'stand against human rights violations carried out by the powerful rather than the powerless.' Excuse me? Putin's many political prisoners would disagree quite strongly, as would the many opposition

members who have had their emails hacked and their phone calls recorded by the KGB in attempts to discredit them. And Snowden could have been more respectful of the many injured and dead among journalists and his fellow whistle-blowers in Russia... As someone who grew up under the all-seeing eye of the KGB and who is fighting its modern rebirth under Vladimir Putin, it is exasperating to hear blithe comparisons between the NSA and other Western spy or law enforcement organizations and the vicious internal security regimes of the USSR and East Germany. The NSA is to the Stasi what a bad hotel is to a maximum security prison. It is not what a government does with data that defines it; but what it does to human beings.

We should hold Kasparov's observations in mind as we follow Snowden's remarks in the Think Inc interview. As a great American friend of mine declared last year, 'Anyone who thinks Obama's America is a police state has never lived in a police state.' Kasparov has. Snowden, ironically, now does—in the name of freedom of expression and freedom from surveillance.

Morrow began by asking Snowden about whistleblowing and its perils. This is a subject close to my own heart as a dissenter from and critic of various aspects of intelligence, security and public policy making. Some years ago, I publicly defended Allan Kessing of Customs when he was accused of leaking a report to the press on organized crime and corruption at Sydney's international airport. The judge in his trial instructed the jury that they were to disregard the public interest argument and confine themselves to the question: had Kessing leaked the report or not? Surely, I urged, the public interest argument must be our decisive criterion in such matters. The findings of the report had been vindicated. Why was Kessing being prosecuted, rather than rewarded? My interest in Snowden stems from these kinds of concern.

He declared, in his Think Inc interview, that we are in the midst of 'a global war on whistle-blowing', not least in the United States, 'where the current president has brought forth more whistleblowing prosecutions than all other presidents combined.' He made no reference at this point to the suppression of whistle-blowers and dissenters in many other countries—Russia high among them; China, Iran and Turkey being others—by far more condign and lawless means than in the United States. Nevertheless, his point is sobering. The president in question, Barack Obama, can hardly be thought of as a nasty, anti-democratic would-be dictator, but the proliferation of prosecutions should give us pause.

As a result of Snowden's stance and the revelations he made possible, Obama actually came forward in January 2014 and said that while he could never condone what Snowden had done, the conversation about surveillance, privacy and legality was important for the nation to have and made the United States stronger as a nation. An 'independent' (government) inquiry was then commissioned to examine the consequences of Snowden's revelations and it concluded 'that despite [the surveillance program] operating for more than ten years it had never stopped a single terrorist attack.' This did not, however, lead to any relief for Snowden. He remained trapped in Moscow, with the US government pressuring all manner of democratic countries—successfully—to deny him asylum. Given that what he leaked is now in the public domain, why can he not be given a fair trial in open court?

One of the most astonishing moments in the conversation was Snowden's observation that he has made clear to the US government that he is perfectly willing to return to America to face trial, provided that he is *given* a fair trial in open court. Here is the passage in which he describes their response:

> From the very moment I departed the United States and this information first hit the newspapers continuing until today, I've told the United States government that I have a single condition for returning; and that's that I'm allowed to make my case to the jury, that I'm allowed to make a public interest defence, that they will not assert again these privileges of government that allowed them to create a closed courtroom—a secret courtroom where the public can't actually see what's going on. And do you know what the government said when I asked them about that? Would they agree with that? They sent me a letter signed by the Attorney General that said we promise not to torture you. I actually have that letter.

Yet Daniel Ellsberg, having leaked *The Pentagon Papers* in 1971, had his day in court and the case against him was thrown out on the basis that the Executive branch had abused its authority in its pursuit of him. Manifestly, things have deteriorated in the United States, if Edward Snowden cannot get a similar judicial hearing.

Snowden outlined in some detail how the system of surveillance works, not only in the United States, but in Australia. This is worth capturing, because the new technologies make possible levels of surveillance never possible in Ellsberg's time or earlier, although domestic espionage and security agencies had long practiced surveillance and the harassment of dissidents in a great many societies, going back thousands of years. Snowden made two separate but important points regarding such technologies and such surveillance: first, that they entail intrusions into our privacy of a systematic kind about which we ought to feel very concerned; secondly that the secrecy with which all this has been done has undermined the accountability of our political representatives and their civil servants in ways we should find troubling.

Since extended excerpts from Snowden's remarks follow, I won't quote them further at length here; but only observe that, listening to him, I found myself taken back in many ways to the 1980s, when I was reading *The Pentagon Papers* as part of the research for my PhD (on US counter-insurgency strategy in Southeast Asia and Central America throughout the Cold War) and found myself admiring Ellsberg for both the integrity of his thinking and the moral clarity of his actions. He stood then and Snowden stands now in what might be called a Socratic position. We might tell ourselves that such actions are in the public interest, but those who take such actions generally cannot count on public support or protection against the hounds of executive authority. Socrates, as I remarked earlier, was condemned to death by a democratic society's court system. Ellsberg has remained a pariah in many circles since 1971, though a hero in others. Snowden remains in exile in Moscow.

Listening to Snowden's responses to questions, first from Julian Morrow and then from the audience, I warmed to him. He was not, I concluded, a hair-brained, narcissistic opportunist (as he had initially been described by those in the US and elsewhere annoyed at what he had done) and he was not a traitor or deluded ideologue. He was a person standing in the tradition of American civil disobedience dating back to Henry David Thoreau, if not earlier; or at least that is how he now comes across. He takes his stance on the evils of secrecy in government, while accepting that some materials should be classified at least temporarily; and on the Bill of Rights—above all the First Amendment to the US Constitution, guaranteeing freedom of speech. Unless we stand with him on such very basic principles and rights, we are not serious about our liberties.

Moreover, as he put it, whistleblowing should not be necessary and should not be our first choice; because we'd like to believe that our institutions are sound enough to detect abuses and correct them internally, without the need for scandal and crisis. Yet our institutions are not doing this sufficiently. He cited the recent revelations of *The Panama Papers* as further evidence of this. And if we do not, as citizens of at least nominally liberal democratic societies, take clear-minded action to restore and maintain the integrity of institutions and hold them accountable, then 'we start allowing these institutional failures to progress and collapse down to the individual level, which ultimately is the level of culture, that is the point at which we become a closed society. And there's no recovering from that shy of revolution.'

He might have added that 'revolution' would itself be rather difficult to organize if there is total surveillance and that, in any case, modern revolutions have all too often yielded not liberation but tyranny of the most appalling and relentless kind. The point is that, as he expressed it, 'we don't want to be in the position where everyone is trying to act as an army for themselves, where everyone is trying to build castles to defend themselves. That's not what free societies are for.' He is, surely correct about this. Therefore, more of us ought to be concerned to understand what is at stake and to insist that, at the very least, someone like Snowden be given a free, open and fair trial for his alleged crimes. In fact, we should, I believe, be insisting that what he did was not criminal at all and that he deserves protection against those who seek to imprison and silence him. Yet the implications of doing that are considerable, since it could be seen as opening the floodgates to leakers with many different motivations.

An interesting parallel here is with Herve Falciani who, in 2008, downloaded an enormous amount of secret data from the computer networks of HSBC in Switzerland revealed massive tax evasion by global elites and the collusion of the bank in the handling of criminal profits and terrorist financing. Falciani's story, written up at length in the 30 May issue of *The New Yorker* this year, underscored the need for whistle-blowers and hackers to unearth these kinds of files, since the institutions in question, with literally trillions of dollars in play, have no incentive at all to come clean. For those who have not yet caught up with this debate, Gabriel Zucman's *The Hidden Wealth of Nations: The Scourge of Tax Havens* (University of Chicago Press, 2015), with a foreword by Thomas Piketty, is required reading.

When Falciani fled Switzerland, he was given asylum in France, because the French government realized what the data showed: that thousands of French citizens had been evading taxation by salting huge sums of money away in Swiss bank accounts. The same turned out—so Falciani's data demonstrated—to be the case for Germany, England, India, Russia, Greece and many other countries. Now, let it be said: there are good reasons for individuals and companies to be able to protect their wealth from the greedy hands of states. We should not view private property as something to which states have the right to help themselves at their own discretion. The question is how to strike the right balance—and do so across jurisdictions in a globalized world. And so it is with data of a non-financial kind. But whereas Falciani was given protection by France, Snowden has only—to this point—been able to find protection in Putin's Russia.

Just to the extent that we, as citizens of Australia, are concerned about the matter of privacy and surveillance, two questions naturally present themselves: what would it take for this country to offer Snowden asylum; and what is the extent of surveillance in Australia, in the name of counter-terrorism and national security? The answers are pretty evident: it is very difficult to imagine any Australian government (unless there was or had been a sudden overwhelming lurch to the Greens) seriously considering offering Edward Snowden asylum. The pressure from Washington to abstain from such a measure would be overwhelming, even if there was an inclination on the part of our own executive branch, or senior civil servants to consider such a step. Quite apart from the fact that our intimate intelligence alliance with the United States inhibits sympathy for Snowden at the official level, our own surveillance practices closely parallel the very things to which he has drawn attention in America.

What, therefore, is to be done by those of us who are paying attention and who feel troubled by these issues? Part of the challenge is simply becoming well informed. I am a scholar of international security affairs, a former senior intelligence analyst, a very freely outspoken critic of government secrecy and intelligence practices who knows the *Pentagon Papers* case probably better than anyone else in Australia; yet, until I listened to Edward Snowden, I remained poorly informed about his character and motives and too busy to have inquired into the revelations he facilitated in other than the most superficial manner. I remain heavily committed even now. This leaves me with the disquieting feeling that I should be doing more than I reasonably can, even as the situation is deteriorating—like the country's economic condition.

Among the most measured things Snowden said to Morrow was that those inclined to heroic activism should keep their powder dry and think about what they do before launching themselves headlong into civil disobedience or protest movements. He pointed out that it is too easy to become passionate and angry and this can inflame a complex situation. Instead, we need to be as quietly persistent and rational about the matter as we can—inquire, network, share information, launch or sign petitions, lobby our representatives and understand both our liberties and the new technologies. We could be in for a rough ride, if, for example, Donald Trump became US President and began to systematically violate the law. But for the time being, both in the US and here, there are many barriers to the breakdown of the rule of law. We should commit ourselves to understanding what courses of action are readily open to us and build a body of concern that is grounded and principled, not paranoid or angry.

By way of underscoring Snowden's basic sanity, it seems worth concluding by drawing attention to the first question put to him, after his interview with Morrow finished. The question was:

> From all the documents you've seen and your work in the NSA and all that, have you seen, or do you have any evidence of who is actually responsible for September 11th and is it the people that the mass media says?

This is a question from Paranoia Central, of course. It is representative of the disturbing plague of conspiracy theories and 'truther' movements that have sprung up in the United States ever since the assassination of President Kennedy in 1963. It was important that Snowden field it intelligently; and he did. As with the whole tenor of his exchange with Morrow, his answer did him credit, both for its rationality and its honesty.

Here is what he said:

> So, there's actually a lot of controversy in the United States right now about the classified annex to the 9/11 report. And the interesting thing about this conspiracy is that it's not saying, you know, that it's an inside job or there were space aliens or pyramids or anything like that. But in fact there were a lot of connections between our allies in the Saudi Arabian government and some of the attackers that continued even while they were within the United States. This is something that the government is not very wild about declassifying because of the diplomatic ramifications; and it's not certain, of course, that there was any actual operational connection there. But it is something that's been concealed from the public for nearly 15 years now and we probably should know.

This is the tone and stance of a man fully in possession of his critical faculties and his sense of proportion. Given what he has been through since leaving the United States and the uncertainties in his current position, it is to his credit that he remains so grounded. That is, perhaps, the most significant take away from the evening organized so well by Think Inc.

5: A splendid paean to art and dissent

Over the past half dozen years, at least three journalists of Australian origin or based in Australia have written first class books about contemporary China. The first was Richard McGregor, in 2010. The second was Rowan Callick, in 2013. The third is Madeleine O'Dea, this year. O'Dea's is easily as good as the other two and completely trumps (if one can now comfortably use that verb) all mealy mouthed apologetics for the repressive China of Xi Jinping.

McGregor's *The Party: The Secret World of China's Communist Rulers* was a brilliantly incisive expose of the huge Communist Mafia that holds the world's largest country under its thumb. It illuminated the structure and practices of the Party in the era prior to the ascension of the overweening premier princeling Xi Jinping, under whom many chickens are coming home to roost.

Callick's *Party Time: Who Runs China and How*, three years later, updated McGregor's work and provided its readers with a wonderfully judicious portrait of a nation teetering between maturing as a modern state and stumbling into an era of renewed tyranny and possibly confounding conflicts.

O'Dea, who spent more time in China than either of the others has done, has given us a beautifully crafted and immensely readable book which moves back and forth between the narrative of historical events and the personal stories and artistic endeavours of some of contemporary China's most imaginative and free-spirited citizens.

The Phoenix Years: Art, Resistance and the Making of Modern China is required reading for all those who seek to understand both how China has stumbled repressively through the past forty years and how its finest citizens have persisted in trying to imagine a better, freer China. In interweaving the macro-economic and political with the personal and artistic, O'Dea does not put a foot wrong.

The book is well-paced, vividly written, based on deeply enriching personal encounters and observations and grounded in completely sound scholarship. Those who keep repeating the weary and fallacious mantra that Chinese culture is incompatible with democratic norms and that the Communist Party, instead of being criticized for human rights abuses should be held in awe for 'lifting hundreds of millions of people out of poverty' in record time, need to have this book thrust under their noses.

O'Dea, as she tells us very early in her book, 'was there for the 'big story', in the 1980s, of how the opening up of China was revolutionising its economy'. She was there again and again in the 1990s and the 2000s. Reading her book, I confess I more than once found myself reflecting that

I should have become a journalist in China instead of an intelligence analyst charged with thinking about it. She was able to travel far more widely doing her work than I was ever permitted to do in the course of mine. Such are the bizarre constraints of the secret intelligence world!

It is immensely refreshing to read O'Dea's well-informed and forthright defences of Wei Jingsheng and Liu Xiaobo, whose lengthy incarcerations by the Communist Party for their principled, articulate and peaceful democratic dissent constitute a damning indictment of the Chinese regime. She tells their stories and quotes their words in context. That is good to see.

Their warnings, about dictatorship coming back if the Party refused to open the path to political reform and liberal democracy, are being borne out under the neo-Maoist Xi Jinping. As O'Dea observes:

> The intense crackdown on China's civil society, which began with the ascension of President Xi Jinping in late 2012, is now in its fourth year and shows no sign of slackening. Instead, an ever widening circle of people is being caught up in a campaign to silence alternative voices. In July 2015 a major police operation targeting China's rights lawyers was launched across the nation. More than 300 people were picked up for questioning and nineteen were charged after months in secret detention. The severity of the charges shocked even seasoned observers of China's human rights record.

She points out that the state conducts surveillance, censorship, repression and the strangling of critical debate to an extent that is both extraordinary by Western standards and profoundly counter-productive from the point of view of China's well-being and further development.

The soul of the book, however, breathes in her account of the lives and artistic endeavours of a range of people whose names are almost certainly unknown to more than a small circle of Australians who have paid attention to Chinese cultural affairs, even in the diaspora, over the past generation: Huang Rui, Zhang Xiaogang, Gonkar Gyatso, Aniwar, Guo Jian, Sheng Qi, Bei Dao, Mang Ke, Cao Fei, Jia Aili and Pei Li, all born between 1952 and 1985.

The link between the two themes or strands of the book is formed early on, where O'Dea informs her readers that 'when China's most famous dissident, Liu Xiaobo, winner of the 2010 Nobel Peace Prize, was writing about what influenced him most deeply in his formative years, he cited the poetry of Bei Dao and Mang Ke and the art of Huang Rui.'

As I read this book, I found myself highlighting numerous passages indicative of the soundness of the author's knowledge, the maturity of her prose and the poignancy of the stories she tells. There are many passages I would have liked to quote. But above all, I found myself thinking that O'Dea has done us all a great service by bringing together the disparate stories of her artists and showing how their creativity has been a constant struggle against regime repression.

That is the direct testimony of these free spirits, for whom the death of Mao in 1976 was a liberation, the 1978 Democracy Wall a spring time of freedom of expression, the open-minded General Secretary Hu Yaobang a hero and the brutal crushing of the popular democracy movement in June 1989 a defining moment. Their vision for China's future should be ours.

6: We must rise to the China challenge

The debate over the rising power and ambition of China is heating up all over Australia. It is important that we have this debate, openly and vigorously. It is even more important that it generate wider and deeper understanding of what is at stake for this country as China presses its evident aspiration to become the hegemonic power in East and Southeast Asia.

The recent brouhaha over Sam Dastyari's indiscretion is only one of many incidents of recent months whose common denominator is China's growing reach and its active attempts to expand both its hard and soft power. Beijing's attempt to sponsor celebrations of Mao Zedong in both Sydney and Melbourne was another; the Ausgrid episode a third; the Kidman investment a fourth. Concerns about Chinese espionage and infiltration of the Chinese community in Australia are yet another aspect of the situation. There have been many others.

Beijing's dismissal of the Hague's ruling on the South China Sea and the muted response to this at the recent ASEAN Forum throw into high relief the geopolitical context within which our concerns closer to home must be seen. Those still befuddled by all the rhetoric on this should read Bill Hayton's *The South China Sea: The Struggle for Power in Asia* (Yale University Press, 2014).

At an even broader level, China's relentlessly increasing military expenditure, which has been growing by double digit increments annually for a generation—points not only to China becoming more powerful, but to it becoming of rapidly increasing concern to many of its neighbours.

Terence Foo's letter to the editor in this newspaper last Thursday brought out the deep confusion that prevails about all this in many quarters. He wrote that 'the amount of China bashing in the media in the past few weeks has been astounding'. He referred to both Paul Dibb and Peter Jennings as 'hawkish anti-China experts' and expressed a worry that 'these people will help put Australia on a warpath with China'.

Doubtless, Foo is more comfortable with Dick Woolcott, Hugh White, Twiggy Forrest, Paul Keating and the late Malcolm Fraser suggesting that Australia distance itself from the United States and 'accommodate' China's ambitions and sense of entitlement. Ross Garnaut declared a few years ago that China is simply resuming its 'natural position' as the greatest power in the world, after an anomalous era of Western preponderance.

Foo concluded: 'It is an insult for Chinese such as me for any Australian to think that China wants to invade us. If China really had the desire, it would have done so 600 years ago during the time of Admiral Zheng He.' This strange remark, rather than being shrugged off as simply eccentric, is worth using to make a few points about present and emerging realities.

The famous voyages of Zheng He, in the early 15th century, before the Ming dynasty became introverted, were the last time China had a respectable blue water navy. Its explicit ambition now is to develop a very substantial one and to become the primary naval power in the Western Pacific and Southeast Asia by the mid-21st century.

These are not the claims of an 'anti-China hawk'. This has been part of China's strategic plan for several decades. That plan is maturing. It is incompatible with US strategic primacy in the Western Pacific and its alliance systems in East and Southeast Asia. These are the most fundamental of current strategic realities. Drawing attention to them is not 'hawkish', or an insult to anyone. It simply means that one is not sleepwalking while the world changes.

We have a very real stake in all this. We depend crucially on the current order. The consequences for us should that order be overturned and replaced by Chinese predominance are anything but attractive, given that China remains a harsh dictatorship that bullies its neighbours. Foo declares that the very idea that 'China wants to invade us' is 'an insult'. But the question is not whether China will invade Australia in the crude military sense. It is how the region will operate should China displace the United States as the dominant power.

In his masterful survey of these issues, *The China Challenge: Shaping the Choices of a Rising Power*, published just last year, Thomas Christensen, former US deputy assistant secretary of state for East Asian and Pacific Affairs, argued that avoiding a Sino-American conflict 'will require a strong US presence in Asia combined with deft diplomacy, to...persuade a large but still developing country with a nationalist chip on its shoulder to contribute to the international system...', rather than seek to shoulder it aside.

In another serious contribution to the debate last year, *China's Coming War with Asia*, Jonathan Holslag articulated a set of concerns about that 'nationalist chip' on China's shoulder and the trouble it foreshadows. What few analysts care to point out is that nationalism is the least of it. The core problem is the Communist Party itself, which foments xenophobia and historical grievance in order to buttress its threadbare political legitimacy.

To complicate all this further, we face the prospect of Donald Trump becoming President of a United States whose redneck heartland also seems to have a nationalist chip on its shoulder. Such a development would make all our lives more dangerous and difficult. But it would not eliminate the underlying reasons for concern about China's rise and behaviour. On the contrary, it would exacerbate them.

Both World Wars and the Cold War were fought to sustain an international order of politically and economically liberal trading states. Australia has always been committed to and has benefited immeasurably from such an international order. That order has always been led by the Anglophone powers.

If that was to change while China remains illiberal and aggrieved, it would be very much to our disadvantage, without 'invasion' even being contemplated. We must rise to this challenge and actively seek to sustain the liberal international order—whatever exertions it takes.

7: The dog day afternoon that confounded the pundits

Just before last weekend's AFL Preliminary Finals, I ran a check on what odds bookies and pundits were offering on the Geelong vs Sydney and GWS vs Bulldogs games. With modest variations, both saw the first game as too hard to call, but the second as heavily favouring GWS. They were wrong in both cases. There are interesting and important lessons to be drawn from that, as regards statistics, prediction markets and gambling.

The single most scientific set of odds I could find—from a professional analyst of the game, not a bookie—put the odds as 50/50 in the Geelong vs Sydney game and 75/25 in favour of GWS against the Bulldogs. These estimates were not gamed to make money. They were based on rigorous analysis of season long data about the four teams and the criteria that had been determining the outcome of matches both this year and in years gone by.

The first lesson, prior to any consideration of the outcome, is how a football fan responds to statistical odds at all. Personally, as a Victorian, I was keen to see both Geelong and the Bulldogs win. Should I have allowed that to weigh in the scales against what the best data analysis was suggesting? Or should I have put good money on the Bulldogs, not simply out of a passion for the perennial Victorian under dogs, but because if they happened to win I'd triple my money?

As it happens, I'm not a gambling man. But betting on sports is now rampant and aggressively marketed, which makes an understanding of odds, statistics and prediction rather important. It has often and rightly been remarked that gambling is a tax on the poor and the stupid. It is a form of folly, in which the overwhelming majority of people inevitably—and predictably—lose their money. But it is possible to be canny about it, as at cards, and it is certainly possible to be scientific about odds and statistics.

What are we to make of the fact that Sydney jumped Geelong and beat them decisively, while the GWS vs Bulldogs game went right down to the proverbial wire and the Bulldogs won? The superficial answer would be that the experts got it wrong and that this shows the hollowness of data analytics and the scientific approach to such matters. The second lesson, however, is that that would be an error. It would be akin to the common illusion that meteorologists are hopelessly inaccurate and that weather cannot be forecast. In reality, meteorology in our time is a very well calibrated science.

The two football outcomes certainly demonstrate the wonderful, irreducible uncertainties in sport (which is why so many of us love it). But they don't by any means suggest that the scientific analysis is a waste of time that generates illusory odds. As with meteorology, though, the amount of random variation among the many variables involved in a game of football means that predictions can only ever be approximations. Over a long series of games, good analytics will do better than the average punter. For most individual games the same will be true. But there will always be outliers.

A little reflection suggests that, of course, this has to be the case. What would be the point of cheering wildly for the underdogs if there was no possibility of them winning? When GWS pulled ahead by 14 points early in the final quarter last Saturday, I found myself thinking 'Here we go! The odds were that this would happen and the Giants are probably going to break the game open now.' Perhaps the Giants themselves thought so at that point. The Dogs, however, had other ideas.

This brings us to the third lesson. Back in the 1990s, then North Melbourne coach Denis Pagan remarked that, at the elite level, 90% of the game is played 'above the shoulders'. Presupposing roughly equal levels of fitness and skill, he was implying, the chaotic psychology of motivation, emotion, morale and team cohesion determined almost everything that happened on a football field. If that's so, how can we ever get the analytics right?

The role of psychology was surely evident last weekend. After a week off, Geelong started the game half asleep and Sydney charged out of the blocks, kicked the first eight goals of the match and were never headed. In the other game, the Giants appear to have come to the game believing their own propaganda and seeing themselves already playing off in the Grand Final against Sydney, whom they had already decisively defeated in the Qualifying Final. The Bulldogs went at them like terriers, would not let go and got over the line by a kick.

How does this square, though, with data analytics? The answer is that the data over time evens out the random variations and psychological flip flops and shows us strong trends and general patterns. As with a game of dice, no roll is predictable, but over large numbers of throws broad statistical patterns are in fact clearly discernible. They don't give us certainty, which is not available; but they do give us our best understanding of what the odds are against which we are betting in any given case.

There is a lot of very good work being done right now in prediction analytics and the analysis of chaotic processes. Sport is simply an arena in which masses of us see the uncertainties and challenges of life literally gamed and we often prefer to run with our hopes and passions rather than with coldly rational calculation. As long as we are not betting the house on the outcome, no harm is done by this. That's where rational calculation comes back in, though: don't bet the house; especially if you have no understanding of the odds.

Come the Grand Final, what odds? My head says Sydney, though my heart hopes the Doggies can go from three to four great wins—against the odds.

8: We need to Locke in our principles of toleration

Several weeks ago, in the wake of the twitter storm about Sonia Kruger and Muslim immigration, I wrote in these pages that we need to keep clearly in mind the distinctions between race and religion, religion and fanaticism. Islam is a religion. It has nothing to do with race, any more than Christianity does. The problem we have is with fanatical Muslims on religious grounds. That problem has to be dealt with in those terms.

Making these distinctions did not save me from abuse by various regressive Leftists, who asserted—like the Foreign Editor of *The Age*, Maher Mughrabi—that the distinctions I had made were a lot of nonsense and that 'of course' criticism of Islam is 'racist'. One lecturer in critical thinking at the University of Sydney, no less, denounced me on Twitter as a high brow version of Neo-Nazi racists, a photo of whom accompanied his text.

Such deeply confused polemics throw into high relief how important it is to hammer these distinctions into our public and political consciousness, so that they set the terms of the debate. For if we are to avoid serious social conflict over the challenge posed to Western secular society by aggressive Islam, it would be in everyone's interest to understand that the issue is, indeed, one of religion and not one of race.

Religious concerns have underpinned recent tentative moves in both the United States and the EU to curtail the massive spending by Saudi Arabia on the building of Wahhabi Islamist infrastructure in the West. Based on principles of toleration hammered out in the West since the 17th century—notably in John Locke's *Letter Concerning Toleration* of 1689—all religions are allowed to worship unmolested. This is not so in Saudi Arabia. There, no religion other than Wahhabi Sunni Islam is permitted. No churches, synagogues, Buddhist or Hindu temples can be built.

Over the past few decades, the Saudi regime has spent a staggering $100 billion to build Wahhabi mosques, madrasas and other facilities around the world. They are used to propagate an objectionable religious culture which is singularly intolerant and reactionary. Belatedly and cautiously, moves are now afoot to curtail the influx of Saudi money to fund such activities. Note well, that the target here is the Wahhabi Sunni sect of Islam. It is not Arabs and least of all Arabs who do not subscribe to this particular religious sect.

As Daniel Pipes, of the Middle East Forum, pointed out a few days ago, 'the Saudis have been arrogantly indiscreet about spending to promote Wahhabism'. The extremist literature provided to the public by Saudi-funded institutions was described more than a decade ago, in a Freedom House report, as 'a grave threat to non-Muslims and to the Muslim community itself.' Riyadh has also pumped money, Pipes points out, into the Council on

American-Islamic Relations, 'the most aggressive and effective Islamist organization in the United States.'

This pattern of Saudi funding and the widespread disturbances being caused by Muslim fanatics directly raise the issues pondered by John Locke, more than three hundred years ago, when he sought to articulate what were to become, most notably in the United States, broad-based principles of religious toleration: the relationship between the freedom to worship and the keeping of the civil peace.

'If solemn assemblies, observations of festivals, public worship be permitted to any one' religious sect, Locke wrote, meaning to Anglicans in England in the first instance, 'all these things ought to be permitted to the Presbyterians, Independents, Anabaptists, Arminians, Quakers, and others, with the same liberty.' He was, in other words, seeking liberty for religious dissenters. He added, however, 'if we may openly speak the truth, and as becomes one man to another, neither Pagan nor Mahometan, nor Jew, ought to be excluded from the civil rights of the commonwealth because of his religion.'

'The Gospel commands no such thing', he argued, 'and the commonwealth, which embraces indifferently all men that are honest, peaceable, and industrious, requires it not.' He was inclined, however, to draw the line at the Catholic religion, which he saw as answerable to a foreign principality—the Papacy—and especially given to inciting civil tumults and religious strife. That objection was overcome in time. It pertains, however, in our time, to various fanatical strands within Islam and must be dealt with.

The crux of the matter is that militant Islam poses a direct and deliberate threat to any secular liberal constitution. We must organize our defences and push back on a coherent and principled basis. When the regressive Left insists that no such defence is warranted and that any attempts to organize it are 'racist', they are not only being intellectually incoherent, they are setting up a situation in which the rise of Islam will inevitably be met by illiberal reactions. No one should want to see that happen.

Liberal democratic norms, properly understood, are not about treating any and every religion as self-contained and beyond criticism. They are about insisting that those who embrace religious beliefs, if they wish to be accepted within the liberal social order, must accept that their beliefs—often incomprehensible or rebarbative to others—are a private matter and must not be practised or propagated in such a way as to disturb the common peace.

Islam, as it is widely practiced and propagated in our time, does not meet these criteria sufficiently to leave the adherents of other religions or no religion at all comfortable with how things are unfolding. Wahhabi Islam, Iranian Shia Islam, the Islam of numerous militant sects in Africa, the Middle East and Asia are incompatible with liberal norms. These are not Arminians, Quakers or Presbyterians, or even Catholics. They seek violent theocratic revolution in the name of reactionary values. We do not owe them any favours or concessions. It is, on the contrary, they who must bow to the principles of toleration—or be excluded from its benefits.

9: Mockery of Islam cannot be forbidden

Last Monday, British journalist and broadcaster Douglas Murray, author of the satirical pamphlet *Islamophilia*, blogged that far from being something that should be frowned upon, mockery of Islam is a much needed antidote to its excessive severity and overweening claims to be taken seriously. He has a point that merits, dare I say it, serious thought.

His remark was all the more notable because it was made in response to the assertion by Mohammed Shafiq that 'our faith is not to be mocked'. Shafiq heads a body called the Ramadhan Foundation, in Manchester, has spoken out against extremism and terrorism since 2001 and has been warned by police of Islamist death threats against him. So he is not what one would call a Muslim firebrand.

Murray's responded to Shafiq that 'there is nothing special about Islam that means it cannot be mocked. In fact, it would be a very good thing (both for Muslims and everyone else) if it were mocked rather more.' This claim ought to be the basis for intelligent discussion in the context of our prolonged and often rather precious discussion of 'hate speech' and the famous '18C'.

Having been raised as a conservative Catholic, I am well acquainted with religious objections to the mockery of the tenets of faith or of ritual practices. Yet, as a young man, I was very struck by two aphorisms coined by Arthur Schopenhauer and Friedrich Nietzsche respectively, which suggested an attitude far closer to Murray's than to that of the parish priests where I grew up.

'What a bad conscience religion must have,' wrote Schopenhauer, 'is to be judged by the fact that it is forbidden under pain of such severe penalties to mock it.' Half a century later, Nietzsche wrote: 'Objection, evasion, happy distrust, pleasure in mockery are signs of health: everything unconditional belongs in pathology.' One might disagree with Schopenhauer and Nietzsche about many things, but these are striking observations.

Douglas Murray is plainly offended by the excessive seriousness with which Islam takes itself and by the violent threats constantly being issued against those who mock either Mohammed or the Qur'an. Anyone interested in civil society, freedom of expression and the principles of toleration ought to reflect open-mindedly on his exchange with Shafiq.

Right now in the cinemas, we can see Louis Theroux's *My Scientology Movie* and this summer the musical comedy *The Book of Mormon* will be staged in a theatre near you. The Scientologists are notoriously litigious, but there seems no danger that the cinemas screening Theroux's film will be bombed, or people coming out of them attacked. Mormons tend to be pretty earnest types and to take their absurd beliefs seriously, but there seems no likelihood that they will storm theatres when the musical is being performed or seek to assassinate its creators.

Why, asks Murray, should Islam be an exception in this regard? There are two reasons. From its inception, as spelled out in the Qur'an, Mohammed built into Islam execrations and dire threats against unbelievers, apostates and what he called 'hypocrites'. Those passages from the 'holy book' of Islam are cited again and again to justify acts of violence against 'blasphemers', apostates and infidels all over the world.

This is both disturbing and unacceptable. But the second reason is, in some ways, even more disturbing. It is that a body of thought has grown up in the West to the effect that criticism of Islam, whether substantive scholarship or sceptical raillery, is 'politically incorrect', 'inflammatory' or 'neo-colonial' in character and should be avoided. Under the aegis of this school of thought, 'toleration' means acceptance of conservative and even militant Islam pretty much on its own terms. This, of course, hamstrings civil society's response to the influx of Muslims into the West and the problem of militant Islam on the global stage.

We need new and better ground rules for civilizing Islam. The first such rule has to be that there can be no justification at all, whatever the Qur'an says, for violence or threats of violence against people for either criticism of Islam, or mockery of it. Toleration does not mean treating the religious beliefs or ideological positions of others as sacrosanct. It means respecting the humanity and civil rights of others, despite their often strange beliefs and feeling perfectly free to differ with them and to josh them about those beliefs.

Now mockery of the Murray kind presupposes something still hotly disputed: that the dogmatic claims of Islam are absurd and many of its conservative practices both objectionable and deserving of parody. Those things can only be established by discursive argument. Within the Muslim world even such argument is largely forbidden. If we intend to win the war of ideas with a resurgent Islam, we must both engage in such argument and insist on our right to do so.

If we are to absorb large numbers of Muslims into Western societies, it cannot be as Wahhabis or Salafists. It has to be as initiates into the freedoms of a secular society, which include scholarship, theatre and journalism that will openly challenge Islam. As with other religions, large and small, those who wish to cling to old traditions and ritual practices will be protected under the law from harassment or persecution. But the militant insistence that 'Islam will dominate' has to be discouraged and dismissed.

Mockery, as Douglas Murray argues, has a part to play in this. We could do with a film about Islam comparable to *The Life of Brian* which would enter into the broader culture and enable people to laugh until they cry about the absurdities at the heart of Islam. But we need, also, to press forward with both critical scholarship on the history of Islam and the active defence of cosmopolitan civil society against both reactionary rhetoric and threats of violence. That way lies a possible future in which dignity and good humour will prevail over prejudice and intimidation.

10: Trump's victory: rub your eyes and read the classics

The original models for modern constitutional democracies were the republics of Athens and Rome. They failed to keep their constitutions viable and fell to dictatorships: Athens to Alexander the Great; Rome to the Caesars. For many centuries after that, the conventional wisdom was that democratic republics do not work. The American founding fathers thought they could prove this wrong. Their design is now being seriously tested.

Each of the classical republics had plenty of warning of the danger of weakening republican institutions being trumped by demagogues and men on horseback. They were unable to remedy their defects and they fell. The victory of Donald Trump in yesterday's Presidential election is one of a series of signs, over the past couple of decades, that the American system of government is in trouble. The question is: can it haul itself back from the brink?

The decay of the Roman republic is still our most instructive case study in how representative institutions can become gridlocked, corrupted and dysfunctional. The rot set in after the defeat and destruction of Carthage, in 146 BCE. For America, the problems seem to date from the end of the Cold War. In Rome's case, a century of growing political crisis—without significant external enemies—culminated in the fall of the republic and the creation of the principate, the rule of Augustus Caesar.

The crisis in US institutions is not yet as grave as that in Rome, even a century before Augustus. But it is serious. And the US does have external enemies who view it with malign intent. We also live in an age in which things can move with extraordinary speed. It is, therefore, vital that the election of this rank demagogue by a disgruntled and largely ignorant mass of American voters concentrate minds about where the great republic in America is heading.

The expressions of alarm that Trump's rise has caused and the spooked reaction of global markets to his electoral victory centre on three things: his apparent incoherence and irresponsibility as regards geopolitics and alliance relationships; his narcissistic and amoral personality; and his populist rhetoric, stoking domestic xenophobia and racism. The markets are bracing themselves for volatility and policy shocks. America's allies, of whom this country is one, are facing years of uncertainty and strategic instability.

Rather than indulge in fevered speculation about the immediate future, we badly need to put Trump into historical perspective. The fate of the classical republics should be a key reference point. A second is the debates by the American founding fathers about how to set up a modern republic that would do better than Greece or Rome. A third is the reflections by Alexis de Tocqueville in his 1830s classic, *Democracy in America*. A fourth is that all modern 'democracies' have gone through crises and have generally emerged stronger from them.

Listening to the Trump campaign kept making me think of the figures who fought over the declining Roman republic; especially Lucius Cornelius Sulla, who seized power as dictator, rammed through constitutional reforms that he claimed would buttress the old order, but which in fact helped to undermine it, then retired and watched the crisis begin to deepen. Sulla was not a populist, as Trump is; but Trump brings Sulla to mind because in the name of reforming a decadent constitutional order he threatens to bring it down.

The famous exchanges, in 1787-88, between Alexander Hamilton, John Jay and James Madison that became known as *The Federalist Papers*, also come pressingly to mind in these circumstances. Those letters by three highly educated founders written to the American people were penned under the name 'Publius', signifying both their consciousness of Roman history and their concern to address a free public.

Their central preoccupation was to define the nature of 'popular government' such that freedom could be exercised without descending into anarchy. They saw themselves as conducting an experiment, as Hamilton expressed it, on behalf of all mankind. They specifically sought to devise what they called 'republican remedies' for 'the diseases most incident to republican government', so that free men could govern themselves well and not require an authoritarian sovereign of the kind prescribed by Thomas Hobbes, in his classic 17th century treatise *Leviathan*.

Tocqueville, a French observer writing half a century later, in the age of that controversial populist President Andrew Jackson, admired the vigour of American democracy. But he was concerned about two things: the dangers of a tyranny of the majority and the implications for public policy of the inevitable closing of the frontier and the 'filling up' of the continent, reducing outlets for the marginalized and disgruntled. On all these points and many others, this is a good time to read or –re-read Tocqueville—as a spur to thinking deeply about American democracy.

As for other democracies, it might be good to reflect on the checkered history of democracy in France since 1789. Hannah Arendt memorably wrote, in *On Revolution* (1963), that the French Revolution, which ended in dictatorship, had become the very model for modern revolutionaries; whereas the American Revolution, which was triumphantly successful, had been largely ignored. Between 1789 and 1958, France swung between republic and monarchy, democracy and dictatorship several times. Hence its current 'Fifth Republic'. Crises need not be terminal.

Alexander Hamilton began his first Federalist letter:

> After an unequivocal experience of the inefficacy of the subsisting federal government, you are called upon to deliberate on a new Constitution for the United States of America. The subject speaks its own importance; comprehending in its consequences nothing less than the existence of the Union, the safety and welfare of the parts of which it is composed, the fate of an empire in many respects the most interesting in the world.

We might all ponder these words, as we rub our eyes in astonishment that Donald Trump has become the embodiment of Uncle Sam in our time. For the American Constitution does need some rethinking. As perhaps does our own, too.

11: The infernal puzzle of anti-Semitism

I have always found anti-Semitism perplexing. I associate Jewishness with a religion that doesn't pester anyone; an intellectual culture that produces a disproportionate number of Nobel Laureates, comedians, musicians, philosophers, economists, novelists and philanthropists; and, perhaps not least, an outsider status with which, as an intellectual, I identify.

When I was a young man, I knew only one set of anti-Semites: Hungarian immigrants, who had come to Australia after the Second World War and the Communist takeover in Eastern Europe. They were neighbours and members of the Catholic parish in which I grew up. They were fine people in so many ways, but they espoused the most irrational and bigoted anti-Semitism. Moreover, they did so openly.

One of these neighbours, who was a wonderful cook and a motherly figure, would tell me that the Jews ran both the Communist movement and the world banks and would get us all one way or the other. I asked her, many years ago, after reading a fine book on the history of Budapest, whether she had frequented the old cafes on the Elizabeth Ring Road when she lived in the city before 1956. 'No,' she responded, 'because they were always full of dirty Jews.'

Another of our Hungarian neighbours, a gentle soul who cooked well and painted, said to me one afternoon, over a cup of tea in his living room, 'You probably think that this sounds crazy, Paul, but back in the 1930s the Jews were taking over everything in Europe and something had to be done.' The stunning dissonance between his quiet statement and the realities to which he was alluding has always astonished me.

I first read about the Holocaust, in William L. Shirer's *The Rise and Fall of the Third Reich*, when I was thirteen. It horrified me and continues to be a central preoccupation in my ongoing project of making what sense I can of the modern world and the human prospect. I simply could not reconcile the evident, basic humanity of these immigrant neighbours with the evils I had read about in appalling detail.

They exhibited no moral recoil at all from what Hitler and his willing executioners had done. For all I knew, they or their circles in Hungary may have been among those willing executioners. What was I supposed to say to them or do about their blatant expressions of racial prejudice and genocidal bigotry? In truth, I regarded these things as strange eccentricities and said nothing to them about the matter.

Yet at the same time, Jewish writers and singers and comedians were among the people I most admired; from Hannah Arendt and George Steiner, to Leonard Cohen and Bob Dylan, to Woody Allen and Jerry Seinfeld. I had been raised a Catholic and had learned to see the Hebrew Bible, or the 'Old Testament', as Christians call it, as a book of remarkable poetry and extraordinary tales. Nothing in it imparted to me the slightest sense that there was anything wrong with the Jews. Quite the contrary.

But for many years, I tended to put all this to one side, thinking that the problem had more or less been solved and that anti-Semitism was now universally condemned and, among all right thinking people, a thing of the past—because of the Holocaust, more than anything else. Only slowly have I come to realize that, alas, this is far from being the case.

The vehement revival of anti-Semitism in our time is often attributed, incorrectly, to the oppression by Israel of the Palestinian Arabs. Sometimes, more honestly, it is attributed to the very existence of Israel as a Jewish state in the Middle East. In these contexts, two things become conflated: anti-Zionism and anti-Semitism. The two are not the same. There have always been Jews who were anti-Zionists. And thoughtful, well-informed argument about the Zionist project, or more narrowly the behaviour of Israel as a state, has never bothered me to any great extent.

But the root of much anti-Zionism is anti-Semitism, not the other way around and this is especially the case within the Muslim world, where it goes back to Muhammad himself and the denunciations of the Jews as such in the Qur'an. Moreover, anti-Semitism in Europe and in North America has been on the rise in troubling ways and it demands explanation, because it is out of all proportion to any empirical evidence or rational justification—as has always been true with this especially long-lasting and pernicious version of racism.

What precipitated my interest in collecting my thoughts on the subject was, of all things, a series of Twitter messages I received a couple of months ago, from an unknown individual called Greg Felton. He appeared out of nowhere on my Twitter feed declaring that Israel has no legitimacy and the whole UN project of creating a Jewish state in Palestine had been a matter of fraud and manipulation.

When I challenged him on this, he became vehement, so I Googled him. I discovered that he is a Canadian Neo-Nazi who, in 2010, had a racist book published. Originally published in 2007, it is called *The Host and the Parasite: How Israel's Fifth Column Consumed America*. His publicity blares out the extraordinary claims that the United States has been totally infiltrated by the Jews; that only a military coup will save it from this invisible Zionist (sic) government; and that such a coup would free the United States to wage 'total war against Israel'.

I twittered him back, saying: 'I've just found out who you are. You're a complete lunatic. I'm going to buy your book and give it the full treatment.' I then blocked him on Twitter and ordered the book. While waiting for it to arrive, I read Daniel Jonah Goldhagen's *The Devil That Never Dies: The Rise and Threat of Global Anti-Semitism* (Little, Brown & Co., 2016).

Goldhagen, of course, is the author of *Hitler's Willing Executioners* and other books on anti-Semitism, each of which has come in for considerable scholarly criticism.

Goldhagen's father, Erich, a retired Harvard professor, is a Holocaust survivor from the Ukraine. Goldhagen himself studied and taught at Harvard for twenty years. During a lecture by Saul Friedländer, he had a 'lightbulb moment', in which he asked himself 'When Hitler ordered the annihilation of the Jews, why did people execute the order?' He set out to investigate who the German men and women had been who killed the Jews and what their reasons were. He came up with the thesis that they did so willingly and even enthusiastically, as bigoted ant-Semites.

His latest book, like his earlier ones, is a polemic against anti-Semitism, whereas Felton's is an anti-Semitic polemic. The comparison is instructive and sobering. Whereas Goldhagen argues that anti-Semitism begins with what he calls the 'foundational anti-Semitic paradigm' in the Christian New Testament and is reinforced within Islam, then in modern nationalist and secular racism, before being amplified and globalized in the 21st century by the effects of the Internet; Felton openly exhibits the anti-Semitic prejudices denounced by Goldhagen and unashamedly advances his variant on the old conspiracy theories about Jewish power and influence.

As I read the two books, I was less inclined to find fault with Goldhagen's indictment of the dark and persistent scandal of anti-Semitism in the Mediterranean world, the Muslim world, the Americas and even elsewhere, than I was with Felton's diatribe. However, the further I read into *The Devil That Never Dies*, the more troubled I became by Goldhagen's chronic tendency to exaggerate and make sweeping claims, without carefully arguing his point. Anti-Semitism, for one thing, surely did not begin with Christianity, as the Book of Esther and the celebration of Purim should have made clear to Goldhagen long ago.

Criticisms of his tendency to polemic have been levelled at Goldhagen again and again, starting with *Hitler's Willing Executioners*, which was seen as overstating its case to the point of anti-German racism. In his 2002 book *A Moral Reckoning: The Role of the Catholic Church in the Holocaust and Its Unfulfilled Duty of Repair*, he indicted the Catholic Church for its deep background role and to some extent direct complicity in the Holocaust. Critics accused him of allowing scholarly standards to lapse for the sake of an anti-Catholic polemic.

His following book *Worse than War: Eliminationism, and the Ongoing Assault on Humanity* (2009) was described by one critic as having been 'undermined by a casual approach to basic research, and by the author's tendency to overreach and overstate his case.' Unfortunately, the same has to be said of *The Devil That Never Dies*. Goldhagen's tendency to see ant-Semitism everywhere and to read 'eliminationism' (genocidal intent) into it, paradoxically deprives the better parts of his case of their force and even their credibility.

What is striking about his argument, nonetheless, is that anti-Semitism has no rational basis in empirical fact, is wholly ideological and yet simply will not go away. Worse than that, the Internet and militant Islam are causing an ominous new wave of anti-Semitism with deeply disturbing implications. The best parts of Goldhagen's book make this clear. The challenge is to find nuance and scruple, complexity and level-headedness in his overall judgements.

This is less of a problem in Felton's case, because his argument lacks even the semblance of sound reasoning or maturity of judgement. There is a strange pair of disclaimers on the opening page of *The Host and the Parasite*, of a kind that immediately makes one wonder what both the author and the publisher are trying to guard themselves against.

The first, headed 'Disclaimer and Reader Agreement', reads, in part: '...Bad Bear Press and the author make no representations as to accuracy, completeness, currentness, suitability or validity of any opinions expressed in this book. Neither Bad Bear Press nor the author shall be liable for any accuracy, errors, adequacy, or timeliness in the content, or for any actions taken in reliance thereon.' The second, headed 'Reader Agreement for Accessing This Book', reads: 'By reading this book, you, the reader, consent to bear sole responsibility for your own decisions to use or read any of this book's material. Bad Bear Press and the author shall not be liable for any damages or costs of any type arising out of any action taken by you or others based upon reliance on any materials in this book.'

In a lifetime of serious reading, I have never seen the like of this. Rather than implicate any of you, my own readers, in this strange farrago, I recommend that you not read Felton's book. It is not worthy of your time or attention and should be allowed to moulder, unread, wherever physical copies exist. Alas, it is representative of a prolific and pernicious literature, both in print and on the web. It embodies what so alarms Daniel Goldhagen and constitutes the kind of evidence that might be adduced in extenuation of Goldhagen's regrettable tendency to over-stating his case.

Now, of course, to write that without then dissecting the book is likely to occur to many readers as tantalizing. What is in this book, with its strange disclaimers, you may well find yourself asking. I confine myself to three indicators of Felton's unhinged approach to reality. Beyond that, should you truly want to read his book, it is over to you.

In his final summation, Felton states that 'a person who subscribes to the 'common sense' world of the official narrative of the last decade, does not question the notion that jet aircraft brought down the Twin Towers, that the US invaded Iraq for oil, or that al-Qaeda exists.' Never mind that these are an odd trio, since the second does not belong in the same analytic set as the first and third. We are, by his own account, literally inside the Matrix here and he tells us that he is Morpheus offering us the red pill and showing us 'how deep the rabbit hole goes.'

A page later, he puts to his readers the proposition that: 'The persistent illusion that the US is still run by a national government precludes consideration of any theory that might prove otherwise.' So, what is the actual government of the United States—at least as you see it after swallowing his fanciful red pill? Well, it is 'Israel's fifth column'—the parasite of his book's title. He calls it, with a rather quaint pun 'AIPAC of wolves'. 'Only a Congress prepared to de-Zionize the country could hope to address the cause of the abuse,' he asserts; without ever having made a plausible case that the US has in fact been taken over by Zionists.

But the climax to his bizarre polemic is in his recommendation, which truly has to be read to be believed:

> In an ideal scenario, the military would stage a coup, arrest the junta's leadership, and set up a provisional government to oversee the drafting of a new Constitution. Such a military government could:
>
> • Institute a Nuremberg style war crimes tribunal to prosecute the leaders of the Lobby and the junta for treason and crimes against humanity
>
> • Declare null and void the Supreme Court confirmations of justices John Roberts and Samuel Alito and void all fascist legislation passed over the last six years, including the USA Patriot Act;
>
> • Call for a proper investigation into the September 11 attack;
>
> • Freeze and liquidate the assets of every Zionist Jewish and Christian organization and place the proceeds into a bank account for distribution to Palestinians, Iraqis and Lebanese;
>
> • Declare military, economic and political war on Israel.
>
> Since the Constitution is, to all intents and purposes, null and void, citizens already have little or no protection against anti-democratic measures like arbitrary arrest, indefinite detention, or warrantless search and seizure, so life under military rule would make little difference. In fact, armed insurrection would help close the gap between political appearance and reality and focus attention on the Zionist enemy within...

You will appreciate, I trust, from this passage not only what Felton really means about taking the red pill and going down the rabbit hole, but why he and his publisher inserted their sweeping disclaimers on the first page of the book. Not only is its scholarship grossly unreliable and its reasoning crackpot; but it is a direct incitement to sedition, insurrection, war and genocide.

After all this, the good master Felton has the hide to conclude with a quotation from, of all people, Marcus Tullius Cicero on the fact that an enemy within is more dangerous than an enemy at the gates. Cicero, of course, was talking about Catiline's conspiracy to overthrow the Republic. He was later to be murdered when Mark Antony and Octavian in fact defeated the last defenders of that Republic. For Felton to invoke Cicero, when he is openly calling for an armed insurrection against the Republic would be comical if it was not for two considerations.

The first of these is that the prescription he offers for what ought to be done and his blatant anti-Semitism are far more redolent of Hitler or the Ku Klux Klan than of Cicero. That he calls the Bush and Obama administrations 'fascist' is simply one more piece of glib and incoherent rhetoric inside his Matrix. Transparently, his own agenda is both fascist and racist.

The second consideration is that the United States has just had a presidential election in which a demagogue with more than a passing resemblance to Catiline (or perhaps Sulla), in the person of Donald Trump, has won a stunning election victory and been elevated to the White House. Rather too many of those who support him openly think more or less like Felton.

By the time this appears in print, we shall be approaching the inauguration of President Trump and a new era in American politics. The danger that Felton's kind of 'thinking' embodies, given the upsurge in populist anger and the demands for sweeping change in America may start to get out of hand. That isn't a reason to read Felton, though it might be a good context in which to read Goldhagen. Felton's writing is a symptom of disturbingly widespread madness. Goldhagen's evident sense of alarm might vitiate his scholarship at various points, but it may well be warranted in present circumstances.

It gives grounds for all of those committed to reason, constitutional democracy and the future of Western civilization—including our many Jewish fellow citizens—to get seriously organized against these darkly pernicious and racist trends. For if we do not, we risk going down less the rabbit hole into Wonderland than an Orwellian memory hole into a dystopia we thought that victory in the Second World War and then in the Cold War had banished.

12: ISIS and the pathology of Islam

The literature on the chaos in the Middle East, on Islam, jihad and terrorism is vast. The recrimination, conspiracy theory and angry rhetoric that swirl around it threaten to spiral out of control. It is vital, therefore, that we find a way through without losing our bearings. Robert Manne has just produced a beautifully crafted and lucid book on this problem. It deserves a very wide readership.

I read *The Mind of the Islamic State* over two days. In between, I attended a concert by Fred Smith, a remarkable individual who spent several tours of duty with the ADF in Afghanistan and emerged from it both sane and full of wry, touching, sometimes hilarious songs. He has not only written a deeply humane book about the experience, *The Dust of Uruzgan* (Allen & Unwin, 2016), but released an album under the same title. I recommend reading Manne and Smith together and getting hold of Smith's wonderful CD.

Of other recent books on ISIS several are sound and instructive: Fawaz Gerges *ISIS: A History* (Princeton University Press, Princeton and Oxford, 2016); Joby Warrick *Black Flags: The Rise of ISIS* (Bantam Press, 2015); Jessica Stern and J. M. Berger *ISIS: The State of Terror* (William Collins, 2015), Daniel Byman *Al Qaeda, the Islamic State and the Global Jihadist Movement: What Everyone Needs to Know* (Oxford University Press, 2015) and Jay Sekulow's *Rise of ISIS: A Threat We Can't Ignore* (Howard Books, 2014).

The upheaval in Syria is so complex and awful that it is a conundrum all on its own. Two recent books by insightful first-hand observers throw its travail into a humanized perspective: Francesca Borri's *Syrian Dust: Reporting from the Heart of the Battle for Aleppo* (Seven Stories Press, New York and Oakland, 2016) and Marwa al-Sabouni's *The Battle for Home: The Memoir of a Syrian Architect* (Thames and Hudson, London, 2015), with a foreword by Roger Scruton.

Finally, Australia's own specialist on counter-insurgency and the pitfalls of the lengthening war against Islamic jihad, David Kilcullen, has contributed two substantial books in three years: *Out of the Mountains: The Coming Age of the Urban Guerrilla* (Scribe, 2013) and *Blood Year: Islamic State and the Failures of the War on Terror* (Black Inc., 2016). Kilcullen is a rare rapporteur on these matters. He is a former highly regarded Australian military officer, who left the Army and went to the US to specialise on the theory of counter-insurgency and counter-terrorism. He worked in both Iraq and Washington DC.

Robert Manne's contribution is among the best of these books. It is, almost certainly, the most challenging and important work Manne has done in a long career as a public intellectual of some standing. Uniquely, it traces the development of radical Islamist doctrine step by step through its key textual outputs, from Sayyid Qutb half a century ago, to *Dabiq*—the organ of the horrifying, apocalyptic vision of the Islamic State in Iraq and Syria, which we have come to call ISIS.

Alongside this litany of thoughtful and useful books, there are others that are abysmal. One of these is Malcolm Nance's bulky recent book *Defeating ISIS: Who They Are, How They Fight, What They Believe* (New York, 2016). His pivotal claim is that the *raison d'être* of ISIS is nothing less than 'to destroy Islam'.

It is important that this paradoxical claim be refuted, lest it add to the already endemic confusion about ISIS. Not the least merit of Robert Manne's book is that it shows in detail the relationship between ISIS and traditional Muslim teaching on jihad, infidels and the apocalypse. His close analysis of these matters contrasts with Nance's sloppy apologetics and textual vacuity.

Several passages give away the poor understanding of history underlying Nance's flimsy assertion that the mission of ISIS is to 'destroy Islam'. Here are two of them, from the heart of the book:

> ISIS believes that it is carrying out a chain of events as prophesied by the Prophet Mohammed. All components of their belief system enjoins (sic) the words in the Qur'an, but instead of interpreting it the way that it has been for the past fourteen centuries, they took another direction...(p. 193)

> The Cult of Jihad now led by ISIS and a close second al-Qaeda seek nothing less than the seizure, dismantling and destruction of the entirety of Islamic thought, culture, jurisprudence and tradition since 632 [when Mohammed died]. All of those centuries of tolerance, discovery and compromise with the rest of the world are weakness to be ruthlessly eliminated. To them, little of Islam can be salvaged—the Muslim world is going to have to be burned to the ground to be saved for God. (p. 216)

He makes these assertions without at any point attempting to substantiate them. The beauty of Robert Manne's book is that he takes us through the debates over jihad and the End Times within the Sunni jihadist movement throughout the past half century and delineates, with often exquisite precision, the cleavages in doctrine and scriptural interpretation that have produced the genocidal propaganda and cruel barbarities of ISIS.

Very early in his book, Manne remarks:

> Like all Jews of my generation, I grew up under the shadow of the Holocaust. As an undergraduate, I had been invited to review Norman Cohn's *Warrant for Genocide*, a history of *The Protocols of the Elders of Zion*, a supposedly authentic document that purported to reveal the secret Jewish war plan for world domination.

In the seven chapters of his book, he reviews, as it were, a set of works which, each in its own way, urged that true Islam requires that Muslims collectively and individually have a moral duty to engage in jihad against both 'apostate' Muslim regimes and against all infidels, until all the world is Islamic.

These works are Sayyid Qutb's *Milestones* (1964); Muhammad Abd Al-Salam Farraj's *The Neglected Duty* (1980); Abdullah Azzam's *Join the Caravan* (1987); Ayman al-Zawahiri's *Knights Under the Prophet's Banner* (2001); Abu Bakr Naji's *The Management of Savagery* (2004); and the serial publication, from 2014, of the ISIS journal *Dabiq*, which Manne describes as 'an elegant and glossy official on-line magazine in several languages...self-evidently written by intellectuals steeped in the theological tradition of Islam, with a deep knowledge of the Qur'an, the hadith and major Islamic scholars.'

The lucidity, historical sensitivity and textual interpretation that Manne lays before us across this dark evolution of insurgent Muslim thought are alike impressive. They lead us, as he himself concludes, from the systematic and sophisticated dogmatism of Sayyid Qutb—a kind of Islamic John Calvin—to 'the Gates of Hell'. Anyone seeking to engage thoughtfully, rather than merely fearfully or angrily, with this body of work, will benefit from reading *The Mind of the Islamic State*.

Given that Manne is Jewish and lives, as he writes, in the shadow of the Holocaust, his restraint in this piece of work, the care with which he picks his way through the darkening landscape, is admirable. The book is not a polemic; not even against the Islamic State. It is a work of moral and intellectual distinction, because it parses grim and repellent debates with close reading, fine discrimination and nuanced evaluation.

There is a lacuna, however, in Manne's reflections. Between the lines, we can see how those whose books of the past half century he has read and thoughtfully analysed, point back to the deep roots of jihad in Muhammad's own practice, in the Qur'an and in the earliest epoch of Islam, as well as in the 14th century, after the Mongol destruction of the Abbasid caliphate. As he observes (at p. 129), Sayyid Qutb understood that 'the Qur'an delivers its secrets only to those whose frame of mind has been shaped in battle.'

In short, the one God of Islam is not the God of Abraham, of Micah, of Isaiah—or of Jesus. Muhammad's deity is a God of war and conquest and the Sunna, the example of the Prophet, is one of jihad and the killing of one's enemies and critics. This fundamental problem Manne does not address.

Islam did not arise or spread by peace or persuasion, nor did Muhammad preach that it should do so. It arose as a religion calling for the violent overthrow of all non-Muslim religions and principalities, in order that the 'truth' might prevail. For several centuries, its adherents strove by all means at their disposal to conquer the whole of Europe and Asia. The much criticized crusades were a belated and relatively small scale response to these wars of conquest.

The Ottomans renewed those wars of conquest and took Constantinople, Greece and the Balkans. Modern jihadists, including Hassan al-Banna, founder of the Muslim Brotherhood, decades before Sayyid Qutb wrote *Milestones*, sought to revive this tradition of Muslim militancy. It is very active now in many parts of the Muslim world and by no means confined to that vicious enclave which calls itself the Islamic State.

This is the larger problem. Sayyid Qutb's master work was *In the Shade of the Qur'an* (1954). Those who insist that ISIS is an aberrant form of Islam and its rise the fault of the West, must reckon with the fact that 'the shade of the Qur'an' is the complacent, but dangerous assumption that Islam is the 'final revelation' and that sooner or later the world must and will become Muslim—through jihad and as the 'will of Allah'. If you are reading Manne's book closely, you will perceive this between the lines—but it is not directly stated or addressed. It needs to be.

13: Splendid study of an absurd war

There is no higher praise for a war historian than calling his work Thucydidean. Pierre Razoux's history of the Iran/Iraq War (1980-88) deserves such praise. It has three Thucydidean characteristics: it is remarkably dispassionate about the many protagonists in the conflict; the author is meticulous in describing military operations year after year; and he situates the war in a larger geopolitical and historical perspective. It is not depicted as having only immediate causes, but as having roots in several centuries of territorial disputes. Moreover, its implications for both Middle Eastern security and global power rivalries are put in judicious perspective.

The book includes 30 detailed military maps, making it comparable to the splendid *Landmark Thucydides* edited by Robert B. Strassler, published in 1996, which throws considerable light on the dense text by the classical historian by inserting many detailed maps of the theatres of operation. Razoux and his editors have done us all a great service in including so many maps in the present history. They enable the reader to follow closely what would otherwise quite often be a bewildering description of terrain and military manoeuvres.

There is also a set of Appendices. In the first of these, Razoux sets out an historical chronology, which rather remarkably begins with the Arab defeat of the Persians at al-Qadisiyya in 636 CE and concludes in February 1991, when the UN ceasefire monitoring force left the Persian Gulf, after the end of the Gulf War. The second is a tabulated comparison of the two states of Iraq and Iran in 1980, covering size, population, geography, ethnic composition, religion, politics, currency and military personnel. The third, a kind of *dramatis personae*, lists the military high command figures in each state. The fourth, running to 27 pages, details the military forces and capabilities on each side at the outbreak of hostilities.

The fifth describes the armed militias facing each of the antagonists in the 1980s, including five separate Kurdish organizations. The sixth specifies the military assistance provided to the antagonists by other countries around the world. We learn that Iraq, which had started the war, received incomparably more assistance than Iran, starting with somewhere between 30 and 45 billion dollars' worth of assistance from the Soviet Union and 17 billion dollars' worth from France. No country provided more than 3 billion dollars' worth of military assistance to Iran, though China and North Korea reached that amount.

The seventh appendix, over seven pages, covers the oil production and exports of the two countries throughout the war, the revenues earned in the process and the damage done to oil tankers in the course of the conflict. The eighth sets out the naval deployments to the Persian Gulf by foreign powers during the course of the war. The ninth and tenth appendices set out the war costs in terms of human casualties and financial losses, including types of aircraft and the means of their destruction, as well as a list of air force 'aces' on either side, i.e. fighter pilots who scored multiple kills during the war.

The cost to the two sides was enormous, not least because nothing was gained by either side at the end of the conflict. The total financial cost to Iraq is estimated at $452 billion; that to Iran $645 billion. The opportunity costs of such immense expenditure, of course, were incalculable. The war deaths totalled some 180,000 in Iraq (including 50,000 Iraqi Kurds) and a stunning 500,000 Iranians. But there were also the wounded and maimed: some 520,000 in Iraq and 1,300,000 in Iran. There were relatively few civilian deaths: about 5,000 in Iraq and 10,000 in Iran, but the military losses were staggering. Moreover, Razoux makes clear that both states were exhausted by the end of the second year of the war, but Iran refused every overture for a settlement until, by July 1988 it was on its knees.

From the outset, Razoux exhibits a masterly *savoir faire* in assessing both the interests and the actions of the protagonists, from major states to Gulf emirates, and from international statesmen to military officers in Iraq or clerics and politicians in Iran. He never condescends or engages in gratuitous moralizing. On several occasions he addresses charges regarding American actions or motives and shows the charges to be unwarranted. Yet, where error or incompetence occurred, he forensically exposes it. This is notably the case with the destruction of Iran Air Flight 655 in July 1988. He describes the event in minute detail, demonstrating that the fault lay neither with Washington nor the Iranians, but with the arrogance and haste of Captain William Rogers, commander of the USS *Vincennes*.

Occasionally, Razoux's French background leaps out at the reader. He likens Saddam's invasion of revolutionary Iran, in September 1980, to the Prussian invasion of France in September 1792, the unexpected French victory at the battle of Valmy and the quickening of the radical revolution which followed. He likens Ali Khamenei to Maximilien Robespierre and Akbar Hashemi Rafsanjani to Georges Danton in their political styles and roles. Unlike Danton, of course, Rafsanjani was not guillotined by the Iranian Robespierre; but the psychological parallels are apt enough in other respects; though only a French historian is likely to have thought of them.

Saddam Hussein, having opportunistically and recklessly started the war and having tried for years from 1982 to end a conflict that had become ruinous, actually won the war in the end. It was a 'Pyrrhic' victory, to be sure; but there is no doubt that Iraq fought the war both resourcefully and successfully. In the final months, an Iraqi army that was four times as large as it had been at the beginning of the war, better armed and battle-hardened, routed the demoralized Iranian forces and forced Tehran to yield. Not the least impressive aspect of

Razoux's history is his mastery of each stage of the war and his understanding of the tactical and strategic thinking that shaped decisions on both sides throughout it.

Saddam's thumping victories in the final months of the war retrieved a parlous situation for him and enabled him to posture as a great Arab hero. But they left him with a dilemma. His huge army was very expensive, but demobilizing it in a bankrupt country looked likely to cause serious social unrest. In an attempt to solve both problems, he invaded Kuwait only two years after settling the war with Iran. In doing so, he took on a power considerably larger than Iran, apparently without appreciating what he was getting himself into. He blustered about giving the coalition forces 'the mother of all battles', but his huge, battle-hardened forces were simply brushed aside by the US forces.

For eight years Iran had hammered away at Iraq, with prodigal expenditure of its soldiers' lives and limbs, without either being able to gain much advantage. It had repeatedly attempted to break through Iraq's defences and open a road to Baghdad, without anything close to success. Then the American superpower, fresh from its geopolitical triumph in the Cold War, marching under a clear United Nations mandate, stepped in and swept Saddam's forces off the table as if they were children's toys. It was a breathtaking display of military power.

Iraq has all but ceased to exist, of course, as a consequence of George W. Bush's war. Iran has gained from that war everything it was unable to gain in the 1980s in its war with Saddam, whom it sought in vain to overthrow. Concerning Iran, Razoux drew a number of lessons. First, that 'the Iranian leadership is perfectly rational and pragmatic and thoroughly understands the notions of ratio of power and deterrence'. Second, that 'any military intervention against Iran would only reinforce the regime by uniting the population behind it, rather than weakening it.' Third, that 'the Iranian government practises asymmetric warfare and does not hesitate to strike first to take its opponent by surprise.' Fourth, that the Iranian political class sees nuclear weapons as a necessary strategic acquisition. Each of these points deserves careful consideration in the present context of disquiet over Iran's nuclear program.

Razoux also concluded, however, that the majority of Iranian citizens 'appear to be awaiting a strong, pragmatic and coherent government that would protect the country from outside interference, send the clergy back to the mosques...and reopen Iran to the outside world to allow for the economic development of a country that has been living in near autarky for the past thirty years.' Just to the extent that these are the realities, we should seek to encourage those developments. Whether the present situation in the Middle East lends itself to the emergence of such a new regime in Iran any time soon is moot, but our goal, at least should be to do whatever we can to reassure both ordinary Iranians and the Iranian political class that that outcome would certainly suit us all better than hostilities, whether hot or cold.

14: Russian ambassador's killing may realign geopolitical stars

The assassination, on Monday, of Russian Ambassador to Turkey, Andrei Karlov, by Mevlut Mert Altintas, seems likely to galvanize closer relations between Ankara and Moscow, rather than derailing them. It has also prompted Donald Trump to call for a fundamental rethinking of the way the 'civilized world' deals with Islamist terrorism, which, he tweeted, 'must be eradicated from the face of the earth'. Contrary to the assassin's hopes, his act may trigger a geopolitical realignment that will cost his cause dearly—but also ours.

The cries of Altintas in the name of Aleppo and Allah, as he shot Karlov, indicate that he sided with the rebels who unsuccessfully defended Aleppo against forces of Bashar al-Assad. What has bedevilled the Arab world for many years, not least since the 'Arab Spring', is radical Muslim rebellion against tyranny, with the demand that it be replaced by Islamic regimes and sharia law. Liberal, secular and non-Muslim rebels have not had such a goal. It seems Karlov's assassin did.

The West's response to Assad's attempts to crush his opponents has been confused by these realities. Neither Turkey nor Russia, nor Iran has been confused about its interests in Syria. Washington and its allies have called for the resignation or overthrow of Assad. Moscow has sought to buttress him. Tehran has done the same. Each has done so for its own reasons. Erdogan's Turkey has been concerned to keep the Syrian Kurds in check and advance a kind of 'Neo-Ottoman' and Islamist influence in Syria.

All this has generated tensions between Washington and Moscow, Moscow and Ankara, Ankara and Washington; with Tehran tenaciously and quietly pursuing its own interests. Our own strategic policy has been aligned with that of Obama's Washington. The response by Donald Trump to the assassination could, however, presage a major shift to alignment with the ruthless *realpolitik* of Vladimir Putin. The broader implications for NATO and for Russia's interests in Eastern Europe will bear watching, as it were.

Putin called Karlov's assassination a provocation intended to sabotage warming ties between Moscow and Ankara and efforts to resolve the Syrian conflict. The two countries have collaborated in evacuating survivors from Aleppo, as Assad's forces entered the city. Erdogan agreed. He declared that the killing was aimed at destabilising a normalisation process that he initiated after a crisis earlier this year, when Turkey shot down a Russian fighter over Syria.

Quite apart from the strife in Syria, there has, of course, been a great deal of strife within Turkey this year, with a spate of bombings and an abortive coup that Erdogan has used to crack down on all kinds of opposition and to strengthen his grip on power. Much of Turkey's population is Sunni Muslim, especially on the Anatolian plateau, around Ankara; and Karlov's assassination has taken place amid days of protests in Turkey over Russia's role in Syria. The protesters have blamed Moscow for human rights violations in Aleppo; with thousands gathering not only in Ankara, but outside the Russian consulate in Istanbul.

It is in the perennial nature of geopolitics that governments, for reasons of *realpolitik*, overlook human rights violations in order to pursue their interests, including their perceived joint interests. The Turkish Foreign Minister Mevlut Cavusoglu was on his way to Moscow for a summit with the Russians and Iranians about the war in Syria when Karlov was shot. He did not turn around and go back. These powers are trying to work out how to achieve their respective goals with a minimum of conflict among themselves. That makes sense, but it has a number of implications.

Meanwhile, the Syrian government called the assassination an atrocious crime. They know about atrocious crimes. They have committed enormous human rights violations over the past four years. As Ben Taub reported in *The New Yorker* in mid-April this year, the documentation, by the Commission for International Justice and Accountability, of tens of thousands of cases of systematic torture and murder by the Assad regime—before the assault on Aleppo had even begun—has culminated in a 400 page legal brief that traces these abuses to 'a written policy approved by Bashar al-Assad, coordinated among his security intelligence agencies and implemented by regime operatives, who reported their successes to their superiors in Damascus.'

These abuses are of no concern to Moscow, or Ankara, or Tehran. Their strategic objectives override any such considerations. Washington has wrung its hands about them, but found no effective means for checking them. Meanwhile, the radical jihadists, both ISIS and the others in Syria, have committed horrors of their own. Anyone moderate, civilized, democratic or just neutral and vulnerable in Syria has been caught between the proverbial 'Devil and the deep blue sea'. Yet the assassin, having cried out 'Aleppo' and 'Allahu Akbar', in Arabic, yelled in Turkish: 'Don't forget about Syria, don't forget about Aleppo. All those who participate in this tyranny will be held accountable.'

That's a nice idea, in principle, though one would hesitate to hand the accounting to the jihadists. But what we are seeing is now a hardening of the lines against those Sunni jihadists. As of 20 January, when Trump enters the White House, there now seems to be a distinct possibility that he will seek, through his pro-Russian Secretaries of State and Defence, to become a fourth member of the summit group now meeting in Moscow. The aim will be to 'eradicate' the Sunni jihadist movement. George W. Bush tried that by launching unsustainable wars. Obama has tried it using drones. We are about to see a whole new approach to the 'Global War on Terror.' Canberra has some serious thinking to do.

Bashar al-Assad has crushed the rebellions in Syria with huge loss of life. His forces have tortured and killed far more people than have the jihadists in Syria.

PART IV: 2017

1: Trump, Putin and the jihadists aren't playing cricket

On 20 January, Donald Trump will be inaugurated as President of the United States. He has been twittering about reigniting the nuclear arms race, punishing America's allies for free-riding, eradicating Islamic jihadism from the face of the earth and starting some kind of trade war with China. He has also been talking up Vladimir Putin as some kind of partner against Islam. The implications for world order are unsettling, to say the least.

But, hey, it's Boxing Day. The test cricket is on at the MCG. It's the Saturnalia and we are eating and drinking Christmas fare. Mind you, we have just breathed a sigh of relief that yet another terrorist plot has been foiled—a plan to set off a bomb in St Paul's Cathedral in Melbourne among 1,400 observant Anglicans. Spare a thought for those, in our national security establishment, whose job it is to actually think through all this—and the prospects of a Trump presidency.

Many who admire Trump do so because they insist he is more honest and realistic than Hillary Clinton or much of the political elite. Admirers here would like to see 'Trumpism' in this country. But how would this affect our national security? It might be worth reflecting on this during the holiday season. What, for instance, do you think of the idea of a Trump partnership with Vladimir Putin—the hard-edged prince of Muscovy—against Islam; or at least against *Sunni* Islam, since Moscow has been even friendlier to Shia Iran than Obama's Washington has been.

This is, in fact, what Trump seems to have in mind, or at least in Twitter. As Peter Beinart pointed out recently in *Defence One*, Trump is 'moving away from an ideological confrontation with authoritarian Russia and toward a civilizational conflict with Islam.' His nominated National Security Advisor, Michael Flynn, as given to tweeting as Trump is, has put out that 'fear of Muslims is rational' and that Islam as such is a kind of 'cancer'. We beat Hitler with Russia's help, he said in August, and it's time to enlist its help to defeat Islam.

If you are a Trump enthusiast, it may be in part because of a fear of Islam. Ongoing terrorist incidents around the world fuel this fear. Let's assume, just for the sake of argument, that such fear is in fact warranted and that the problem is, indeed, Islam as such, rather than a narrower problem to do with certain strands of Islam or certain sources of agitation and violent anger within the Muslim world. How and why might a partnership with Russia actually help? And, since this is Boxing Day, one might ask in genteel terms, 'Would such a partnership be 'cricket'?'

Michael Flynn's line is, 'Remember the war against Hitler!' Perish the thought that we are about to enter into violence on the scale of the Second World War. But his point was that

Stalin (a totalitarian tyrant) was an ally against Hitler; so why should we recoil from allying ourselves with Putin (a mere secular dictator) to fight a current form of common, fascistic enemy? This isn't a time for insisting on the niceties of liberal internationalism. It's a matter of realpolitik: the enemy of my enemy is my friend. So the elementary logic of the argument runs.

This is itself a sign of the times. As John Bew, of King's College London, remarks in his very useful introduction to the subject, *Realpolitik: A History*, published this year, 'The optimism and sense of triumph that crept into Anglo-American political thought following the end of the Cold War and peaked with the toppling of Saddam Hussein's statue in Baghdad's Firdos Square in April 2003, have been replaced by the 'return of history', the 'revenge of geography' and 'the 'end of dreams.'' Realpolitik, in other words, is back and strategic expediency is on the agenda.

Putin rose to power on the back of a brutal war against the Chechens and consolidated it through the suppression, including assassination, of his political rivals and critics. He has invaded Georgia and Ukraine (twice) and waged cyber war against Estonia. NATO's protectorates in Eastern Europe and the Baltic are seriously concerned about him. He is an aggressive Russian nationalist. But Flynn is right that Stalin was much worse and that, once Hitler attacked Stalin, the West made common cause with Russia.

The question, therefore, is what might we gain through a partnership with Russia against Islam? Could 'Islam' be similarly defeated? How, exactly? And what would the 'post-war settlement' look like? Remember that, in 1945, Stalin's forces occupied the whole of Eastern Europe and the Baltic states as well as North Korea, imposing totalitarian dictatorships across the board. They also handed masses of Japanese weapons to the Chinese communists, enabling them to overthrow the Nationalist regime in China. The Cold War followed. What might be the ramifications of a Russo-American war to 'eradicate' radical Islam?

The larger context in which to think about all this, as you watch the opening day of the Boxing Day test against Pakistan at the MCG or in front of your TV, is that world order is at stake. Since 1945, for all its faults, the United States has been the linchpin of a liberal international world order. It kept communism at bay while rebuilding a shattered non-communist world and extending security and free trade to an unprecedented extent. The 9/11 attacks were a direct challenge to that order. Fifteen years on, it is in trouble.

The forthcoming issue of *Foreign Affairs*, the journal of the New York based Council on Foreign Relations, is about the crisis in international institutions. That crisis is real. Trump, Putin and the jihadists they vow to crush, say 'Bring it on!' The rest of us have good reason to feel alarmed and we cannot afford to remain mere spectators, as if all this was just a cricket match at the MCG.

2: Thomas Piketty's errors regarding inequality need correcting

The Trump victory in the United States was a reaction, at root, to the real and perceived costs of globalization: inequality and immigration flows. Now that he is in office, there are serious possibilities of disruptive changes to the global trading system, as we saw with his instant dismissal of the Trans Pacific Partnership. For Xi Jinping, head of state of the world's most mercantilist country, to stand up at Davos and extol free trade, while Donald Trump, head of the supposedly most ideologically free trade state on the planet vows to set up tariff barriers has been a remarkable turn of events in the first weeks of 2017.

More than ever, we must get our collective minds around the roots of inequality, the best data on the subject and the structures that undergird world trade. French economist Thomas Picketty has been contributing path-breaking work on the trends in economic inequality for some years. He made a name for himself in 2014 with *Capital in the 21st Century*, an instant best-seller, arguing that inequality is increasing across the developed world and that something needs to be done to arrest this trend. Trump's rise to power was plainly premised on both those claims, though his prescriptions for change may not align with Picketty's social philosophy.

Picketty was in Australia some months ago, speaking at Melbourne Town Hall. His speech was notable for three things: his delightful—or as John Cleese famously expressed it in *Monty Python and the Holy Grail*, his 'outrageous'—French accent; the lucid presentation of his data on income, taxation and inequality around the world in general; and his completely daft statements about the history and causes of inequality in the Middle East. The first was enjoyable; the second fascinating; the third deeply puzzling. The third set off alarm bells in my mind. If Picketty could be so demonstrably wrong and wrong-headed about the Middle East, what else might he be getting fundamentally wrong?

His core claim regarding the growth of inequality was that the era of 'neo-liberalism' has seen income differentials widen, taxation become less progressive and wealth disparities widen, across the OECD. He and his research team have gathered long-term data on inequality and its causes. That's why his book is interesting. There is a hunger out there for such data, based on a widespread sense that inequality has, indeed, increased and that this is due to questionable macro-economic policies.

Picketty points out that both Karl Marx and Simon Kuznets were mistaken in their prognoses (one hundred years apart) about how development would affect income distribution. Marx, in the mid-19th century, forecast growing immiseration and revolution. This is not what happened. Instead, growing wealth and moderate social policies contributed to a narrowing of income inequalities in the capitalist world and the rise of a broad middle class. Kuznets, in the mid-20th century, forecast growing equality and prosperity, but for thirty years now his prediction, also, has been falsified. Piketty's data set shows this and also points to some of the underlying causes. This is much the most interesting aspect of his research.

His much older and smaller book, *The Economics of Inequality*, first published in 1997, but republished last year, centred on the claim that, in the industrialized world, the ratio of national income going to capital and labour has hovered around one third to two thirds over the long run, varying only marginally. He added that, while distribution could modify this to a certain extent, there seemed very little scope for radical alteration of the ratio. Attempts to radically alter it, in the case of communist states, had simply led to economic gridlock and entrenched poverty.

In *Capital in the 21st Century*, he greatly deepened his enquiry, under four basic heads: Income and Capital; The Dynamics of the Capital/Income Ratio; The Structure of Inequality; and Regulating Capital in the 21st Century. His speech last year covered much of this ground in brief and was notable for its moderate tone, largely sensible observations and emphasis on the role of sound institutions in fostering growth, constructive fiscal policy and a modicum of egalitarianism. Unfortunately, of course, it is precisely the failure of such institutions, in both the US and the EU, that has led to the present impasse at which we find ourselves. Indeed, institutional failures in Japan and growing ones in China point to very serious challenges to global economic governance for the foreseeable future.

However, Piketty's work contains a strange omission with regard to the factors behind the recent increases in inequality. Kuznets argued, in the 1950s, that industrialization generally sharpened inequalities at first, then stabilized, then caused them to diminish, with the growth of a broad middle class and higher wages for workers. Piketty claims that this trend held true only until the 1980s, then went into an unexpected reverse. What he does not appear to consider is that globalization and the surge in technological innovation may well be causing a *second wave* of the phenomenon suggested by Kuznets: widening inequalities on an at least temporary basis due to the successes of the capitalist system, rather than its failures.

Just to the extent that Kuznets was correct about the first wave of industrialization, it is possible that a sharp increase in inequality would be a natural corollary of the globalized surge of industrialization and urbanization—China leading the charge—since the 1980s. The collapse of the Soviet bloc and the integration of Eastern Europe and Russia into the world economy, the abandonment of socialism by India and much of Africa and their rapid growth have all contributed to this second wave Kuznets phenomenon. This has had indirect flow-on effects in the 'advanced' world. Moreover, the massive shifts in resource allocation and the dynastic fortunes being made in new technologies surely mean that the recent growth in inequality in the United States and elsewhere is not particularly surprising.

This is the issue I had hoped Piketty would discuss in his talk. He didn't. But what was even more disturbing was that, having specified the Middle East as the most economically and socially inegalitarian region of the world, he completely flubbed the question of its historical and institutional causes. He stated flatly that the problem in the Middle East was 'oil and finance' and not culture or historical social stratification. He is demonstrably in error on both counts. The strangest moment in his speech came when he made the gratuitous assertion that 'there has been no slavery in the Middle East since the rise of Islam', so that slavery could not be seen to be (as he claimed it to be in the United States) a root cause of inequality.

This was an astounding claim. Slavery was endemic in the Muslim world from the start. The Arabs enslaved so many Berbers in the Maghreb, for instance, in the late 7th and early 8th centuries that they triggered a massive rebellion. They ran a large scale slave trade along the coast of East Africa for a thousand years. The Ottoman slave trade in the Mediterranean was only ended by European and American intervention in North Africa in the 19th century. Slavery persisted in Saudi Arabia into the 1960s. Piketty's statement, in short, was so at odds with reality that one is left wondering whether he has any grasp of Islamic history at all. How can he have made so grave an error? One is left with the disquieting thought that it was due to that endemic 'political correctness' which shys away from any criticism of the Islamic world as inadmissible 'Orientalism' or 'neo-colonialism'.

As for 'oil and finance' causing inequality in the Middle East, one has only to ponder the facts that he himself drew attention to about oil and finance fuelling American growth and the *reduction* of inequality in mid-20th century America to appreciate that these things do not, in themselves, cause inequality. Oil is widely seen as inducing macro-economic inertia and corrupting political systems, enabling reactionary elites to buy off their peoples and avoid structural reforms. This did not happen in the United States. But it has happened right across the Islamic world, to varying degrees. The two claims—that there has been no slavery in the Muslim world and that oil and finance explain inequality in the Middle East—taken together cast grave doubts on Piketty's reliability as an economic historian and as a systematic thinker.

I walked away from the Town Hall bemused. The contemporary debate over economic inequality and what to do about it is an important one. Piketty's books are a very stimulating contribution. But his confusion about the Middle East and his failure to factor globalization or rapid technological innovation into his analysis are serious shortcomings. The first is almost inexplicable. The second is where the most serious analytical attention needs to be focused. Now that Donald Trump is President of the United States and seems bent on radical protectionism, these issues are only going to become more acute and more important. We need to get our bearings and political correctness of this kind about the non-Anglo-American world will not help us one little bit.

3: Popper and the pelvis: an essay on conjectures and refutations

In the last issue of this magazine, it was pointed out by Todd Kliendienst (Organiser of the Karl Popper Philosophy Meetup Group, Brisbane), in a letter to the editor; that, while he enjoyed what I had written about Karl Popper, he felt obliged to point out that I was in error on a point of detail. I wrote, towards the end of the essay on Popper:

> Popper did not venture into the arena of biology, but a similar story holds in that regard, of course. The bold conjecture by Charles Darwin that natural selection had driven a process of evolution and that the observable changes in the biological world were due to such selection pressures, opened up the biosphere and the human past to inquiry in a way that no creation myth had ever done.
>
> The 20th century saw developments and refinements of this theory, with the integration of genetics into the picture and then the realization, only thirty years or so ago, that evolution had proceeded not through a gradual, progressive process, but via many changes and catastrophes of a quite haphazard nature—punctuated equilibrium. Little by little, our understanding had to be adjusted in the light of the refutation of assumptions or poor inferences embedded in the original conjecture.

All this was fine, Todd pointed out, except that Popper *had* ventured into the philosophy of biology.

This was freshly on my mind late last year when I got hold of the November/December issue of *American Scientist*, which features a story about new discoveries in palaeoanthropology that upend the conventional wisdom about the evolution of the human pelvis. What a happy coincidence, I thought, that an article in a serious magazine about conjectures and refutations in evolutionary biology—and human evolution, in particular—should appear in print even as I was being corrected on the matter of Popper and biology!

The article in question is titled 'An Updated Prehistory of the Human Pelvis.' It is by Caroline VanSickle, a specialist on anatomical sex differences in hominins base on the fossil record. It is a made to order case study not only in evolutionary biology, but in Popperian critical rationalism. The larger context for the piece, as she wrote is 'The mystery of how humans came to be the only species of their kind on the planet.' The problem, as she also points out, is that trying to figure this out is 'a lot like working on a never-ending jigsaw puzzle without a box-lid for guidance and with most of the puzzle pieces missing.' How could any intelligent person, at this point of her piece, not want to read on?

Here is her summary of what, in fact, passes for the box-lid—the up to date conjecture of specialists about the course of human evolution:

> Sometime between 7 million and 13 million years ago, our lineage diverged form
> that of Pan troglodytes, the chimpanzee…At the end of the nineteenth century, when
> Charles Darwin was writing about human evolution, many scholars thought the
> evolutionary path to humans was a straight line. This conception seemed reasonable
> at a time when we hadn't yet found many types of hominin fossils…Today, however,
> we have a lot more fossils to fit into the hominin lineage and what we've found is that
> evolution rarely proceeds in a straight line…This situation means that whenever fossil
> evidence of a new species is discovered, it has the potential to change the entire 'map'
> of human evolution. Lately, the map has begun to look less like a direct route than
> the roadways of a complex city, complete with dead ends, detours, roundabouts and
> side roads, representing both the fossils we know and the hominin species we haven't
> discovered yet.

Having sketched out this lid box for us, she then cuts to the chase. Her own field is the evolution of the human pelvis. This, she hastens to advise the naïve reader, 'is an important part of our evolutionary story, because the pelvis of hominins differs dramatically from that of the chimpanzee—and possibly, therefore, from that of our last common ancestor.'

The conventional wisdom for some considerable time has been that the shape of the pelvis changed to accommodate the bipedal gait and upright posture that our ancestors adopted from well over three million years ago. The Laetoli footprints, from Tanzania, show that there were fully upright and bipedal hominins not less than 3.6 million years ago. The chimpanzee birth canal is elongated and spacious, allowing their small-brained infants an easy passage. The human birth canal is smaller and the infant's brain larger, which results in the painful and difficult birth process for our species. It has long been assumed that as upright posture made birth more complex, the pelvis adapted to the emerging challenge. It just never quite adapted sufficiently to save human females the pangs of childbirth.

New evidence now suggests that this conjecture is false. Popper, I feel sure, would be fascinated. Up until about 15 years ago, VanSickle tells us, the available fossil evidence suggested that pelvic evolution had moved in only one direction, with the pelvis adapting imperfectly but steadily to accommodate bipedalism and upright posture. But in those past fifteen years, 'a terrific sequence of fossil finds has provided enough additional evidence to change the picture.' Here is the Popperian deductive process at work:

> It now appears that paleoanthropologists need to find a different explanation for
> hominin pelvis variation than birth adaptations, because the old model does not fit the
> new evidence.

The most astounding such new evidence surfaced only in 2015, in the Rising Star Cave outside Johannesburg, where more than 1,500 human fossils were discovered; an extraordinary, even unprecedented abundance of fossil material.

As VanSickle remarks:

> To find more than 1,500 fossils of the same species, representing nearly every part
> of the skeleton, including 41 pelvic fragments—often from multiple individuals of
> different ages—was like winning the paleoanthropological lottery. But there was
> a catch: What these new fossils told us about hominin evolution was confusing...
> Suddenly, it appears that mixing primitive and modern pelvic traits was relatively
> common in the past.

The scale of the find and its radical implications reminds me of the discovery of the Nag
Hammadi Library in Egypt in the 1940s, with its trove of gnostic gospels and their implications,
which threw open the field of New Testament scholarship. But the Rising Star Cave finds takes
us back a whole lot further than anything in the Bible ever did! And its holdings confront us
with a beautiful Popperian question. In VanSickle's words: 'If birth constraints do not explain
the pelvic variation of the past, that must mean we don't really understand why human pelvises
look the way they do today. In the absence of any simple answer...paleoanthropologists have
started to consider more complicated possibilities.'

There are now several hypotheses being considered, one of which is that human pelvis
shape has been shaped by diet and that a carbohydrate heavy diet, after the invention of
agriculture, has been the main cause of problems with the birth canal. This, at least, ought to
be fairly readily testable. In any case, as VanSickle observes, testing this and other hypotheses
'will call for developing a better understanding of what causes variation in the shape of the
modern human pelvis'. She adds a salutary comment about the nature of inquiry:

> It seems to me very likely that we scientists have spent so much time focused on
> figuring out how birth explains the evolution of the hominin pelvis (only to realize
> belatedly that it might not), that the real explanation may be something we haven't
> thought of yet.

So it goes when inquiry is open and scientific. This plays directly into Popper's argument for
critical rationalism and freedom of discussion. We need to revitalize that argument right
now, because there are far too many parties abroad in the world whose approach to matters of
knowledge is dogmatic, sectarian, partisan and anti-liberal.

As Popper wrote in 1963, in *Conjectures and Refutations* (p. 352):

> Truth is not manifest; and it is not easy to come by. The search for truth demands at
> least
>
> 1). Imagination
> 2). Trial and error
> 3). The gradual discovery of our prejudices by way of a and b and of critical discussion
>
> The Western rationalist tradition, which derives from the Greeks, is the tradition of

critical discussion—of examining and testing propositions or theories by attempting to refute them. This critical rational method must not be mistaken for a method of proof, that is to say for a method of finally establishing truth; nor is it a method which always secures agreements. Its value lies, rather, in the fact that participants in a discussion will, to some extent, change their minds, and part as wiser men.

It is striking that he wrote 'men', in 1963; but we can be confident that this was a linguistic convention, not a prejudice on his part. We might add, moreover, that it was too sweeping to say that critical rationalism derived from 'the Greeks', as if it had been a racial or cultural trait. It was not. It was the brainchild of a small subset of Greek thinkers, who (like Anaxagoras and Socrates) were at times persecuted for their critical rationalism.

Such thinking is a human possibility. Variations in its occurrence and practice, like variations in the shape of the pelvis across evolutionary time, call for careful analysis and explanation, not glib assumptions. The statement that the 'Western' rationalist tradition has the quality of considering and testing hypotheses is less narrowly racial than the claim that 'the Greeks' hold pride of place, but it has the same limitation. The great majority of people in the Western world have never been any more scientific or devoted to critical rationalism than human beings elsewhere. Those things have always been the work of a sub-culture and they require constant nourishment, institutional embodiment and active exercise in order to survive. That is as true now as ever and if we are to bring a viable new global economic and ecological order to birth in the 21st century, we will need to work hard at getting the cultural birth canal into shape. Let's go to it.

4: James Packer gambled and lost

There is a scene towards the end of Kostantinos Gavros's 1982 film, *Missing*, in which a hard-edged US military officer tells Ed Horman, played by Jack Lemmon, 'Suppose I went up to your town and started messing around with the Mafia and I wind up dead in the East River and my wife or my father complains to the police because they didn't protect me. They really wouldn't have much of a case, would they? You play with fire, you get burned.'

James Packer, gambling tycoon, played with fire in China and has just been burned. Eighteen of his staff from Crown have been arrested, three of them top Australian executives. Crown's share price has tumbled. As its single biggest shareholder, with more than 48% of the stock, Packer, lost half a billion dollars in the process. Does he have much of a case?

China has laws; lots of them. One of those laws stipulates that one cannot explicitly advertise gambling in China. The eighteen Crown staff are alleged to have violated that law by seeking to entice high rollers, so-called 'whales' to gambling resorts in Australia, given some of the recent strictures on resorts in Macau. In other words, they seem to have been messing around with the Mafia. They are now likely, at least metaphorically, to wind up dead in the East River.

While Packer and his Crown colleagues meet and confer about how to handle this problem and he expresses concern about and support for his detained staff; what are the rest of us to make of the situation? We should recall to mind that the law is more than usually an ass in China; since the Communist Party chooses with studied arbitrariness when or whether to uphold its own laws; and there is nothing available in China resembling what we in Australia or elsewhere in the West think of as 'due process'.

The superficial and naïve interpretation of the eighteen arrests is that unscrupulous foreigners fell afoul of a perfectly clear Chinese law and deserve the penalties they will now get. Xi Jinping has been cracking down on corruption and these arrests are of a piece with his sweeping anti-corruption campaign. But to leave the matter here would be to overlook everything that really matters about the case.

Given that the Party chooses very selectively when and how to enforce its own laws, we need to ask why it has in this specific case. Given that the detainees will not receive a fair trial, we will be left wondering about the truth of the matter. And given that some of those detained and facing prison are Australian citizens, we need to think about the understanding we have with China regarding such incarcerations.

There are now a large number of very wealthy people in China, including a great many of the Communist Party elite. They have indulged, many of them, in gambling for a long time, especially through Stanley Ho's casinos in Macau. What is it that makes the enticing of such whales to other gambling precincts unwelcome? Are they not at liberty to spend or throw away their own money as they see fit? Well, no, not altogether. And one reason for that is that so many of them are gambling with ill-gotten gains. Gambling casinos have been a means for laundering such gains.

There have also been reports that the immediate trigger for the arrests was irritation among powerful figures in China at Crown's attempts to collect the gambling debts that an unnamed Chinese tycoon incurred at a Melbourne casino—to the tune of $15 million. Who'd have thought that strings might be pulled back in the mother country and Crown hit hard to teach it a lesson?

Well, anyone familiar with how the Chinese Communist Party does business, frankly. Did James Packer and his people not foresee such a possibility? They deal in risk. It seems that here they failed to calculate the odds. In truth, if we talk of whales and such, the New York Mafia are little minnows compared with the Chinese Communist Party. If he was strangely unaware of this before now, Mr Packer has just been brutally reminded of that reality.

'I am respectful that these detentions have occurred in another country and are therefore subject to their sovereign rules and investigative processes', he has stated for public consumption. It's a good bet that, behind closed doors, he has been swearing violently in the manner we all associate with his late father. It will be interesting to observe how the game now plays out.

Those who do business in China will remember the raid on Rio Tinto's offices in Shanghai a few years ago and the imprisonment of Stern Hu; as well as the trumping up of charges against Matthew Ng and his long imprisonment in Guangzhou. Crown's Jason O'Connor may fare better, because the Communist Party tends to treat Chinese expatriates more harshly than 'round eyes'. But the process is unlikely to be any fairer or more transparent.

How does the 'justice' system work in China in such cases? The charges are poorly specified; the defence counsel is not provided with the charge sheet of evidence until shortly before the trial; the detainees are pressured into making confession while in prison; the trial is not accessible to the press; and even consular access to foreign prisoners can be hard to obtain. Expect all these 'rules' to apply in the Crown case.

Does all this mean that those who do business in China must learn more than ever to 'keep their noses clean'? Well, it's not clear how exactly that is to be done, Chinese law being what it is. What stands out is that, despite calls in China since the late 1970s for the 'rule of law' to replace the arbitrary rule of power holders, no such thing has occurred. Until it does, doing any kind of business in China will remain something of a gamble.

5: The defence strategy debate we have to have

Each of these books is worth reading, if you have any interest in Australian defence and security. Both are timely, lucid, scholarly and readable. The first is a handy introduction to current debates about the ANZUS alliance, China and our security, which avoids over heated language and shows a deft familiarity with the scholarly literature. The second is something of a *tour de force* on strategic thinking as such in Australia. It could have benefited from a little editing to clean up typographical errors and infelicities of expression, but it provides an unusually incisive critique of the history and theory of defence strategy in Australia. It also offers the elements of a fresh approach, against the background of emerging strategic realities.

Lockyer's book is much the more important of the two. A twice the length of Curran's book, it covers a great deal more ground. Whereas Curran focuses almost entirely on the history of Australia's alliance with the United States; Lockyer sets our strategic choices in the far wider context of the great power aspirations of India, Indonesia and Japan, as well as China and the United States. He critically re-examines a hundred years of strategic thinking in this country. He creates an analytical framework for evaluating all the main competing schools of thought on our contemporary defence strategy. He finds all of them wanting and suggests a new defence strategy which has a good deal to recommend it.

Curran's book is significant because it will enable whoever reads it to put into fairly well-informed perspective the extravagant language we have been getting from a number of our elder statesmen in recent years, to the effect that the ANZUS alliance has reached its use by date, that we should distance ourselves from the United States and move closer to China. The late Malcolm Fraser lobbied for this in his last years and wrote a whole book on the subject. Paul Keating, in his Keith Murdoch Oration in 2013, urged that we cut adrift from the Anglosphere and 'strike out on our own'—by making Indonesia our new 'great and powerful friend'. John Brumby, Bob Carr and Stephen Fitzgerald have been insisting that we now live in 'a Chinese world' and need to turn our attention increasingly to Beijing.

Curran's position, set out very early in his short book, is that we have had our differences with the United States in the past and are likely to have increasing differences with them in the future, especially as regards the rivalries of the great powers in East Asia and the Western Pacific. He does not, however, suggest that we go so far as to break off the alliance in the ill-considered manner urged by Fraser and Keating. What we need, if we are to stake out a new position, he argues, is a better common understanding of the history of the relationship. He quotes Henry Kissinger's *World Order* (2014) on the need for security affairs to be grounded in more depth of perspective than Twitter or Facebook—or the impetuous outbursts of elder statesmen. He positions himself modestly, by quoting the respected Australian historian Keith Hancock, from back in 1954, that the historian is not someone who 'knows all the answers', but simply someone who 'has come to grips with a few very difficult questions.' He urges that we do attempt to do so now.

This stance is refreshing to read in the work of a rising young historian, after the rhetorical excesses of so many much older public figures. Like too many other debates in recent years, the one over the American alliance risks becoming unmoored from serious thinking about 'very difficult questions'. Not the least virtue of Curran's book is that it is studiously non-partisan. There is no shrill invective, rhetorical overkill or ideological cant in it. Indeed, he shows even-handedly how the same public figures who now like roundly to denounce the United States for its 'foreign adventurism' have in the past enthusiastically backed American power. Paul Keating declared to Fran Kelly, in 1994, that Desert Storm, in 1990, should not have stopped at liberating Kuwait. It should have gone all the way to Baghdad and overthrown Saddam Hussein. A more partisan book might have passed over such an episode in silence.

Curran concludes his historical reflection with three general observations: that, in the Trump era, we need to disabuse senior US policy makers of the notion that Australian support can be taken for granted; that it is time to re-examine our alliance with fresh eyes in order for it to last well into the 21st century; and that we need to be smarter in our rhetoric and 'less prone to sonorous declarations of support than to hard thinking informed by a greater sense of history.' His argument is largely persuasive. If, however, we are to do these things, we need more than the brief historical survey he has provided. We need something like Adam Lockyer's sustained reflection on our own strategic tradition, the emerging strategic environment and the realistic defence strategy options among which we need to choose.

Lockyer dedicated his book to his father, WO1 Phil Lockyer, who enlisted in the Royal Australian Infantry on 25 March 1970 and 'now, after four and a half decades of continuous service, is one of the last remaining Vietnam veterans still serving in the Australian Army'. He issued a vote of thanks, in his Acknowledgements, to Professor Alan Dupont, 'one of Australia's most prominent defence thinkers', under whose tutelage, at the University of New South Wales, he did the research that forms the basis for his book. These statements might have signalled a partisan stance, but he is strikingly dispassionate and fair-minded in his overview of the field:

> I found myself convinced by Professor Paul Dibb over breakfast, swayed by Professor Hugh White during lunch and persuaded by Professor Michael Evans over dinner. Being pulled in so many directions prompted the central question of this book: how would we know a 'good' defence strategy if we saw one?

He offers, in this book, a clear and practical set of ideas about how we might in fact know a good strategy if we saw one. He applies these ideas to the various competing schools of thought, concludes that there is 'still considerable work to be done to develop a good defence strategy for Australia'; then proposes what he suggests might actually be a good strategy, evaluated against the criteria he has set out.

His argument is refreshing in that it combines history, game theory, geography, geopolitics and economics in an incisive critique of all the contending approaches that have been offered for many years now in Australian defence debates. He identifies these as the Defence of Australia school, with variants espoused by Paul Dibb and Hugh White; the Flexible Deterrence school of Ross Babbage; the Status Quo school, with variants espoused by Michael Evans and Rory Medcalf; and the Security school articulated by Alan Dupont. He finds fault with all of them, including the thinking of his own mentor, Alan Dupont. He then reframes the debate and argues that we need to distinguish between defence of continental Australia as our ultimate strategic *interest* and prevention of a threat to continental Australia as our primary strategic *objective*. The latter, not the former, should be what drives our defence strategy, he argues and he sketches out a new approach to how this might be done in the emerging strategic environment.

He calls his new approach a 'Corbettian maritime denial strategy', after the British naval historian and strategic theorist Julian Corbett (1854-1922). Corbett differed radically from the famous Alfred Thayer Mahan in arguing that naval force was best used to control sea lanes and blockade ports, rather than to fight massive naval battles to destroy the enemy's force in being. Lockyer's argument is that Australia should develop a maritime strategy centred on the Indo-Pacific Arc (across our northern perimeter) and the Melanesian Arc (across the South West Pacific), rather than areas further abroad. Above all, we should focus on denial of control of the Malacca Strait or of the seaways on either side of it to any would-be hegemonic power. Our air and land forces should be configured to support such a strategy, including the development of amphibious assault forces for seizing key chokepoints along such sea lanes in the event of crisis or conflict.

The way in which he arrives at this prescription is impressive. His analytical framework is transparent and his way of assessing the merits of various strategies is a judicious mixture of the empirical, the probabilistic and the game theoretic. The breadth of his reading is outstanding and it is clear that he has read not in order to buttress a preconceived theory, but in order to think more deeply and break new ground. His book is a genuinely thought-provoking introduction to the great strategic debate we have to have. Indeed, there has probably never been a better such introduction.

6: Expert knowledge and scientific thinking under siege

A special Issue of *New Scientist*, dated 1 April 2017, was devoted to the question 'What is Knowledge?' The sub-title was 'The Biggest Questions about Facts, Truth, Lies and Belief'. It was clearly not intended as an April Fool's Day joke, but there would be plenty of scope for a spoof which had done just that, given the bizarre beliefs and attitudes to truth held by altogether too many human beings. As Carl Sagan expressed it some thirty years ago, we have created a scientific civilization, but have allowed a situation to develop in which the vast majority of people do *not* think scientifically—and that is a recipe for disaster.

This is more important in our time than at any time in human history. It is important in general, because we need the citizens of a scientific civilization to understand things in a non-superstitious, non-religious, non-ideological way, which is to say in terms of sound evidence, probability and good reasoning, not fantasy, dogma or authority. It is important, in our time, because the rate and scope of scientific discoveries, since the middle of the 20th century, have overwhelmed the folk culture and traditional belief systems even of Western societies. Globally, traditional folk and religious belief systems are hopelessly at odds with the scientific worldview and the gap is widening, not narrowing.

Moreover, the distortions of thinking we see all around us gravely aggravate the practical problems we face in strengthening the foundations of the nascent global civilization of the 21st century. The ecological stresses of the human impact on the biosphere have been of growing concern since at least the 1960s. But they are at the outer margin of a set of problems that begin with the most elementary matters of public policy and mass education. Religious opposition to the findings of evolutionary biology is not merely the eccentricity of a few cranks, but the symptom of a deeper cultural problem which surfaces in the plague of conspiracy theories that beset the world, or the movement against vaccination, or the widespread confusion about anthropogenic global warming and what to do about it.

Tom Nichols, a Professor of International Security Affairs at the US Naval War College, has just contributed a thoughtful little book on this subject, with the disconcerting title *The Death of Expertise: The Campaign Against Established Knowledge and Why It Matters* (Oxford University Press, 2017). He also has an essay in the March/April issue of *Foreign Affairs*; an issue devoted to pondering 'Trump's World'. He doesn't mean that expertise itself is dying out. He means that the willingness of altogether too many people—including Donald Trump—to accept the judgements of experts is under threat and that this poses a fundamental problem for both scientific civilization and democratic governance. It is a potentially lethal pathology in a civilization overwhelmingly *dependent* on good science, but overwhelmingly *ignorant* of the science itself and addicted to poor thinking, prejudice and tribalism.

By experts, Nichols means specialists within their fields, whether tradesmen or astrophysicists, school teachers or professors of economics. 'Something is going terribly wrong', he writes. 'The United States is now a country obsessed with the worship of its own ignorance.' He plainly does not mean the best thinkers in the country, of whom there are many in countless fields. He means a large mass of the population, including student activists at Ivy League universities and all manner of common citizens harvesting factoids and narratives from the Googleplex. 'Never have so many people had so much access to so much knowledge and yet have been so resistant to learning anything', he laments.

His is a cry from the heart of a serious and dispassionate scholar. It centres on the premise that:

> we are witnessing the death of the ideal of expertise itself, a Google-fuelled, Wikipedia-based, blog-sodden collapse of any division between professionals and laypeople, students and teachers, knowers and wonderers—in other words, between those of any achievement in an area and those with none at all.

He infers from this that:

> The death of expertise is not just a rejection of existing knowledge. It is fundamentally a rejection of science and dispassionate rationality, which are the foundations of modern civilization.

These two claims make his book a must read for those dedicated to critical rationalism and the kind of 'open society' that some of us have attempted to build, based on such thinking. He would be the first to confess that the field is complex and that his evidence is impressionistic rather than encyclopaedic. But his arguments ought to prompt serious debate—of precisely the kind he champions against the 'blog-sodden', anti-expert, tribal culture whose rise he deplores.

Experts have long had their critics, of course, both in the name of brute reality and the name of 'common sense'. Harry Truman famously declared, in the late 1940s, that he longed to meet a one handed economist, because all the ones he had met would forever say to him 'on the one hand, but then again on the other hand'. He wanted less *qualified* advice, one might say. And one might then comment, 'Be careful what you wish for.' In Fred Schepisi's acclaimed 1990 film of John Le Carre's *The Russia House,* CIA chief Russell (Roy Scheider) exclaims in exasperation at one point, concerning the ambivalence of his experts on Soviet nuclear missile capabilities 'For experts, there's no toilet deep enough!'

Conversely, the failure of experts to persuade democratic masses to heed the voice of reason and restraint is age-old and by no means a problem only in our time. There is a famous scene in the sixth book of Thucydides' history of the Peloponnesian war, in which the veteran and sober-minded general Nicias attempts to dissuade the Athenian popular assembly from mounting an invasion of Sicily. When his warnings about how ill-advised this would be fall on deaf ears, he attempts a little reverse psychology, telling the assembly that to ensure success they would need to double down on the number of men and ships they sent to Sicily—which they then enthusiastically do; putting him in command. This was, decidedly, not a case of the 'wisdom of crowds'—a topic that Nichols also touches on quite intelligently.

His observations about the role of experts in forecasting, as distinct from explaining complexities or implementing skilled routines are interesting. He has read the best recent work on the subject of forecasting, such as James Surowiecki's *The Wisdom of Crowds* (2004), Philip Tetlock's *Political Experts* (2006) and Nate Silver's *The Signal and the Noise: The Art and Science of Prediction* (2012). He praises Tetlock's work on the failures of expert forecasting, but correctly observes that too many opinionated people have drawn precisely the wrong conclusion from this: that they are smarter than the experts and that their own fanciful opinions are as likely to be correct as anyone else's. In fact, crowds need close curation and disciplined procedures to produce useful forecasts. It's just that such methods can yield surprisingly useful results. I am currently engaged in developing a platform based on such methods, with the hi-tech start-up Dysrupt Labs.

Nichols does not argue that experts always get things right. But he does express concern at shoddy and overheated thinking getting out of control, causing growing problems for the Western democracies. Crucially, he remarks that:

> Experts are often wrong, and the good ones among them are the first to admit it—because their own professional disciplines are based not on some ideal of perfect knowledge and competence, but on a constant process of identifying errors and correcting them, which ultimately drives intellectual progress.

This is Popperian. There is nothing pretentious or obscure about it. His concern is that an increasingly anti-intellectual culture, in which experts are derided as egg heads and all manner of ignorance, prejudice and conspiracy theory is propagated virally on the Internet, presages a grim future for the open society, in which both serious scientific inquiry and more or less effective public policy may become more and more difficult to sustain.

He concedes that anti-intellectualism in America has quite a pedigree. He quotes Alexis de Tocqueville as referring to it in the 1830s as a cultural trait of many Americans. His concern is that this is now getting out of hand. The American republic was founded by educated men who believed that sound public policy depended upon an informed citizenry electing responsible representatives to legislate on their behalf. Even in a relatively homogeneous and slow-moving America, this proved problematic and the American Civil War showed that the system had failed abysmally to resolve the single greatest challenge it faced in the first half of the 19th century. But

Nichols argues that America is now afflicted by hi-tech egalitarianism undermining the very idea of intellectual authority or high standards of critical thinking. While he does not discuss the 19th century failures, he fears there will be grave 21st century ones.

He draws attention to the fairly well-known Dunning Krueger effect: the research finding that the less rational or intellectually gifted a person is the likelier they are to believe that they can make accurate judgements about things that are in fact beyond their grasp. This kind of problem was supposed to be overcome by mass education; but mass education, he argues, has had unintended side-effects. Among them is the problem that since the 1970s, educational institutions have flattered students at every level about their abilities, diluting the intellectual standards to which they are held; creating a growing class of conceited and outspoken young people who actually have poorly developed thinking skills, deficient knowledge of reality and an absurd and truculent sense of their own opinions and entitlements. His remarks on this subject are especially worth reflecting on.

But as if this was not bad enough, he adds, the Internet has generated a runaway proliferation of toxic websites that feed ignorance, prejudice and conspiracy theory at the expense of serious reading, thinking and engagement with the opinions and writings of experts. He doesn't offer a finely calibrated set of data on just how many people fall into these categories and how many are still well-informed and reasonably rational. He simply points to some basic indications that there are worrying trends and that those of us concerned to foster and reinforce a culture of critical rationality, scientific education and sound public policy would be well advised to take such trends and their implications very seriously. A bastion of such concern should be our universities, but he expresses serious alarm that they, too, are being overrun by a plague bacillus of anti-intellectualism and lowered standards.

It is easy enough to poke fun at or feel dismayed by the confusion and ignorance of the patently under-educated, but the situation at even Ivy League (never mind second or third tier) universities is not reassuring, Nichols argues:

> The most important of...intellectual capabilities and the one most under attack in American universities is critical thinking: the ability to examine new information and competing ideas dispassionately, logically and without emotional or personal preconceptions...Universities have now become, especially in the second and third strata, 'an expensive educational buffet laden mostly with intellectual junk food, with very little adult supervision to ensure that the students choose nutrition over nonsense.'...Make no mistake: campuses in the United States are increasingly surrendering their intellectual authority not only to children, but also to activists who are directly attacking the traditions of free inquiry that scholarly communities are supposed to defend.

Each of his chapters addresses a different aspect of the problem, concisely, lucidly and forcefully; but those on higher education and the dark side of the World Wide Web are the most troubling.

Hubert Krivine's *The Earth: From Myths to Knowledge* (2015), Shawn Otto's *The War on Science* (2016) and Seth Mnookin's *The Panic Virus: Fear, Myth and the Vaccination Debate* (2016) are recent books attempting directly to address the epistemological and factual confusion that besets our society. Another excellent recent contribution is James Lawrence Powell's *Four Revolutions in the Earth Sciences: From Heresy to Truth;* which looks at the discovery of Deep Time, continental drift, meteorite impact and global warming. One would very much like to think that such books would be read very, very widely and would help to form the minds of a mass of citizens in a scientific and democratic society. Unfortunately, only a small number of people read such books, while—as Nichols argues with anxiety and disdain—a vastly larger number surf their favoured websites and browse, all too often, on junk, including anti-scientific ranting or conspiracy theories.

Two things need to be brought into focus here that Nichols does not address. The first is that the human brain, as recent cognitive psychology has shown, is what Daniel Kahneman called 'a machine for jumping to conclusions'. It is hard-wired to make certain kinds of errors in judgment and inference. Only systematic education in critical thinking and scientific method can correct for these cognitive deficiencies. This has serious implications in a society based on complex problems and large data sets. The invention of behavioural economics has been an attempt to integrate these insights into macro-economic and indeed micro-economic thinking. But the whole educational curriculum needs to bring them into play very seriously and systematically.

The second thing is that we have been here before, but almost no-one—even highly educated historians—is aware of the antecedent. As Lucio Russo pointed out in *The Forgotten Revolution: How Science Was Born in 300 BC and Why It Had to be Reborn* (Springer Verlag, 2004), the 3rd century BCE Hellenistic scientists (not the Pre-Socratics or Plato and Aristotle) invented science as we know it and began to produce theories, experiments and results of a kind we associate with modern science—but then, from the mid-2nd century BCE, it ground to a halt. His explanation as to why is arresting and runs contrary to the conventional Enlightenment narrative about 'barbarism and religion' being the problem. In reality, he claims, the problem was the inability of Greco-Roman society itself to allow scientific thinking to take root and flourish. It stagnated and then died on the vine. He wrote his book as a warning that this could occur again and that we should not be complacent about the problem. Tom Nichols would agree.

7: Undoing the confusions of the intuitive brain

Michael Lewis writes good books. They tend to be concise, highly readable, immensely lucid and concerned with fascinating matters of human confusion and how to find one's way through it. He also tends to be highly interested in thinkers who operate outside the range or authority of both popular prejudice and conventional intellectual wisdom.

His first book, *Liar's Poker* (1989), was about his strange experience in a Wall Street bank's bond trading department. Since then, he has written a string of best sellers. Perhaps the most famous of them have been *Moneyball* (2003) and *The Big Short* (2010). His latest book, *The Undoing Project: A Friendship That Changed the World* (2016) is less exciting than any of these other three—not being about sport or the corruptions and stupidities of Wall St and the US government—but it is a wonderful story and Lewis is a first rate raconteur.

The story is that of the extraordinary intellectual friendship between Amos Tversky and Daniel Kahneman, which took cognitive psychology to new levels and ended up generating the new discipline of behavioural economics, with profound implications for public policy and the whole conversation about choice and human rationality. As with the heroes of *Moneyball* and *The Big Short*, the heroes of this story were highly intelligent, somewhat eccentric outsiders addicted to asking curly questions and digging relentlessly for the answers.

Lewis uses as the epigraph to his book a quip by Voltaire: 'Doubt is not a pleasant condition, but certainty is an absurd one.' One might add that a fog of confusion is the most common human experience and that bringing about tolerable clarity—to say nothing of certainty—is a very exacting task. Yet our economists argued for a long time that human beings were 'utility-maximizing rationalists' and that this was why market economies worked—and worked better than command economies. There is a lot to this, but...

Behavioural economics, based on the insights of Kahneman and Tversky, is based on a substantial correction of that assumption and, as Richard Thaler (one of the founders of that discipline and another of Lewis's outsiders) and Cass Sunstein (a brilliant Chicago University professor of jurisprudence and political science) point out in *Nudge: Improving Decisions About Health, Wealth and Happiness* (2009), if we *want* our citizens to make rational choices, we need to give careful thought to how the choices are *presented* to them, lest they make predictably irrational choices.

Daniel Kahneman was awarded the Nobel Prize in Economic Sciences (2002) for decades of work on prospect theory, human biases and cognitive illusions. His 2011 book *Thinking, Fast and Slow*, helped to popularize many of his (and Tversky's) most seminal insights. Like Lewis's work, it is both highly readable and very lucid—the two by no means always go together. It's key maxim is that the human brain is 'a machine for jumping to conclusions'—the 'fast' mode—and that it often jumps to strangely *erroneous* conclusions because of certain hard-wired biases that must be very consciously and deliberately corrected for if we want to avoid such errors—the 'slow' thinking part.

Tversky was widely regarded as the more brilliant of the two. It used to be said, as early as the late 1970s, that there was something called the Tversky Intelligence Test: 'The faster you realized that Tversky was smarter than you, the smarter you were.' But he and Kahneman developed their ideas like two master duelling banjo players, bouncing insights and hypotheses off one another and spending so much time in one another's company that it was almost as if they were lovers. It was a classic intellectual friendship.

Both were Israeli Jews and their casts of mind and intellectual preoccupations were wonderfully representative of that Jewish intellectual culture that has generated so very many first class minds in the modern era. Neither was religious. Tversky was born in Haifa, in the British Mandate of Palestine, in 1937, but grew to adulthood in the besieged state of Israel. He received his undergraduate education at the Hebrew University of Jerusalem, but his doctorate from the University of Michigan, Ann Arbor, in 1964. He fought in Israel's wars and was awarded for bravery. He died of a metastatic melanoma in 1996. He was fascinated by chance and the roots of misperception.

Kahneman was born in Tel Aviv, in the British Mandate of Palestine in 1934, where his mother was visiting relatives. He spent his childhood years in Paris, however, where his parents had emigrated from Lithuania in the early 1920s. They were in Paris when it was occupied by the Nazis in 1940. His father was picked up in the first major round-up of French Jews, but was released upon the intervention of his employer. The family, on the run for the remainder of the war, survived except for Kahneman's father, who died from diabetes in 1944. The rest of the family moved to British Mandatory Palestine in 1948, just before the creation of the state of Israel. Kahneman's fixation on randomness and error was psychologically rooted in his precarious childhood.

The origin of Lewis's book about these two men lay in a review of *Moneyball*, by Richard Thaler and Cass Sunstein, in 2003. Lewis's summary of what they wrote about his own work and the impression this made on him is beautifully characteristic of his trademark modesty and as good an introduction to why he wrote *The Undoing Project* and why the story it tells matters as one could hope to find. Thaler and Sunstein, he wrote:

> Agreed that it was interesting that any market for professional athletes might be so screwed up that a poor team like the Oakland A's could beat most rich teams simply by exploiting the inefficiencies. But—they went on to say—the author of *Moneyball* did

not seem to realize the deeper reason for the inefficiencies in the market for baseball players: They sprang directly from the inner workings of the human mind. The ways in which some baseball expert might misjudge baseball players—the ways in which any expert's judgements might be warped by the expert's own mind—had been described years ago by a pair of Israeli psychologists, Daniel Kahneman and Amos Tversky. My book wasn't original. It was simply an illustration of ideas that had been floating around for decades and had yet to be fully appreciated by, among others, me. That was an understatement.

He refers here to the flaws in the judgement of 'experts', but those flaws are human universals. They are just more interesting when they surface in the errors of experts.

If you are yourself a specialist in prospect theory or cognitive science more broadly, or almost any field of rigorous thinking, you may already be familiar with the findings of Tversky and Kahneman and those lesser known figures, such as Paul Slovic, who created this rich set of insights. But you may well not be acquainted with the personal and intellectual journey that led to these insights. Lewis has written the story of that journey in his distinctive manner. It is a beautiful piece of work. Read it and enjoy the journey of two brilliant human beings.

8: Were there Russian moles in ASIO? Yes, Prime Minister.

The final volume of the official history of ASIO admits, in muted tones, that there were multiple Soviet moles in the organization during the Cold War. Not one or a possible one, as so often rumoured in the past; but a number of them. The language is vague and elliptical, but the statement is there and it is buttressed by the rhetorical question with which the authors finish the whole work: 'how extensive was the betrayal and how extensive was the damage?' The official history was the best possible place to answer this question, but its authors were forbidden by ASIO itself to do this. The highly classified 1994 Cook Report contains the truth. The official history does not. As a consequence, we the people, for whose sake ASIO exists in the first place, are being kept in the dark about its betrayal from within and consequent grave failures during the Cold War. We must have the truth in this matter—clear and unredacted.

Speaking on national television last year, one of the three authors of the three volume official history John Blaxland, stated that there had been a 'handful' of Soviet moles in ASIO; that the official historians had seen the documents and know the names of the moles in question; that it was 'deeply shocking' to finally realize what had happened and that the damage done had been 'devastating'. Yet none of this was printed in the official history. All that ASIO would allow into print was the oblique statement that there were a number of moles and that the whole story is still being kept secret for undisclosed reasons. As someone who is a former senior intelligence analyst and has written about this matter for many years—claiming that there had been four or more moles in ASIO—I feel both vindicated by the official history and badly let down by it.

This is a big story. In 1981, in the *National Times*, Brian Toohey wrote that the KGB had been 'more successful in its penetration operations in Australia than in any other country, according to hard evidence available to the American Central Intelligence Agency.' It is worth quoting him at length on this, because last year he played a completely different tune in reviewing the official history:

> The CIA evidence has been built up over many years from defectors, its own agents in Moscow and intercepts of Soviet communications. It shows that the KGB consistently has been able to obtain a much higher level of classified information from Canberra than from anywhere else. The special value of the leaks is that they include sensitive US information given to Australia under intelligence and other swapping arrangements...A top CIA source told the *National Times* that, despite intensive efforts, the agency had been bamboozled in trying to work out just who were the KGB penetration agents in Australia. But he said CIA studies of what they knew was turning up in Moscow demonstrated that the KGB had magnificent sources in Australia. 'The product was better than anything else they were getting—and still is.'...According

to this source, who at one stage in the 1970s was head of the division that included CIA activities in Australia, the KGB operation in Australia had the hallmarks of a penetration that went back at least 30 years.

This assessment has now been vindicated by the official historians—but not in the official history, except in the most muted possible language.

ASIO and both sides of politics, at the highest levels, have known the truth since 1994, but have been withholding it from the public. The Russians, of course, have known it all along. Those concealing the Cook Report's findings have been aided and abetted by those who think that talk of moles is just the old hunt for 'reds under the bed', which was always misguided and should be consigned to the dustbin of history. In reviewing the third volume of the official history last year, Brian Toohey, of all people, took the position that the history provided no evidence that there had been Soviet penetration of ASIO; that it wouldn't matter if there had been; and that Dennis Richardson, in the early years of this century, had justifiably stripped away ASIO's counter-intelligence capability to concentrate resources on counter-terrorism.

Toohey has lost the plot. The muted manner in which the official history admitted that there had, indeed, been penetrations is a fig-leaf over the organization's acute embarrassment about the grim truth. Hostile penetration matters a great deal. The stripping away of what counter-intelligence (CI) capacity had presumably been put in place since 1994, if that is indeed what happened in the 2000s, is astonishing. A very tightly held AFP and DSD program dubbed Operation Liver reviewed and cleaned out ASIO in 1993-94.

The 1994 Cook Report laid out the evidence of how rotten ASIO had been in the Cold War. It has been dubbed 'the report no-one is allowed to read'. Given, however, that ASIO was established in the first place (in 1949) because Canberra was leaking like a sieve and that throughout the Cold War it was supposed to be the guardian of our intelligence alliance with our Anglophone allies, the discovery that there were multiple Soviet moles inside it for much of its history calls into question the very rationale for having such an organization at all.

There were rumours right through the 1970s and 1980s that ASIO (and possibly other parts of the Australian government) had been penetrated. But the general tendency was to assume that Australia was an intelligence backwater and to insist, as Toohey still does, that hunting for moles is a dangerous and unjustified 'witch-hunt'. Yet it was discovered, in the late 1940s, that there was a large Soviet spy ring in Canberra. This ring was not uncovered due to a witch hunt, but by cable traffic intercepts and skilled decryption of Soviet codes. The fourteen spies in question were not working at the margins of Australian society, but in the offices of the Minister for External Affairs (H. V. Evatt), the Secretary for External Affairs (John Burton), and on the staff of Paul Hasluck (in External Affairs and at the United Nations).

The late Des Ball, doyen of Australian scholars on intelligence matters, declared in his last years that he believed both Evatt and Burton were knowing collaborators in this espionage in the 1940s. Both were resistant to the establishment of ASIO and to any vetting of External Affairs staff. Evatt notoriously remarked in the House of Representatives, in the mid-1950s, that there were no Soviet spies in Australia. He had asked the Soviet Foreign Minister Vyacheslav Molotov and been reassured of this, he told his astounded fellow parliamentarians. Those, like Toohey, who now play down the penetration of ASIO are in the same category as the half-mad Evatt.

The Hope Royal Commission of 1974-77 and later investigations worried about possible Soviet penetration of ASIO. No truly serious investigation was conducted, however, until the Keating government, in 1992-93, learned disturbing things from unreleased portions of the Mitrokhin archive about KGB operations in Australia. Operation Liver and the Cook Report were commissioned by Keating to get to the bottom of the problem. What they found, however, was so disturbing that the evidence was buried by the Keating government. The final chapter of the official history's final volume, 'Looking for Moles', begins:

> Allegations of penetration—that the [KGB or GRU] might have placed moles within ASIO—have circulated for years. We now know...that penetrating Australia's intelligence agencies was one of the KGB's objectives following the resumption of diplomatic relations between Australia and the Soviet Union in 1959. It now appears evident...that they succeeded, although in most instances, the fact of penetration during these years was revealed through information that only came to light after the Berlin Wall fell...

This is an evasion of what the historians actually found and what Cook had long ago reported to the Keating government. The truth is that ASIO was deeply compromised and foiled, from very early on, in performing its most fundamental task.

ASIO's counter-intelligence function, never robust, was broken in the Whitlam years. Lionel Murphy, as Attorney General, in 1973-74, actually forbad ASIO to bug the Soviet Embassy. As Blaxland and Crawley express it:

> At its peak, in 1969, D5 had nine staff, but it had shrunk to only three people by 1974. By the mid-1970s, ASIO's counter-intelligence capabilities were so poor, despite the continuing efforts of some judicious officers, that they were almost non-existent.

Yet in those very years we now know that a highly effective KGB officer, Gerontiy Lazovik was active in Canberra, recruiting inside the Australian intelligence services.

At a telling point, based on knowledge of who the moles turned out to be, the official historians comment:

In hindsight, it seems that the difficult questions were often avoided or not considered. Explanations were settled on, such as indiscreet agents, with no evidence, and these were accepted over the more sinister possibility that a mole was busy undermining ASIO's efforts. All the while, as later intelligence would suggest, a number of moles were left to continue their treachery.

The wording here warrants close attention. *Later intelligence would 'suggest'* that *a number of moles* were at work within ASIO as of 1981. What exactly that intelligence was or is, the official historians do not disclose. Operation Liver and the Cook Report are the answers. We need their findings finally to come out. There can be no excuse, a generation after the end of the Cold War, for concealing from the Australian public what has always been known in Moscow and has long been known in tight circles in Canberra.

Lazovik was not the first or last successful Soviet intelligence officer in Australia. In 1988, just as the Cold War ended, ASIO learned from KGB defector Oleg Gordievsky that Lazovik's recruit had almost certainly been in ASIO and that 'the next two KGB residents, Gennady Nayanov and Lev Koshlyakov had also had successful tours of Australia'. Koshlyakov was here from 1978 to 1984 and is to this day a consultant to the Putin regime. He has been described as 'one of the most dangerous KGB officers ever posted to Australia.' Why are we still being told so little about his activities in the 1980s? If Brian Toohey is right and none of this matters, there is no reason to censor the record. But the official historians have stated that what happened was 'shocking' and 'devastating'. It must, therefore, be brought to light and explained.

In May 2016, Paul Dibb—who was head of National Assessments in the Joint Intelligence Organization (JIO) in the mid-1970s, then later Deputy Director of JIO, head of the Defence strategic policy and force structure review for Kim Beazley in 1985-86, Director General of JIO and then Deputy Secretary of Defence for Strategy and Intelligence as the Cold War ended; spoke to *The Australian's* Cameron Stewart about having been an undercover agent for ASIO throughout the Lazovik and Koshlyakov years. He expressed annoyance at the fact that innuendo had surrounded him for decades, claiming that he had been 'cleared' by the Cook Report. That claim was the first time anyone had claimed to be so much as a subject of the Cook Report or openly admitted its very existence.

Dibb stated that he had approached the Soviet Embassy in 1965 as a young geographer, been photographed by ASIO and then recruited by ASIO's Deputy Director, no less, to cultivate Soviet Embassy officials and try to both identify intelligence officers and open lines for possible defections. By his own account, he performed this role for twenty one years, even as he rose through the ranks of JIO and completed the famous Dibb Review for Kim Beazley.

He became closely acquainted with the top KGB officers in Canberra, most notably Lev Koshlyakov. There is a story to tell here. Dibb himself has not told the half of it. Yet neither the second nor the third volume of the official history has so much as an entry in its Index under 'Dibb, Paul'. Why is this story, too, so secret?

The official history concludes with oblique objections to the veil of secrecy that has been cast over the whole matter of Soviet moles:

> The question remains over the whole issue of penetration and whether the veil of secrecy needs to be maintained' and 'secrecy for secrecy's sake can on occasion prove counterproductive.

Aldrich Ames and Robert Hanssen, 'men who compromised American intelligence operations and whose actions led to the deaths of scores of Soviet agents who were prepared to risk their lives collaborating with Western intelligence agencies', are both behind bars and books have been written about them, the historians point out. But in Australia the moles remain at large and unpunished. All the official historians offer us, however, is a question to which they know the answers: '...how extensive was the betrayal and how extensive was the damage?' They know, but ASIO has forbidden them to disclose the facts.

What possible justification is there for keeping these things classified? Five years ago, I put that question to Michael Cook himself, who now lives in retirement in London. He responded by email that:

> ...[Neither Paul] Keating, nor anybody else, told me or even suggested to me that I give my report a high security classification. That I decided on my own for what I thought, and still think, were good reasons, which is why..., as you correctly recall, I would not do as you asked.

He declined to disclose the reasons themselves. Given that the official history has now both confirmed the existence of the Cook Report and the existence of 'a handful' of moles (meaning four or five) inside ASIO, we might reasonably speculate about those reasons. It could be that the Keating government did not want what would have been a scandal far more explosive than anything else in ASIO's history. It therefore suppressed things that the public had and has a right to know. It did this not for our sake, or for the sake of national security, but purely to spare itself embarrassment and vexatious trouble.

But in that case, why did the Howard government not release the Cook Report after 1996? There must be *bipartisan* reasons for the matter being kept secret. The most plausible is that what CI sleuths see as compelling is not always what a court of law will find convincing. A consensus therefore arose that the whole thing was too messy to drag out into the light of the courts and the media. Yet the official historians say they know who the moles were and that the evidence is clear enough to be shocking. So the argument about the evidence being inconclusive looks somewhat tenuous.

There may be another reason, but the official historians do not provide one and seem sceptical themselves about the decision. Given all that they have seen, that should itself be regarded as a compelling argument for the nonsense to end and for the Cook Report finally to be released. Until it is, we will know that ASIO failed in the Cold War, but we will have no grounds for believing that its old weaknesses have been remedied, rather than merely papered over in a *Yes, Prime Minister* kind of way. This in an era of unprecedented Chinese penetration of Australian society and institutions. But that is a story for another time.

9: Syrian atrocities: fact, propaganda and realpolitik

The Syrian government stands accused of mass killing, in its war against both Sunni jihadists and unarmed political dissenters. The latest claim is that it is incinerating bodies at Saydnaya prison to disguise the evidence of its mass murder. This it categorically denies, declaring the claim a 'Hollywood plot' and a bunch of 'lies' intended to justify aggression and intervention against it. What should we believe?

It's an old maxim that 'truth is the first casualty of war'. Lies and propaganda are used by all sides, due to exaggeration in the heat of battle, to damn the enemy, mobilize the moral passion of one's own side and justify the brutal measures resorted to in an effort to win. As John Dower pointed out in his study of the Pacific war of 1941-45, *War Without Mercy*, savage racist propaganda was used by both sides and the brutality of the fighting escalated relentlessly; culminating in the nuclear bombing of Japan that ended the war.

There are those who declare that claims of mass atrocities by the Assad regime are only anti-regime propaganda drummed up by its enemies; that, indeed, the Western media and human rights organizations have been duped by the Sunni jihadists again and again and that it is they—the 'head choppers' as one old friend of mine describes the Sunni jihadists—who are the true enemy of human rights in Syria. We should, according to this school of thought, put aside misguided criticisms of Assad and back him and his Russian and Iranian allies against the Sunnis.

We need, however, to keep the two issues of atrocity allegations and *realpolitik* distinct. Let's suppose, for the sake of argument, that the evidence showed unambiguously that the battle in Syria comes down to a choice between Assad's secular dictatorship and a radical Sunni regime. Let's suppose further that we lean towards Assad in this regard. Would it follow that Assad could not be guilty of horrific war crimes? Surely not; but we might well feel ill at ease about admitting or criticizing them, because this appears to lend moral support to the other side.

The tendency to want to deny Assad's crimes would be strong in such a case. But facts are stubborn things. It might be easiest to get this in perspective by historical analogy. During the Spanish Civil War (1936-39) there were large scale atrocities on both sides and within the Republican side. Fascist death squads executed an estimated 220,000 people, according to historian of that war Paul Preston, in his monumental study *The Spanish Holocaust* (2012). Hundreds of thousands of others died in the war itself.

This didn't bother Franco's allies, Hitler and Mussolini. Nor was it played up by London or Paris, who strove to remain neutral throughout the civil war. But Stalin's NKVD death squads also killed large numbers of Trotskyists and anarchists within Republican ranks and the latter were not innocent themselves; killing priests, landowners, bourgeois Republicans and Stalinists. These atrocities, in turn, tended to be played down by the anti-fascist front organizations. It has taken a great deal of historical spadework to, literally, exhume the truth. So it is with the Syrian civil war.

As one veteran reporter on Middle Eastern conflicts put it last year, 'the Syrian rebellion today is dominated in its entirety by Sunni Islamist forces. And the most powerful of these are the most radical...In the now extremely unlikely event of the Islamist rebels defeating the Assad regime and reuniting Syria under their rule, the country would become a Sunni Islamist dictatorship.' The defeat of Assad, therefore, would be a serious setback for the West in its struggle with radical Islam. We should not want that—neither from our own point of view, nor for the people of Syria, nor for the Middle East.

This leaves us, however, with the kind of intractable moral dilemma that arises again and again in world affairs. When there is no viable good option—no 'white knight'—to back, what do you do? If we seek to undermine Assad and his allies, we risk strengthening the hand of the Sunni radicals. As it is, Saudi Arabia and Qatar are backing those radicals and the West is at best playing a weak or equivocal hand behind the scenes. If we back Assad, we are aligning ourselves with his allies, Putin's Russia and the ruthless Shiite mullahs in Tehran. If we stand on the sidelines, we can expect others to determine the outcome. What, therefore, is to be done?

The problem becomes even more acute once we accept—as I believe we should—that there *have*, in fact, been large scale atrocities committed by the Assad regime: tens of thousands of political prisoners tortured and executed since the uprising began five years ago. For such atrocities, whether we like it or not, buttress the radical Sunni cause. If we stand with Assad—especially without drawing attention to and condemning his crimes—we make ourselves, more than ever, the enemies of the radical Sunnis. Vengefully bitter terrorism will follow, as night follows day.

Perhaps that is why our Western governments have been all over the map in trying to deal with this geopolitical quagmire. Assad does not deserve our support and his allies are repellent. But the radical Sunnis do not represent an attractive alternative and their allies, the Saudis and Qataris, have been the arch-funders of radical Sunni Islam—Salafism and Wahhabism—globally for many years now.

It is tempting to cry 'A plague on both your houses!' and stand aside, but that leaves us with the horrific spectacle of the war, a mass of refugees, the resentment of both parties and the scorn of Putin and the mullahs. In the circumstances, the very least we must do is work hard to sift fact from propaganda and be willing to look unblinkingly at the grim realities. That is a pre-condition for taking any form of responsible action.

10: Islam, nihilism and the 'suicide' of Europe

Douglas Murray was born in July 1979, half way between the Ayatollah Khomeini flying from Paris to Tehran to lead his Shia Muslim revolution against the Shah, in January, and the Soviet invasion of Afghanistan, in December, which triggered a global Sunni Muslim jihadist reaction. On 22 September 1979, Khomeini made a speech to university students in Tehran, declaring that 'those intellectuals who say that the clergy should leave politics and go back to the mosque speak on behalf of Satan.' Alas, the clergy in question have not left politics.

During Murray's childhood, Khomeini established a theocratic state in Iran. Just after he reached adulthood, the Sunni jihad movement declared war on the United States. Just after he turned 22, al-Qaeda's planes crashed into the World Trade Centre and the Pentagon and the US retaliated by invading Afghanistan to hunt down al-Qaeda's leadership. Throughout Murray's life, jihadist terrorism has grown worse and worse, while Muslim immigration to and activism within Europe have increased relentlessly.

In short, Douglas Murray has lived all his life against a background of Muslim insurgency and terrorism, as well as massive and now all but unrestricted Muslim immigration into Europe. *The Strange Death of Europe* is about the danger he believes this poses to the future of Europe. It is intended as a clarion call to Western societies, but above all Western European societies. The opening sentence of his book reads: 'Europe is committing suicide'. That is an extraordinary claim. Extraordinary claims require extraordinary evidence. He provides what might be described as such evidence. This makes his book important, indeed compelling reading.

He declares that 'by the end of the lifespans of most people currently alive, Europe will not be Europe and the peoples of Europe will have lost the only place we had to call home.' If you find this claim shocking or wildly implausible, you should read his book and absorb the full weight of his argument. For, though you may jump to the conclusion that he is being a bit hysterical, he is a highly educated and deeply humane individual and the case he makes is troubling, just because it is *not* hysterical. He is gay and committed to Western freedoms. What he fears is the rise of reactionary and homophobic Islam in the West.

He argues in some of most thoughtful and interesting chapters—'Prophets without honour', 'The tyranny of guilt', 'Tiredness' and 'The feeling that the story has run out'—that Europe has lost its moorings and is now a ship in serious danger of capsizing. He thinks 'nihilism' has eviscerated Europe, so that it no longer believes in itself and has lost the instincts needed even for cultural survival. Whatever your point of entry to this debate—even if you are a Muslim—these chapters make thought-provoking reading and are highly recommended.

Nihilism is not a concept common to human cultures. It is chiefly associated with the self-critique of Western culture since the late 19th century and especially with the writings of Friedrich Nietzsche, who wrote in the winter of 1887:

> What I write is the history of the next two centuries. I describe what is coming, what can no longer come differently: the advent of nihilism. This history can be related even now; for necessity itself is at work here. This future speaks even now in a hundred signs...

Murray believes he is seeing those signs all around him and they alarm him deeply.

His evidence for this is richly varied. Some of it comes in direct quotes from prominent political and intellectual figures who have openly declared that Europe does not have a culture worth defending and that Islam has much to offer the West. He sees this as a deeply confused and culturally suicidal attitude and is pessimistic, because he is largely persuaded that this attitude is now too deeply entrenched to be changed, short of a cultural and geopolitical upheaval.

He dismisses scornfully the retort that such attitudes as his are merely irrational or racist 'Islamophobia'. He marshals a wide array of evidence about immigration, multiculturalism, crime, public opinion polls, terrorism and craven political correctness that is both documented closely and presented calmly. The net effect, on a close reading, is quite deeply disconcerting; not because Murray seems unhinged, but because Europe itself does—or at least far too many of its political and opinion leaders.

Against that background, he reflects on the angry last writings of the great Italian journalist Oriana Fallaci, denouncing what she saw as the betrayal of the West and the capitulation of its leaders to Iranian and Sunni jihadist intimidation. In *The Rage and the Pride* (2002), written as a furious response to the 9/11 assault on New York (where she lived in Manhattan), Fallaci excoriated those who were refusing to defy Islamic totalitarianism, Shia and Sunni alike. Murray comments that her language was at times excessive, but her fury warranted.

Elsewhere, he draws attention to two French novels, written 42 years apart, that each prophesied a strange capitulation by France to Islam. The first, in 1973, was Jean Raspail's *The Camp of the Saints*. The second, in 2015, was Michel Houellebecq's *Submission*. Raspail eerily foresaw a tidal wave of Muslim immigrants coming to France and the country unable or unwilling to turn them away. Houellebecq, notoriously, writes of Muslim political figures taking over France in 2020, equally without resistance, and the novel's key character—the decadent scion of a culture at its fag end—converting to Islam for the sake of money, polygamy and a teaching job.

His discussion of the two novels is illuminating. If you have read Houellebecq's *Submission* and found yourself queerly drawn to its demoralized sense of European capitulation and emptiness, Murray's book is for you. It offers empirical evidence in place of novelistic imagination and serious thinking in place of disconcerting and provocative fantasy. The beauty of the book is that it constitutes a systematic and morally coherent argument.

One may freely challenge the argument, but this is at the very least a presentation of it with which as many of us as possible must engage. Murray travelled widely and collected a great deal of data for his book. He visited the European frontiers where the immigrants have been pouring in. He interviewed people across the spectrum from genuine refugees to political figures. He has put the problem in historical, continental, political and cultural context. He is literate, dignified and highly articulate.

Reading his book, I found myself thinking uncomfortably of the Gothic and other Germanic migrations into the Roman Empire from the 3rd century to the 5th; and the Arab migrations of the 7th and 8th centuries which swamped the southern and eastern littorals of the Roman world and overran the Persian and Turkish worlds. He clearly sees these historical antecedents and their implications as relevant points of reference. It is not clear that he is in error. It would be reassuring, however, if a serious and temperate debate was to be prompted by his book and policies put in place to prevent what he fears from coming about.

11: Hellas: prejudice, pragmatism and scientific culture

We live in an era of extraordinary scientific and technological innovation, but also of swirling controversies, anti-intellectual political and religious movements and widespread popular ignorance. Misgivings about 'Western civilization' or, more broadly, about science and industrialism, mix with all manner of confused belief systems. Is it possible that all this could bring down modern science; that scientific progress could end up being reversed or stopped in its tracks?

Twenty years ago, the Italian polymath Lucio Russo pondered this question in a remarkable book called *The Forgotten Revolution: How Science Was Born in 300 BC and Why It Had to be Reborn*. It was first published by Feltrinelli in Milan in 1996. It appeared in English, via Springer Verlag (Berlin, Heidelberg and New York) in 2004. It was drawn to my attention in 2009, by another polymath, Mark Elvin, an old friend, by then working in Heidelberg on the history and philosophy of science. It is an enormously interesting and thought-provoking book and should be on the reading list of any critical rationalist.

Russo's thesis is simple: science as we understand the term in the modern world did not begin in the 17th century of the Common Era (CE), but in the 3rd century *before* the Common Era (BCE), in the Hellenistic world. It was not the work of the pre-Socratics or of Plato and Aristotle. It began *after* Aristotle, was not governed by his preconceptions and began to discover things that would be forgotten and not rediscovered until the century after Galileo. It got off to an impressive start, but then came to a halt. Not only that, but it was largely erased from cultural memory. Most of its key figures and their work were almost wholly forgotten.

Why did this happen? His answer to that question revolutionizes what might be called the standard Enlightenment narrative, which might be summed up in the proposition that the Greeks and Romans, in some collective sense, were broadly enlightened and scientific, but then were overcome by 'barbarism and religion'. Western civilization then regressed, only recovering when the ancient world was rediscovered and science began to displace religion in the 17th century. This has been disputed on various grounds by Christians (the religion part of the equation) for many years, chiefly by arguing that it was religion that saved Western civilization—from the barbarians.

Russo has a more interesting and in some ways more disturbing story to tell than either of these conventional and somewhat myopic narratives. His argument, supported by a magnificent marshalling of primary evidence, is that the Hellenistic era (from the time of Alexander's conquests in the late 4th century BCE to the Roman conquest of the eastern Mediterranean world in the 2nd and 1st centuries BCE) saw 'an explosion of objective knowledge about the external world' and 'the appearance of science as we understand it now'; but that:

> not long after this golden period, much of this extraordinary development had been reversed. Rome borrowed what it was capable of from the Greeks and kept it for a little while yet, but created very little science of its own. Europe was soon smothered in the obscurantism and stasis that blocked most avenues of intellectual development for a thousand years.

Science had been a sub-culture within the Greek world and never took root in the Roman world. The Roman Empire actually disrupted the nascent scientific culture of the Greek world and it did not recover from that disruption. There was an afterglow for a few centuries, then things deteriorated further—until the Renaissance and the modern scientific revolution.

Russo argues that this should alert us to a danger in our own time, even though science has taken incomparably greater strides since 1600 than it ever took in the Hellenistic era:

> The naïve idea that progress is a one way flow automatically powered by scientific development could never have taken hold, as it did during the 1800s, if the ancient defeat of science had not been forgotten. Today, such dangerous illusions no longer prevail absolutely, and we may have a chance to learn from the lessons of the past. Those who engage in defending scientific rationality against the waves that buffet it from many directions would do well to be forearmed with the awareness that this is a battle that was lost once, with consequences that affected every aspect of civilization for a thousand years and more.

An iconic figure from that lost era is Archimedes, whose death at the hands of a Roman soldier during the Roman sack of Syracuse in 212 BCE can be seen as marking the beginning of the assault on Greek science that would come to a head seventy years later, when the Greek scientific community in Alexandria was almost entirely destroyed.

The *name* Archimedes tends to be remembered. Many others, however, have been forgotten. Russo brings them back into the picture. In doing so, he shows us a scientific culture at work:

> Not only do we see physicians conducting controlled experiments, scientists using mathematics and mechanics to build better weapons, painters applying geometry to their art, but even the notion of language changes: poetry becomes a playground for experimentation, while words are consciously assigned precise new meanings in technical fields, a procedure that would not become familiar again until the nineteenth century.

All this began to decay after the Roman conquests of Greece, the Levant and Egypt. Classical Athens continued to be celebrated, but the achievements and theoretical works of the great thinkers of the Hellenistic period were lost, in many cases irretrievably. As Russo put it, even now 'the Hellenistic period often continues to appear as one whose cultural heritage is for us less essential than that of the classical period.'

Do you find yourself responding intuitively with the thought that the classical period *is* more essential as a cultural heritage? We more automatically think of Aeschylus and Sophocles, Pericles and Thucydides, Socrates and Alcibiades, Plato and Aristotle than we do of Archimedes and Euclid or...Well, the list trails off very quickly, doesn't it? And that is precisely Russo's point. If we only knew the history and achievements of the 3rd century BCE, we would see things differently. That would be especially so with regard to scientific culture. But a book like his has been necessary even to make this case—yet few of us read it, to say nothing of taking its argument to heart.

He makes this point right at the start, in section 1.1 of his book 'The Erasure of the Scientific Revolution':

> Let's consider three great beacons of the scientific revolution: Euclid of Alexandria, Archimedes of Syracuse and Herophilus of Chalcedon. What does an educated person know about them? About Herophilus nothing. About Archimedes one remembers that he did strange things...he is remembered, yes, but as a legendary character outside of history. One ends up forgetting that he was a scientist...whose results continue to be part of scientific education at many levels...Euclidean geometry has remained, throughout the centuries, the framework for basic mathematical teaching. But Euclid himself has been taken out of history...he is offered to us without any historical context, laying down 'Euclidean geometry' as if it were something that had always been there at mankind's disposal...

Herophilus was the pioneer of anatomy and physiology. He discovered the optic nerve and the nervous system in general and corrected Aristotle's mistaken belief that the brain was merely an organ for cooling the blood and not the seat of human cognition. Do the names Strato of Lampsacus, Ctesibius, Eratosthenes, Aristarchus, Chrysippus, Seleucus, or Hipparchus mean anything to you? All were Hellenistic scientists of note.

Almost all the writings of that era have been lost. A few scientific works survived the 'deluge' to be handed down via Byzantium and the Arabs (who inherited them when they conquered the Greek world in the 7th century CE), but the best and most original works were lost. This last point requires emphasis. Russo writes:

> Unfortunately, the optimistic view that 'classical civilization' handed down certain fundamental works that managed to include the knowledge contained in the lost writings has proved groundless. In fact, in the face of a general regression in the level of civilization, it's never the best works that will be saved through an automatic process of natural selection...Late Antiquity and the Middle Ages favoured compilations or at

least books written in a language still understandable to a civilization that had returned to the pre-scientific stage. Thus, we have Varro's work on agriculture and Vitruvius' on architecture, but not their Hellenistic sources; we have Lucretius' splendid poem on nature, but not the works of Strato of Lampsacus, who according to some indications may have originated natural science in the true sense.

Strato (335–269 BCE) was the third head of the library and research establishment created by Aristotle (after Aristotle himself and Theophrastus): the Lyceum, in Athens. He was an atheist who did not believe there was any need for the hypothesis of a god or gods to explain the universe and did not believe in the immortality of a soul. He believed in scientific research and natural law, was a materialist who refined the atomism of Democritus, and a theorist of space, time and energy. He criticised the work of Plato and Aristotle. We have none of his books.

Alexander's empire, after 335 BCE, constituted a cosmopolitan world of ideas that flourished briefly, but was suffocated. Apart from textual losses and cultural amnesia, we suffer from the lack of serious archaeological work even in Egypt, where the submerged remains of Alexandria 'only began to be explored systematically in 1995'. No such work has been done for Hellenistic states other than Egypt, such as the Seleucid kingdom, which included Mesopotamia; or Bactria, which was a channel between India, China and the Hellenistic world. In other words, 500 years after the Renaissance, we still have a great deal to learn about the antecedents to our own scientific culture, partly because so little effort has so far been made to recover them.

How serious are the implications of all this for our time? Read Russo's wonderful book and ponder that question. But consider this: the Renaissance began with the recovery of largely humanistic and philosophical texts. Suppose we were able now to recover more fully the roots of critical rationalism and scientific method in their cultural context? Might that not help to revitalize our own scientific culture, at a time when it faces so many challenges? Might it not enable those of us committed to a scientific worldview to pivot on a new foundation and champion the possibilities of humanity with a refreshed vigour? I'd like to think so. Reading Russo encourages such bright thoughts.

12: Arthur Kroeber: China's immediate economic future

The mining boom triggered a dramatic shift in Australian perceptions of our relationship with China. In the course of fifteen years, it went from being a large country to our north that we vaguely hoped would prosper without becoming dangerous, to being our largest trading partner and vital to our economic future. Then the mining boom stopped. What happens next? Well, that depends not only on what we do, but on what occurs within China itself. Arthur Kroeber, an economist working in Beijing, wrote a very interesting paper earlier this year on that precise subject. It is worth pondering what he wrote.

The paper appeared in a book called *China Matters*, in which every other chapter was written by either Linda Jakobson or Bates Gill or both of them together. The book's long sub-title is 'Getting It Right for Australia: What We Need to Know for Today and Tomorrow'. Kroeber's chapter is titled 'China's Economic Transition: Will It Succeed?' The economic relationship has two ends to it and China's is the big end. If it fails to make what Kroeber calls its 'transition', the implications for Australia could be very serious. Conversely, if it succeeds in that transition, the implications are enormous.

So, what is the transition Kroeber is pondering? He means that the explosive era of growth in China since the 1980s of 10% per annum and huge imports of commodities to fuel and enact gigantic overhauls of urban and industrial infrastructure has come to an end. What happens next needs to be an era of lower, consumption-driven growth. He outlines two alternative scenarios for the immediate future, with dramatically different implications. In Scenario 1, China undertakes economic major reforms and is able to sustain an annual growth rate of around 5% through the 2020s. In Scenario 2, it fails to bring about such reforms, precipitating an economic crisis that causes its growth to flat-line to between 0% and 2% per annum in the 2020s.

His single most dramatic point in an admirably lucid paper is that unless the major reforms in question are undertaken *in the immediate future*, Scenario 2 is likely to occur 'by 2020 at the latest and quite possibly sooner' (p. 68). That is a very near timeline. It isn't a matter of vaguely saying that something could go seriously wrong *somewhere down the line*. This is urgent right now. And with the Communist Party's 19th Party Congress coming up next month (October 2017), all eyes should be on Beijing to see whether the Party shares his sense of urgency and looming crisis.

What makes his paper even more interesting is that he spells out exactly what reforms he believes are necessary and states:

> There is no question that achieving this outcome would be difficult and would require far more commitment to deep reforms—and a much greater willingness to surrender state control in key parts of the economy—than the Xi government has shown so far.

In fact, under Xi Jinping, the Communist Party has been reinforcing state control and the repression of both dissent and organizational freedom across the board. Had it been edging in the direction of reform and opening, one might have said that it needed to go much further and that this would require strong leadership. In reality, it would have to radically *reverse* direction.

So, what are the reforms that Kroeber believes are necessary? There are six sets of reforms, each of them complex and formidable:

1. Cutting back excess capacity in heavy industry, especially coal and steel.
2. Rationalizing remaining SOEs (state owned industries) through financial and market discipline, allowing bankruptcies and restructuring.
3. Deregulating major service sectors—telecommunications, aviation, logistics, finance, health care and non-compulsory education—thus allowing much greater domestic and foreign private investment.
4. Recapitalizing the country's banking system, with bad loans being hived off, special credit lines to SOEs ended and government guidance on the financing of firms curtailed.
5. Restructuring local government finances, so that such governments are prohibited from bank borrowing and required to raise their revenues through taxation on consumption and property.
6. Moving the renminbi (China's currency) exchange rate to a Singapore-style trade-weighted basket peg with minimal central bank intervention.

One has only to read this to register that this is a massive agenda for any government, never mind one that is intent on remaining firmly in the driver's seat politically and economically. To say that pushing it through will be difficult is an understatement. It could only happen if, in fact, contrary to all appearances, Xi Jinping has been centralizing power precisely with the view to *enacting* such reforms over the heads of any independent power centres or interest groups. If that is his intention, however, he has successfully kept the secret to himself.

Let us imagine, however, that (a) Kroeber is correct, that all these reforms are indispensable and (b) that Xi Jinping is seized of these realities and is both willing and able to act. What would successful reform look like? Many millions of workers would be laid off in the heavy industries and SOEs targeted by the reforms. Credit growth would slow drastically, curtailing the ballooning debt that threatens to cripple China's economic expansion. The outlook for private sector investment would brighten appreciably. The private sector's share of fixed-asset investment would, Kroeber argues, be likely to increase from its current 65% to around 80% and this would provide a solid foundation for ongoing consumer-driven economic growth. That growth would be half what it has been for the past thirty years, but from a high base and therefore even more impressive than the industrialization surge since the 1980s.

If all this happens, he reasons, the household consumption share of GDP would probably increase from its current 38% to around 45% by 2025 and 50% by 2030. That's what a consumption driven growth rate of 5% per annum throughout the 2020s would look like. But even then, in Kroeber's own words, this would only bring household consumption as a share of GDP in China to 'a level that is more or less in line with other middle-income Asian countries.' Yet he believes that *unless* all the proposed reforms are enacted, China will become *trapped* in the middle income economic doldrums. It seems that, in fact, merely to remain comfortably *within* the middle income bracket, it must enact these reforms. If it does *not* it risks being trapped in a sub-optimal lower income bracket.

We have become so accustomed to hype about China's economic performance and its future rise to world power that thoughts such as these come from left field. That's why Kroeber's paper is refreshing and thought-provoking. Many pundits have been asserting that China rode out the GFC because of the robustness of its economic management and that it is well down the track already to the economic transition Kroeber calls for—away from a capital intensive and toward a consumption-driven economic growth model.

He cautions that the optimism inherent in such assessments is misplaced:

> The transition is far from complete and there are serious concerns about the sustainability of growth at anything close to its 2015-16 trend rate of around 6.5%. The main issue is that the economy-wide return on capital is falling, dragged down by the deteriorating returns in the SOE sector.

Productivity is not growing as it needs to and capital investment is becoming increasingly inefficient, with the consequence that the debt to GDP ratio is climbing and already sits at 160%, one of the highest in the world. Without the reforms he has listed, Kroeber argues, this will climb to 300% in the near future and that could blow the economy up and cause growth to stall.

Crucially, he observes that a financial crisis, if it comes, will not be based on foreign creditors calling in their loans, because China's debt is overwhelmingly internal. Partly for that reason, it has been able to postpone correction. But a day of reckoning is coming. When and if it does, he argues, the Party would very likely respond with 'quick and massive countermeasures'. Such measures would head off total collapse, but would be likely to lock China into 'an extended period of GDP growth in the 0-2% range, similar to Japan's lost decade of the 1990s'. The problem is that such stagnation would be far more socially and therefore politically costly to China than it was for Japan, because Japan was already far wealthier by 1990 than China will be in 2020 and it was not a one party dictatorship. The overall consequences, therefore, are likely to prove very challenging indeed.

Kroeber closes his paper by pointing out that even Scenario 1 (successful reform) would produce a China that posed serious challenges to other actors in the world economy, especially with regard to foreign investment. We have already seen that this is a challenge for Australia and has required reform of the Foreign Investment Review Board. Under the successful reform scenario, Kroeber anticipates, these problems would increase, not diminish. Under Scenario 2, on the other hand, the tide of China's rising global influence would begin to ebb. The threat of China seeking to displace the liberal rules-based economic order and to dominate it would recede, but the costs to the global economy would be severe.

In other words, China faces a serious challenge, but whatever happens in China, we face a serious challenge. The world economy—and Australia not least—needs China to keep growing, but if it does we will have to think hard about how to deal with it. Kroeber offers thoughtful observations on Australia's options under Scenario 1 and his paper is well worth reading in that regard. But the central question posed by his paper is whether or not reform will occur at all.

Kroeber presents this question in a deliberately simplified form. He states early:

> There are many possible trajectories for China's economic future. For analytical clarity, it is convenient to consider two basic scenarios.

But he doesn't weigh the *relative probability* of these two scenarios in other than the most general manner. Given what is at stake, this surely needs to be done. It might begin with the consideration, which he himself mentions, that the reforms he calls for were already noted at the 18th Party Congress in 2013, but have not been enacted. Will they be now?

We need new methods for assessing the probability that they *will* be enacted in the wake of the 19th Party Congress. What is the extent of our confidence, or doubt? We need probability-based forecasts with regular updates, rather than vague rhetoric about general possibilities. Otherwise, we are flying almost blind. Why do that when so very much is at stake?

13: Grappling with the rise of China

The rise of China is the biggest story in geopolitics. We fuss about where we stand between China and the United States; the end of the commodities boom and our future place in China's economic development; the uncertainties engendered by Donald Trump's leadership style; and the systematic efforts of the Chinese Communist Party to buy influence within our institutions and stifle criticism of its own policies and mode of government.

These three books should be read and discussed, in order to enliven debate. From an Australian point of view, the most useful is *China Matters*. From the point of view of international security and geopolitics, Allison's *Destined For War* is the most important. Fenby's book is a very useful supplement to the other two, especially to Arthur Kroeber's chapter on the Chinese economy in *China Matters*.

Jakobson and Gill came to Australia from abroad. Jakobson created a forum called China Matters to bring together specialists from business, government, academia and journalism. Her book, with the always quietly thoughtful Bates Gill, builds on that foundation.

They remark:

> Upon moving to this country several years ago, we were both struck by a sense that Australians do not entirely grasp how vast China's impact will be on Australia's future.

Among their many recommendations, they urge that:

> Australia needs a national peak body with a mandate to advance the Australia-China relationship as it enters an unpredictable and challenging era.

Also that:

> Asian literacy needs to be institutionalized. Learning about Asian cultures and societies should be made compulsory from Year 1 onward.

These and other suggestions call for critical assessment.

A peak body of the kind they urge would run the risk of being captured by interest groups and infiltrated by Chinese money. Think of Bob Carr's institute (ACRI) in Sydney, so determinedly committed to avoiding acrimony in Sino-Australian relations, because of the ACRI money flowing to it from Chinese sources. It's not a 'peak body' that we need, but serious scholarship and policy engagement among our universities and research institutes to bring new ideas and voices into the policy debates and to build broader understanding of the challenges ahead.

Kevin Rudd poured sixty million dollars into the Centre for China in the World at ANU. It has shown a very poor return on that investment in terms of strategic analysis, real world scholarship, or public outreach. Any new initiative must be based not on the casual whims of politicians, but on robust principles designed to deliver outcomes in the national interest. And it must not take Chinese money—whether directly from the Chinese government or through billionaire 'philanthropists' with close links to the Chinese Communist Party.

A mandatory curriculum is also problematic. We don't teach our children any coherent course on *Western* civilization. How, then, are we going to teach them about a multitude of Asian histories and cultures? The proposal also shows a lack of awareness of the institutional restraints on mandatory curricula innovation in Australia's state-based schools system and little familiarity with the last thirty years of educational debate on Asia literacy in this country.

Rather than another foray into ill-conceived mass education, we need a few good university seminars comparing and contrasting classical Mediterranean and classical Chinese history. One such might be the parallel between the history of classical Greece and Rome and that of China during the warring states period and the rise of the Qin and Han empires—in both cases running from roughly 500 BCE to 50 BCE.

Arthur Kroeber, a veteran analyst of the Chinese economy resident in Beijing, in his chapter 'China's Economic Transition: Will It Succeed?', makes the striking judgement that:

> If current trends continue unabated, it is likely that China's debt burden will trigger either a financial crisis or a severe growth slowdown by 2020 at the latest and quite possibly sooner.

That is a very near time frame. He argues that major reforms are imperative if growth of around 5% per annum is to be sustained beyond 2020, that these are unlikely to be achieved and that growth could stall, as it did in Japan in the 1990s or in the EU in recent years. This argument needs to be rigorously tested.

Fenby argues that China will *not* dominate the 21st century, because it's growth probably will stall, trapping China in the middle income bracket so that it grows old before it grows rich; bedevilling the Party's determined efforts to remain in control. He also argues that China's soft power offensive will fail, because it's narcissistic view of itself as the 'Middle Kingdom' and its overweening ambitions alienate almost all its neighbours and lack the cosmopolitanism of the Western culture that has created globalization.

Allison, a Harvard scholar of international security affairs, urges us all to 're-read' Thucydides' history of the Peloponnesian War, in order to think seriously about the psychology of conflict and the logic of power. He is generous, since most of his audience have surely never read Thucydides at all. But he believes that Thucydides teaches a vital lesson that we should heed before it's too late: a rising power (read China) tends to challenge a declining one (read America)—and we should not want a Sino-American war.

He offers a number of historical analogies in an attempt to show that Thucydides was right about rising and declining powers. But his central lesson is ill-founded. The 'declining' power in ancient Greece (Sparta) won the war. The rising power (Athens) lost. And the lessons Thucydides offers us are much more complex than the one Allison wishes to draw.

In any case, his history of China is embarrassingly clichéd and at a number of significant points just factually wrong. He uncritically buys into the '5,000 years of civilization' mystique and the notion that the Chinese think far ahead in ways that we in the West do not. This is nonsense. Their utter failure to do such things under the Ming (14th to 17th centuries) and Manchus (17th to early 20th centuries), in stark contrast with the Japanese, for example, from 1868, hobbled them.

He writes uncritically about China being the globally dominant state for 'millennia' before the Western powers 'humiliated' it in the 19th century. It was nothing of the kind. It fragmented in the middle of the first millennium CE on several occasions; and was conquered by the Mongols in the 13th century and by the Manchus in the 17th century. Even their empires, far larger than China, under any of its native dynasties, did *not* dominate the world. And, if anything, both sets of invaders held China back.

The Manchus were foreign and resented; but it was them, not the Han Chinese, who conquered Central Asia, Mongolia and Tibet, in the 18th century. Allison writes of their downfall without any reference to the huge civil wars within China such as the Taiping Rebellion, the belated constitutional reforms in the 1900s, the non-communist republican movement or the serious intellectual debates in China about modernity and liberty.

He uncritically reproduces the cliché about Mao Zedong's party saving China 'from domination by foreign imperialists'. It was the United States that saved China by defeating Japan in the Pacific War. Mao's guerrillas faced crushing defeat by Chiang Kaishek, had it not been for the Japanese invasion, the American defeat of Japan and the Soviet occupation of Manchuria and arming of the Chinese Communist forces.

He writes that Japan took over Manchuria in 1894. It did not do so until 1931. In the decades prior to that, it had invested intensively in Manchurian infrastructure and industrialization. By the early 1930s, Manchuria was the most developed and prosperous area of a China otherwise mired in internal warlordism.

He writes that Taiwan's 23 million people are descended from those who fled Mao in 1949. In fact, only 15% of Taiwan's population is of that lineage. The rest have far deeper roots on the island. The native Taiwanese resented the imposition of Nationalist rule from the mainland in 1945, openly rose against it in 1947 and were brutally crushed. This was the seedbed of the independence and democracy movements and of the Democratic Progressive Party which governs Taiwan now—and of resistance to the idea of rule from Beijing.

All this is rather disturbing, given that Allison urges the rest of us to study history carefully ourselves. That an emeritus strategic thinker at Harvard, surrounded by China scholars, could make so many elementary errors about his core topic is dismaying. That topic is important and the book addresses a debate we have to have. Alas, the Harvard professor gets it off on the wrong foot. It is to be hoped that he will rethink and rework his understanding of China. In the interim, however, by all means take his advice and read Thucydides, who really was a great historian.

14: Warming up to our global challenges

These three short books are contributions, from distinctly different angles, to the long running and thus far not very productive climate debate in this country. They are all easy reads. They are all lively and passionate. Of the three, Flannery's is by far the most interesting and constructive. He engages the imagination by first sketching a picture of Malthusian environmental apocalypse and then arguing that by 2050, with wisdom and determination and lots of innovation, we could live in a much *better* world than we do now.

Mark Butler is the shadow minister for the environment and has written a lucid and interesting political pamphlet. It is marred by its blatant political partisanship in asserting that the ALP and only the ALP can save the country from climate catastrophe, or at least put policies in place consistent with both our international obligations as he understands them and the country's economic viability. The argument is worth having, but he presents only one side of it. It would be interesting to see a considered and dispassionate response from both Green and Coalition perspectives.

Not the least interesting aspect of Anna Krien's quarterly essay is that she fires more than one broadside at the ALP, both federally and in Queensland, in ways directly at odds with Butler's attempt to depict the Party as the white knight of climate policy and environmental politics. Her primary concern is the Great Barrier Reef and, if her analysis is correct, we are bidding not a long goodbye to it so much as a rapid farewell. Her essay suffers from a flaw common, unfortunately, to quite a few of the quarterly essays—much as one may enjoy reading them—which is a tendency to embed a serious argument in a highly discursive and often personalized narrative that obscures more than it illuminates the central points at issue.

Tim Flannery is a celebrity and a folk hero, because he writes books that both popularize and dramatize the geophysical and economic challenges we face in the 21st century, given our huge numbers and our soaring appetites for materials consumption, food and water, with all the strains this is clearly putting on the ecosphere. This new book is among his best. Parts of its are really first rate in drawing attention both to the pollution of the Earth and the fascinating innovations that are arising in response to our problems. His chapters on solar energy technologies and on aquaculture and the uses of kelp are wonderfully thought provoking.

His observations concerning the shocking condition of China's soil, air and water, as a direct consequence of its hectic and very poorly regulated industrial and urban development over the past few decades, are well informed and very sobering. But China's environmental problems were serious even before this. As Judith Shapiro pointed out, in *Mao's War Against Nature* (2001), even unsuccessful efforts at development can cause grave harm. The longer perspective was sketched out brilliantly by Mark Elvin a generation ago in a long essay called 'Three Thousand Years of Unsustainable Development in China', which looks like a droll oxymoron. His magisterial study *The Retreat of the Elephants: An Environmental History of China* (2004) showed that there was nothing at all droll about the matter.

Flannery's opening chapter is called 'The Population Bomb'. He endorses Paul Ehrlich and the Club of Rome on the population 'bomb' and the 'limits to growth'. Yet he goes on to predict not only that the global human population will stabilize in the 21st century somewhere around 9 billion, but that innovation, imagination and determination will enable us to feed all these people at a pleasant standard of living in a greener and more pleasant world than now, by 2050.

A pessimist will embrace the first claim and dismiss the second. An optimist will embrace the second claim and dismiss the first as merely 'Malthusian', with an assertion that technological innovation and global markets will give us this outcome—provided that utopian socialists and ecological enthusiasts don't derail growth in the meantime. Flannery wants to have it both ways. What's interesting is to consider that he may actually be right. At least he is not simply predicting doom and disaster. What is not clear is how, exactly, he thinks the utopian vision he sketches out is to be achieved by 2050 and what he means by 'determination'.

Across the spectrum, the climate and environment debate is too often characterized by extraordinary vagueness and even complete ignorance of climate science. All three of these authors take the IPCC's warnings as a benchmark. None of them discusses the deeper background to the matter. Yet that deeper background is vital if we are, collectively, to get a handle on this ominous and confused controversy and act in ways that might, if not by 2050 then within this century, get us to something like the world of Flannery's dreams: clean energy, green cities and abundant, nutritious food.

We need to remind ourselves that almost everything we know about the geophysical history of the Earth and the ecosphere has been learned very, very recently. This is particularly true of the long term history of Earth's climate. Over the last several million years, as our human ancestors evolved, the global climate was highly changeable and for long periods highly volatile, with abrupt and dramatic changes in global average temperature much greater than are being forecast even by alarmists for the 21st century. The problem was not greenhouse gases, but other things.

The Holocene, which is the period since the end of the most recent ice age, has been *unusually* stable. That *stability*—a kind of climate homeostasis (as Anna Krien observes in a neat little footnote)—has been the precondition for the flourishing of our species and the development of agriculture, cities and trade. Brian Fagan's *The Long Summer: How Climate*

Changed Civilization (2004) is a very good introduction to the subject. This 'long summer' has seen a number of fluctuations in global temperature, both warming and cooling, and these have had appreciable consequences. Our present concern is about whether we are ourselves generating the *largest* shift seen within the Holocene—and also a mass extinction.

The prehistory of all this is beautifully set out by William J. Burroughs, in *Climate Change in Prehistory: The End of the Reign of Chaos* (2005). If you are serious about understanding climate science, read this book as a matter of priority. The primary problem we have had in generating agreement about what is happening, what it signifies and what to do about it is that the matter has only in recent decades come into scientific focus, it is highly complex and the overwhelming majority of people simply do not grasp the science at all. The consequence has been a slanging match between interest groups and advocacy groups which has failed to advance the debate in enlightening ways.

But even if we had overwhelming consensus on the science—as it is widely claimed we do—getting clarity and consensus in public policy in short order is another matter again. It would have been good to see Mark Butler reflect on this. A very good introduction to the problem is David G. Victor's *Global Warming Gridlock: Creating More Effective Strategies for Protecting the Planet* (2011).

To get your mind around the economics and risk analysis questions, a good place to start is William Nordhaus *The Climate Casino: Risk, Uncertainty and Economics for a Warming World* (2013). And regarding the overall attempt of our lot to actually manage the Earth, as distinct from feeling dependent on its natural cycles—and as distinct from recklessly plundering it—a fine start is Richard B. Alley's *Earth: An Operator's Manual* (2011).

The politics of all this are vitally important. In a passage at the end of his little book, the visionary in Flannery looks back a century and asks who, in 1916, when 'there was not a single communist country on earth', would have anticipated that by 1950 there would have been such a spread of communism, as well as massive technological innovation, including the invention of jet aircraft and nuclear weapons.

He refers to all this simply as 'technological and social change'. He does not pause to reflect on the fact that the communist revolutions, born of utopian vision and ruthless political violence, were catastrophic. Their approaches to public policy, to history, to science and above all to economics were reckless and destructive. The environmental movement must not see them as in any way a model for rapid and radical change.

Both Stalin's forced collectivization (1929-31)—undertaken at speed against the express, cautious advice of his state planning organization, GOSPLAN—caused a man-made famine that took millions of lives and impoverished the Soviet agrarian economy for generations.

Mao's so-called Great Leap Forward (1959-61) was even more calamitous. It caused the largest man-made famine in history, taking the lives of an estimated 35 to 45 million people; all because Mao thought he could overtake the West in five to ten years.

Assume, for the sake of argument, that the basic scientific picture of climate and environment right now is accurate; getting to anything like what Flannery hopes for by 2050 will require highly intelligent policies. Given the current rate of innovation and growing awareness of the scale of the problem, we would do well to heed the political lessons of the 20th century and go by the old maxim 'more haste, less speed' in rising to our collective challenges. That will require steady nerves and improved capacity for conducting fruitful, complex debates.

The massacre of journalists at the magazine Charlie Hebdo inspired widespread revulsion, but self-censorship for fear of Islamist violence also remains widespread.

PART V (2018)

1: The myth of Bolshevism dies hard

At the half-way point in Warren Beatty's 1981 film *Reds*, about John Reed and the Russian Revolution, Reed and his wife Louise Bryant march in a joyous candle lit procession through the streets of Petrograd in late October 1917; and stroll into the Winter Palace as if it is already a quiet museum; all to the stirring sounds of the Internationale. It would be difficult better to encapsulate the notion that Lenin's seizure of power was an event to celebrate and consisted in the popular overthrow of a reactionary few by the liberated masses. The following year, 1982, Sheila Fitzpatrick's book *The Russian Revolution* enshrined this myth by describing the Bolshevik coup against the Provisional Revolutionary Government as 'the overthrow of the bourgeoisie by the proletariat.' It was nothing of the kind. It was the seizure of arbitrary power by an unscrupulous coterie who let nothing stand in their way and then imposed their rule ruthlessly on the majority of the population, not least the workers and peasants.

There is a long running and, alas, still unresolved debate about modern revolutions which type-casts them in terms of the 'progressive, radical Left' and the 'reactionary, counter-revolutionary Right', with everyone in between cast as waverers or petit bourgeois opportunists. The language is Marxist-Leninist, but the dichotomy dates back to the French Revolution and it bedevils democratic politics in the West and around the world even now. We badly need to be rid of it. The Russian Revolution, even more than the French, entrenched the dichotomy in political discourse and despite all the terrors and privations caused by Leninism, Stalinism and Maoism in the decades after 1917, the pernicious dichotomy persists. It has the grievous consequence that many of those whose philosophical and political views are decidedly enlightened, responsible and moderate can be dismissed as 'reactionary' or 'Right-wing' in the name of the most hair-brained or bigoted of causes, merely because the latter style themselves 'Left-wing' or 'progressive'.

If we are to get these matters tolerably clear, we need to go back again and again over the language and history of modern revolutions. One of the most enlightening observations in the literature is still Hannah Arendt's remark, in *On Revolution* (1963 and 1965) that:

> It was the French and not the American Revolution that set the world on fire and it
> was consequently from the course of the French Revolution and not from the course
> of events in America or from the acts of the Founding Fathers that our present use of
> the word 'revolution' received its connotations and overtones everywhere.

At a time when the American republic itself is struggling under the strains of ideological and social confrontations and when its constitutional system is being seriously tested, it is more important than ever to reflect on this. For it was the French, not the American revolution, that gave us the polarizing terms 'Left' and 'Right' and gave us the guillotine and the terror instead of the division of powers and the attempt, at least, to set the principles and processes of republican government on lasting foundations.

Hannah Arendt had, of course, come to the United States as a refugee from Nazi tyranny in Europe and appreciated the American republic's virtues, even while being critical of its flaws and the dangers of its subversion, as she spelled out in *Crises of the Republic* (1973). An earlier European observer of the United States, a century before Arendt, was Alexis de Tocqueville. His classic study *Democracy in America* (1835) should be getting widely read right now. It was an extraordinarily perceptive piece of work and remains illuminating still, despite the immense changes that have occurred in America and the world since he wrote it. Twenty years later, he wrote his mature reflections on the French Revolution—*The Old Regime and the French Revolution* (1856). It was and remains a beautifully nuanced and perceptive reflection on the causes and course of the revolution, the ironies of history and the tragedy of the radical violence that swept France between 1789 and 1794, only to end in the establishment of Napoleon's dictatorship.

It is a symptom of the failure of far too many scholars (and activists) to absorb the lessons drawn by Arendt and Tocqueville that Timothy Tackett, in his *The Coming of the Terror in the French Revolution* (Belknap Press, Harvard, 2015) still repeated like a mantra the tired old assertion that all 'major' revolutions necessarily follow the course of the French Revolution, because they involve the mobilization and enactment of:

> ...intense convictions that the society must and can be changed, convictions that
> easily breed impatience and intolerance with opposition. All revolutions engender
> counterrevolutionary opposition among those whose interests and values are
> threatened...All revolutions can be pushed in unanticipated directions through the
> influence of the popular masses. And it may well be that all major revolutions are beset
> by periods of conspiracy obsession, of intense suspicion and lack of trust, of agonizing
> uncertainty as to who are one's friends and who are one's enemies...

One cannot say that this is an 'eccentric' interpretation of the French Revolution as the very model of a modern major revolution. It is, alas, the conventional interpretation and one repeated again and again by those who style themselves 'progressives' and see the Jacobins and, all too often the Bolsheviks and Maoists, as the 'impatient' agents of 'progress'. Yet they were not. They were, in each case, political conspirators who created a form of government that was far more tyrannical than the 'reactionary' governments they overthrew—something that was *not* true of the American Revolution.

It does not appear to have occurred to Tackett that 'intense convictions that society can and must be changed' constitute a form of *fanaticism* and that such fanaticism is *inherently unlikely* to result in constructive or even durable change, much less in liberty and social peace. It is, moreover, simply untrue to assert that the so-called 'major' revolutions have been the bringers of progress. Tocqueville pointed out in 1856 that the French Revolution had destroyed stability and legitimacy in France and had swept away not only much that was genuinely corrupt and decadent, but a great deal that it would have been better to maintain. The Russian Revolution did far worse. The Chinese Revolution worse again and the nadir was surely reached in the late 1970s, when Pol Pot and his cronies inflicted an unprecedented catastrophe on Cambodia in the name of 'revolution'. The Khmer Rouge founders were not only inspired by the French Revolution and its avatars, but actually taught by Stalinists and self-styled theorists of 'liberation' in Paris itself. Khieu Samphan (Brother No. 5 and the Khmer Rouge head of state) actually took a PhD from the Sorbonne, in 1956. Philip Short's *Pol Pot: The History of a Nightmare* (John Murray 2004) is the outstanding biography of Brother No. 1, Pol Pot.

This being it's centenary, the Russian Revolution badly needs to be put into a framework of historical and even counterfactual perspective that the 'progressive Left' somehow seem never to contemplate. The great myth of the revolution is, broadly speaking, that Lenin's 'workers and peasants' overthrew the old regime, established a radical communism that was emancipatory and visionary, but were then set upon by Whites and foreign interventionists, forcing the poor innocent Reds to defend themselves, which alas led to regrettable excesses. The capitalist powers attempted to strangle the 'revolution' in its cradle by denying the Bolshevik regime investment or credit or even diplomatic recognition. This was all deplorable. Stalin then pulled things together and 'made the best of a bad job' by building 'socialism in one country' through forced collectivization and state-led heavy industrialization. These things worked, even if things got nasty along the way, and Stalin was vindicated when his newly industrialized state beat off the Nazis after June 1941. He should not, therefore, be too severely criticized and those who denounce his rule are simply reactionary 'Cold Warriors' who don't 'get it'.

As Sean McMeekin has laboured to point out in *The Russian Revolution: A New History* (Profile Books, London, 2017), this myth is a delusion at virtually every point. In the two decades before 1914, under the last Tsar (Nicholas II), Russia had begun to develop and industrialize rapidly. Its growth in the 1900s and early 1910s resembled that of China in recent years at 8 to 10% per annum. Foreign investment was pouring in and exports were growing, railroads were being built, industries were sprouting up, oil was being discovered. That there were inequalities in this process, that there were still high levels of poverty and that the system of government was monarchical and often genuinely 'reactionary' is all true. But as the Tsar's great prime minister of order and development Peter Stolypin declared to the Russian Leftist deputies in the Duma in 1907:

> You people want a great upheaval. We want a great Russia. Give me twenty five years of peace and you will not recognize Russia!

Stolypin was assassinated four years later. After 25 years from 1907, in 1932, Russia was being ground beneath the Stalinist jackboot, famine and terror stalked the country and there was no Duma, no liberal intelligentsia, no freedom of dissent. Russia had become a nightmare of despotic state-dominated 'development'. The alternative had been a constitutional monarchy with a diverse legislature and thriving economic relations with the outside world—Stolypin's great Russia.

At a time when fewer and fewer of our students elect to study serious history and those who do are often taught by ideologues of 'intense conviction' like Timothy Tackett, no such understanding of the colossal tragedy of the Russian Revolution enters into the minds of the populations of the Western democracies. This needs to be corrected. But here is the thing: such correction is likely to be dismissed by all too many as merely being a 'reactionary' or 'Right-wing' version of events. This is pernicious. It is the very problem that the Left/Right dichotomy has entrenched for about two centuries or more. It is neither 'Left' nor 'Right' wing to point out that Lenin was illiberal, that his catastrophic economic policies led to the collapse of trade, investment and industry and to an appalling famine that killed millions; that his terror killed more people *by two orders of magnitude* in five years than had been executed under the Tsars in the last hundred years of their rule; that he dispersed the elected Constituent Assembly and replaced it with an arbitrary dictatorship which never sought an electoral mandate and that Stalin then took all this to the next level of repressive totalitarian government. These are checkable empirical facts. The question is, what do we think about politics and 'revolution' in the light of such facts?

McMeekin addresses all these matters of historical fact and others besides at book length. He expresses concern that historical ignorance and increasingly intense convictions about the 1% and inequality in the context of globalization have led various people to start talking again of Karl Marx having been 'right'—which is to say 'left', of course. He points to the popularity of Thomas Piketty's *Capital in the Twenty-First Century* and the rise of rancorous populism of various stripes and says that those who seek 'revolution' ought to be careful what they wish for, since they just might get it. He means that however much the Gini co-efficient may point to rising levels of inequality and however unjust or corrupt certain practices or policies may be, there are approaches to rebellion against these things that we should be wise enough not only to avoid, but prudent and firm minded enough to suppress if it comes to that. Had the Provisional Revolutionary Government, a century ago, been wiser and more prudent, it might have pulled together the forces that would have made it possible to suppress Bolshevism pre-emptively. Its failure to do so, closely analysed by McMeekin, opened the door to dreadful things.

'Ah,' one can hear the 'progressives' intoning, almost in a chorus, 'so you are an extreme Right-wing reactionary! You actually believe Bolshevism should have been suppressed!' Others, styling themselves 'realists' will respond by saying, with an affected (or, let's be charitable, a sincere) wearied worldliness, that Bolshevism was fated to win and that the system of government the Communists built was simply 'Russian' in character, since the *muzhiks* (Russian peasants) had only ever responded to the knout (scourging whip). It seems to me terribly important that we not settle for or succumb to such cant. Bolshevism was in no sense fated to win and the Russia that it took over was far more civilized than it then became. We need to dwell on this, because it is the lesson we all need to imbibe and share in the interests of civilized and liberal government—here and elsewhere—in the 21st century. The old regime had Bolshevism well in hand before 1917. Its victory in 1917 was highly contingent and the revolutionaries it overthrew (for it overthrew the Provisional Revolutionary Government, *not* the old regime) were far more civilized than Lenin and his minions—as indeed the old regime itself had been.

There is a moment in David Lean's famously romantic film *Doctor Zhivago* where Victor Komarovsky says to Yuri Zhivago that he admires the Bolsheviks because 'they may win'. This is around Christmas 1913, eight months before the Great War began. The screenplay is by Robert Bolt and the words he put into Komarovsky's mouth in the mid-1960s were flagrantly anachronistic and historically misleading. By 1913, the Tsar's secret police, the Okhrana, had Bolshevism pinned down, with Lenin and many of his leading followers in exile abroad or in Siberia. Both then and almost until the Germans shipped him to Petrograd, in April 1917, with bags full of money to make mischief, Lenin himself had not believed Bolshevism could overthrow the old regime. Seeing that it had been overthrown for him, but that the Provisional Revolutionary Government (PRG) was making every kind of tactical and political error in its inept attempt to govern, Lenin saw an opportunity to seize power. His colleagues, including Stalin, argued that this was a dubious idea, even in terms of Marxian historicism. Undeterred, he led them to an attempted putsch in July. When this did not result in their suppression, he had another crack at it in October and this time knocked Kerensky and the PRG off their perch in Petrograd.

McMeekin's coverage of the German gambit—using Lenin as a 'catalyst of chaos' to break Russia and drive it out of the war—is a study in contingency and cynicism. Anyone who believes that the October 1917 seizure of power by the Bolsheviks was in any sense 'fated' to occur, or that it was a matter of a popular uprising by the fabled 'workers and peasants' needs to read McMeekin's book. Had the PRG been willing or able to assume legitimacy from the Tsarist regime and to keep its secret police and army in working order, it could very easily have suppressed Lenin and his crew, as the old regime had done. That it was unable to do so was not a matter of 'historical necessity', but due to the fact that the PRG consisted of a broad and unstable coalition of constitutional monarchists, liberals, socialist revolutionaries and social democrats who simply could not agree on what to do. The irony of their overthrow is that it was possible precisely because they would not act to suppress violent fanatics when they could and then found that their emasculation of the forces of order and the army made suppression impossible when the chips were really down—in October. The Bolsheviks didn't overthrow 'reactionaries'. They overthrew genuine, democratically inclined but disorganized and inexperienced revolutionaries.

This was confirmed in November 1917 when, despite the Bolshevik seizure of power and declaration that they were the government of Russia, elections for a national Constituent Assembly that the PRG had arranged went ahead. The turnout, in the circumstances of war and growing chaos, was remarkable: fully 50% of eligible voters or almost 42 million people participated. The Bolsheviks, with all the advantages of 'incumbency', won 175 seats out of 707, or just under a quarter. The Socialist Revolutionaries won 410, of which the Left SRs won 40. The Bolsheviks refused to ratify the vote until 'electoral abuses' could be investigated and, when the Constituent Assembly was finally convened, in the Tauride Palace, Petrograd, they derided it, then dispersed it by force. In the interim, as McMeekin points out, they declared the outright confiscation of all the savings and bullion deposits in Russia's banks above 5,000 roubles in the name of 'revolution', repudiated the country's international debt obligations and initiated a process of unilateral disengagement from the war. By these means they effectively abolished private property, brought the economy to a halt, alienated Russia's wartime allies and capitulated to Germany. And that was just the beginning.

In *Doctor Zhivago*—the film, not the novel—the voiceover of Alec Guinness, as Yuri's half-brother Yevgraf, a Bolshevik, declares as the war begins, 'Our task was to organize defeat, because from defeat would come revolution and revolution meant victory for us.' But this, again, is anachronistic. As McMeekin argues in detail, the war right through to the end of 1916 was far from being the disaster for Russia that popular and 'progressive' opinion has long seen it to have been. Bolshevik penetration of the ranks did not occur in any serious manner until after Lenin returned to Petrograd in April 1917 with piles of German money to spend on propaganda and agitation. German military opinion before 1914 had been that Russia was rapidly developing and was on the verge of becoming a formidable military power. The course of the war actually demonstrated this and Russia, while struggling to deal with the German military, had the Austro-Hungarian and Ottoman Empires very much on the back foot by 1916. The PRG, from February 1917, however, in the name of 'revolution' undermined the officer corps, even though it wished to prosecute the war vigorously. This was a serious error of judgement and, in combination with the German use of Lenin as a wrecking ball, opened the door to the Bolsheviks and crippled the Imperial Army as a fighting force by late 1917.

Nowhere was the ineptitude of the PRG better illustrated than in the Kornilov affair of August/September 1917, in which Alexander Kerensky mistakenly and fatefully undermined and removed from office General Lavr Kornilov, commander in chief of the Imperial Army, who might otherwise have both held the Army together and protected the PRG against the Bolsheviks. Kornilov, as McMeekin points out, 'represented the Russian Imperial Army at its best, ascending from the humblest of origins (with a peasant-soldier father and a Turkic mother in Kazakhstan) to the top of the officer corps on talent alone'. He was polylingual, an explorer, a scientist and a military intelligence specialist. Succumbing to fears that Kornilov was party to a 'Right wing' coup plot, Kerensky had him arrested. Kerensky would later state that he believed the danger he faced was from the right rather than the left. He was wrong. Kornilov, after being released, would join forces with his senior colleague General Mikhail Alekseev in an attempt in 1918 to raise a force that could defeat the Bolsheviks and restore the Constituent Assembly. He died in that attempt.

McMeekin's coverage of this matter is meticulous. This is important, because earlier accounts differ and the official Soviet view for decades was that Kornilov had been a monarchist intent on overthrowing the PRG and restoring the Tsar, or becoming a dictator in his own right. This, it seems, was not the case. What Kornilov sought to do was to stiffen the resistance of the PRG to the Bolsheviks in the wake of their attempted putsch in July 1917. Kerensky, jumping at shadows, had him dismissed and arrested, which completed the demoralization of the officer corps. In an extraordinary move, which proved fatal to his government, he had dozens of Russia's most patriotic and professional senior officers thrown in jail and, at the same time, released from jail Leon Trotsky, who had been so instrumental in the abortive July putsch. He also abolished the very counterintelligence organization that had conducted the investigation into the events of July and the Bolshevik use of German money. Let off the hook, the Bolsheviks proceeded to seize forty thousand rifles from a government arsenal. A month later, they overthrew the PRG and Kerensky fled from Petrograd.

None of this might matter very much had Lenin and the Bolsheviks truly been a 'progressive' force, which is to say committed to a regime in which the actual, tangible well-being and civil rights of human beings mattered and in which deliberation and accountability in politics were to be institutionalized. Had they been so inclined, they might have left us the Russian equivalent of the *Federalist Papers*, debating how best to achieve these things in a country that had been heavily damaged and traumatized by the Great War. They would, surely, have sought to form a coalition with the PRG liberals, socialists and others, perhaps with the Socialist Revolutionaries who had an actual majority anyway (370 out of just over 700 seats) and campaigned for greater support in the years that followed among a newly enfranchised Russian public. Or they might have accepted minority status in the Constituent Assembly, adopting the role of a loyal opposition. Kerensky bent over backwards to leave this path open to them. They did not take that path. They took power and within six weeks (on 7 December 1918) Lenin created the Cheka—the Extraordinary Commission for Combating Counterrevolution, Speculation and Sabotage. Counterrevolution, it soon became apparent meant everything from seeking to defend one's private property to being a Socialist Revolutionary, never mind a liberal, a monarchist or for that matter an anarchist.

Would it have been an extreme reactionary Right wing thing to have suppressed the Bolsheviks in 1917 and prevented them from ever taking power? To have prevented, therefore, the dispersal of the Constituent Assembly, the creation of the Cheka, the unleashing of civil war and the Red Terror, the abolition of private property by decree and the collapse of the Russian economy, the armed confiscations of grain from the peasants and the consequent famine and epidemic which took an estimated five million lives? Would the restoration of some form of constitutional monarchy or fledgling democracy that put Russia more or less back on the path of growth and liberalization envisaged by Peter Stolypin in 1907 have been 'Right wing'? Would a regime that was based on private property, trade and the rule of law, with considerable civil liberties and freedom of the press have been 'Right wing', compared with what emerged in monstrous form in the 1920s and 1930s, under first Lenin and then Stalin? Are there not, to say the least, numerous gradations of political constitution and opinion between what actually happened and being an outright reactionary?

Of course there are. That is the whole meaning of an open society—the ideal of the modern liberal. It was in order to make this clear and defend the idea of such an open society against Leninism that, dare I say it, the Congress for Cultural Freedom was set up and *Quadrant* founded under its auspices, in the 1950s. If public policy and related matters are to be discussed in a constructive and intelligent manner, it is necessary that there be voices that cover a wide spectrum of opinion. In any matter of significance, this is rather likely to be the case. Attempts to prevent the expression of such diverse opinions in the name of a 'truth' proclaimed by some party or other of, shall we say, 'intense convictions' intrudes on intelligent and civilized discourse. What this means is that a liberal constitution requires the defence of a number of civil and political liberties. The American Constitution was an attempt to define and institutionalize those liberties. Leninism systematically and violently *abolished* them. They are, in our time, under attack from many quarters—as the current trial of Jiang Tianyong in China testifies, even in the wake of the death in gaol of Liu Xiaobo—and must be defended by all means.

It has been estimated that the average longevity of creative individuals—novelists, poets, artists, composers—who left Russia to escape Bolshevism was 72, while that of those who stayed behind was 45. Vitaly Shentalinsky's *Arrested Voices: Resurrecting the Disappeared Writers of the Soviet Regime* (Martin Kessler, New York, 1996) is the classic account. Among the many who fled after October 1917 were the Nabokovs. Andrea Pitzer's *The Secret History of Vladimir Nabokov* (Pegasus, New York and London, 2013) tells the story exquisitely and poignantly. Vladimir Dmitrievich Nabokov, the father of the novelist Vladimir Nabokov, was a leading liberal political figure in Russia in the years before war and revolution threw it into chaos. He worked for democratization, argued against the death penalty and in favour of liberalization of laws against homosexuality. He was threatened by monarchists before 1917 and by the Bolsheviks both then and after 1917. He was a senior member of the PRG. His property was seized by the Bolsheviks after October 1917 and he was driven into exile, only to be assassinated in Berlin by a monarchist. His son's novels are haunted by this and what followed.

The creation of the Cheka was the signature of the Bolshevik 'revolution'. It led almost at once to the creation of what would become the notorious GULAG Archipelago. We now have good histories of the GULAG, notably those by Anne Applebaum and Oleg Khlevniuk. Applebaum's *GULAG: A History of the Soviet Camps* (Allen Lane, 2003) and her *Iron Curtain: The Crushing of Eastern Europe 1944-56* (Allen Lane, 2012) should be core reading in a mandatory course in modern history and the nature of political liberty at our universities. Her Epilogue to the book on the GULAG is poignant in drawing attention to the fact that there seems to be a pervasive amnesia about the matter—wilful in Putin's Russia, neglectful in the West. Putin has long openly called himself a Chekist and still honours the Soviet and KGB past. Unless that past is understood in the West, the myth will persist that the Cold War was somehow due to an unjustified paranoia about Communism and that the Communist revolutions were, in fact, 'progressive', so that efforts to prevent or contain them were unjustified and merely 'reactionary'.

McMeekin argues that the total number of people executed in Tsarist Russia between the reigns of Nicholas I (1825-39) and Nicholas II (1894-1917) was about six and half thousand, including *both* criminal and political executions. That figure might be contested, but it is almost certainly close to the right order of magnitude, as Russia was, paradoxically, at the forefront in civilizing penal codes in the 19th century. In the first five years of Lenin's rule (until he was cut down by strokes), with the Cheka under his direct control, it has been estimated that between 200,000 and 250,000 people were executed on *political* grounds without anything resembling the kind of trial most of those executed under the Tsars had received. In an Appendix to her history of the GULAG, Anne Applebaum addressed the question of how many people died unnecessarily as a consequence of the Bolshevik revolution. It is a scrupulous and sobering attempt to reckon with a grim and controversial subject. Rather than being simply an appendix to a book, it might well serve as the introductory text for a course, provoking students to inquire into sources, methods and meanings.

Timothy Tackett seems prepared to accept that 'intense convictions' are a reasonable explanation and even excuse for political terror. He would not agree that this held in the case of the Nazis, but he appears to suggest that it did do so in the case of the French Revolution and other 'major' revolutions. Yet what those revolutions wrought was political regression of the worst kind. Education in their malformation of Russian, Chinese and Cambodian (or Ethiopian and from 1979 Iranian) society ought be part of a core curriculum in the West. There should be a mantra among all of us that says of this history, as of the Holocaust, 'Never again! Never again!' Whatever our differences of opinion, we should be united in our commitment to civil liberties, constitutional checks on the abuse of power and willingness to defend these things against those who are programmatically committed to destroying them. For there are such parties or organizations still and well-ordered liberty is far from being the natural or default setting of human societies. It requires informed, principled and active exercise to maintain. The centenary of the Bolshevik *coup d'état* is a good time to reflect on all this.

2: Icons of liberty and their common humanity

Thomas Edwin Ricks, who was born in 1955, is the best kind of American journalist and writer: forensic, dispassionate, judicious and lucid. His two books on the Iraq War, *Fiasco* (2006) and *The Gamble* (2009) are among the best written by anyone on that controversial conflict. Prior to those books, he was a reporter in Somalia, Haiti, Korea, Bosnia, Kosovo, Macedonia, Kuwait, Turkey and Afghanistan. On the virtues of *Fiasco*, he was given extraordinarily privileged access by General David Petraeus in Iraq to research and write *The Gamble*.

These experiences set him up beautifully to write about Winston Churchill and George Orwell as observers of war and writers about power and conflict. What's striking is that he chose to juxtapose the two lives. He has done a very fine job. The book reads exceptionally well and is distinguished by the maturity and incisiveness of the author's judgements.

In certain respects, Churchill and Orwell are a study in contrasts: the conservative aristocrat with hereditary access to high politics and a love of the British Empire, who led his country through one of the gravest crises in its history and lived into his nineties in comfortable retirement; versus the impoverished journalist and social democrat who worked obscurely, struggled to make ends meet most of his life, detested the British class system and Empire and died of tuberculosis at the age of forty six.

Yet Ricks shows that there were striking similarities between the two. Ten are worth singling out, given the overarching fact that the two Englishmen have become icons of the cause of freedom from tyranny: since 1940, in Churchill's case, and 1945 in Orwell's case, with the publication of *Animal Farm*, or perhaps 1949, with the appearance of *Nineteen Eighty-Four*. Both men had lonely boyhoods, with fathers who neglected and in some respects despised them. Both sought immersion in reality abroad in their youth: Churchill in India and Africa, Orwell in Burma, in the imperial service. Both had what Ricks describes as an 'anarchic aristocratic outlook'.

This led Churchill to challenge, defect from, re-join and finally (if briefly) dominate the Conservative Party; and Orwell to empathize with the poor and downtrodden, but to detest their smell and to long for higher values than working class culture could deliver. Both believed passionately in individual liberty and practised it. Neither was ever willing to be the drummer boy or apparatchik of anyone else's party or ideological cause and each believed fiercely in the vital importance of *Habeas Corpus* to liberal democracy. Both were, also, passionate about nature and colour.

Both men abominated fakery, incompetence and treason. Both were astringent prose stylists, although Orwell somewhat more astringent than the at times florid Churchill.

Both, in the early 1940s, felt a growing apprehension about the prospects for the post-Second World War order. Finally, the strain of the war years seriously undermined the health of each of them.

Their common emphasis on the importance of *Habeas Corpus* goes to the root of their distinctly English sense of justice and individual liberty. From as early as the reign of King Henry II, in the late 12th century, English monarchs could require of any party who had detained one of their subjects within the realm that the detainee be brought before a regular court or released without charge. This is what makes sense of the famous lines in Shakespeare's *Henry IV Part 2*, in which young Prince Hal says to his circle:

> This is the English, not the Turkish court; not Amurath an Amurath succeeds, but
> Harry Harry.

This is why Thomas More felt able—mistakenly, as it turned out—to take shelter behind the common law from the demands of King Henry VIII himself.

Churchill, a descendent of the Duke of Marlborough, and Orwell, the offspring of a low-ranking bureaucrat in the Indian civil service, who oversaw the production of opium in the early 20th century; imbibed very early an instinctive sense of the rights of subjects of the Crown and the liberties of an Anglo-Saxon. Each then lived doggedly by this sense and each has become identified with the defence of such liberty.

Ricks engagingly opens his book with the reflection that both came within an inch of being killed before achieving the things that have made them icons of the cause of liberty: Churchill in a car accident in New York in 1931; Orwell when shot in the throat fighting as an anarchist in Catalonia in the Spanish civil war in 1937.

Just a very slight alteration in the timing of the accident or the impact of the bullet, he reflects, and either or both men might have been consigned to obscurity. Instead, they lived to become among the most celebrated figures of the 20th century.

Peter Davison's anthology of George Orwell's journalism and essays, published in 2014, is titled *Seeing Things As They Are*. Ricks argues that this was, indeed, a defining characteristic of Orwell's worldview and writing. But he adds that both Orwell and Churchill had a gift not only for seeing everyday realities as they were, but for grasping the bigger picture and seeing above and beyond ideological slogans and the myopia of many of their contemporaries.

He closes his book with a philosophical remark which could serve as a thought provoking point of entry for a good graduate seminar discussion:

> The struggle to see things as they are is perhaps the fundamental driver of Western
> civilization. There is a long but direct line from Aristotle and Archimedes to Locke,
> Hume, Mill and Darwin and from there through Orwell and Churchill to [Martin

Luther King Jr's] 'Letter from Birmingham City Jail'. It is the agreement that objective reality exists, that people of goodwill can perceive it, and that other people will change their views when presented with the facts of the matter.

This belief in objective reality, he argues throughout the book, is the key to Orwell's inquiries, his curiosity and his political satire. It was also the key to Churchill's stand against appeasement of Hitler in the 1930s; his belief, in 1940-42, that the Anglo-Saxon powers could and would prevail against Nazi tyranny and his clarion call in 1946 for the war-weary West to face down the threat from Stalin's sinister totalitarian regime. It is a ringing note on which to end a fine book.

3: *Senectus mentis*: Glen Bowersock on Islam

Glen Warren Bowersock, now 81 years of age, is by any measure one of the West's most distinguished scholars of classical civilization. His chosen field, from the start, was the history of the ancient Mediterranean world: Greece, Rome and the Near East. He is a prize winning graduate of Harvard (1957) and Oxford (1959, as a Rhodes Scholar) Universities. His doctorate at Oxford (1962) was on Augustus and the Greek world. He has served as lecturer in Ancient History at Balliol, Magdalen, and New Colleges, Oxford (1960–62), Professor of Classics and History, at Harvard (1962–80) and was Professor of Ancient History at the Institute for Advanced Study at Princeton University from 1980 until his retirement in 2006. He is the author of over a dozen books and has published over 400 articles on Greek, Roman, and Near Eastern history and culture as well as the classical tradition.

The list of his honours is long and impressive and the titles of his books and the number of his scholarly articles are alike the stuff of open mouthed awe on the part of any aspiring student of classical civilization. They include a book based on his doctoral dissertation, *Augustus and the Greek World* (Oxford, 1965), *Greek Sophists in the Roman Empire* (Oxford, 1969), *Julian the Apostate*, Harvard, 1978), *Gibbon's Historical Imagination* (Stanford, 1988), *Roman Arabia* (Harvard, 1983), *Late Antiquity: A Guide to the Post-Classical World* (edited with Peter Brown and Oleg Grabar, Harvard, 1999), *Interpreting Late Antiquity* (Harvard 2001), *Mosaics as History: The Near East from Late Antiquity to Islam* (Harvard, 2006), *Lorenzo Valla: On the Donation of Constantine* (edition and translation, Harvard, 2007), *From Gibbon to Auden: Essays on the Classical Tradition* (Oxford, 2009) and *The Throne of Adulis: Red Sea Wars on the Eve of Islam* (Oxford, 2013).

This is a wonderful body of work and an indication of what our best universities in the West have been able to produce, even if all too many of our students in the 21st century read very little of it. Having read several of Professor Bowersock's earlier works, not least his very recent and fascinating study of pre-Islamic Arabia and Christian Ethiopia, *The Throne of Adulis*, I was prompted to buy and read at once his latest offering, *The Crucible of Islam* (Harvard, 2017). I was dismayed, therefore, to discover that something strange has affected the mind of the great scholar, leading both to some startling, basic errors of history and an approach to his subject that would have astonished Edward Gibbon, whose 'historical imagination' had exercised Bowersock in his prime. I had expected mature insights and fresh perspectives from this book, concise though it is, at only 220 pages. Instead, I found myself astonished by its errors and omissions and recoiling from its deference to Islam.

We might anchor a reflection on Bowersock's writing about the origins of Islam in the famous remarks by Gibbon himself, in the fiftieth and fifty first chapters of his celebrated history of *The Decline and Fall of the Roman Empire*. He makes the sardonic remark that:

> The birth of Mohammed was fortunately placed in the most degenerate and disorderly period of the Persians, the Romans and the barbarians of Europe: the empires of Trajan, or even of Constantine or Charlemagne, would have repelled the assault of the naked Saracens, and the torrent of fanaticism might have been obscurely lost in the sands of Arabia.

These lines have a curious and disturbing resonance in our time, a generation after the end of the Cold War and in the midst of violent upheavals in the name of Islam, not least in the Middle East. They also show Gibbon's characteristic turn of phrase and sceptical outlook. 'Fortunately placed' was not an indication that he believed the Arab conquests to have been fortunate for the conquered, but rather that the Arabs got lucky and hence their desert fanaticism was able to spread far and wide. Bowersock set out to explore the roots of that 'fortunate' turn of events in his two most recent books, *The Throne of Adulis* and *The Crucible of Islam*.

The first of these throws light into some rather dark corners of standard Western historiography. The second is a far more questionable contribution to our shared understanding of the ancient world. It would be, in some respects, ungracious of one to direct too withering a broadside at Professor Bowersock, given his distinguished career and great learning. But the errors and the general tone of this book on Islam cannot go without comment. Sadly, they may be a reflection of an aging intelligence—a *senectus mentis*. They are certainly a cause for concern about failures of editorial assistance at Harvard University Press. But above all, they need correction for the sake of the common interest we all have in understanding accurately how Islam arose and what it represents as a force in history.

The errors that struck me most forcefully are of a kind that would surely have been corrected had any competent scholar or editor checked the book before it was published. How they were committed by an emeritus professor of classical history at the Princeton Institute of Advanced Studies and overlooked by the editors at Harvard University Press quite eludes me. To take one example: Bowersock refers (at p. 16) to Jewish settlers in Arabia having migrated there 'in the aftermath of the revolt against Titus in Jerusalem'. Yet the Jewish revolt against the Romans in 66 CE, which lasted until the sack of Masada in 73 (or, archaeologists and historians tell us, perhaps 74) CE, was in no sense a revolt against Titus. Given the weight of his classical learning, Bowersock has to know this.

Reading Bowersock, one cannot readily tell whether Titus is supposed to have been emperor at the time of the revolt, or perhaps the governor of Judaea against whom the Jews rebelled. He was neither. They revolted against the taxation policies of the Roman governor Gessius Florus. After local efforts to quell it had failed in 66, Vespasian was appointed, in 67, to conduct a large scale counter-insurgency operation. Titus was his son and second in command. When Vespasian departed for the west in 69 to bid for imperial power in the famous Year of Four Emperors, Titus took command of what was already a three year campaign against the Jews. He then took Jerusalem and completed the suppression of the Jewish rebellion.

Another breathtaking lapse is Bowersock's remark that the ferment in Arabia in the second half of the 6th century and the early 7th century—the rise of a Jewish kingdom in Yemen, the invasion of Arabia by the Christian Ethiopians and the first stirrings of what would become Islam—prefigured possible upheaval and 'neither Byzantium nor Baghdad could ignore this possibility' (p. 105). There are two solecisms here. Constantinople was not generally known as Byzantium at that time, even if that had been its name before Constantine made it his capital. But this is a minor point. Far more significant is the reference to Baghdad as the Persian capital, when Baghdad did not exist at all until after 762, when it was built by the Abbasid caliphs. The Persian capital was Ctesiphon. Again, Bowersock has to know this. How many of his readers will be jarred by this kind of error and how many will entirely fail to notice it? It is disturbing to think that his general readership will take it to be no error at all and will imagine Baghdad to have indeed been the Persian capital.

Yet he repeats this error at p. 120, where he states that 'After the Persian capture of the city [Jerusalem] in 614, the Christians had been dispossessed and the relics of the True Cross removed to Baghdad.' Those relics were removed to no such place, since Baghdad did not exist at that point and would not do so for almost another century and a half. Such an error is all the more mystifying in that, in his Acknowledgements, he expresses glowing gratitude to two other eminent classicists, Peter Brown and Christopher Jones, for their interest in and close attention to the book as a project and for improving his pages with their 'perceptive observations and searching questions'. Evidently, neither of them noted his strangely anachronistic references to Baghdad or his description of Titus as the object of the Great Revolt by the Jews.

An equally strange and disturbing error comes at p. 142, where Bowersock, in discussing the Dome of the Rock as sitting on Mount Moriah, where Solomon's Temple stood before the sack of the city in 587 BCE, describes that sacking as the occasion on which 'the Assyrians took the Jews of Jerusalem into captivity in Babylon.' How is it possible that a scholar of ancient history in an Ivy League university could make so basic an error as to state that the *Assyrians* took the Jews to Babylon? Assyria had ceased to exist a generation before that date, destroyed by the Babylonians themselves and the Medes; the climax being the destruction of the Assyrian capital at Nineveh. It was the Babylonian King Nebuchadnezzar who took the Jews into exile in 587-86 BCE. This is such a famous story that it is astonishing to see a senior and distinguished scholar get it so obviously wrong.

Egregious errors of this nature do much to undermine one's confidence in the credibility of an author, or at least of a book. If Bowersock was just starting out, publishing a book marred by such howlers would surely obstruct the development of his academic career. Ironically, just because he has long since become a distinguished and decorated scholar, neither his most brilliant and learned colleagues, nor the copy editors at one of the wold's most prestigious publishing houses saw fit to closely check his accuracy. Well before I finished reading the book, however, I was shaking my head in disbelief. Yet it is not only the obvious mistakes that trouble one. It is the consideration that, if he can get things like this wrong, how can we rely on his judgement and accuracy in points of more minute detail, regarding the obscure origins and controversial rise of Islam at the end of the classical era?

Nor is it only errors of fact that mar this book. Drawing upon well over a century of scholarship that has been seeking to pin down the actual history of early Islam, as distinct from the myths and dogmas hallowed by Muslim tradition, Bowersock consistently fails to display any of the qualities of irony, literary flair or sardonic humour that make Gibbon such an education to read. He long ago made a close study of Gibbon's historical imagination. What can have possessed him to immerse himself for a lifetime in the very materials studied by the 18th century Englishman and yet acquire none of the little master's genius for inflection and Olympian detachment? This is especially so with regard to Islam as a set of beliefs and practices. Gibbon has been much berated for his slyly irreverent asides about Christian theology, if not for his salacious footnotes often disguised, as William Beckford long ago observed, in the obscurity of the original Greek and Latin. Regrettably, no-one could accuse Bowersock of such things in his work on Islam.

Anyone who has had the pleasure of reading *The Decline and Fall of the Roman Empire*, or taken the time at least to do so, is likely to carry with them ever afterwards some of Gibbon's famous quips or beautifully constructed passages of historiographic rhetoric. I love the writings of St Augustine, but cannot forget Gibbon's acid footnote to the effect that Augustine's learning was too often borrowed and his arguments too often his own. Or his wonderfully droll footnote about the Roman Emperor Gordian II, who left behind on his death 'twenty-two acknowledged concubines, and a library of sixty-two thousand volumes'. If the number of his progeny and his literary productions were any indication, Gibbon drily remarked, then both the women and the library had been intended 'for use rather than ostentation.' Bowersock's tone stands in marked contrast with that of Gibbon precisely on account of its painful and humourless deference to Muslim traditions and dogmatic claims.

Despite the wealth of serious archaeology and history available to him, which he explicitly acknowledges and cites, Bowersock refers again and again, without the least trace of irony or scepticism, to the Prophet Muhammad, the 'revelations' to Muhammad from the Archangel Gabriel, even the night flight of Muhammad to Jerusalem and his meeting there with Gabriel, as if such things had the status of actual historical fact. It seems vanishingly unlikely that he actually believes these things, yet he betrays not an iota of scepticism or irony as he slips such phrases into an otherwise resolutely secular and earnest history. Why is this? His oblique reference at p. 70 to what he calls the 'now notorious story of the so-called Satanic verses that Satan himself was alleged to have induced the Prophet to include in his Qur'an' may be an indirect clue as to why he adopts the tone that he does.

Salman Rushdie notoriously suffered a *fatwa* condemning him to death for writing *The Satanic Verses* (1988) and publishers and distributors of the book were verbally and physically attacked for doing so. Its Japanese translator, Hitoshi Igarashi, for example, was stabbed and killed. Its Italian translator Ettore Capriolo was seriously injured in a stabbing, and there were quite a few other acts of incredible violence committed under the sign of the *fatwa* by fanatics. Many incidents of violence have occurred since, in which critics of Islam or Muhammad have been assaulted for their words or drawings. It seems disturbingly possible that Bowersock, eminent scholar of Harvard, Oxford and Princeton, was pulling possible punches and avoiding all irony in order to avoid incurring the anger of fanatical Muslims, whether Sunni or Shia. This is all the more remarkable given his observation at the outset that it has taken a long time for Islam to be subjected to the same kind of textual and historical criticism that, from the Renaissance onwards, steadily undermined the dogmatic claims of established Christianity.

He is worth quoting on this, because this caution, hesitancy and self-censorship, on his part go to the heart of a dilemma that has confronted the West since the 1980s and has grown steadily more acute in recent years. On p. 2, he states:

> The pioneering generation of Islamicists in the West, including Theodor Noldeke,
> Julius Wellhausen and Ignaz Goldziher, applied the methods of classical philology
> as they had been successfully imported into the study of the New Testament and
> the Hebrew Bible by Erasmus and Gesenius. As these scholars recognized, the
> transmission of these old texts was susceptible to critical analysis, which in the fullness
> of time could be supplemented by surviving documents on stone, papyri and coins
> and eventually the discoveries of archaeological excavation. For Islam, the authority
> of the Qur'an, being the revealed word of God, notoriously resisted the Erasmian

challenge, because of the vast hiatus between its creation, at whatever time and by whatever means, and very much later reports of the context from which it came. It took nearly two centuries for Islamic exegetes to acquire a corpus of what was known about the genesis of their religion. By then a complex process of textual contamination had already taken place.

The better part of his book attempts to build upon this foundation. It is vitiated by his regrettable tendency to concede by indirection that the Qur'an was, in fact, a 'revelation' from Gabriel to Muhammad and that Muhammad was, indeed, the singular progenitor of the religion that, from the late 7th century and especially after the Abbasid revolution in the mid-8th century, became the state religion of the Arab empire stretching from Central Asia to Spain.

Much that Bowersock relates in his short book will be a revelation, if one may use that word in its secular sense, to the naïve reader. He offers something of a synthesis of a century and more of secular scholarship of the Erasmian kind on the origins of Islam. But given the startling errors of basic fact and the disturbing deference to Muslim religious sensitivities that characterize the book, one has to caution any reader with the time-honoured Latin phrase *caveat emptor*—buyer beware, or read with care. The great scholar wants to write a summary account of the rise of Islam, but he gets elementary historical facts in his own field flat wrong and shows marked signs of not wishing to offend any believing Muslim. From this starting point, we need to take *cum grano salis,* to use another Latin term (with a grain of salt), his assertions that Islam did begin almost exactly as Muslim tradition asserts: with revelations to Muhammad, the creation of the base (al-qaeda) at Medina, the triumph at Mecca and the rapid diffusion of original and pure Islam across the stricken Roman and Persian empires by inspired Muslim armies after 632, when Muhammad reportedly died at Mecca.

Perhaps there is an explanation for all this that has eluded me. Perhaps a more charitable explanation for the errors of fact and the lack of scepticism and irony in Bowersock's history of Islam is that it is all a very sly and artfully constructed polemic. Perhaps he knows very well that the errors I have pointed out are flagrant and has included them as an indirect way of arguing that the history of Islam he offers should not be relied upon either. I am, of course, being sardonic. It is surely inconceivable that Harvard University Press would lend itself to such a strange exercise, or that scholars like Peter Brown and Christopher Jones would connive in it. Yet short of such a far-fetched apology for what has been published in this book, one can only lament the author's evidently failing powers and the travesty of scholarship that has resulted. Readers should be advised to turn, instead, to Ibn Warraq's *The Quest for the Historical Muhammad* (2000), Tom Holland's *In the Shadow of the Sword* (2012), or Karl-Heinz Ohlig's *Early Islam: A Critical Reconstruction Based on Contemporary Sources* (2013).

Bowersock goes out of his way to dismiss the argument by the late Patricia Crone (1945-2015) that Mecca was not the trading city of Muslim tradition and that there are good reasons for doubting the conventional story of Islam having arisen there from whole cloth. He would have done well to have urged his readers to linger in such territory, as Holland does, for example, and to recognize that the history is far more uncertain than the religious believers assert. It is, for example, the opinion of Moshe Sharon, a specialist on these matters of considerably more learning about the origins of Islam than Glen Bowersock (whose work has overwhelmingly been on Greece and Rome) that it arose from several discordant and geographically dispersed centres, which were pulled together by force under the Umayyads, then made into a state religion for the Arab Empire in the late 7th century. Sharon may be in error, but Bowersock does not so much as entertain such an intriguing hypothesis.

The best scholarship on the subject does *not* point to the neat and pious conclusions that Bowersock seems determined to offer us in *The Crucible of Islam*. It points, rather, to Arab monotheisms having germinated in multiple places, as Sharon argues, as Arab migrations overran the exhausted Roman and Persian empires in the 7th century. The Ghassanid and Lakhmid Arab states in what is now Syria and Iraq had been client states of the Romans and Persians, respectively, throughout the climactic wars of the 6th and 7th centuries. When the Persians overran the Roman Empire and were then decisively defeated by the Emperor Heraclius in the 620s, frontiers opened up to the Arabs that had been closed for centuries; much as such opportunities opened up in the West for the Goths and other Germanic peoples as the Roman Empire imploded in the 4th and 5th centuries.

Arab tribes then migrated widely and, like the Goths in Italy, southern France and Spain, established new principalities within the provinces of the old empires. The Umayyads then pulled all this into a single empire by force, including the conquest of Mecca and Medina in the late 7th century. Abd al-Malik completed the task and built the Dome of the Rock in Jerusalem to signify and assert, for the first time, that Islam was the state religion and the purest of monotheisms. Early the following century, Arabs and Berbers broke into Visigothic Spain and overran it. Half a century later again, it was taken over by Abd al-Rahman, an Umayyad princeling who had survived the overthrow and wholesale massacre of his family by the insurgent Abbasids, who had come out of Khorasan (Central Asia), not out of Arabia, in the late 740s.

I bought and read Bowersock's book believing that it would add to my stock of knowledge of these matters. It dismays me to report that it did nothing of the kind, but rather reinforced a sense that Western scholarship on Islam has found itself caught between objectivity and fanatical religion in a manner that it has not been (with regard to Christianity) for almost three centuries. It is very important that this not be permitted. The efforts by a number of powerful and well-resourced Muslim movements to get criticism of Islam banned in the West and broadly defined anti-'blasphemy' laws introduced must be resisted strenuously. Liberty itself is at stake in such matters. If a society based on broadly liberal norms and freedoms is to be maintained—and, indeed, extended more widely around the world, not least to the Muslim world itself—then we simply cannot bend to an alien religion which would forbid us so much as to inquire critically into its claims. I would like to believe that Glen Bowersock would agree.

4: The mountains of the Anthropocene

If you have not yet seen Jennifer Peedom's documentary film *Mountain*, do so. It is a sublime masterpiece. She should, surely, get awards for this beautiful composition. The sound track—performed by the Australian Chamber Orchestra—is magnificent, the cinematography is breathtaking, the narration by acclaimed actor Willem Dafoe is beautifully paced, economical and has well-honed gravitas. In both concept and execution, this is a singular achievement and it is exhilarating to know that it is an Australian production, backed by Screen Australia, directed by an Australian and with the music performed by an Australian orchestra.

It is about the way an obsession with mountains and wild landscapes, mountain climbing, skiing and extreme sports has grown around the world in the very recent past. Very early in the film, Dafoe's voice intones that, until three centuries ago, the idea of trying to climb serious mountains—as distinct from by-passing them, finding ways through or around them, or gazing up at them in awe as the abodes of gods or monsters—would have struck human beings as a lunatic idea. The film's theme is how this has radically changed in those three centuries, but above all in the past century and at an exponentially accelerating rate.

Very early in the film, after we glimpse Dafoe and the musicians getting ready to record, we are shown a huge rock face, many hundreds of sheer feet high, with a tiny red figure, almost like a beetle from a distance, crawling up it; a dizzying drop below and a soaring cliff above. Then the camera—perhaps a drone—zooms in and we realize first that this is a human being and secondly that he has no harness or protection of any kind. He is climbing this immense bluff, which looks almost smooth and without ledge or crevice to the amateur viewer's eye, with no grappling gear, no safety rope, no parachute. It is stunning to observe. Then he pauses, pivots on his toes and drops his arms to his sides to shake out his hands before resuming his climb. 'That's what I'm talking about!', as the saying has it.

This film could only have been made in our time, because the technology to execute it in the astonishing manner that Peedom and her team have done did not exist until quite recently. Nor did human beings so much as attempt most of the things filmed until very recently. But the climbing of mountains goes back before cameras could do any justice to the heroics involved. Anyone who has read Wade Davis's superb book *Into the Silence: The Great War, Mallory and the Conquest of Everest*, will appreciate the difference between his evocation in well-crafted words and still, black and white photographs of Mallory's early 1920s expeditions and the exquisite aerial and close-range colour photography that the Peedom crew were able to bring to the subject.

Film and text are in many ways non-transitive media. There are things you can do with the skilled use of words that no piece of film can accomplish. But the reverse is also true and *Mountain* is a truly breathtaking illustration of what can be done with film. Not only do its cameras soar high above many of the most majestic mountain landscapes in the world; they show us climbers in real time doing remarkable things; they show us skiers performing staggering exploits of various kinds; they show us people walking tightropes strung between immense mesas in the Grand Canyon; they show us, from perfect aerial vantage points, people riding mountain bikes straight off high cliffs—and then releasing parachutes to soften and control their descent; they show us the changes of seasons in mountain landscapes or crowds of skiers and mountain climbers doing what they do in sped-up, time-delayed footage, as well as slow-motion images of rushing rivers and wildlife, volcanic eruptions and acts of stunning bravado; and they show us magnificently enlarged and close-in shots of snowflake crystals tumbling through chill air, which no words could adequately describe or evoke.

The musical sound track was conducted and enhanced by Richard Tognetti. It includes works by Beethoven, Chopin, Grieg, Arvo Part, Sculthorpe and Vivaldi and vocal work that hoists us into the heights we are seeing on the large screen. Beethoven's Violin Concerto (Opus 61) and Fifth Piano Concerto (Opus 73) are used to beautiful effect near the end. After seeing the film for the fifth time, I went home and immersed myself again in Phil Grabsky's wonderful documentary *In Search of Beethoven* (2005); if only to contemplate, once more, how music, also, has climbed extraordinary peaks in the past three centuries. The technology of musical production, recording and playing has, of course, gone ahead by leaps and bounds during that time. Beethoven himself was constantly pressing piano makers to create bigger, more powerful, better tuned instruments on which he could exhibit his abounding energy and genius.

That brings us to a consideration that the film prompts, without touching upon it directly: that when Dafoe describes the emergence, over the past three centuries, of a human obsession (initially very much a Western one) with climbing mountains and 'turning mystery into mastery', to the point where the climbing of Everest is now less exploration than 'crowd control', he is describing the Anthropocene. This is a term of recent coinage to describe the era of human dominance in the biosphere—and it's very mixed implications, from the ominous to the inspirational. That dominance has its roots in the inventiveness our species began to exhibit even in the Upper Palaeolithic, but is most reasonably confined to the past three centuries—since the Scientific Revolution and above all since the technological revolutions and population explosion of the past hundred years or so. We have, across the board, been turning mystery into mastery and exploration into crowd control.

Mark Denny's new little book, *Making the Most of the Anthropocene* (Johns Hopkins University Press, 2017), is a breezy introduction to the Anthropocene and its possibilities. But here I want simply to make the point that Jennifer Peedom, in *Mountain*, has exhibited brilliantly a single facet of the Anthropocene, without drawing attention to the wider significance of what she is showing us; perhaps without quite realizing it herself. Towards the end of the film, Dafoe's voice tells us, quietly and with measured conviction, that the mountains exist, unlike us, in Deep Time and are the symphony of the Earth, rising and falling over aeons too vast for the human mind to rightly comprehend. They are, he comments, indifferent to us and want nothing from us, neither love nor fear. In small doses, he adds, this insight is exhilarating, but in full form it is annihilating. This situates us in the natural world where we belong and demands of us a major reckoning concerning our purposes now—in the Anthropocene.

We can pitch that imperative in ecological terms, in economic and political terms and in moral terms. But, watching Peedom's *Mountain*, one comes to appreciate that we can and must also interpret it in terms of individual psychology and human ontology. If there is a book of philosophy that I would see as the most appropriate companion piece to *Mountain*, it would not be any classical text—Plato, Aristotle, Lucretius, Epictetus—but Peter Sloterdijk's *tour de force* of 2006 (English translation 2013): *You Must Change Your Life*. Never, since reading Nietzsche's books as a youth, have I discovered a philosophical thinker who provides such a brilliant invitation to what he calls *practices* of transcendence and 'acrobatic ethics'. His title is derived from the final line of a famous sonnet by Rainer Maria Rilke 'Archaic Torso of Apollo'. Thinking about *Mountain*, as distinct from merely gasping at it or becoming dreamily lost in its imagery and music, induces similar thoughts. Here's a recommendation: see the film, then read Sloterdijk's book—while listening to Beethoven's concertos.

The American poet and critic James Pollock reminds us[8] that Apollo was the Greek god of poetry and that Rilke wrote the poem after working as August Rodin's personal secretary, in Paris. Rodin had him visiting art museums nearly every day. His advice to the young poet was that an artist must always be at work and the example he set, 'tirelessly labouring to transform the perishable bodies of his human models into durable bronze statues with great spiritual power', had a profound effect on Rilke. It changed him into a poet whose calling was to transmute the impermanent things of this world into a higher order of reality within himself and for others. That is the effect—or ought, I think, to be the effect—on us of Jennifer Peedom's fabulous documentary. In colour, in sound, in concept and execution, in implicit thought and provocation to wider thinking, this film is calling out to us, like Rilke's archaic torso of Apollo: You must change your life.

---

8   https://voltagepoetry.com/2014/02/24/1311/

5: Jabotinsky and the state of Israel

Daniel Kupfert Heller is assistant professor of Jewish Studies at McGill University, Montreal, Canada's most prestigious university. *Jabotinsky's Children* is his first book and was based on a PhD dissertation completed at Stanford University in 2012. It is a great start to an academic career. We shall hear more of him, if this book is any guide to his talents.

Both his subject and the scholarly acumen with which he has approached it have deep roots in his tertiary education. He singles out a number of mentors whose influence shaped him as a young historian. Were it not for Derek Penslar at the University of Toronto, he remarks, 'I would never have considered a career as a historian'. Several of Penslar's classes on the history of the Jews in Europe and the Middle East captivated him. Anna Shternshis and Piotr Wrobel opened avenues for him to extend his interest in the Jews of Eastern Europe.

Aron Rodrigue, Norman Naimark and Steven Zipperstein at Stanford then guided his immersion, as a graduate student, in the history of both the European and Jewish Right and his development as a thinker. He pays particular tribute to Zipperstein for his 'extraordinary level of commitment to training historians as thinkers, teachers and writers.' He was fortunate, indeed, to have such a mentor. Zipperstein's own work on the Jews of Eastern Europe is of the first rank; but the mentoring of young scholars to high standards is a priceless service and here Zipperstein has also excelled.

How bold it was of Heller to begin with a study of Jabotinsky, such a seminal figure in the history of Zionism. From more or less the beginning of his career, Jabotinsky, as Heller shows, clashed with the mainstream Zionists on two grounds: he believed that a state of Israel would require a military force to delineate and defend it; and he believed that socialism would impoverish it and could generate a Leninist politics of the kind he had seen arise in his native Russia. Zionism, he argued, should be resolutely capitalist. The first claim was hammered home in the 1930s, in resistance to Arab pogroms in Palestine. It led to the creation of the Haganah as a Jewish self-defence force.

The second argument took much longer to prevail. Perhaps it was only the economic reforms of the 2000s, when Ariel Sharon was Prime Minister and Benjamin Netanyahu Minister of Finance that Zionist capitalism really came into its own—albeit with social consequences that caused considerable and ongoing disquiet. They did, however, trigger an economic boom in Israel, turning it into a hi-tech start-up nation and the most dynamic economy in the Middle East or Eastern Mediterranean world.

The influence of Jabotinsky on the use of force by the Zionist movement has been a matter of profound controversy for many decades. So much so, that when one opens such books as Avi Shlaim's *The Iron Wall: Israel and the Arab World* (2000), Bruce Hoffman's *Anonymous Soldiers: The Struggle For Israel 1917-1947* (2015) or Padraig O'Malley's *The Two State Delusion: Israel and Palestine—A Tale of Two Narratives* (2016), almost the first thing one does, is turn to the Index and look under 'Jabotinsky, Vladimir'. Shlaim devotes five pages in his Prologue to Jabotinsky; which is unsurprising, since the very title of his book is derived from Jabotinsky's writing in the 1920s. Hoffman's whole book is about Revisionist Zionism and the question of terrorism.

Jabotinsky is widely seen as the man who inspired and justified the hard-line militarism of Irgun and the Stern Gang, as well as the more widespread militaristic hubris attributed to Israel after 1948 and more particularly since 1967. His figure looms behind those of Avraham Stern, Menachem Begin and Yitzhak Shamir, Ariel Sharon and Benjamin Netanyahu. His ideas, more than those of Theodor Herzl, Chaim Weizmann or David Ben-Gurion, lend themselves to citation as evidence that Zionism was always a self-consciously racist and nationalist project aimed at displacing the Arabs from Palestine, not co-existing with them. Stern and a few others, of course fantasised about an Israel extending from the Nile to the Euphrates.

For this reason, Heller's book on Jabotinsky and the Eastern European roots of Revisionist Zionism is a vital contribution. The miracle is that he has given us a wonderfully well researched, finely nuanced and deeply informative history, rather than an ideological polemic. The story he has to tell fills a large and important gap in our common understanding of Revisionist Zionism in general, Jabotinsky personally and the genesis of that militarism which flowed, via several streams, into the founding of the state of Israel and its political development. This is no mean achievement and it is a great tribute to both the young historian and his supervisors that he has accomplished it—masterfully.

The crucible, he shows, was Eastern Europe and above all Poland in the 1920s and 1930s. Poland had a long history, but for centuries had been ruled by others—Germans, Russians, Austro-Hungarians. After the First World War, it was one of several new nations carved out of the defeated or collapsed empires and it was struggling to define itself, not least with relation to its various ethnic minorities, among whom the Jews were a substantial and often resented presence. Various strands of Judaism and Zionism existed and competed in this context. Heller shows us those various strands and their conflicts scrupulously and then demonstrates how Revisionist Zionism modelled itself on Pilsudski's Polish nationalism and militarism in the 1920s and 1930s—seeing Poland as a parallel to Palestine.

Jabotinsky, born in Odessa, in pre-revolutionary Russia, was already a Zionist when the First World War broke out and his worldview was decisively shaped by both the realities of that upheaval, the Balfour Declaration and the Bolshevik Revolution, which uprooted the world in which he had grown and been educated. Steven Zipperstein's work on the Jews of Odessa made him an ideal supervisor for Heller in dealing with all this. But the crucial development for Jabotinsky was founding the Jewish Legion in Palestine during the war, in collaboration with Joseph Trumpeldor. One is reminded, reading Heller's account of all this, of Gershom Scholem's 1913-19 diaries, *Lamentations of Youth* (Belknap, Harvard, 2007).

As Heller shows, Jabotinsky found such lamentations in Pilsudski's Poland after 1919 and helped create Jewish youth movements with a martial character: Betar, HaTzohar and, finally, the Irgun. Menachem Begin rose through Betar and, as a young man who admired Jabotinsky, but challenged him in the late 1930s for being too equivocal and out of touch with the martial nationalism of Revisionist youth. The older man died in New York in early August 1940, with Nazism rampant and Israel far from established. The majority of those who had rallied to Betar in Poland perished in the Holocaust. Begin survived—in Lithuania and Russia—and made it to Palestine with his famous maxim 'I fight, therefore I exist'.

Heller does not argue that Revisionist Zionism has been vindicated. He concludes by taking issue with Benjamin Netanyahu's interpretation, in 1993, of a speech given by Jabotinsky to a Jewish audience in Warsaw in August 1938. That interpretation was proffered as a critique of the Oslo accords and a warning that the Jewish inclination to pacifism had led millions to the slaughterhouses of the Nazis. The Jews had to be prepared to fight their neighbours and instil fear in them. Heller notes that Jabotinsky had not foreseen the Holocaust and that his 1938 speech should not, therefore, be used to imply that he had.

He is, nonetheless, more generous to Netanyahu than Ben Caspit, whose new biography *The Netanyahu Years*, delivers a damning indictment of the prime minister as a person and a politician that will confirm the view Moshe Arens expressed in a *Ha'aretz* op ed five years ago: that *Ma'ariv* had moved to the political Left, 'forsaking the right-wing readership that was loyal to it for years.' Of all countries in the Middle East, it is only in Israel that such a biography of a leader in power could have been written at all. And this, too, is consistent with the vision of the Jabotinsky Heller shows us. His parsing of the history is Talmudic in the finest sense and one imagines that Jabotinsky, were he alive today, would be both moved and impressed by what this young Jewish scholar has written.

6: Voluntary assisted dying, philosophy and Christianity

As I write, the Victorian Legislative Council is set to debate the Voluntary Assisted Dying (VAD) Bill. The vote is balanced on a knife edge, with a handful of undecided votes set to determine whether the bill will become law or be shunted aside[9]. Like most complex issues, the matter of VAD is open to all manner of confused arguments and emotional stances. It is to our credit as a state that the deliberation and debate that went into this bill have been conducted with great care and seriousness. Yet there is not a clear consensus on its merits. What are we to think, say or do, in these circumstances?

I should lay a few cards on the table. I am in complete remission from metastatic melanoma and was taken off immunotherapy last February. Before that time, I pondered carefully what my options might be should things go badly. I spoke at length with Rod Syme, long-time campaigner for VAD and author of *A Good Death: An Argument for Voluntary Euthanasia*. I was raised as a Catholic and am conversant with Catholic teaching on life, death and responsibility. Yet, from a young age, I have been much affected by elements of the philosophical tradition, both classical and modern, that have depicted suicide, under certain circumstances, as a matter of dignified moral and existential choice. I am strongly inclined to claim a natural right to such a choice and therefore to VAD.

Where does all this leave me right now? The Prime Minister, Malcolm Turnbull, and two former Prime Ministers, Paul Keating and Tony Abbott, have all publicly stated their opposition to the VAD legislation. All three are Catholics. The root of Catholic opposition to suicide, including VAD, is the argument by Augustine of Hippo, in *The City of God* that suicide contravenes the commandment 'Thou shalt not kill'. This argument is grounded in the prior supposition that the Bible, where this commandment is attributed to the Deity, is an infallible guide to moral truth. Suppose, however, that this supposition was to be rejected—as it is by a great many people in the modern era? We would, surely, have to fall back on 'natural law'—and reason. Where might that lead us?

Going down this road, we need to distinguish both between suicide as such and VAD, which is a very special case of suicide; and between unreasoning impulse and rational choice in the ending of one's own life, which is treacherous terrain, but crucial to the VAD debate. The current legislation has been carefully framed so as to give the greatest possible support to people making a rational and considered choice and not either being pressured into ending their lives or doing so without due consideration. We also need to reflect more generally on

---

9   The bill was subsequently passed, after a great deal of lobbying and politicking on both sides.

our cultural attitude towards mortality, suffering and compassion. We are all mortal, but we do not by any means endure the same sufferings. Also, we consider it compassionate to end the terminal sufferings of beloved animals, but recoil from doing the same for beloved human beings. Why?

Albert Camus famously began his reflection on absurdity and human existence, *The Myth of Sisyphus*, with the words:

> There is but one truly serious philosophical problem and that is suicide. (Il n'y a qu'un problème philosophique vraiment sérieux : c'est le suicide)

Is life worth living and if so, what conditions would terminally change our minds on that point? The classical philosophers discussed this in the light of reason and natural law and arrived at differing conclusions, but certainly not at Augustine's blanket ban. As Marzio Barbagli puts it in his recent history of suicide, in the classical world, all free human beings:

> ...had the right...to take their own life for a variety of reasons: illness, physical pain, fear, the desire for revenge, loss of a dear one, furor, namely a fit of rage, insania or inability to control their actions, or the experience of rape or military defeat. However, suicide was not just tolerated. Among the intellectual elite...it was regarded as the highest expression of liberty, the only form that allowed humans to be equal to and even to exceed the gods, who were destined to be immortal. This explains why the act of suicide was public, almost theatrical, and was carried out calmly, without betraying anger, desperation or fear, in front of numerous witnesses.

It would be difficult to think of a better way to express what the current VAD legislation is seeking to make available to people suffering terminal illness and intolerable deprivation of quality of life. Yet it is precisely such an attitude—chiefly among the Stoics—that Augustine roundly condemned and, indeed, ridiculed, in Book XIX of *The City of God* 'Philosophy and Christianity on Man's End', most notably in Chapter 4.

His argument, however, was not that a law or philosophy legitimizing suicide would pave the way to barbarism and indiscriminate killing of the vulnerable. He simply argued that the problem for the Stoics was that they did not believe in a heavenly beatitude after death and therefore tied themselves in knots arguing that the happy life on Earth should include a dignified right to end one's life. He wrote:

> It is because the philosophers will not believe in this beatitude which they cannot see that they go on trying to fabricate here below an utterly fraudulent felicity built on virtue filled with pride and bound to fail them in the end.

From this, however, it might be deduced that if a great many people do not, indeed, believe in the 'beatitude' of another life beyond the grave, it would seem strange to insist that they endure suffering in extremis rather than end it. From which it might further be deduced that a just law would offer citizens of a pluralistic society the choice between enduring all sufferings with patience and the hope in eternal felicity hereafter, or accepting their natural mortality and putting a term to their sufferings as a matter of dignified volition arrived at in consultation with their doctors and friends. This latter is what the VAD legislation seeks to make available.

A key founder of Stoicism was Chrysippus (279-206 BCE), a brilliant philosopher whose powers of reasoning demonstrably exceeded those of Augustine, but did not lead him to belief in salvation beyond the grave. It has been written of this man that he developed the science of logic well beyond where Aristotle had left it, delving into propositional logic in a manner that would not be repeated or improved upon until the late 19th and early 20th century. Unfortunately, unlike the *Elements* of Euclid, the works of Chrysippus on propositional logic did not survive the decay of the classical world; only citations and fragments sufficient to point to his achievement.

His thinking, however, was firmly grounded in both natural science and rational thought and this makes him, in important respects, more of a forbear to our 21st century culture than Augustine. We might consider them as the poles of the debate about VAD. Yet Emile Durkheim, whose work on suicide was one of the outstanding contributions to modern social science, argued, a century ago, on largely Kantian grounds, that suicide was immoral. These are the key antecedents to the debate in which we are immersed, or so it appears to me.

In April this year, I visited the Museo del Prado, in Madrid, with my partner. After we had spent some hours viewing and discussing many great works of art, she asked me which painting had made the most profound impression on me. I said it was *La Muerte de Seneca* (*The Death of Seneca*) by Rubens. Why? I had the VAD debate on my mind and the Stoic in me was responding to the idea of choice, dignity and liberty. Seneca (4 BCE—65 CE) ended his own life rather than suffer indignities at the hands of Nero. He was a Stoic and had given long thought to the matter. He had long hesitated and plainly would much have preferred to live, had there been a felicitous option for doing so. There was not.

He faced reality and died voluntarily surrounded by friends. I cannot find it in myself to either ridicule or condemn his action. And I believe I have a perfect natural right, should circumstances come down to a choice between voluntary death and intolerable suffering, to emulate Seneca, defy fate and take my life in my own hands. In short, I align with the Stoics and not with Augustine. But if we are to have norms which both allow this and regulate recourse to it to avoid excesses or the use of lugubrious and traumatic methods for ending life, we need something like the VAD legislation. By the time this essay appears in print, our Legislative Council will have indicated whether or not they agree and why. I would like to think that their thinking will more or less align with mine.

7: Epicurus and the garden of human civilization

Reading Matthew Walker's *Why We Sleep* (2017) recently, I was very struck by the way in which neuroscience in our time has been establishing the *materiality* of the mind. The philosophical implications took me back to the conjectures of Democritus and Epicurus, the classical atomists, and prompted this essay. At pp. 112 of his book, Walker cites the great Roman master of rhetoric and education Quintilian (35-100 CE) as having written:

> It is a curious fact, of which the reason is not obvious, that the interval of a single night will greatly increase the strength of the memory...Whatever the cause, things which could not be recalled on the spot are easily coordinated the next day and time itself, which is generally accounted one of the causes of forgetfulness, actually serves to strengthen the memory.

Walker goes on to show how the neuroscience of NREM and REM sleep and the use of brain scans has enabled us, step by step, since the 1950s, to identify how important sleep in fact is to the creation of coherent and enduring memories, among other things.

The materialism of the atomists was a more serious challenge both to mind/body dualism and the great (and petty) religions than were the other schools of Greek philosophy—Platonism, Aristotelianism, Stoicism, Scepticism—because it repudiated the very idea of immortal souls, divine providence and creationism; attributing the causes of all things to the movements of atoms and to chance. Lucretius, in his famous first century BCE philosophical poem *On the Nature of Things*, famously laid out precisely this argument. But whatever its intrinsic appeal, it was not vindicated until modern atomism finally began to get far more precisely to the causes of things—and the Periodic Table.

On the Nature of Things is the only book Lucretius wrote. After converting to the philosophy of Epicurus (341-270 BCE), he set out to persuade others of its truth. He declared that he was working only and directly from the work of Epicurus and it can be seen that his six books closely follow the first fifteen books of Epicurus's foundational thirty-seven book treatise *On Nature*. They address successively:

I. Matter and Void
II. The Dance of Atoms
III. Mortality and the Soul
IV. The Senses
V. Cosmos and Civilization
VI. Weather and the Earth

Here is the transmission of Hellenistic science and philosophy into the Roman world, as well as a clear antecedent to modern science and our contemporary worldview. Scientific inquiry was not a Roman strong point and Epicureanism, though grounded in materialism, centred more on ethics than on scientific inquiry. Yet as Stephen Greenblatt argued, in *The Swerve: How the Renaissance Began* (2011), Lucretius exerted a major influence on the revival of scientific inquiry in the modern world.

In his Introduction to a new (2007) translation of *On the Nature of Things* by A. E. Stallings, Richard Jenkyns, Professor of the Classical Tradition at Oxford, wrote:

> One of the achievements of the Greek mind between the eighth and fifth centuries
> (BCE) was a process which might be called separation or differentiation. They
> discovered that fact is different from fiction and that history is different from myth,
> that theology and philosophy are different ways of talking about the world, and that
> each of these is different from natural science.

In fact, of course, it was not 'the Greek mind' that generated these distinctions, but only a small number of specific Greek minds—as Thucydides made clear in the proem to his path-breaking history of the Peloponnesian War. And Roman culture, though committed to liberal education, was not inclined to scientific inquiry. Lucretius' liberal poem communicates and recommends the theories of Epicurus, but it does not deepen their foundations.

One of the foundations of Epicureanism, famously expounded by Lucretius, is that because death is simply the physical dissolution of a compound of atoms, there is nothing to fear in terms of punishment and nothing to hope for in terms of reward in any afterlife. We can, therefore, live a serene, secure and rational existence and then pass back into the material world from which we arose to begin with. This, of course, is at odds with religious teachings and was so even in the pre-Christian world. But Lucretius extolled Epicurus precisely for trampling religion under foot and setting people free from it. If we are to revere anything, he argues, it is the facts of nature and the practice of a rational way of living. Life's beauty can be celebrated and suffering mitigated, but without reference to arbitrary or punitive deities.

Lucretius lived two hundred years after Epicurus and, by then, Epicureanism had spread widely in the classical world, from its central school—the Garden of Epicurus—in Athens. He praised Athens as the cradle of civilization, not least because Epicurus had developed his thinking there. In Lucretius' time, the leading Epicurean scholar and teacher in Italy was Philodemus of Gadara, who had studied in Athens under Zeno of Sidon, taught in Sicily, until he was expelled for causing religious offence (without, perhaps, giving 'trigger warnings'?) and then settled at Herculaneum, at the foot of Mount Vesuvius, to educate the Roman elite. There, it seems, he taught, among others, the future Roman poets Horace and Virgil.

We know of Philodemus from various late classical sources, including Diogenes Laertius, who wrote biographies of the Greek philosophers in the 3rd century CE. But in the 18th century, digging around amidst the ruins in Campania long before buried by the eruption of Mount Vesuvius, British aristocrats discovered the library of Philodemus: in the remains of a magnificent Roman villa that had belonged to Lucius Calpurnius Piso, the father-in-law of Julius Caesar, in the first half of the last century BCE—150 years before it was destroyed by the volcanic eruption. The library was fossilised by volcanic ash and only advanced 20th century technologies made it possible to recover considerable parts of it from oblivion.

Philodemus owned multiple editions of Epicurus's *On Nature* and cited it frequently. He also wrote extensively himself, including a multi-volume history of philosophy, critiques of the Stoics and Academics, numerous books on rhetoric, poetry, music and ethics and at least four books on epistemology. It is astounding to have recovered a library of such scope from the 1st century BCE, buried in the late 1st century CE, when we consider the poverty of even institutional libraries in the Middle Ages. But as David Sedley points out, one thing notably lacking from the work of Philodemus is any inquiry into physics—150 years after the pioneering work of Archimedes. Conquered Greece may have civilized Rome, as Horace famously remarked, but it did not convert it to scientific inquiry.

Sedley is the author of *Creationism and Its Critics in Antiquity* (2007), which delves into the speculations of the leading Greek philosophers regarding the origins and evolution of the cosmos. But even Epicurus and certainly Philodemus were more concerned with wisdom, approaches to well-being and emotional therapy than with physics, to say nothing of chemistry. Epicurus believed that what he called 'pleasure' was the greatest good, but that the way to attain such pleasure was to live modestly, gain knowledge of the workings of the world, and limit one's desires. This would lead one to tranquillity (*ataraxia*), freedom from fear and absence of bodily pain (*aponia*). This is not a philosophy that seeks to transform the world or bring about social justice. It is a philosophy of withdrawal to one's garden and library.

James Warren, author of *Epicurus and Democritean Ethics: An Archaeology of Ataraxia* (2002) and *Facing Death: Epicurus and His Critics* (2004), explores the uses of Epicurus' worldview in a scientific age. Just as we can enjoy Lucretius without confining ourselves to his scientifically limited outlook, so can we see Democritus and Epicurus as ancestral to our worldview, without limiting ourselves to their conclusions. As Warren remarks, in his Introduction to *The Cambridge Companion to Epicureanism* (2009):

> ...The Epicureans saw our world...as just one among indefinitely many which are generated and destroyed in the infinite and everlasting universe simply as a result of the unceasing motion of atoms in a void. [It] is not the product of...rational design, nor are any of its constituents or inhabitants as they are because of some kind of natural teleology. The Epicureans saw humans, as a consequence, as free to seek their own natural well-being, fitted as a result of natural processes of selection with the faculties

of perception and reason which allow them to acquire reliable knowledge of the world about them and with the means to live a good and fulfilling life free from the constraints of any external divine authority.

The Roman Sulla destroyed the Garden of Epicurus in 86 BCE, when he sacked Athens, but we have inherited a good part of Epicurus's thought and a scientific world that strikingly vindicates his atomism—extending it in ways that would have astounded him. This is now our Garden.

8: Trump, Putin and collusion: what to believe?

Steven Spielberg's latest film, *The Post*, is a beautiful reconstruction of the debates at the *Washington Post*, in 1971, over whether or not to publish the newly leaked *Pentagon Papers*, after the Nixon administration had issued an injunction restraining the *New York Times*. With Meryl Streep playing the *Post's* owner, Katherine Graham and Tom Hanks playing its editor, Ben Bradlee, the film is a wonderful study in old media at its best, standing up to an overweening and mendacious Executive. If you don't know the story or have become vague about it, don't miss the film. It's deeply refreshing in the present climate.

Of course, the *Pentagon Papers*—seven thousand pages of classified documents—were a huge leak in 1971, though quantitatively pretty small beer by Wikileaks standards. What was striking about them and how they were handled by the press in 1971, however, is that they were a coherent body of documentation and analysis setting out a clear story. These days, getting almost any story clear seems paradoxically harder than ever, because of both the deluge of material leaked or printed or circulated on electronic media and because so much of it is polemical, partisan, ill-informed, reactive or unevaluated.

A fascinating case study in this problem is the controversy over whether Donald Trump has been in collusion with Vladimir Putin and, if so, what the implications are for his presidency, American foreign policy and national security and the US constitution. If you are reading this magazine, you will be well aware of how convoluted and polemical the debate about the Steele dossier has become since late 2016. Follow the story on Fox News or *The Washington Times* and you will be informed, in the words of Mark Steyn, that in truth 'everybody has been colluding with the Russians *except* Trump', specifically including Hillary Clinton and the Democratic National Committee. The *Post's* own Bob Woodward denounced the Steele dossier as garbage.

Yet, read Luke Harding—journalist, writer, award winning correspondent for the *Guardian*, including a stint as its Moscow Bureau Chief—and you come away with a seemingly compelling case that Trump and his inner circle have been in cahoots with Putin and his intelligence operatives for many years and that Trump is in Putin's pocket. Harding's book, *Collusion: How Russia Helped Trump Win the White House*, is vastly more detailed and closely argued than the 35 page dossier that Christopher Steele put together in 2016. And it comes on the back of his 2016 book *A Very Expensive Poison: The Definitive Story of the Murder of Litvinenko and Russia's War With the West*.

That book built on a trenchant argument advanced in 2007 by Martin Sixsmith in *The Litvinenko File: The True Story of a Death Foretold*. Both belong alongside Edward Lucas's *Deception: Spies, Lies and How Russia Dupes the West* (2012) and Garry Kasparov's *Winter Is*

Coming (2015). All paint a dark picture of Putin's regime and its attempts to break up the EU and NATO, undermine democratic politics in the West and funnel tens of billions of dollars of stolen money out of Russia into Western or offshore bank accounts and properties. Anna Politkovskaya's diary, published in London in 2007, after she was murdered in her apartment bloc, in 2006, is a study in how feral Russian politics became under Putin. This is the dark milieu out of which the allegations about Trump have sprung—not the Steele dossier alone.

David Satter's *The Less You Know, the Better You Sleep: Russia's Road to Terror and Dictatorship under Yeltsin and Putin* (Yale University Press, 2016) goes so far as to argue in detail that Yeltsin and Putin had elements of the FSB (Russia's security service) carry out bombings inside Russia in 1999, blamed them on the Chechens and used this as a pretext to launch the second Chechnya war, catapulting Putin into power. Yet a good friend, Robert Horvath, an expert on Putin's Russia, a serious and deeply informed critic of the Putin regime and the history of human rights, the KGB and political dissent in the old Soviet Union, says that he does not accept Satter's argument and believes it was, in fact, the Chechens who carried out the notorious bombings in question.

All these considerations led me, over the past week, to read Luke Harding's *Collusion* very closely and to ponder a crucial question. That question is not: *Are Donald Trump and his cronies in league with Putin or in thrall to him?* It is the classic philosophical or epistemological question: *How are we to determine what is the truth in such a case?* For all manner of political biases, geopolitical fears and susceptibilities to the dramatic implications of various allegations impinge on our judgement. A blizzard of polemical commentary and speculation makes the task of discerning the truth harder as time passes. As a veteran of both intelligence analysis and many years as a consultant and trainer in critical thinking skills, this epistemological question seems to me to be not only more fundamental than the political one, but actually far more interesting.

It was the Nobel laureate Daniel Kahneman who wrote, in his lovely book *Thinking, fast and slow* (2011), that the human brain is 'a machine for jumping to conclusions'. Social media and political partisanship aggravate that problem. So, we might ask ourselves: What are the various contributions to a debate or inquiry of this kind (Trump/Putin) by social media, old media (think *The New York Times* or *The Washington Post* and Spielberg's film), serious expert writers working at book length (think Luke Harding) and official judicial inquiries (think Robert Mueller and the Justice Department's ongoing inquiry into Trump's affairs and his links with the Kremlin)? Which of these is most prone to jumping to conclusions? Which is most addicted to polemic and tribal partisanship? Yet, conversely, which facilitates the greatest access to information and the most rapid fact checking or cross-examination of claims? This is the world we now live in.

'In a digital world', asked William Powers at the beginning of *Hamlet's Blackberry* (2010), 'where's the depth?' He added a couple of pages later, with regard to the kind of deeper inquiry I am talking about here, 'Few of us are eager to take on such questions and, even if we were, who has the time?' That's what I'm talking about here. I took the time to read *Collusion* because I assumed, knowing a little about Harding, that he would be more reliable and better informed than anything I might find on Facebook or Twitter, on Fox News or CNN. Yet I was aware of Robert Horvath's cautionary remarks about David Satter's argument and alert to the various ways in which even an apparently well-researched and responsible book can turn out to be in error or can so bear one along with a plausible and dramatic narrative that one's critical faculties lose their way.

It is not my purpose in this column to offer a conclusion about *Collusion*—except to recommend it as a seemingly sound and very thought-provoking book—but only to remind RSA members and readers of this magazine of how interesting and important dispassionate, critical rationalism is in sorting truth from fiction. I'd like to more or less close, therefore, with a quote from the Introduction the historian Hugh Trevor-Roper wrote, in 1966, to Mark Lane's indictment of the Warren Commission, *Rush to Judgement*:

> Between complete acceptance of a questionable argument and the assumption
> that such an argument is deliberately fraudulent there are many gradations; and
> miscarriages of justice, or misinterpretations of history, when they arise, generally arise
> not from corrupt purpose but from human error. When a man, or a body of men, are
> seeking the truth in a tangle of evidence, they are inevitably engaged in a process of
> simplification. We cannot complain that they seem eager to extract a clear pattern out
> of an amorphous mass of testimony. That is their business. But it is very easy to see the
> pattern for which one is looking too soon; and, once it has been seen, it is even easier
> to read the evidence as sustaining that pattern: to emphasize such evidence as seems
> to support it and to overlook or extenuate or explain away such evidence as might
> undermine it. There is no dishonesty in this, no indecency in suggesting it. It is a well-
> known psychological fact, and the most reputable scholars fall into the error.

Where we are not exercising due caution, because our passions are up, we are, of course, highly susceptible to these traps. I am inclined to think that Harding has largely avoided them. I expect Robert Mueller to do so. But I remain uncertain of the final verdict, not because I am partial to either Trump or Putin, but precisely because I have a deep antipathy to both. And, as it turns out, Mark Lane and Hugh Trevor-Roper were both in error about the Kennedy assassination and the Warren Commission. There ends the lesson for today.

9: Daniel Ellsberg and the Doomsday Machine

There are a great many newly published books that might be interesting, instructive or entertaining to read. There are relatively few that can rightly be called *required* reading. This is one of them. Every literate person should read it—now.

It is about a deadly existential threat to human civilization and even life on Earth: nuclear arms and the danger of nuclear winter. It is written by a person unusually well informed on this particular subject, having worked at the highest levels with extraordinary access to the most secret plans and discussions and fully conversant with the subject.

He is a brilliant individual whose specialty for sixty years and more has been decision making under conditions of uncertainty. His book is uncommonly lucid, highly readable and remarkably dispassionate. At eighty six, he writes as crisply and incisively as he did in his youth and with uncommon humanity and wisdom.

Ellsberg has been a hero of mine for decades: as a thinker, a Harvard, RAND and Pentagon prodigy, a dissident against the Vietnam War from the late 1960s, the leaker of the famous *Pentagon Papers* to the *New York Times* and eighteen other newspapers in 1971 (as depicted in the current film *The Post*), the object of a vendetta by the Nixon administration that brought down Nixon himself instead and the author *Papers on the War* (Simon and Schuster, 1972).

He was, also, the subject of a classic study by Peter Schrag *Test of Loyalty: Daniel Ellsberg and the Rituals of Secret Government* (Simon and Schuster, New York, 1974), the author of an exceptional memoir *Secrets: A Memoir of Vietnam and the Pentagon Papers* (Viking, 2002) and the subject of a first class documentary by Judith Ehrlich and Rick Goldsmith *The Most Dangerous Man in America: Daniel Ellsberg and the Pentagon Papers* (2009). If you haven't seen that film, do so.

His *Papers on the War* and the *Pentagon Papers* themselves, as well as Schrag's book, were all grist for my mill when I wrote my doctoral dissertation thirty years ago and more. Ellsberg's evident brilliance, his all but unrestricted access to secret files and his deeply thoughtful and moral questions made a profound impression. His 2002 memoir and the 2009 film were belated confirmations of what I had (mostly) long known.

What I had *not* known, or at least not registered adequately, was that his work on the Vietnam War was small beer compared with his work on nuclear war fighting strategy between 1957 and 1971. Nor did I have the slightest idea that, in 1971, as he copied 7,000 pages of secret documents on the Vietnam War, he also copied 8,000 pages of even more highly classified documents about nuclear war plans, which he fully intended to leak as well.

His account of how and why he came to this point in 1971, why he leaked the Vietnam papers first and then *lost* the nuclear war papers in an attempt to conceal them from the FBI, makes astonishing reading. But the really eye-opening points in the narrative are twofold: that it was because Nixon and Kissinger believed Ellsberg had the nuclear plans that he was called 'the most dangerous man in America', *not* because of the Vietnam papers; and that he intended to leak these far more important and deeply disturbing documents, because he *knew* that American plans for a nuclear first strike threatened to inflict 'one hundred Holocausts' on the human world and believed that they simply should *never*, as plans or possibilities, ever have come into existence.

He referred briefly to this aspect of his concerns in *Secrets* (pp. 57-59), in 2002, but remarked in that book that the book on American nuclear strategy remained to be written. I have a small library of books on nuclear weapons, including studies of the US, British, Soviet, Chinese, Israeli, North Korean, Iraqi and Iranian nuclear programs. I have books on the origins of the bomb, espionage and the bomb, strategic arms talks, the Cuban missile crisis and the nuclear scientists.

But I had for years waited, in vain I thought, for Daniel Ellsberg to write his *own* account of what he learned from inside the system in the 1950s and 1960s. He has at last done that and it is a stunning book. As soon as I saw it—by chance in a small bookshop down by the sea—I snapped it up, knowing what it was likely to contain. My expectations were exceeded. He says it will be his last book. If so, it is a remarkable way to conclude what has been a remarkable life.

The book has two Parts: The Bomb and I and The Road to Doomsday. It begins with asking how he could ever have become involved in working on nuclear war planning and concludes with an impassioned, but closely reasoned call for an unequivocal US declaration of no first use of nuclear weapons, the dismantling of the still vast nuclear arsenals of the major powers and a serious global commitment not simply to non-proliferation but to the *abolition* of nuclear weapons.

There are many highlights both in detail and in theme. Thematically, two stand out. The first is Ellsberg's honest examination of the psychology of his own work sixty years ago and that of the thousands of security cleared colleagues, civilian and military, who built the American nuclear arsenal at that time. The second is the acute fragility of command and control systems—contrary to public claims and widespread naïve assumptions—as a consequence of how the system was designed and how it was and is maintained.

Ray Monk's *Inside the Centre: The Life of J. Robert Oppenheimer* (Jonathan Cape, London, 2012) is a first rate exploration of the thinking and moral qualms of the man who led the Manhattan Project (from a scientific angle) but opposed the building of thermonuclear weapons later. Ellsberg was a schoolboy when Oppenheimer was master-minding the creation of the bombs that destroyed Hiroshima and Nagasaki.

But Oppenheimer was stripped of his clearances for opposing the H-bomb. Ellsberg joined RAND at the age of 26, in 1957, with the nuclear build-up well under way, knowing full well that the US had a large arsenal of ICBMs and bombers armed with thermonuclear weapons. The access he got at that very young age is striking. It was because he was seen as a brilliant theoretician of decision theory and decision-making under uncertainty.

RAND's job was to think through the acute uncertainties of nuclear strategy and Ellsberg became one of it's—and the Pentagon's—golden haired boys on this terrifying subject for well over a decade. An interesting point of comparison with his memoir is that of Raymond Garthoff, who joined RAND before Ellsberg and stayed far longer in the system than he did: *A Journey Through the Cold War: A Memoir of Containment and Co-Existence* (Brookings Institution, 2001).

Garthoff never broke ranks like Ellsberg, though both knew basically the same things. Both were and are highly intelligent and decent men. The differences in their attitudes and actions are, therefore, highly instructive. Garthoff's latest book (2015) is *Soviet Leaders and Intelligence: Assessing the American Adversary during the Cold War.* In the whole of his 2001 memoir, he mentions Ellsberg only once, in passing.

But Ellsberg's memoir is by far the more compelling of the two. Beginning as someone who genuinely felt that at RAND he was among an intellectual elite trying to solve excruciating problems in good faith, he was stunned by the realities he discovered at first hand and concluded that in fact the whole nuclear arms race, having sprung from flawed premises, was clinically and criminally insane and had to be stopped—by ensuring that the American public was informed of what was really going on and how perilous the situation was.

Ellsberg was closely involved with the famous Cuban Missile Crisis in 1962 and provides hair raising insights into what happened and how the thinking was being done during that fortnight, again based on flawed premises and seriously deficient knowledge. He knew, by then, of very serious weaknesses in the system and of a culture within the Strategic Air Command (SAC), run by Curtis LeMay and Thomas Power, that was fully prepared to unleash thermonuclear war and was morally blind to its consequences.

In 1964, when Stanley Kubrick's celebrated black comedy *Doctor Strangelove* was released, Ellsberg and his senior RAND colleague Henry Rowen went to see it during the workday 'for professional reasons'. He says they 'came out into the afternoon sunlight, dazed by the light and the film, both agreeing that what we had just seen was, essentially, a documentary.' Knowing what he did about the command and control flaws and SAC, he wondered how the film makers had picked up the insights that they had. You can now pick up those and a vast amount more by reading this gripping and deeply thought-provoking book. Do so. There is no better book on the subject.

10: Memo to Twiggy: the Beijing problem is real

At a recent Lunar New Year dinner in Perth hosted by the Australia China Business Council, Twiggy Forrest, billionaire founder of Fortescue Metals Group which sells China a lot of iron ore, denounced what he called 'immature commentary' about China. 'This has to stop,' he declared, as it fuels 'distrust, paranoia and a loss of respect.'

Adam Handley of Minter Ellison, West Australian president of the ACBC, agreed. They spoke of China as being 'an ally', which we need more than it needs us and which has been 'neglected in recent times, as Australia lost sight of its long term national interests.'

Just so we're all clear here: when they said that the debate has to stop, they were not objecting to Hugh White calling for Australia to distance itself from America and make large concessions to China. Nor were they calling for Bob Carr to pipe down in his unapologetic apologetics for Beijing. Nor were they calling on Paul Keating to quieten down.

It's Clive Hamilton and his many sources they want to shut up. His book is based on research by some of this country's finest investigative journalists, serious academics and security intelligence analysts, collated by Hamilton's brilliant young research assistant, Alex Joske. It is the work of these people that they are stigmatizing and deploring.

If, however, Forrest, Handley, Carr and others seriously believe that all this investigation and commentary is 'immature' and 'must stop', they will need to make their case a lot better than they have so far. Indeed, they have hoist themselves by their own petard in calling for it to stop.

Either they are in the market for mature debate, or they aspire to do as the Chinese Communist Party (CCP) routinely and ruthlessly does: suppress information and opinions at variance with its perceived interests and disdain open debate altogether. Do they seriously believe that this would be in our country's national interest, in either the short or the long term?

There has, of course, been an unending stream of opinion from a striking range of well-known public figures taking a line very similar to that laid down at the Perth dinner. Bob Carr's Australia China Relations Institute is only one of many outlets for pro-CCP commentary in the name of our national interest. Paul Keating's characteristically blunt and insensitive remarks perhaps strike Twiggy Forrest as 'mature', but they are patently partisan.

In any case, both Forrest and Handley are confused. China is *not* an 'ally' of Australia; it is a trading partner. We have many trading partners: the United States, the EU, the UK, Japan, South Korea, Taiwan, Vietnam, Indonesia and others. Many of them have their differences with China and are engaged in trying to think through their security in the context of China's rising power and its overweening ambitions.

Those ambitions have been made explicit by Xi Jinping, now unrivalled autocrat in China's one party state: to replace the United States as the world's greatest economic and military power by the middle of this century. Time was when the political character and ideology of that state would have caused political and business figures here to recoil and treat it with the greatest circumspection. Now the merest suggestion that we debate this is denounced by many of them as paranoia and something that must stop. Why? We all know the answer: fear and greed.

Do they believe we *are or should* be Xi Jinping's ally in his strategic ambitions? This being a country in which one is at liberty to advance forthright opinions on almost any subject, they are perfectly free to express such an opinion. What they are *not* entitled to do is to insist that those who hold a different opinion shut their mouths, put down their pens and toe the line.

Hamilton's book has been denounced as hysterical or misguided by people who, one suspects, haven't even read it. One senior ALP figure described it to me as 'deeply flawed'—without specifying any flaws. Graeme Richardson called for it and its author to be banished from public respectability. Had he done more than glance at its title? It's neither hysterical, nor misguided. It's lucid and important. Allen and Unwin backed away from publishing it. To their credit, Hardie Grant have done so. They are to be congratulated for their political courage. The stunning thing is that it required courage.

Silent Invasion should by no means be banished, as the old 'whatever it takes' warhorse, Richo, urges; nor is it 'odd', as one think tank director suggested to me. It should be read as widely as possible and openly discussed. Writing in these pages, I have stated the same with regard to Hugh White's Quarterly Essay, *Without America*, which takes a very different line to Clive Hamilton. If Twiggy Forrest believes that the central arguments of *Silent Invasion* are in error, let him and his allies make that case in a mature debate. But there is no case for *suppressing* this debate. It is one whose time is now.

What is in this book that so many pundits, big end of town types and former political figures would like to see suppressed? It has thirteen chapters and you should read every one of them—not excluding the endnotes, which are meticulous. It begins with a recollection of the disturbing manner in which the Chinese Embassy secretly mobilized many thousands of Chinese residents in Australia and brought them to Canberra, in 2008, to stifle calls for China to be sanctioned over its actions in Tibet and calls for the Beijing Olympic Games to be boycotted.

Chapter 1, 'Dyeing Australia Red' draws to our attention the strategic decision, taken in Beijing in 2003-04, under Hu Jintao, that Australia should be drawn away from the United States and included within China's sphere of influence economically, politically, culturally, in all ways. If you think that it would be just fine to be brought under the dominant influence of the CCP, you ought to be required—as a citizen of this liberal democratic and Anglophone society—to make your case. But make no mistake, this is the forest that the founder of Fortescue Metals doesn't want to you to see. The rest of the book shows you the trees that make up that forest.

Chapter 2 is about how the powers that be in China see themselves and the world. This is not a matter of open debate in China itself. It is a matter of intensive indoctrination and political dictation from the Politburo down. Those who suggest otherwise are either sadly ignorant or under the sway of the Chinese regime and its agents of influence. There is no point in mincing words here. If you believe that Beijing is benignly disposed to us as a free country, you are a naïf.

Chapter 3 'Qiaowu and the Chinese diaspora' is about Beijing's systematic program, orchestrated through the Overseas Chinese Affairs Office, the United Front Work Department and the China Council for the Promotion of Peaceful National Reunification, to exert sway over Chinese communities here and around the world and infiltrate democratic political systems. Someone needs to tell Twiggy Forrest about it. But it would be better that he read the book for himself and give the matter some serious, quiet thought, before he makes further sweeping claims.

Chapter 4 'Dark Money' and Chapter 5 'Beijing Bob' are among the parts of the book that have been upsetting some of the pro-Beijing people, especially in the Australian Labour Party. Read them for yourselves. They are closely argued and sourced. Chapters 6 and 7, 'Trade, Invest, Control' and 'Seduction and Coercion' cover topics that have upset the pro-Beijing people at various points. Read them. Don't be a mushroom.

Then read Chapters 8 through 13: 'Spies old and new', 'Malicious insiders and scientific organisations', 'Engineering souls at Australia's universities', 'Culture wars', 'Friends of China' and 'The Price of Freedom'. If you *don't* read this whole book, you are—whether you acknowledge this or not—actually withdrawing from the serious debate we have to have.

Alexander Downer declared with regard to expressions of concern by ASIO and other elements of the Australian intelligence system, 'I don't know what's wrong with Australia. It's not a John Le Carré novel.' Someone needs to point out to our former conservative Foreign Minister and High Commissioner to London that we are, indeed, *not* in the midst of a Le Carré novel.

For one thing, what's happening isn't fiction. For another, it is far more serious than anything Le Carré ever dreamed up. We face a challenge, in terms of foreign influence and infiltration the like of which we never faced even at the height of the Cold War—precisely *because* China is our largest trading partner.

If we are to address this subject with the maturity that Forrest and Handley call for, we need the debate to be open. We need leading journals, such as the new *Australian Journal of Foreign Affairs*, to foster it, not retreat into denunciations and huffery puffery. It's second issue, just released, shows some promise of being able and willing to engage such subjects at a mature level.

The contributions to this issue by Andrew Davies, David Kilcullen, Kim Beazley with L. Gordon Flake, and Michael Wesley are diverse and intellectually serious. The Back Page on the Munich Analogy is excellent. A minor contribution is a letter from Professor John Fitzgerald on the tensions between the Chinese community in Australia and strategic subversion by the CCP. It is well worth reading as a coda to Hamilton's book length analysis of what we are facing.

For those unfamiliar with his work, Fitzgerald is a prize-winning historian of modern Chinese politics and history, for his book *Awakening China: Politics, Culture and Class in the Nationalist Revolution* (1996) and *Big White Lie: Chinese Australians in White Australia* (2007). He is a specialist on the history of the Chinese community here and former head of the Ford Foundation in China. If you are a newcomer to Chinese political history and serious about wishing to understand how China's revolution fell into the Leninist trap, you would do well to read *Awakening China*.

You might also look up and read Professor Edmund Fung's *The Intellectual Foundations of Chinese Modernity: Cultural and Political Thought in the Republican Era* (2010). Fung, an Australian citizen, is one of many Chinese Australians who have made major contributions to the understanding of modern and contemporary China in Australia.

Over a century ago, Liang Qichao, a leading political reformer in late imperial China, came to Australia to observe Federation. He wrote to his countrymen from Sydney that China should seek to adopt the new Australian model of political democracy and federal government. How about that? Get the word to Twiggy and Adam. Quick.

11: Plato, Atlantis and 'alternative facts'

Plato (428-348 BCE) stands close to the beginnings of Western philosophy and has exerted a remarkably enduring influence on the development of Western thought. Writing in 1929, in his book *Process and Reality*, the American philosopher Alfred North Whitehead famously remarked that: 'The safest general characterization of the European philosophical tradition is that it consists of a series of footnotes to Plato.'

Unfortunately, one of the strands in Plato's writings that has inspired far more footnotes that it warrants is the fable of the lost continent of Atlantis. Stephen P. Kershaw, a veteran classicist from Oxford University, has now provided us with a critical digest of the endless fantasies about Atlantis, showing how Plato's political fable has inspired speculation in the ancient world and rampant charlatanry in the modern world. It's worth a read this summer.

For those not already acquainted with the fable, it is set out in Plato's brief dialogues *Timaeus* and *Critias*—the second of which was abandoned unfinished, along with a planned third dialogue that he never wrote, *Hermocrates*. His erstwhile student Aristotle later wrote that he was confident Plato only ever intended the story about Atlantis as a fiction. Others were not so sure and, given the extraordinary vagueness of geographical knowledge at that time, uncertainty lingered.

The central idea was that the Greek statesman Solon had been told the story of Atlantis by Egyptian priests: a lost civilization which, 9,000 years earlier, had dominated a vast continent out in the Atlantic Ocean and much of North Africa; had invaded the Mediterranean world, but been defeated by none other than the primeval Athenians; only to be swallowed up by natural catastrophes and vanish beneath the waves.

Those familiar with J. R. R. Tolkien's tales will recognize the broad similarities between this legend and Tolkien's tale of the glory and downfall of Numenor. But Plato was outlining a general theory of cosmology and the creation of the world in the *Timaeus* and the seriousness with which he was taken in general and with which his cosmology was long taken seem to have led more than a few disciples long ago to believe that Atlantis had actually existed—and fallen.

The beauty of Kershaw's book is that he puts Plato himself and the sequence of his writings in historical context, showing why the philosopher was attempting to think through theories of politics and Athenian history and why he began to create the Atlantis tale for the purposes of political philosophy. That he abandoned it and, instead, left us with the far more substantial political works *Republic* and *Laws* suggests that he decided it would not serve a serious purpose.

Kershaw's first three chapters guide the reader through both the history of Plato's era, the confused and often fable-ridden historical and geographical thinking of that time and, not least, Plato's own travels, writings and thinking, as a background for grasping why he wrote the *Timaeus*, began the *Critias*, then left it unfinished and never wrote the *Hermocrates*. His fourth and fifth chapters give us the core (Atlantis) parts of the *Timaeus* and *Critias* with commentary.

The rest of the book—chapters 6 to 16—provides a fascinating examination of how the tale has been thought about, refuted and resurrected from the Hellenistic world through into the 20th century. He makes the pivotal point early—and returns to its significance more than once—that the myth of Atlantis is unique in the whole corpus of Greek mythology in that it has no antecedent prior to Plato and is to be found in no source other than Plato's dialogues.

As he writes:

> The Greek myths are not 'standalone' stories that exist in isolation. They form an intimately interconnected web of stories, but the Atlantis tale is entirely self-contained—it sprang fully formed from the head of Plato, rather like the birth of Athena from the head of Zeus.

Not only that, but Plato locates the continental kingdom of Atlantis on a vast continent in the middle of the Atlantic. It was unclear to the ancients what exactly lay out beyond the famous Pillars of Hercules in the ocean. We, however, know beyond doubt now that there never was any continent in the Atlantic that sank beneath the waves. Atlantis was always entirely imaginary.

Arguably, Plato was relating the story with a sly wink all along. Critias states, early in the *Timaeus*, that he had heard it, as a child, from a ninety year old relative. The old man told him that he had himself heard the story from Solon and that, if Solon had not been so deeply engaged in political affairs, he might have written an epic poem to rival the works of Homer and Hesiod. He might have preserved a tale otherwise lost in 'the lapse of time and the destruction of the actors.'

Plato then followed Solon. He left the tale of Atlantis unfinished and concentrated on more serious political and philosophical reflections. These were so fertile in their numerous ideas and serious questions that Whitehead was prompted to see almost all of Western philosophy since then as deriving its research program from Plato. In this context, Plato's most famous fable, the Cave Simile, was always understood as a thought experiment. The status of Atlantis was less clear.

Having been planted by Plato in his cosmology, the alluring and tragic epic of Atlantis never really went away and was debated for the next thousand years, from Theopompus of Chios and Aristotle in the 4th century BCE (both of whom rejected it as a confabulation) to the Neo-Platonist Proclus in the 5th century CE (who was inclined to take it seriously) and the Christian geographer Cosmas Indicopleustes, in the 6th century CE, who concluded that it was a fiction.

The great puzzle in the case is why Atlantis resurfaced, as it were, in the modern world after, as Kershaw rather sweetly phrases it, 'God had submerged it in Cosmas Indicopleustes *Christian Topography*'. Kershaw's account of this, in his chapters 8, 9 and 10 is one of the joys of the book as a piece of scholarship and is recommended reading. Once the Americas were discovered, there was renewed speculation about Atlantis, which was dismissed by Montaigne as incoherent.

Nineteenth century Romanticism and its theosophical and unhinged offshoots, however, inflicted upon the modern world not mere scholarly curiosity about Plato's old cosmology, but an unquenchable mania to find the 'lost continent' and its primal civilization. Occultists and alternative geography charlatans galore entered the field at this point and, in a blizzard of fantasy, began looking for Atlantis in all manner of places other than the Atlantic seabed— from the North Pole to the Antarctic, from the Caucasus to the Mediterranean.

Kershaw's chapters 11 to 16 on all this make highly enjoyable reading. He shows how ill-founded all these searches have been. They are entirely without credibility. His is a patient and illuminating study in the now pandemic phenomenon of 'alternative facts' and the epistemological anarchism that uses them to generate all manner of impostures, delusions, superstitions and ideological fantasies. It's worth reading for this secondary reason, apart from being intrinsically diverting.

I've long kept a little file of Atlantis clippings inside my copy of the wonderful Bollingen book *Plato: The Collected Dialogues*. It includes one, dated 5 April 1981, in which Soviet geographers claimed to have discovered Atlantis on the Atlantic seabed 720 kilometres west of Portugal. Another, dated 29 December 1997, reported that a different Soviet team had located the ruins of Atlantis 128 kilometres off Land's End, England. These claims were, of course, unfounded.

A third, dated 16 November 2004, reports that American 'researcher' Robert Sarmast claimed to have found 'the lost city of Atlantis...under the Mediterranean seabed beneath Cyprus and Syria (sic)'. Sarmast held a press conference and declared 'If this isn't it, what is?' He claimed that his findings 'matched almost perfectly every clue in Plato's description of the legendary city state.' That was demonstrably false in multiple ways. But, of course, it was always going to be so.

However, there's no quenching the strange appetite for finding Atlantis. In the January/February 2018 issue of the fringe magazine *Atlantis Rising*, one Frank Joseph contributed an essay headed 'Atlantis the Religious: Do We Know What the Natives Believed?' He opened his piece with the fervid declaration to his readers that '*Atlantis Rising* readers have learned much over the last twenty three years about the geological fate and checkered history of the sunken civilization from which our magazine derives its name.'

Alas, poor souls, they have learned nothing at all, since the 'sunken civilization' never existed to begin with. They need to read Kershaw and sober up. But those of you who are already sober might find the book useful as a reflection on how the whole thing got started and has, paradoxically, become a veritable cult in a supposedly scientific age. It's a reminder of how much nonsense is 'out there'.

12: Pierre Ryckmans and the Heavenly Kingdom

Almost exactly forty years ago (November 1978), a special issue of this magazine was edited by Simon Leys, the well-known alias of the late Pierre Ryckmans (1935-2014). It featured a red cover with a snippet of Mao Zedong's very own calligraphy, in black. The meaning in English of that snippet was:

> by verification of the facts, get at the truth; strive to eliminate all empty talk

It was fired at the deeply corrupted world of China 'scholarship' in 1978 and remains apt now, as we ponder the rise of China to a level of wealth, power and strategic ambition it never had in Mao's day. We are in the midst of debates about the use of that wealth and power by the overweening autocrat, Xi Jinping. Simon Leys is an important reference point in setting the tone for these debates.

Morry Schwartz's publishing house, Black Inc, has done us all a service by publishing Simon Leys' *The Hall of Uselessness: Collected Essays* (2011) and Philippe Paquet's biography *Simon Leys: Navigator Between Worlds* (2017), translated by Julie Rose, a recipient of the PEN Medallion and the NSW Premier's translation prize. Black Inc also published Leys' novel *The Death of Napoleon* in 2006 and his reflection *With Stendhal* in 2010. Schwartz is also, of course, publisher of *The Monthly*, which was set up in explicit antagonism to *Quadrant*, in 2005, as a way for Robert Manne to reposition himself, after he resigned as editor of this magazine, twenty years ago.

Although the two magazines compete, Simon Leys is a figure that spans the divide between them. He was, however, more of a *Quadrant* conservative than a politically correct social democrat in the manner of *The Monthly*. He was multi-lingual, mandarin, cosmopolitan, a conservative Catholic who nonetheless admired Stendhal; a classical moralist and satirist in the vein of Juvenal or Swift, not a politically correct 'inner city latte-sipping' type. He was a believer in what he unflinchingly called the *aristocratic* logic of higher education and a remorseless and mordant critic of those who lionized Mao Zedong, depicting his Cultural Revolution as a great 'experiment' in social emancipation that should inspire the smashing of capitalism and 'bourgeois' culture in the West itself.

The Hall of Uselessness has six sections: Quixotism, Literature, China, The Sea, University and Marginalia. The section on China has twelve essays, the variety of which demonstrates not only the breadth of the man's scholarship and lines of inquiry, but his Olympian detachment from the destructive and craven polemics of the Cold War anti-anti-communists. The essays include reflections on the Chinese attitude to the past as exhibited, among other things, in their architecture; Chinese calligraphy; Confucius (whose *Analects* he translated into French and then into English); Chinese classical aesthetics in both poetry and painting; the relationship between ethics and aesthetics in classical Chinese culture; Edward Said's mutton-headed polemics about 'Orientalism'; and the subtle attractions and substantive importance of serious Sinology.

They include, also, pieces on the political prejudices and scholarly errors of the 'China experts'; Zhou Enlai and his deeply compromised role in Mao's regime; the great Hungarian Jesuit and China watcher Laszlo Ladany; the Tiananmen massacre of 1989; and the Cambodian genocide under Pol Pot. That, surely, is an impressive set of essays for someone who also had keen interests in art, calligraphy, architecture, ethics and poetry; was a translator, a novelist and a writer about the sea. That such a man remained a Chestertonian Catholic all his life and a free spirit when it came to politics and education only increases the fascination he ought to hold for all of us. His essays should be required reading for anyone claiming to be a China scholar or a contemporary public intellectual. The biography by Paquet places all this in a deeper perspective and deserves a wide readership.

Opening his essay on Zhou Enlai, Ryckmans wrote, in that characteristically subtle and yet biting style of his:

> Alone among the Maoist leaders, Zhou Enlai had cosmopolitan sophistication, charm, wit and style. He certainly was one of the greatest and most successful comedians of our century. He had a talent for telling blatant lies with angelic suavity. He was the kind of man who could stick a knife in your back and do it with such disarming grace that you would still feel compelled to thank him for the deed. He gave a human face (and a very good looking one) to Chinese communism. Everyone loved him. He repeatedly and literally got away with murder. No wonder politicians from all over the world unanimously worshipped him.

This capacity for razor sharp dissection of the pretensions and posturing of Zhou Enlai and the Chinese Communist Party makes Leys required reading right now. The systematic strategic effort by the Party to infiltrate, corrupt and suborn Australian institutions would be seriously hampered if only everyone approached by its minions and fellow travellers had graduated from the Simon Leys seminar in Sinology.

In his Foreword to the special issue of this magazine forty years ago, he wrote:

> The momentous events which have taken place in China in recent years...have provoked everywhere in the world painful and dramatic revisions of the rosy images which the travelling salesmen of Maoism had previously succeeded in imposing upon the public. In its blessed isolation, Australia alone, it seems, has so far escaped from such a shocking encounter with reality. It usually takes a few years for world events to register here—if their impact is being felt at all...

Yet we now find that rosy images of the China of Xi Jinping have seamlessly displaced those circulated in the past about the China of Mao (whose portrait still sits above the Gate of Heavenly Peace) and that the Australian public is again being urged to trust China and distance itself from the United States. *Plus ça change*, as they say in Leys' native French.

He saw that special issue, in 1978, as a matter of throwing *un pave dans la mare* (a cobblestone into the pond) and wrote that the essays chosen for the issue were intended

> to challenge the conventional propaganda images by providing factual information and scholarly analyses, to raise questions, to provoke reflection. The only common denominator of the papers we are presenting here resides in the soundness and reliability of their information; otherwise they are quite heterogeneous...

How very refreshing. He added:

> Though we tried to achieve some pluralism, we did not feel the need to include also the official Peking view: this can be obtained free of charge either from the Chinese Embassy in Canberra, or by tuning in to the public lectures of some of our prominent China scholars.

Remarkably, after forty years, extraordinarily little has changed in this regard, as the Chinese Communist Party continues to run a relentlessly propagandist public information campaign and far more people in this country and abroad now succumb to or collaborate with it than was ever the case at the height of Maoism and the Cold War. The Turnbull government, disturbed by the growing evidence of this, has begun taking steps to retrieve the situation—steps which Kevin Rudd has denounced as 'McCarthyism'. In this context, it is timely to see a full length biography of Ryckmans, precisely under the *nom de plume* that he used as the scourge of the Party and its fellow travellers in days gone by.

I was tempted, given Ryckmans' pen name, his Catholicism, his Sinology and his elite intellectual interests, to call this essay 'Simon Peter (or Simon Pierre or Saint Pierre) and the Heavenly Kingdom', but none quite seemed to work. So I settled for the more straight-forward 'Pierre Ryckmans and the Heavenly Kingdom'. Ryckmans was, as his biographer calls him, a navigator between worlds. Unlike all too many others, he did not succumb to the exoticism and mystique of China that the Party hides behind, but observed it with both the aesthetic fascination and the scientific curiosity of a lepidopterist. One thinks of Nabokov and his interest in butterflies. Yet if Ryckmans was a kind of intellectual lepidopterist, he was, in his own way, also a species of delicate butterfly. In terms of the Greek etymology of *Lepidoptera*, his *lepis* (scale or psychological carapace) was his Catholic cultural background. His *pteroi* (wings) were his elite intellectual attainments. He was a fascinating being in his own right.

Paquet's biography has five parts: 'The Law, Art and Faith', 'The Other Pole of Human Experience', 'Communism in Action', 'The Inner China' and 'The Sea and the Motherland'.

The first two show us the cocoon in which Ryckmans was formed. The other three show him in flight. It also has a brief Foreword by Julian Barnes, written especially for the Black Inc translation, which is a delightful little essay in its own right. Barnes writes:

> I first came to know him thanks to *The Death of Napoleon*, that bravura piece of droll, wrong-footing counterfactual fiction. This made his name widely known, but, typically, he never wrote another novel. He evidently had no sense of a literary 'career': rather, a sense of where he would go and what he would write next…His work fits no previous or current literary profile. As Merimee wrote of Stendhal, he was 'original in all matters—a rare achievement in this age of greyness and timidity.'

Barnes reminds us that Leys chose to become a resident of Australia and finally a citizen of this country. He never sought notoriety, fame or placement in the best seller lists. He lived by the maxim of Confucius that 'A gentleman resents his incompetence; he does not resent his obscurity.' Barnes concluded, '*He* may not have resented his comparative obscurity; but with his death, the rest of us are liberated to resent it on his behalf.'

The biographer begins by invoking this sense of the sublime 'obscurity' of the Confucian gentleman (or Catholic contemplative) by analogy with Victor Hugo declaring of his exile in Guernsey that it left him with only two interlocutors: God and the ocean. Exile from Napoleon III's France was for Hugo a second birth and the most productive period of his life. Simon Leys, domiciled in what Paul Keating notoriously dubbed 'the arse end of the Earth', wrote eighty percent of his oeuvre in English, his third language. He also wrote in French and Chinese with distinction. He thought it remarkable, says Paquet, that writers, such as Joseph Conrad, Vikram Seth, V. S. Naipaul and Kazuo Ishiguro, had been able to excel in English, even though it was their second language. He was pleased to be in their company. But he developed, early, a habit of seclusion, in order to devote himself to reading and writing—and the company of his beloved muse and companion in life, Hanfang.

This Catholic/Confucian gentleman/érudit/recluse was born to one of Belgium's most eminent bourgeois families in Brussels, on 28 September 1935. By coincidence, that is the official birthday of Confucius. Perhaps, therefore, we might indulge the notion that his magisterial translation of Confucius' *Analects* was 'predestined'. He translated it first into French (1987), his native tongue; then into English (1997) and would write, looking back on both, that he very much favoured the second. 'French', he wrote, 'is a beautiful language but, compared to English, it has the rigidity of one that's half dead. For a translator, it's torture. Whereas the suppleness of English, the richness of its vocabulary, the flexibility of its syntax, allow us to play on a bigger keyboard.' That is, in fact, the key to the life of Pierre Ryckmans and his alter ego, Simon Leys: the aspiration to play on a bigger keyboard and the art of doing so.

Paquet provides a beautifully nuanced account of the Ryckmans family and its deep roots in upper middle class Belgian society: in law, government, colonial administration, religion, education and publishing. The Index to the book in English contains the names of no fewer than thirty family members. The grandfather of Leys, Alphonse Ryckmans, born in 1857, became a distinguished lawyer and politician, married a very strong woman, Clémence Van Rijn, in 1881, fathered eight children and raised them in a 'vast seventeenth century house'. Leys' father was Etienne Ryckmans. But the family member who most shaped Leys' development was 'his uncle, the homonymous Pierre Ryckmans' (1891-1959), who had a brilliant career as a military officer, senior public servant and 'the best governor-general the Belgian Congo ever had'. The historian of the Congo David Van Reybrouck, described him as standing out for 'his great intelligence and moral integrity', and as resembling Albert Camus in this respect and even in appearance. His nephew idolized him.

The Ryckmanses were fervent Catholics, which did much to shape the personality of Simon Leys. As Paquet writes, this was an inextricable part of his character and was exhibited in 'his passion for writers like Pascal, Simone Weil and G. K. Chesterton' in 'a never-ending spiritual quest'. Another of his uncles, Gonzague Ryckmans (1887-1969), was a priest, a brilliant linguist and a student of comparative religion, especially in the Middle East. He took a doctorate in Semitic languages from the Louvain, wrote the first Akkadian grammar in French, spent many years in relative isolation in Palestine and conducted learned expeditions into Saudi Arabia, looking for textual evidence of pre-Islamic cultures. Like his brother Pierre, Gonzague was a man of great integrity as well as deep learning and high intelligence. He inspired his nephew both directly and indirectly, urging him to go even further and deeper into 'the East'. He had Uncle Gonzague in mind, Leys confessed, when he wrote his scathing review of Edward Said's *Orientalism*.

Yet another uncle was Albert Ryckmans (1893-1967), also ordained a priest, who, like Gonzague, took a doctorate from the Louvain; in his case, Thomistic philosophy. He became a lecturer in moral philosophy, giving passionate lectures in defence of intractable moral positions. Leys' aunt Elizabeth (Lily) who, widowed in 1930, when she was scarcely forty years of age and had five children in her care, was a daredevil adventurer and traveller and a great lover of the work of Marcel Proust. She introduced young Pierre to *In Search of Lost Time*, volume by volume. It ignited in him a contagious passion. He became so absorbed in it that, for the first and only time at university, in the second year of a doctorate of law at Louvain, he failed an exam.

In short, the young Ryckmans had an upbringing that was singularly rich and provided openings and stimulants to learning wider than those available to less fortunate mortals; but also a strong and conservative moral and intellectual formation, which was crucial to how he saw and developed those enviable opportunities. His father, Etienne, died of throat cancer when Pierre was only nineteen years old. His mother, Marguerite Ryckmans nee Steels (1901-80) played a key role, both before and after that, in fostering the development of her brilliant young son. She was an exceptional woman: elegant, highly educated (including fluency in English), musical (she loved playing Liszt and Schumann on the piano), kind and compassionate. The young Pierre was fortunate in her, as in so many other ways.

Of course, having been born in 1935, he spent the second half of his boyhood in Nazi occupied Belgium. Curiously, his education appears not to have been adversely affected by that or by the war. He was enrolled in an elite and progressive Catholic school and remained there until 1953, graduating in ancient humanities, with an emphasis on Latin and Greek. His passions during these years were reading, nature, drawing and painting. This was the young bourgeois boy who would become Simon Leys, nemesis of Maoism and its feckless Western acolytes, with a lifelong passion for rigorous higher education.

Months after his father's death, he had the opportunity to visit China with a group of Belgian students. As Paquet writes, the young man:

> ...focussed until then on his courses and the next exams, enamoured of Western art and in love with French literature, the sum total of his reading on China being the adventures of Tintin, was suddenly plunged into an entirely unknown universe, exploring at a rapid pace what he later referred to, quoting Malraux, as 'the other pole of human experience'.

He naively thought of the Chinese revolution as a 'prodigious awakening', crucial to the future of the world, which all of Asia was watching. The invitation was, in fact, part of a Party program to generate fellow travellers. Paquet covers this initial journey in detail and shows, step by step, how youthful illusions fell like scales from the young man's eyes in the years after 1955. It's worth reading the biography on this account alone.

The starry eyed youngster of 1955, so amazed by China as such, awed by meeting Zhou Enlai, so ingenuous about revolution and 'awakening', kept learning and thinking—unlike so very many young idealists lured to Stalin's Russia in the 1930s or Mao's China in the 1950s, 1960s and 1970s. The core of Paquet's book is, naturally, devoted to the odyssey that took Ryckmans from his 1955 enthusiasm to his brilliant and unsparing dissection, in the 1970s, of the monstrous crimes and stupidities of the Chinese Communist Party. It is very well done. And it pivots on an observation Leys was to make thirty years later and which remains pertinent in the 21st century.

He wrote, in the mid-1980s, as China's reforms began to look promising:

> All the other great civilizations are either dead (Egypt, Mesopotamia, pre-Colombian
> America), or too exclusively absorbed in the problems of surviving in extreme
> conditions (primitive cultures), or too close to us (Islamic cultures, India) to offer such
> a total contrast, such a complete otherness, such a radical and illuminating originality
> as China. It's only when we look at China that we can finally take a more exact measure
> of our own identity and that we begin to see what part of our heritage derives from
> universal humanity, and what part merely reflects simple Indo-European idiosyncrasies.
> China is that fundamental Other without which, if it never encounters it, the West
> cannot really become conscious of the contours and limits of its cultural self.

This remark is worth pondering. He was not only deeply 'Western', while being a Sinologist of the first water; he was deeply and tenaciously Catholic. He does not appear to have seen Catholicism as a 'simple Indo-European idiosyncrasy'. Nor did he believe that, in the quest for a more universal grasp of our humanity, we should abandon our Western heritage and fawn on the mandarins in Beijing. This combination of deep commitment to the culture of the West *and* deep appreciation of Chinese culture is what we are badly in need of right now—in Australia, not least.

I skip reluctantly over the many chapters of Paquet's biography dealing with the development of Simon Leys. I commend them to others. They are, in general, the better known aspects of the life under consideration, to which Paquet adds nuance and depth of perspective. Likewise, I shall pass over—with commendation—the chapters on the damning indictments of Mao's China by Simon Leys, in *The Chairman's New Clothes*, *Chinese Shadows* and *The Burning Forest*; as well as the reaction of the precious cabal of Maoists and other Leftists whose conceits and delusions he exposed. Richard Wolin's *The Wind from the East: French Intellectuals, the Cultural Revolution and the Legacy of the 1960s* (Princeton 2010) mention Leys scantily, while indulgently treating the French intelligentsia as a brilliant vanguard that made a few mistakes. Tiphaine Samoyault of the Sorbonne, in her biography of Roland Barthes (2017), whom Leys excoriated for his stupidity on China, mentions Leys once, in passing. These omissions are made up for by Paquet's detailed account of the matter.

Those issues are certainly germane to our current debates and Paquet's book should definitely be read on their account. However, it raises some other issues that have received less attention over time and these, also, warrant our collective attention. Perhaps I should say the attention of as many *individuals* as possible. For this is not a matter of ideology, or the presumed need for a 'collective' consensus on the fascinating and important issues raised by the life and work of one unusually talented and intellectually intrepid person. There is, for example, the issue of his writings on matters *other* than China, such as his meditation on shipwreck and humanity, *The Wreck of the Batavia*; his novel about Napoleon's last years and his passion for the personality and writings of Stendhal. There is, also and vitally, his attitude to education in general and higher education in particular; since this is a very pressing matter right now, requiring our attention.

The Dutch ship *Batavia*, captained by Francisco Pelsart, was wrecked on a coral reef in the Abrolhos Islands, off the coast of Western Australia, in 1629, on its maiden voyage. Pelsart and a number of his staff set off for the Dutch colonial outpost of Batavia in a small boat, leaving numerous passengers and crew behind, men, women and children. In his absence, some of the crew mutinied, massacred many of the others and ran a tiny, but brutal piratical state. Pelsart returned, captured them and had them flogged, keel-hauled and hung. In the 1980s, against the background of the atrocious rule in Mao's China, in Stalin's Soviet Union before it and in Pol Pot's Kampuchea in the immediate past, Leys studied this obscure incident and wrote of it much as William Goldman wrote of human nature in *Lord of the Flies;* except that this was history, not fiction.

Paquet's chapter on the writing of this book is titled 'The Little Gulag Archipelago' because the interest Leys took in the matter had to do with his attempt to get to the bottom of human nature and our proclivities for both good and evil. The virtues and advantages he had inherited from his bourgeois Catholic upbringing never made him naïve or dulled the edge of his curiosity about human behaviour. Looking at what occurred on an atoll off the coast of Australia in the early 17th century was a remarkable, almost clinical way to delve into the psychological propensities which had, in the 20th century, generated the colossal abuses of the Nazi, Stalinist, Maoist and Khmer Rouge regimes (among others). He might have settled for some platitude about 'fallen man' and the Garden of Eden, but instead he undertook a painstaking empirical, historical and forensic investigation. The book would not be published until 2005, but his long labours on it are as good a key to Leys' worldview as any of his writings on China.

His novella, *The Death of Napoleon*, originally drafted in 1967, but not published until 1986, was, Paquet argues, yet 'another way for him to approach the phenomenon of totalitarianism.' Leys placed an epigraph at the front of the little book, which provides a clue as to his motivation for writing it. It is a remark by the French poet Paul Valery (1871-1945):

> What a pity to see a mind as great as Napoleon's devoted to trivial things such as
> empires, historic events, the thundering of cannons and of men; he believed in glory,
> in posterity, in Caesar; nations in turmoil and other trifles absorbed all his attention...
> How could he fail to see that what really mattered was something else entirely?

This was similar to the attitude that Boris Pasternak (and Anna Akhmatova even more) adopted towards the Bolshevik regime and Stalinism. The central conceit of the little novel is that Napoleon escapes from his final exile on St Helena and returns to France, only to find that no-one recognizes him and he has to try to rediscover who he is and what it means to be an ordinary human being, rather than an emperor.

Paquet does a wonderful job in setting this out, for those who are either unfamiliar with the book, or who may be tempted to imagine that Leys was succumbing to delusions of grandeur and projecting himself into the shoes of the 'great man' unrecognized by others. He also reveals, however, that there was a fascinatingly personal root to the choice of Napoleon as a subject for the novel. The Ryckmans family had longstanding links with Waterloo itself—several of them live there to this day, Paquet reveals. Pierre Ryckmans himself, long before he became Simon Leys, went to school at the College Cardinal Mercier not far from the battlefield. Rather than being a strange exercise in megalomania, therefore, the novella was an attempt by the thirty two year old Ryckmans to reflect creatively on his childhood and what it means to be human. He would be fifty one when the book was finally published. A dozen publishers had rejected it. The more fool them. It was hugely successful, was translated into eight languages, won a lot of prizes and was turned into a film.

With Stendhal, published by Black Inc in 2010, is a highly idiosyncratic book about a highly idiosyncratic individual, Henri Beyle (1783-1842), whose writings and personality fascinated Leys. Beyle, like Ryckmans, adopted a *nom de plume*: Stendhal. Like Ryckmans, he had a passion for reading and writing. Like Ryckmans, also, he had a passion for colour and art. Like Leys, he wrote books without regard to their potential market, simply to give expression to what he cared about. He liked to say that he wrote for those 'happy few'—they might be no more than twenty—who would understand what he felt and was attempting to communicate. At the front of *With Stendhal*, Leys placed a one line dedication: To the happy few. This book was not about totalitarianism, but about its antithesis: the free and creative individual, scornful of authority and convention, but passionately reflective and creative.

It says a lot about the breadth of Leys' mind that he was so taken with Stendhal, who was in many ways very different from him. Leys remained a Chestertonian Catholic all his life; Stendhal detested Catholicism and priests. He once wrote 'All religions are founded on the fear of the many and the cleverness of the few'. Perhaps his most famous witticism is 'God's only excuse is that He doesn't exist.' Stendhal was a bohemian, where Leys was a mandarin aesthete. Stendhal had no ear for poetry, even in French. Leys was finely attuned to poetry in at least three languages. Stendhal wrote in a rather impulsive and unpolished manner. Leys was a fastidious stylist, who wrote pure and lucid prose. What, therefore, can have attracted the 20th century writer to the 19th century one? Quite simply, his freedom of mind, his passion for creativity and his *aristocratic* attitude to all things: his disdain for all pettiness, cowardice, money-grubbing and vulgar celebrity.

This idea of *aristocratic* values was carried over by Leys into his biting critique of the drift of Western universities—specifically including Australian ones—from the standards he applauded to practices and standards that he execrated. The penultimate chapter of Paquet's biography is titled 'The University Under Siege'. It should not be skimmed over by those reading the book hastily. Leys set exacting standards for himself and believed that any education worth the name must set such standards; especially if it wanted to claim the exalted status of *higher* education. He was appalled when the Université Catholique de Louvain, out of a concern to preserve good relations with the Chinese Communist Party, requested that, if invited there to talk about China, he avoid talking about 'controversial' contemporary issues. As Paquet writes, 'Leys declined the offer because he wasn't available, but in any case this extravagant restriction on academic independence was unacceptable.'

Leys once quipped that what makes a university is 'a community of educated people and a good library'. Material resources and students are important, but secondary to these first two requirements. He argued forcefully that we needed to shatter the illusion that education should or could be egalitarian and democratic. He wrote, in a paper headed 'An Idea of the University':

> The demand for equality is noble and must be fully supported, but only within its own sphere, which is that of social justice. It has no place anywhere else....in its own field, education must be ruthlessly aristocratic and high-brow, shamelessly geared towards excellence.

Many years before he wrote that paper, he had written an essay for *Quadrant*, in 1987, under the title 'Do We Need Universities?—Things That Must Not Be Said in Public'. This was in the midst of the Dawkins 'reforms', which might better be dubbed the Dawkins *deforms*. He lacerated the Dawkins agenda as reducing universities to 'an incoherent soukh, a bazaar, where a thousand wares are spread haphazardly, while the scholars themselves are turned into pedlars, touts and pimps, desperately competing to hustle a few more suckers.' He repeated the fireworks in March 1994, again in the pages of this magazine. Things have not improved since. But those aspiring to an authentic education could do worse than read the collected works of Simon Leys. They could do a lot worse, actually: they could get a piece of paper in media studies or post-colonial mumbo-jumbo from one of our contemporary 'universities'. To appreciate why they would be better off with Leys, they would do well to begin by reading Philippe Paquet's splendid biography of the man.

13: The archaeology and future of Eurasia

Have you heard the news today: OBOR? One Belt, One Road, is the vast Chinese project to deepen commercial infrastructure across Eurasia. It's sometimes simplified to Belt and Road (BAR), because it is far larger and more complex than the word 'One' suggests. These two books are an excellent way to grasp both the prehistory of such infrastructure across Eurasia and the rapidly deepening linkages emerging in the 21st century.

Bruno Macaes is a fast moving, hard hitting thinker from Portugal. He's very plugged in: simultaneously a senior adviser on geopolitics at Flint Global, London; a senior fellow at Renmin University, Beijing; and a fellow at the Hudson Institute, Washington DC. His book on Eurasia is a *tour de force*.

His central argument is that the whole vast super continent that extends from the Atlantic to the Pacific and from the Arctic to the Persian Gulf and the Bay of Bengal is now, for the first time, becoming a single, integrated economic unit—and that this has geopolitical implications for which the European Union is unprepared.

Barry Cunliffe provides, however, what Macaes does not: the prehistory of Eurasia. He enriches enormously the abstract and anecdotal character of Macaes' concise briefing on what is unfolding before our eyes. It is magnificently illustrated, including 94 coloured maps that are an education in themselves. At p. 39, for instance, he offers a set of four maps showing the changing vegetation patterns in the Levant either side of the Younger Dryas, between 13,000 and 7500 BCE. It's a wonderful micro-study in climate change.

Beginning with the geophysical setting and the very tectonic formation of the vast landmass, Cunliffe takes us through the state of human settlement at the end of the most recent ice age and the beginnings of agriculture in the Fertile Crescent, then guides us back and forth across Eurasia down to the 14th century—the eve of the era of Western colonialism. The Mongol ascendancy and the Black Death mark the end of his history—around 1400 CE.

By the time we reach those points, we have seen the spread of agriculture from the Fertile Crescent throughout Europe, the Middle East and India, as well as its emergence in China. We have witnessed the emergence of Neolithic and then metallurgical technologies, writing and record keeping, the rise and fall of city states, empires, nomad cultures on the steppes and the endless and often violent migrations of horse riding nomads into the agrarian zones—what Sellar and Yeatman, in their comedic masterpiece *1066 and All That* (1932) described as that 'great series of waves of which history chiefly consists'. Here it is laid out with unrivalled clarity and learning.

The book should be read right across Eurasia—and here, too, at 'the arse end of the Earth'—since it is a superb introduction to the world of which we are a peripheral part. The extraordinary progress that scientific archaeology and historical studies have made in recent decades is fully reflected in Cunliffe's grand synthesis. Our own place in this vast canvas is perhaps best captured in the new book by Billy Griffiths, *Deep Time Dreaming: Uncovering Ancient Australia* (Black Inc, 2018). Juxtaposing that book with Cunliffe's shows, in staggering depth of perspective, how stranded indigenous Australians were after the end of the ice age, as the continent became both more isolated and more parched; compared with the vast and fertile intermingling and the endless technological innovation that took place across Eurasia.

Raoul McLaughlin's *The Roman Empire and the Silk Routes: The Ancient World Economy and the Empires of Parthia, Central Asia and Han China* (2016) is a basic introduction to part of the vast span Cunliffe covers, but it cannot compare in richness of detail, sweep of time or cosmopolitan sophistication. If you are curious about the old Silk Road tales and the opening up of trade between Europe and Asia—and you should be—Cunliffe's book is a must read. But then read Macaes for a concise briefing on the realities of our time.

Cunliffe is a wonderful scholar. Macaes is a contemporary politician and analyst at the top of his game who exhibits an unusual and refreshing capacity to appreciate the human and the local in the midst of the economic and the geopolitical. His range of empathies is remarkable and he has been able to secure unusual access right across the immensity of the geo-economic landscape he surveys.

If he has an antipathy, one would have to say it is Putin's Russia. He has form in this regard. Only a few years ago, while serving as Portugal's 'Europe Minister', he vigorously pushed for the EU to look west and build its energy infrastructure around imports from North America, in order to counter Russia's manipulation of oil and gas markets for geopolitical ends. He was a kind of anti-Gerhard Schroeder, as it were.

His fifth, sixth and seventh chapters: 'Chinese Dreams', 'The Island' and 'Russia Turns East' are, perhaps, the pivotal ones in his book. He begins the second of these with the remark: 'Russian officials will never say it in public, but in private they confess to increasing worries about Chinese encirclement'. He sees Russia as feeling trapped between Europe, where it is not welcome; and China, which it sees as alluring and impressive, but alien and dangerous.

His reflections on Russia are striking, because they do not constitute a polemic or a superficial geopolitical gloss, but are very well informed and thoughtful. He reaches back through Russian history, reads contemporary Russian novels, converses with leading Russian intellectuals and political figures and while critical of Putin's aims and ambitions, is fully able to empathize with Russian dilemmas, aspirations and cultural confusion in the aftermath of the communist debacle.

In some ways, he argues, the very idea of 'Eurasia' was a Russian invention, in the writings of the exiled aristocratic linguist Nikolai Sergeyevich Trubetzkoy (1890-1938) who argued, in the 1920s, that Russia was the heir not simply of Rome and Constantinople, but of Genghis Khan. Its destiny was to transcend the Western European Enlightenment and champion a more spiritual civilization bringing East and West together.

He also draws Lev Gumilev (1902-1992) into our understanding of modern Russia. Gumilev, the son of the great anti-Bolshevik poet Anna Akhmatova and her ill-fated husband Nikolai Gumilev, suffered enormously under Stalin. He became, however, a Romantic Russian nationalist and Eurasianist, who called upon Russia to free itself from the West and find allies among the Turks and Mongols. It is the implications of all this for the EU's orderly and comfortable world that most concern Macaes.

That concern forms a direct link between Macaes' reflections and the magnificent historical survey by Cunliffe. For Russia straddles the Eurasian steppes and, as Cunliffe shows so beautifully, it was in and through those steppes that those riders on the storms of history, the horsed nomads, moved for more than four thousand years—invading Europe and China and the Middle East alike. If the BAR is to be raised, the disposition of Russia will be central to how or whether it can be done. Macaes is on the money. Cunliffe shows us where all the bodies are buried.

14: Five principles of religious freedom

We are in the midst of a public inquiry about freedom of religion, at a time when record numbers of Australians declare on census returns that they are *not* religious. The subject is both important and deeply contentious. Reasonable and civilized people differ widely in their opinions on the subject and generating social wisdom on it is a non-trivial challenge. I'd like to propose five principles on which, perhaps, the debate might be constructively furthered.

The subject of religion in general and religious freedom in particular is *important*, because religion has played a profound role in the development of human civilization since the Palaeolithic. Those secularists sceptical of this claim should read Roy Rappaport's *Ritual and Religion in the Making of Humanity* (1999) or Robert Bellah's *Religion in Human Evolution: From the Palaeolithic to the Axial Age* (2011).

The debate over religious freedom is *contentious,* however, because religious claims have become increasingly problematic in the light of the modern sciences and because there are numerous religions from the mainstream to the marginal, with conflicting claims. What do we *mean* by religious freedom, in this context? Freedom from persecution? Freedom to proselytize without restriction? Freedom from criticism or from civil law in certain cases?

The modern era has seen various radical secular attacks on religion and on religious freedom in general. The French Revolution involved radical Jacobin attempts to uproot the Catholic Church. The Russian Revolution involved wholesale assaults on the Russian Orthodox religion by Lenin's League of Militant Atheists. The Turkish Revolution suppressed Islam.

The Chinese Communist Party guarantees freedom of religion constitutionally, but in fact suppresses it and seeks to keep a very tight rein on religious practices. A decade ago, the young arch-rationalist, Sam Harris, called for the *abolition* within a generation, no less, of the monotheistic religions worldwide, lest they bring down civilization. He has since considerably modified his youthful position, but remains a robust critic of 'good old time religion'.

A besetting problem with rather too many participants in this debate, whether religious or secular, is the *sectarian* nature of their thinking. Either they adhere to some specific religious body and see its claims as unchallengeable and in some sense 'transcendent', or they, like Sam Harris, the late Christopher Hitchens or Richard Dawkins, see religion as baneful and benighted and would like to replace it with some form or other of post-religious, more or less 'scientific' social culture.

There are quite a few others—and I count myself among them—who no longer lend credence to religious dogmas or claims of revelation, but who come from long cultural traditions which they cherish in often subtle, humanistic ways and do not want to see these ransacked or assaulted. My personal 'index' for this is my love of Christian music, from Gregorian chant and Ave Marias to Palestrina's madrigals, Bach's cantatas and the great requiem masses, climaxing, arguably, with Verdi's magnificent 1874 requiem for Alessandro Manzoni.

While the debate about religious freedom currently seems to centre on a number of moral issues, such as the status of homosexuality, birth control and abortion or genital mutilation and so forth, we need to remind ourselves that its roots lie far deeper and have profound implications for 21st century civilization. This is about far more than the baking of wedding cakes, as the US Supreme Court tacitly acknowledged, in its 7-2 decision overruling the Colorado Civil Rights Commission in the Jack Philips case a few days ago.

Fanatical and violent conflict between religious sectarians and persecution of heretics, apostates or infidels go back right through the histories of the three famous 'Abrahamic' religions and earlier—as witness the upheaval in Egypt in the 14th century BCE over monotheism, dramatically rendered in Philip Glass's 1983 opera *Akhnaten*.

All this included not simply persecution of these religions by 'pagans' or by one another, but persecution of internal dissenters and non-conformists of many kinds. The brutal suppression of the Manichaean Cathars by the Catholic Church in the 13th century and the ferocious wars between Catholics and Protestants in the 16th and 17th centuries are only among the better known cases.

Those unfamiliar with these complex histories are not well placed to discuss religious freedom. Those who *are* should be chastened by them. It was notable that, at the Second Vatican Council, the Catholic Church reversed its longstanding opposition to freedom of religion. It called for abstention from all coercion in matters of belief and the pursuit of inter-faith dialogue about what different religions have in common, as regards both questions and answers.

Yet some Catholic conservatives still speak and write as if Western civilization depends upon Catholicism and badly needs to turn back to even its most arcane and dubious dogmas and 'mysteries' to avoid irremediable decay. This, too, is on the table when we talk about religious freedom in the contemporary world and what we are trying to accomplish.

There is an ancient and civilized way to approach this matter that seems worth considering. It might be called *educated condescension* towards religious contention and dogmatism. There is a famous story in the Acts of the Apostles (18: 12-17) about the Roman governor in Achaea, Gallio (brother of Seneca, the famous Stoic philosopher and adviser to the Emperor Nero). Asked to resolve a dispute between St Paul and the Jews, Gallio told them to resolve their differences peaceably and disdained to be the judge between them.

Two hundred years earlier, writing for an educated Greek elite, the historian Polybius expressed the view that his readers, like educated Romans, did *not*, of course, believe in the gods.

The Romans, however, were perhaps more pragmatic than the Greeks, he suggested, because they understood that religion had certain social functions which could not readily be replaced by philosophy or secular law. They therefore kept up traditional cults to foster social cohesion.

This attitude made something of a comeback during the 18th century Enlightenment, on its more sceptical and conservative wing. David Hume and Edward Gibbon are representative of this attitude, as were many of the American Founding Fathers, most of whom were Deists or Unitarians, even Epicureans, rather than dogmatic Christians. Their view was that the dogmatic claims of the major religions were erroneous and prone to be pestiferous.

Provided, however, that they did not disrupt the civil peace, conducting themselves with dignity, they should not actively be suppressed. In the wake of the centuries of war and persecution between sects within Christendom and between the Christian and Muslim worlds, this was surely a very restrained attitude. Alas, the Enlightenment radicals—the Jacobins and their heirs—did not settle for such restraint and actively attacked established religion. Anti-clericalism remains a strong force in France to this day.

The upheavals of the 20th century and widespread militancy in the Islamic world over the past generation or so raise questions from across a spectrum of concerns about freedom of religion: its relationship with secular society, its subordination to civil law and its tractability with regard to textual or archaeological criticism or the findings of the rigorous sciences. Attitudes to the face-off between 'creationism' and evolutionary biology are a touchstone in this regard.

But even this should not be viewed in simple-minded binary terms, as David Sloan Wilson has shown in *Darwin's Cathedral: Evolution, Religion and the Nature of Society* (2002). Religion is a complex, many-faceted phenomenon and needs to be understood with some sophistication, if the debate about freedom of religion is to proceed on a *constructive,* rather than a radical or acrimonious basis.

Tara Westover observes in *Educated: A Memoir* (2018) that breaking free from a survivalist Mormon family in Idaho and getting a serious education in philosophy and history created a painful gulf between her and her family. Apostasy very often exacts this kind of price; all the more so within conservative religious traditions, or from cults that actively coerce their devotees. Conversely, as Peter Sloterdijk argues in *You Must Change Your Life* (2013), the religions have been wellsprings of *metanoia*—visionary and motivational thinking—since ancient times and need to be understood in this complex, psychological context, rather than on a simplistic propositional basis.

Terry Eagleton, similarly, in *Radical Sacrifice* (2018) argues that our religious tradition, more than the secular philosophical one, has motivated many human beings to look beyond their own, private utilitarian calculus and to think with compassion of others and of the possibilities for social renovation. All this is at stake in our debate over religious freedom.

I would like, then, against this summary background, to advance five principles that might constructively inform the debate we are having; which will certainly not conclude with the report that Philip Ruddock is preparing for the Federal government. In doing so, I have in mind as a model Timothy Garton Ash's *Free Speech: Ten Principles for a Connected World* (2016). The principles are not derived from any religious tradition.

They are philosophical in nature and owe their reasoning chiefly to the tradition of critical thinking that is associated with such figures as Aristotle, Locke, Kant and Russell, rather than with the claims of theologians or clerics of any kind. But they will, nonetheless, surely make sense to any who see themselves as grounded in the more tolerant and eirenic religious traditions, such as Moravian or Quaker Christians, Reform Judaism, Sufi Islam, Baha'i or certain strands of Buddhist thinking. Their intention is to facilitate the development of sound, civilized norms that advance human well-being and mitigate conflicts based on bigotry or excessive dogmatism.

First principle: Each and every religion, sect or cult will be encouraged to accept that it is based on a *story* that others do *not* share and that such stories are seen by others as fables or myths, not 'revelations' or truths.

Second principle: Dialogue *across* religious boundaries or between intra-religious sects will proceed on the basis of getting to *understand the story* that others live inside and the motivations this provides them to live according to certain rules, practice certain kinds of rituals or observances, or dissent from them.

Third principle: Provided such rules, rituals or observances do not violate the civil law or infringe the ultimate freedom and dignity of individuals, whether within or outside the religion in question, there will be no restriction on or interference in the freedom of believers to conduct themselves in their chosen manner.

Fourth principle: No dogmatic claim or 'sacred scripture' will be accorded immunity from criticism in society at large, nor will assertions based on these things be accorded 'sacrosanct' status. It will simply be agreed that these things are constitutive of the story which binds together the religious communion in question.

Fifth principle: There will be active dialogue about the larger story of science and human civilization which transcends the stories constitutive of religious communions, in order that their members may exercise informed choice about adherence to their communities and that the larger society may cohere around agreed realities and meta-rules.

It will be immediately apparent that these principles are broadly consistent with the outlook of Polybius or that of Hume or Kant, but less so with the passionate beliefs of sectarians of all kinds, including radical secularists. But they are intended to generate workability, progress and civil peace, not recrimination, sectarian conflict or the ascendancy of any given set of religious doctrines—even Christian ones, despite the long role of Christianity in Western society at large and in Australian society.

What do I mean by 'story' here? The term 'narrative' is often used in such cases. The simplest and most obvious instances are the Bible story or stories, or the Muslim stories about Muhammad's real or apocryphal 'revelations' and deeds. The story of creation in the Book of Genesis, or of Moses and the Exodus, or of the public life and crucifixion of Jesus of Nazareth are cases in point. None of these stand up well as *history*, but all are impressive simply as *stories* and have held religious communities together for millennia.

But let's take a more recent case, that of the *Book of Mormon* and its fable about the origins of the Native Americans in Judaea in the 6th century BCE. No-one but a Mormon gives this any credence and the scientific evidence against it is conclusive. Yet there are millions of Mormons, in the United States and around the world, who seem to believe it. It is constitutive of their story. My suggestion is that the five principles enunciated above allow us to grasp this, dialogue with Mormons, respect their liberty and humanity and embrace them within civil society.

Some thirty five years ago, I dated a number of young Mormon women, whom I'd met through two old Catholic school friends who, to my fascination and puzzlement, had converted to Mormonism. One of the Mormon women, after an evening out, said to me that she couldn't marry me unless I converted to Mormonism. Since I hadn't even raised the possibility of marriage with her, I was rather surprised by this statement on her part. I responded candidly that it was inconceivable that I would ever become a Mormon, but that I liked her and wished her well.

She subsequently gave me a copy of the *King James Bible* in its Mormon version as a parting gift, before she headed off to California to work as a Mormon missionary. Inside it, in the neatest handwriting, she had written a personal letter. I share it here because, after many years, it seems to me to illustrate the spirit in which the five principles I have proposed can be acted upon without those of genuine religious belief or none at all coming to blows or recrimination, even if they go their separate ways.

She wrote:

> To my friend Paul
> As the days grow nearer to our Saviour's return, I reflect on the meaning and
> importance of our life here on Earth. At these times, it is gratifying to have friendships
> that I know are never ending.

May I urge you to read this most inspired book of books, with a mind and heart receptive to the promptings of the Holy Ghost. We are all given the gift of life itself and are on a path leading back to our Heavenly Father. How joyful to be able to return and live with him ever more. Paul, I know the Church of Jesus Christ of Latter Day Saints is the one, true Church and I leave this testimony with you in the name of our Lord Jesus Christ. Amen.

It has been a wonderful experience to get to know you and I wish all the best of everything to you in your future. Love, (—)

Whatever our differences in religious or philosophical belief, whatever the stories we live inside, if we can all communicate in this spirit, we will not have a problem with religion in 21ˢᵗ century society. My proposed principles are conceived with a view to furthering that possibility.

ACKNOWLEDGEMENTS

This book is a companion volume to *Opinions and Reflections* and it is a delight to have been able to see it into print. The idea for it occurred to me when I realized that I had had almost as many opinion pieces and reflective essays published between mid-2015 and the beginning of 2018 as I had had published in *Opinions and Reflections* and that they covered a really wide range of materials. My great and much loved friend John Spooner, in drawing a portrait of me for *Opinions and Reflections*, remarked that he had drawn me looking serious rather than smiling because he wished to show what a fearless and candid writer I am. This new book, I'd like to think, exhibits the qualities he had in mind. It tackles many dictators and espouses more than a few 'dangerous' ideas. Hence its title.

Just over a year ago, an old girlfriend of mine gave her mother, Shirley, a copy of *Opinions and Reflections*. Shirley then wrote me a very heart-warming letter – not having met me for forty years, but having been an admirer of my writing since I began contributing to the serious press in the early 1990s – declaring:

> I would like to thank you for autographing my copy of your treasure house of a book...I could well sweep all the other books off my shelves. I am 89 and the contents of your book, with your thoughts and all the references, could last me a lifetime.

This from a woman who, in her late eighties was still reading the likes of Daniel Kahneman and Peter Bernstein, was a wonderful compliment; the kind that every author lives for, let's face it. Deeply touched by it, I wrote back to her

> What a delight it was to receive your letter of 23 May. I am deeply touched by your generous remarks about *Opinions and Reflections*. Given the range and quality of your reading, it is a remarkable thing to say that you feel as though you might well sweep all other books off your shelves. Susan has told me at intervals over the years that you would clip out some piece or other of mine and mail it to her. Unfortunately, with the decline and near collapse of our newspapers, outlets for this kind of writing have been shrinking. Perhaps I got in just in time? In any case, *Opinions and Reflections* would not exist as a book had not Claudia requested, when I was quite ill in 2014, that I bring together a set of my better opinion and review pieces for her. The introductory essay turned into a brief autobiography and it was quite interesting looking back on almost half a century of reading and exploration—and the vicissitudes of an intellectual's life!

I feel rather inclined now to send her a copy of this new book and ask whether, perhaps, it might find an honoured place on her shelves alongside *Opinions and Reflections*.

Neither book would have come into being had it not been for the interest in my writing of many other people and the outlets for my ideas in newspapers and magazines. Since 2015, regrettably, *The Age* has declined relentlessly and I have ceased writing for it. The three things that finished it off in my estimation were its sacking of John Spooner, its retrenchment of Sushi Das and its refusal to give me right of reply when its foreign editor Maher Mughrabi denounced me as a 'racist' for my criticisms of Islam. However, I have written numerous opinion pieces, book reviews and reflective essays for *The Australian*, that *bete noir* of the politically correct and the broad Left. I have worked fruitfully and happily with Stephen Romei, Jennifer Campbell and a couple of opinion editors there, and have now struck up a productive working relationship with the current one. I have also continued to publish essays in *Quadrant*, another object of execration from those who imagine that only their own political and cultural views are respectable.

I have published a long string of reviews and thought pieces in the *Australia Israel Review*, yet another outlet that is held in disdain by the broad Left and by anti-Zionists of all stripes. At the same time, I have published many columns in *The Australian Rationalist*, having been invited by the President of the Rationalist Society of Australia (RSA), Meredith Doig, to join both the Society and the editorial board of its magazine. She and the editor, David James, have been a pleasure to work with. Its readership are rather different from that of *The Australian*, *Quadrant* or the *Australia Israel Review*, but as a rationalist and a liberal I have found wide scope for writing pieces for it. The themes are pretty consistently about critical rationalism, scientific thinking and being a thoughtful inhabitant of the 21st century world. It is a source of real pleasure to me to have been able to gather between two covers the full range of my pieces for the RSA's little magazine and so give them, I hope, both greater longevity and wider impact.

During the past five years, I have fought off metastatic melanoma. The constraints on me of years of illness and treatment have, in considerable measure, shaped my output over that time. As of March this year I am officially and finally in complete remission and have launched on a set of really ambitious writing projects. This book serves to round out the production schedule of the borderline years. I am delighted to have been able to see a series of books into print though Ian Gordon's marvellous little workshop – my Aldine Press, as I think of it – and am especially pleased to have his sister Cathy, an artist, illustrate this one. She did a set of wonderful etchings for *Darkness Over Love: A Writer's Workbook*, in 2014 and has done beautifully again in this case. I take enormous aesthetic and personal pleasure in seeing the handsome books I have published with Echo Books sitting on the top shelf in my private library and slowly growing in number as the years pass. It was truly fortuitous making Ian's acquaintance some fourteen years ago and it has been an incredibly creative and rewarding friendship.

Every year since 2005 I have had occasion to thank the medical team at Peter McCallum Cancer Centre for keeping me alive and able to write. They have done their work with unfailing professionalism, human warmth and striking effectiveness. David Speakman has become a good friend and in 2016 we travelled to Brazil together, attended a major international cancer conference in Sao Paulo and visited Rio and Iguazu Falls, all of which was unforgettable. It has been delightful to be able to present him with personal copies of each of my books in turn, including *The Secret Gospel According to Mark,* earlier this year. Ben Brady declares that he has an extra reason now for wanting to ensure I stay alive at least a little bit longer: he wants to read the big historical novel I've set out to write. After the results of my PET scan in March, he declared to me 'You really are the cat with nine lives! You're completely tumour free now!' I was certainly at that point the author with nine books. This will make it ten and I'm not done yet. The truth is, as both he and David have more than once said to me, that I have consistently defied the odds and the population data. Only because that has been so have any of these books been able to be written. That has been a remarkable existential experience.

One person I have never, in print, thanked enough and probably could never thank sufficiently is my mother, Brenda Monk. She fostered my interest in reading from my tenderest years and has been unwaveringly loving through every vicissitude of this explorer's life, enthusing in my accomplishments, supportive when things came apart or looked like doing so. I derive from her, both congenitally and by her example and mothering, my sense of humour, my interest in reading, in poetry, in classical music and opera and, not least, in history. Though, like many women of her generation, she did not get the opportunity to attend university, she has never lost her keen and intelligent interest in authentic literacy and world affairs. She was immensely impressed by *The Secret Gospel According to Mark,* dubbing it 'THE book', which, in the context of my whole life and upbringing was incredibly moving to be told by her in particular. This book, too, I hope, though not as intimately as that one, will be treasured by her as the work of her most bibliomaniacal child.

Last, but by no means least, I must once more express my love and gratitude to my muse and soulmate Claudia Maria Alvarez Ortiz, who occasionally, in outbursts of affectionate enthusiasm calls herself Claudia Monk. We have now been married for just under fourteen years and for ten of those years have lived on opposite sides of the world. Yet we have grown closer and closer as two human beings and she has been a remarkable source of inspiration. From almost the time we first met by chance, in the early winter of 2004, she has urged me to fulfil myself as a writer and a poet. I wrote at some length about this in *Darkness Over Love: A Writer's Workbook* and will not reiterate here the observations I made there, except to recall once more that she has been a perfect muse and has spurred me on even while tackling formidable challenges in her native Venezuela and never allowing the flame of her energy, idealism, intelligence and imagination to be quenched by the sad condition of that grossly misgoverned country. Given that it is now virtually a dictatorship, this book is, once again, dedicated to her in love and solidarity.

INDEX

www.ingramcontent.com/pod-product-compliance
Lightning Source LLC
Chambersburg PA
CBHW061754260326
41914CB00006B/1105